CLASS, ETHNICITY AND DEMOCRACY IN NIGERIA

Class, Ethnicity and Democracy in Nigeria

The Failure of the First Republic

Larry Diamond

Syracuse University Press

First published in the United States by

Syracuse University Press
Syracuse, New York 13244–5160

and in Great Britain by
The Macmillan Press Ltd
Houndmills, Basingstoke, Hampshire,
and London WC2R 3LF

First edition

95 94 93 92 91 **90** **89** **88**   5 4 3 2 1

Manufactured in Hong **Kong**

Library of Congress Cataloguing-in-Publication **Data**
Diamond, Larry Jay.
Class, ethnicity, and democracy in Nigeria/Larry Diamond.
p. cm.
Bibliography: p.
Includes index.
ISBN 0–8156–2422–0
1. Nigeria—Politics and government—1960–1975.   2. Social
classes—Nigeria.   3. Nigeria—Ethnic relations.   I. Title.
DT515.832.D53 1988
966.9′05—dc19   87–18132
                                                        CIP

In memory of James Smoot Coleman,
who led the way

Contents

Tables, Maps and Figures

TABLES

MAP AND FIGURES

Preface

As the most populous nation in Africa, with perhaps a fifth of the continent's entire population, Nigeria is inevitably a focus of attention. Its rich and volatile mix of cultures, abundant natural wealth and powerful democratic impulses have also made it a focus of analysis about politics in Africa. Since its independence in 1960, Nigeria has been widely regarded as having one of the best prospects for democratic government in Africa.

Despite the breakdown of the first democratic constitution, a traumatic civil war, five military coups and the failure of the recent Second Republic, Nigeria retains considerable democratic promise. At both the elite and mass levels, democratic values have considerable resonance. Efforts to impose authoritarian rule have been frustrated by the intensely pluralistic character of the society and the deep popular attachment to personal freedom and political participation. Repeatedly, these pressures have thrust the quest for democracy to the centre of the political agenda, but they have not been sufficient to sustain democratic government. Hence, Nigeria has been trapped in a painful dilemma. For the past quarter-century, no form of authority has been stable.

This is a book about the failure of Nigeria's First Republic, in the first five years of independence. Using the tools of comparative historical analysis and the propositions of democratic theory, it seeks to determine precisely the web of causation behind that crucial historical development. In doing so, it also illuminates common pivotal factors underlying the failure of Nigeria's second attempt at democratic government and of democratic attempts in so many other Third World nations as well. In this sense, it is also a book about the general conditions for stable democracy in developing countries.

This book began (in much longer form) as a doctoral thesis in the Department of Sociology at Stanford University in 1979 and 1980. Although my thinking and analysis have evolved since then – a process stimulated by the publication of significant new theoretical and historical materials – the theoretical framework of the study and most of the historical work derive largely from that earlier effort. I am thus greatly indebted to the outstanding scholars and teachers with whom I was privileged to work. My principal thesis advisor, Alex Inkeles, was a source of tremendous intellectual inspiration and support, a keen reader and shrewd and sympathetic critic. Students of democratic theory will readily recognise the large intellectual debt I owe to Seymour Martin Lipset, who has profoundly influenced my thinking about the conditions for stable democracy while also giving wise and timely advice on this study. I am also grateful to John W. Meyer, who influenced my thinking about the state and development, and to David B. Abernethy, whose assiduous and sensitive reading of the Nigerian case study resulted in a number of often subtle but very important modifications to my analysis. In addition to these thesis advisors, several other professors influenced its conception, framework or method. For this I thank especially Gabriel Almond, Alexander George, Bernard P. Cohen and Morris Zelditch, Jr. Every scholar should be so fortunate to have such teachers, colleagues and friends.

My treatment of the Nigerian case owes most deeply to the extraordinarily generous and insightful advice of two of the original and leading students of modern Nigerian politics, Richard L. Sklar and the late James S. Coleman of UCLA. In addition to his extensive and provocative suggestions throughout my writing and rewriting of the study, Professor Sklar reviewed the entire book manuscript with painstaking care. His penetrating insights, exhaustive knowledge of the historical case and sharp sense of nuance corrected many errors of fact, interpretation and implication, and helped greatly to refine my arguments. As he had done for so many generations of students of Africa, Professor Coleman offered disarmingly energetic and supportive comments at a critical early stage of my work, drawing out the implications of my analysis with effortless grace, portraying his trenchant observations as mere extensions of my own arguments. His pathbreaking work, *Nigeria: Background to Nationalism*, was for me what it has been for two decades and will remain for many more: the essential starting point for the study of modern, democratic politics in Nigeria. His sudden death at the age of 66, deeply mourned by African and American scholars alike, has robbed the field of a founding father and sage guide. This book is dedicated to his memory and his legacy.

I have also benefited from the advice and support of many other people. Gail Ullman was of great assistance in suggesting ways to cut the dissertation and recast it in book form. Paul Lubeck offered numerous comments on the manuscript, many of which I found helpful. Robert Melson gave me valuable feedback on Chapters 6 and 9. Although this study is primarily a synthesis and reinterpretation of secondary historical materials, it was greatly aided by access to the periodicals and political documents in the superb African Collection of the Hoover Institution. I am much indebted to the Curator of that collection, Peter Duignan, and to Deputy Curator Karen Fung. In addition, the final revision and preparation of the manuscript benefited from the support and stimulation the Hoover Institution has given me as a Senior Research Fellow. Support from the Institute of Contemporary Studies, where I was a Public Policy Fellow while writing my thesis, is also gratefully acknowledged. Portions and versions of the manuscript have been typed with care and diligence by Barbara Law, Gayle Ganster, Jo Anne Bradford, Juana Cain and most recently, Margaret Berger. From my colleagues and students at Vanderbilt University and Bayero University, Kano, I drew support and inspiration while rewriting sections of the manuscript, and I thank in particular my Nigerian students for their keen interest and ideas. Finally, and most of all, I thank my parents, without whose many years of faith and generous support this would not have been possible.

Stanford, California   LARRY DIAMOND

'If all moral and material advantages depend on those who hold power, there is no baseness that will not be resorted to in order to please them; just as there is no act of chicanery or violence that will not be resorted to in order to attain power, in other words, to belong to the number of those who hand out the cake rather than to the larger number of those who have to rest content with the slices that are doled out to them.' – Gaetano Mosca, *The Ruling Class* (1939: 144)

1 Introduction

'Metaphorically speaking, most Africans today live under the dictatorship of material poverty. The poverty of dictatorship in Africa is equally apparent. It offends the renowned African tradition of community-wide participation in decision-making. By contrast with dictatorship, democracy is a developing idea and an increasingly sophisticated form of political organisation. The development of democracy in Africa has become a major determinant of its progress in the world.' Richard L. Sklar, 'Democracy in Africa,' Presidential Address to the 1982 annual meeting of the African Association (Sklar, 1982: 21).

Since the wave of decolonisation following World War II, a number of Third World nations, most of them former British colonies, have attempted to govern themselves through Western-style democratic institutions. Almost all of them have failed. This pervasive failure, often heralded by successions of military coups and long periods of political instability, has been a subject of intensive study in the past two decades.

Theories of democratic stability and explanations of democratic failure span the range of almost every type of social science variable imaginable. Some have been developed specifically with the unhappy record of Third World regimes in mind. Others have pondered the requirements for the success of any democratic government. But all of them point broadly in the same direction: as poor nations, with massive socioeconomic development needs and high popular expectations; as poorly integrated nations, with deep ethnic and/or class divisions; and as politically underdeveloped nations, with fragile party systems, weak administrative bureaucracies, and little experience with the give-and-take of large-scale representative institutions, Third World nations, at their present levels of development, have little realistic hope of sustaining democratic institutions.

Some scholars have suggested almost an 'iron law of development', such that below a certain level of economic development stable democratic government is very nearly impossible. Yet Third World peoples have refused to accept this academic verdict. In Asia, Africa, and Latin America, democracies and democrats have been overthrown, ridiculed, banished, and tortured, but the popular aspiration for democratic government has refused to die. Elected rulers quash and jail the opposition, and mock democracy in orgies of self-aggrandisement. Military leaders sweep away discredited electoral regimes, and populist administrations that challenge too fundamentally the established order. But invariably, popular pressure for representative and responsive government reasserts itself. If the story of the 1960s and 1970s in the Third World was the failure of democracy, the 1980s appear to mark the failure and rejection of authoritarianism. Wherever pluralism in social and economic life has not been wholly crushed, diverse interests press for the restoration of political liberties and electoral competition. Such pressure brought down the authoritarian coup of Indira Gandhi in India in the late 1970s and more recently the authoritarian regime of Marcos in the Philippines. Today it is pressing for liberalisation throughout much of the rest of East and Southeast Asia. In stunning fashion, it swept away a brutal dictatorship in Argentina. Elsewhere in Latin America, it has repealed bureaucratic authoritarian regimes whose ruthlessness in eliminating opposition and institutionalisation of corporatist dominance were thought by some to augur prolonged rule.

In Africa, this democratic renaissance had been led by the continent's wealthiest and most populous nation, Nigeria, which has long been viewed as a kind of model and testing ground for the rest of black Africa. It was with great expectations and much fanfare that the Nigerian military returned power to civilian elected government in 1979, after thirteen years of military rule, a ghastly civil war, and one of the most imaginative and carefully designed transitions ever staged by a withdrawing military government. For many observers (e.g. Herskovits, 1980; Sklar, 1982), this was to be the crucial test of liberal democracy in Africa. In little more than four years, it collapsed under the weight of massive corruption, mismanagement, and electoral violence and fraud.

The military coup of 31 December 1983 was not the first to overthrow a democratic constitution in Nigeria that had failed to perform and so lost popular legitimacy. The first coup, seventeen years before it, displaced a parliamentary government that was widely regarded at Nigerian Independence in 1960 as the most promising hope for democracy on the African continent, its leadership a landmark of moderation and reason in a sea of extreme passions. Partly in the hope of avoiding a replay of that tragedy, numerous scholars have closely studied the failure of Nigeria's first attempt at democratic government (what is termed here 'the First Republic,' although Nigeria did not formally become a Republic until more than half-way into that five-year experience). With its record of chronic and ultimately catastrophic ethnic and regional conflict in mind, Nigeria's military rulers, and the drafters of the Constitution that launched the Second Republic in 1979, devised elaborate federal and constitutional mechanisms for crosscutting and decentralising ethnic conflict in politics. These succeeded in reducing the scale and intensity of ethnic political conflict in the Second Republic but did not make for a workable democracy.

To some extent, the Second Republic failed because the underlying causes of the First Republic's failure were never fully and clearly discerned. These causes tap dimensions of socioeconomic structure that are less amenable to revision than the federal structure or the party system. To understand why democratic government has repeatedly failed in Nigeria, despite a broad and deeply felt aspiration for it in the country, we must go back to its origins in the waning period of British colonial rule, and its first, ill-fated experience in the 1960s. We must go beneath the surface of ethnic and regional conflict to fathom the fundamental social forces that doomed that experience. In so doing, we will not only develop a fuller understanding of the nature of ethnic conflict and the process of conflict polarisation, we will also see that the development of stable democracy in developing nations such as Nigeria depends on much more than the effective management of subcultural cleavage. It may also require basic changes in the economy and society and the way these articulate with a rapidly growing state. In directing attention to these structural issues, the failure of the First Republic represents a crucial and profoundly suggestive case for the future of liberal democracy not only in Nigeria, but in many other developing nations as well.

This study is not meant to suggest that every nation ought to have Western-style, liberal democratic government. Such democratic principles as limited government and accountability of rulers to the ruled may take a variety of forms, as is being demonstrated in the experimentation of contemporary African regimes (Sklar, 1982). Moreover, the choice of political system involves a host of other social and economic choices as well, in which basic values such as freedom and equality, political participation and economic growth may conflict. As Huntington and Nelson (1976) suggest, this is 'no easy choice'. It is one that must be worked out in the peculiar context of each nation, by the people themselves. Nevertheless, this study is to some extent motivated by the belief that political liberty is an important value, and that the people of each nation should be free to develop their own form of government – free not only from the imperialism of foreign models and preferences but also from the autocracy of a self-appointed and self-aggrandising indigenous elite.

THEORIES OF DEMOCRACY

As a concept, democracy is pervasive in modern value systems but elusive in definition. By the same word, different theorists and ideologies mean many different things. Notions of freedom and economic equality frequently become confused. Here we wish to separate them. Democracy, or liberal democracy (what Robert Dahl terms 'polyarchy'), is here defined as a political system which meets three essential conditions: meaningful and extensive *competition* among individuals and organised groups (especially political parties), either directly or indirectly, for the major positions of government power; a 'highly̅ inclusive' level of *political participation* in the selection of leaders and policies, at least through regular and fair elections, such that no major (adult) social group is excluded; and a level of *civil and political liberties* – freedom of expression, freedom of the press, freedom to form and join organisations – sufficient to ensure the integrity of political competition and participation (Dahl, 1971: 3–20; c.f. Schumpeter, 1942; Lipset, 1960: 27; Linz, 1978: 5). All of this is, definitionally, independent of the economic and social system, though the empirical linkage is a primary issue in the analysis.

The concern of this study is not simply with democracy but with democratic stability, the persistence and durability of liberal democracy, the likelihood of its enduring over time, particularly through periods of unusual conflict, crisis and strain. From this definition, it is only a short step to the hypothesis that the more challenges a system has survived and successfully managed, the more stable it will be, while the more crises and conflicts cumulate over time without successful resolution, the more unstable the system will be (Lipset, 1960; Binder *et al.*, 1971). More specifically, democratic theorists stress the peculiar degree to which the stability of democracy depends on a widespread popular belief in its *legitimacy*, which in turn heavily depends upon the *effectiveness* of democratic government. A long record of effective performance, of economic growth and political order, builds a reservoir of legitimacy which enables a regime to endure challenges and crises that might otherwise overwhelm it. Regimes lacking such deep legitimacy depend more precariously on current performance, and are vulnerable to collapse in periods of economic and social distress (Lipset, 1960: 64–70; Dahl, 1971: 129–50; Linz, 1978: 16–23). New regimes are inherently vulnerable because they lack a record of past achievements to which they might 'point as proof of the regime's efficacy in the face of their presumably temporary failures' (Linz, 1978: 21). This was one of the many problems that beset Nigeria's First Republic.

One of the important dimensions of regime performance is the management of conflict. Here again, democratic regimes require an unusually high degree of effectiveness. As institutionalised systems of competition and conflict, they are especially liable to witness the disintegration of competition into enmity, of conflict into chaos. If freedom and free competition are not to descend into extremism, polarisation and violence, there must be mechanisms to moderate competition and to contain conflict within certain behavioural boundaries. But at the same time, the regulation of cleavage and conflict must not suppress them entirely, for cleavage is essential if the articulation and representation of discrete interests is to be more than a sham (Almond and Verba, 1963: 357). The theoretical search for these regulatory mechanisms has centred on culture, social structure, and political structure.

Perhaps the largest body of literature on the conditions for stable democracy is that which posits necessary cultural values and psychological propensities. Most prominent here is *tolerance* for opposing political beliefs and positions, and for social and cultural differences in general. Since tolerance is essential to the unfettered exercise of freedoms of belief and action, it is almost by definition, a prerequisite of a liberal society. But tolerance is also necessary for democratic stability. Without it, political opponents become enemies to be conquered and eliminated, and political competition becomes a kind of warfare between camps of dogmatic 'true believers'. If conflict is to be managed effectively, opposing camps must be willing to *compromise*. This implies not simply recognition of the opposition's right to hold its views and campaign for them, but also some degree of moderation in political positions and partisan identifications. Extremist viewpoints and intense attachments obstruct the accommodation and bargaining necessary for effective conflict management. Similarly, political paralysis, polarisation and violence will be less likely when social and cultural interaction is not heavily politicised, when the tone of political discourse remains decent and respectful, and when a measure of trust exists between opposing social and political groups (Lipset, 1960; Almond and Verba, 1963; Verba, 1965; Dahl, 1971).

These features of a democratic political culture must be reinforced by complementary social and political structures. Because political conflict can unleash powerful centrifugal forces, the burden of its regulation cannot be borne by political culture alone; in the heat of crisis, even substantially democratic values and orientations can be overwhelmed by the structural imperatives of polarised competition. To a great extent, the sociological and constitutional challenge is to minimise the possibility of social and political polarisation. In this sense, *crosscutting social cleavages* have been widely assumed to contribute to democratic stability by moderating the tone and intensity of politics (Kornhauser, 1959; Lipset, 1960; Verba, 1965). To the extent that individuals and groups 'have a large number of crosscutting, politically relevant affiliations', they are pulled in conflicting political directions, and thus 'have an interest in reducing the intensity of political conflict'. Such 'multiple and politically inconsistent affiliations, loyalties and stimuli reduce the emotion and aggressiveness involved in political choice' and increase tolerance of opposing forces (Lipset, 1960: 77–8). By contrast, a coinciding pattern of loyalties and affiliations tends to be associated with extreme and uncompromising political orientations. These reinforcing cleavages produce the most intense conflict when they cumulate around two competing social formations or political poles. Such polarisation dissolves the middle ground in politics, and hence any basis for moderation and accommodation. Consequently, each side is induced to go to any lengths necessary to prevail. Since victory will be total, the conflict becomes desperate and brutal.

The assumed relationship between crosscutting cleavages and political moderation has been questioned by Nordlinger (1972), who posits that such cleavages will generate effective crosspressures only if they are equally salient and simultaneously experienced (see also Rabushka and Shepsle, 1972: 57–9). Otherwise, the stronger affiliation may overwhelm weaker, crosscutting ones, or the individual will be able to compartmentalise conflicting affiliations and respond to each separately and intensely over time. Nordlinger also doubts the relevance of the theory to deeply divided societies where few crosscutting cleavages exist. For such societies, Lijphart (1968, 1969, 1972) argues for a 'consociational' form of democracy, in which hostile subcultures are completely separated and then protected by mechanisms of mutual security. The features of such a political system – grand coalition of cultural elites at the centre, autonomy for each subculture over its own affairs, veto power for each group over major national policies, and proportionality in the distribution of representation, resources and rewards (Lijphart, 1977: 25–52) – seek to overcome what is widely and persuasively asserted to be an inverse relationship between the extent and depth of subcultural or ethnic cleavage and the likelihood of stable democracy (Dahl, 1971: 108–11; Emerson, 1971: 247–8).

Rabushka and Shepsle (1972: 62–92) argue that 'democracy . . . is simply not viable in an environment of intense ethnic preferences'. In such 'plural societies' (where different cultural groups have incompatible values and cohesive political organisation, and ethnicity is of high salience), pre-independence ethnic cooperation gives way to intense ethnic political conflict. With independence, distributive issues become primary, the multi-ethnic nationalist coalition becomes oversized, and ambitious communal politicians emerge to 'ethnicise' politics. As the salience of ethnicity increases, multiethnic coalitions and other brokerage institutions disappear, interparty cooperation declines, collective goods such as education become 'ethnicised', and ethnic moderation becomes untenable. Eventually and inevitably, Rabushka and Shepsle maintain, this leads to a breakdown of democratic procedures. Their argument is buttressed not only by their own numerous case studies, but by considerable quantitative, cross-national evidence (e.g. Hannan and Carroll, 1981). A recent study finds that acute ethnic fractionalisation is associated with high levels of deadly political violence, which in turn severely strains the democratic fabric (Powell, 1982: 44–7, 50–53, 157).

Because ethnic conflict has so frequently been associated with democratic instablity in the Third World, a theory of the conditions for democracy must take account of theories of ethnic conflict. Functionalist theories see cultural cleavages as a primordial phenomenon which recedes with socioeconomic modernisation. Industrialisation generates crosscutting economic and class cleavages that defuse and displace ethnic conflict (Lipset and Rokkan, 1967). This assumption has been proven untenable by a wealth of recent theory and evidence, which demonstrate that socioeconomic development and state expansion widen and intensify ethnic identifications and stimulate pervasive competition on the basis of these enlarged cultural identities (Melson and Wolpe, 1971; Bates, 1974; Young, 1976; Nagel and Olzak, 1981). In particular, migration and urbanisation generate larger-scale ethnic identities and provide the essential conditions and stimulus for large-scale ethnic organisation (Wallerstein, 1964; Cohen, 1969; Horowitz, 1975; Young, 1976; Nnoli, 1978). Since ethnic conflict is rooted in competition for resources and power rather than conflict over cultural values, 'ethnicity is . . . basically a political and not a cultural phenomenon' (Cohen, 1969: 190). It has also been interpreted as a class phenomenon, in that dominant social classes may deliberately stimulate and manipulate ethnic consciousness and conflict to mask their class action and advance their class interests (Sklar, 1967; Mafeje, 1970; Nnoli, 1978). Ethnic conflict, Horowitz (1971) suggests, will be more likely in a 'centralised' ethnic structure, in which a few large and powerful groups predominate, than in a 'dispersed' structure where the fragmented and parochial nature of ethnic identities provides the flexibility necessary for intergroup bargaining and mediation by the state. Somewhat differently, Lijphart (1978: 55–61) emphasises that bargaining and accommodation will be more likely where there is an approximate balance or equilibrium between ethnic groups that are more than two but not extreme in number. A key assumption of either theory is that no group have the potential to constitute a unilateral majority.

Pluralist theories of democracy also consider the shape of the class structure, or *distribution of wealth*, an important determinant of democratic stability. Again, pluralist theories stress the importance of avoiding deep, reinforcing and intensely felt divisions (Lipset, 1960: 51; Dahl, 1971: 84–104). When wealth, income, land and other valued resources are relatively equitably distributed, or when inequities are at least dispersed so that actors who are impoverished with respect to one type of resource have reasonable access to another, class is unlikely to become a source of political polarisation and democracy is more likely to be stable. Pluralist theory also emphasises the importance for stable democracy of *autonomous intermediate groups* – based on class, occupation, region, ethnicity, religion, etc. – that can 'provide the basis for the limitation of state power, hence for the control of the state by society, and hence for democratic political institutions as the most effective means of exercising that control' (Huntington, 1984: 203; Kornhauser, 1959).

From this perspective, ethnic fragmentation may provide a pluralistic foundation for democracy (Lipset, 1963). Both Marxist and non-Marxist theorists have seen the development of an autonomous bourgeoisie as a factor of particular importance (Moore, 1966; Huntington, 1984: 204).

The constitutional and party structures are also seen to shape the conflict-regulating capacity of democratic systems. While these conditions are not viewed as necessary for stable democracy, nor as equivalent in importance to conditions of social structure (Lipset, 1960: 80), they become more significant as the conditions of political culture become less favourable. By far the most important constitutional condition for stable democracy is *federalism*. Where the constituent units are demarcated so as not to reinforce other cleavages, a federal structure overlays a crosscutting pattern of regional or state interests atop existing lines of cleavage, breaking up subcultural solidarities. Alternatively, where subcultural cleavage is regionally based, federalism may be an indispensable component of a consociational system, further encapsulating each major group and guaranteeing it autonomy over its own affairs (Lijphart, 1977: 41–4). Federalism may also strengthen democracy by inhibiting the centralisation of power, training new political leaders at sub-national levels, and 'giving the out party a stake in the system as a whole' through control of some state governments (Lipset, 1960: 81).

Constitutional structure also shapes party structure. A *two-party system* is more likely in a presidential system, and wherever the legislature is elected from single-member districts, requiring parties to win pluralities in specific districts and so reducing the prospects of narrow, fringe parties (Lipset, 1963: 336; Powell, 1982: 82). A two-party system is considered the most likely to produce moderation, accommodation and aggregation of diverse interests because it compels each party to fashion broad political appeals (Lipset, 1963: 338–58; Almond and Powell, 1966), in contrast to a multiparty system, where each party typically seeks to consolidate and mobilise its limited base with stridently ideological or divisive appeals. Huntington (1968) also sees the parties in a two-party system as more adaptable to new social pressures and more autonomous from other types of social groupings, but for Huntington, the key structural determinants of democratic stability are the scope of party support and the degree of party *institutionalisation*, as indicated by the adaptability, autonomy, coherence and complexity of the parties.

A two-party system is not necessarily the best regulator of conflict, however. Lipset (1963: 353–5) sees its positive contribution as contingent on crosscutting cleavages. Where party division coincides with other accumulated social cleavages (such as ethnicity and religion), a two-party system may only further polarise conflict that might be softened by the existence of centre parties of sufficient strength to mediate between the two political extremes. Under conditions of 'centrifugal competition', Linz (1978: 24) finds that a two-party system 'is either destroyed or paves the way to a confrontation that takes the shape of Civil War'. The more important distinction, he suggests, may be between moderate (fewer than five) and extreme multi-party systems, the latter increasing significantly the probability of democratic breakdown (Linz, 1978: 25–7). But the decisive underlying variable would appear to be not the number of parties *per se* but the degree to which a multiparty system gives rise to 'polarised pluralism', in which ideological polarisation, extremist, antisystem parties, irresponsible oppositions and the consequent 'politics of outbidding' generate centrifugal drives that obstruct effective and responsible government (Linz, 1978: 26). Indeed, Powell (1982: 154–7) finds that while support for extremist parties is positively associated with political violence, the degree of multipartyism (legislative fractionalisation) has a negative association. He suggests that a 'representational' party system, in which numerous parties exhibit strong linkages to distinct social groups, may contribute to democratic stability by facilitating the involvement of potentially disaffected groups in legitimate political channels and so inhibiting mass turmoil – provided that extremist parties are unable to gain significant support (Powell, 1982: 206, 222–3). Like Lijphart, he stresses the importance of elite coopera-tion and accommodation if democracy is to work in such a context of deeply segmented, coinciding cleavage (Powell, 1982: 224–5).

Whatever the party structure and social context, the skill and democratic commitment of political leaders may have a significant independent effect on the prospect for stable democracy. Linz in particular rejects the socioeconomic determinism of many formula-tions by emphasising the role of elite decision and choice in hastening or averting democratic breakdown. This is crucial in terms of both effective governance (which must begin with a realistic agenda) and democratic behaviour. Democracy requires loyal oppositions, which commit themselves strictly to the constitutional pursuit of power, reject both the use of violence and the rhetoric of violence, eschew collaboration with antisystem parties or extra-constitutional appeals to the armed forces, and emphatically refuse to condone, excuse, or tolerate anti-democratic actions of other participants. Party leaders (including those in power) must manifest a commitment to the democratic system, and an unwavering adherence to its 'rules of the game', even in times of stress, and at the potential expense of substantive political goals (Linz, 1978: 27–38). In part, this is to reiterate the special importance of democratic values and behavioural commitments among the elite (Dahl, 1971). But political strategy and skill are also crucial: when a democratic regime is under strain and incumbent leaders equivocate on critical issues or miscalculate the balance of forces, their actions may precipitate a democratic breakdown that was not inevitable, as Stepan (1978) argues in the case of Brazil.

Powell's cross-national analysis strikingly confirms this emphasis on elite choices and behaviour: deadly political violence is a product 'of the strategic efforts of small groups of political elites,' and 'reactions to deadly violence by leaders of the major contending parties are extremely important to the ability of democracy to survive violent shocks' (Powell, 1982: 155–7). Where all major political parties and factions stand united against violence and terror, democracy survives; where political parties are divided in their view of violent actions and demands, especially where parties actively support or themselves organise political violence, the suspension or overthrow of the democratic regime is highly probable (Powell, 1982: 157–170). Moreover, military intervention rarely occurs where the major political actors remain committed to the democratic process, and where it is attempted it fails. The breakdown of democracy (by either executive or military coup) is commonly preceded by 'renunciations of the democratic faith by its elected leaders' (Powell, 1982: 174).

It is largely from the assumptions about political culture and social structure that generations of democratic theorists have asserted a positive relationship between the *level of socioeconomic development* and democracy. Socioeconomic development is seen to change fundamentally the way individuals and groups relate to the political process. An advanced level of economic development tends to reduce socioeconomic inequality and mitigate feelings of relative deprivation and injustice among the lower class. This in turn reduces the likelihood of extremist politics. In a now classic formulation, Lipset has stated, 'Economic development, producing increased income, greater economic security, and widespread higher education largely determines the form of "class struggle" by permitting those in the lower strata to develop longer time perspectives and more complex and gradualist views of politics' (Lipset, 1960: 45). Moreover, economic development disperses the substantial inequalities that remain, generating the pluralist distribution of resources that is, in itself, an important condition for democracy (Dahl, 1971: 86–7; c.f. Mosca, 1939: 143).

Increased national wealth also tends to enlarge the middle class, which has long been associated in political theory with moderation, tolerance and democracy (Lipset, 1960: 51; Dahl, 1971: 81). But equally significant is the effect of a low level of economic development on the political attitudes and behaviour of the upper class.

> The poorer a country and the lower the absolute standard of living of the lower classes, the greater the pressure on the upper strata to treat the lower as vulgar, innately inferior. . . . Consequently, the upper strata . . . tend to regard political rights for the lower strata, particularly the right to share power, as absurd and immoral. The upper strata not only resist democracy themselves; their often arrogant political behavior serves to intensify extremist reactions on the part of the lower classes. (Lipset, 1960: 51).

In addition, impoverished conditions may intensify the competition for power by increasing the stakes for political actors. If a nation has sufficient wealth to enable some redistribution without greatly threatening privileged classes, 'it is easier to accept the idea that it does not matter greatly which side is in power. But if loss of office means serious losses for major power groups, they will seek to retain or secure office by any means available' (Lipset, 1960: 51). So also will the struggle for power become desperate and violent where there is a great void 'between the material rewards of office and the subsistence level poverty of almost all the rest of the society,' (Emerson, 1971: 247).

The danger of an excessive premium on political power was trenchantly identified by Gaetano Mosca at the turn of the century (see the quotation that introduces this work). Mosca's particular concern was with the increasing coincidence of economic and political power in society, the tendency for the state to 'absorb and distribute a larger and larger portion of the public wealth'. Anticipating the staggering growth of the state sector in the twentieth century, he observed:

One of the most important reasons for the decline of the parliamentary system is the relatively huge number of offices, contracts for public works and other favors of an economic character which the governing class is in a position to distribute ... ; and the drawbacks of that system are greater in proportion as the amount of wealth that the government or local elective bodies absorb and distribute is greater, and the harder it becomes, therefore, to secure an independent position and an honest living without relying in some respect or other upon public administration. (Mosca, 1939: 143).

This may help to explain why a market-oriented economy appears to be a necessary condition for liberal democracy (Lindblom, 1977: 161–9); 'the dispersion of economic power creates alternatives and counters to state power' (Huntington, 1984: 204). This assertion is supported by recent cross-national, quantitative research that finds a negative relationship between liberal democracy and state control of the economy (Bollen, 1979). And it also serves to reiterate, from a somewhat different perspective, the thesis that democracy requires 'a large class of people whose economic position is virtually independent of those who hold supreme power and who have sufficient means to be able to devote a portion of their time to ... acquiring that interest in the public weal ... which alone can induce people to serve their country with no other satisfactions than those that come from individual pride and self-respect' (Mosca, 1939: 144).

Socioeconomic development has other social-structural and psychological effects that are salutary for democracy. Encompassing a richer and more complex associational life, it exposes the lower classes to a more potent variety of moderating crosspressures, and generates more autonomous, intermediary organisations to shield the individual from mobilisation or domination by the mass movement or the state (Kornhauser, 1959; Huntington, 1984). Increasing personal income and education are empirically associated with higher level of participation, tolerance, trust, and commitment to democratic values and practices (Almond and Verba, 1963; Lipset, 1960: 39–40). And as Mosca (1939: 145) implied, a high level of national development is in itself associated with higher levels of tolerance, trust, and democratic values among a nation's citizens (Inkeles and Diamond, 1980).

Given such an accumulation of theory and evidence, it is hardly surprising that so many empirical analyses have demonstrated a close association between the level of economic development and stable democratic government (Lipset, 1960: 27–63, 1981: 469–476; Cutright, 1963; McCrone and Cnudde, 1967; Olsen, 1968; Dahl, 1971: 62–70; Bollen, 1979, 1983; Hannan and Carroll, 1981; Diamond, 1980: 88–9; Huntington, 1984). But the mere fact of this relationship is no longer especially interesting or revealing. For one, it may disguise important counter-trends and pressures, such that the *process* of modernisation may be destabilising even though modernity brings stability (Huntington, 1968); or that the strains produced by capitalist industrialisation, bureaucratisation and popular mobilisation, in a context of economic dependence, may produce a more enduring form of 'bureaucratic-authoritarianism' (O'Donnell, 1973; Collier, 1979). What is problematic is not so much the extent to which liberal democracy in developing nations has been successful, but rather, to what extent the explanations advanced for its recurrent failures are valid, and to what extent the features of the development process that explain this democratic failure may in fact be avoidable.

EXPLANATIONS OF THE FAILURE OF THE FIRST REPUBLIC

Most of the principal theories of democratic stability and ethnic conflict have had their advocates in the contending historical explanations of the failure of the First Republic and the subsequent civil war. The conventional wisdom has argued that Nigeria simply wasn't sufficiently developed to sustain a democratic system. In particular, democracy failed in Nigeria because of an undemocratic political culture, which had so little appreciation for 'the conventions or rules on which western democratic forms depend' that 'nothing the British could have done would have affected the introduction of Nigerian methods into public life' (Mackintosh, 1966: 617–8). Alternatively, the core deficiency is seen in the social and economic structure, the absence of a 'secure economic base' that could 'deliver the goods', and the absence of a large and influential middle class with its characteristic 'attitude of moderation and balance' and capacity to eschew limitless corruption (Akintunde, 1967: 6–9).

A second conventional wisdom of the time was that Nigeria simply fell victim to the centrifugal tendencies inherent in all the multiethnic new states of the Third World, and especially in the highly artificial nations clumsily carved for colonial convenience. From this perspective, democratic order collapsed because the historic competing nationalisms of Nigeria's three largest tribal nations were never successfully reconciled and united into an overarching Nigerian identity (Schwarz, 1966). Democracy in Britain and the US was not evolved to, and 'was never intended and has never managed to settle the range of questions, the whole position of tribes, the domination of the country by one or two areas, . . . open to political determination in Nigeria' (Mackintosh, 1966: 619). Proponents of the theory of ethnic competition have traced Nigeria's tragedy not to the mere fact of ethnic pluralism, nor to primordial culture tensions or historical legacies of conflict, but to the ethnic competition that was generated by socioeconomic and political modernisation (Melson and Wolpe, 1971; Young, 1976: 274–326). This perspective has also recognised the polarising effect of the coinciding cleavages that resulted from the drawing of regional boundaries (and then, inevitably, party divisions as well) atop the major, tripartite ethnic division.

Other analyses have centred around political structure. Most forcefully, Whitaker (1981) has attributed the primary responsibility for democratic failure to the strains and contradictions in the constitutional structure, which – in generating coinciding cleavages, consolidating regional inequalities, and assigning such immense powers to so few regions – encouraged ethnic political mobilisation, made regional dominance the prerequisite and the basis for intense national political competition, and so only heightened regional and cultural insecurity. Prominent analyses of the time noted the acutely destabilising contradiction between the federal structure, which allocated the dominant share of government power to the more populous North, and the social structure, in which the South's vast advantage in education and economic development gave it the natural power advantage and claim (Sklar, 1965a; Dudley, 1966). To the tragically flawed federal structure Kirk-Greene (1971: 3–24) traces not only the failure of the Republic but also the civil war.

A synthesis of ethnic and institutional explanations stresses the failure of political integration – rooted in the colonial legacy of flawed institutional arrangements, regional disparities, and a restricted political process – while conceptualising 'tribalism' somewhat distinctively as rooted in the ethnic competition between elites (O'Connell, 1967, 1970). A similar synthetic analysis gives still stronger emphasis to the elite basis of ethnic competition for resources and rewards (Post and Vickers, 1973).

The latter approaches the more explicit class analysis of Richard

Sklar (1963, 1965a, 1967, 1971, 1981), who exposes the relationship of the twin curses of Nigerial politics, tribalism and regionalism, to the process of class formation. From this perspective, the cause of democratic failure is rooted in the use of tribalist ideologies and oppressive regional power 'by the new men of power in furtherance of their own special interests which are, time and again, the constitutive interests of emerging social classes' (1967: 6). Ethnic conflict, and even ethnic socioeconomic competition, are thus seen as only proximate causes, underlying which is the phenomenon of class action, and the political repression necessary to protect it. By contrast, the dependency perspective traces political instability in Nigeria to an external source of class dominance – the social and economic contradictions imposed by colonial, and subsequently neo-colonial, capitalist economic relations (Williams, 1976; Nnoli, 1978).

Theoretically, this study builds upon Sklar's class analytic perspective. It does not deny the significance of other cultural and structural variables, but argues for the necessity of sorting out the intervening from the more truly independent variables, the proximate from the basic causes. It will become apparent that Nigerial political attitudes and behaviour played a large role in the demise of democracy. But the antidemocratic currents of political culture – the intolerance and constitutional abuse – only beg the question of why Nigerians, and especially Nigerian politicians, believed and behaved this way. Cultural traditions do not suffice here as an explanation. The focus on political structure alerts us to the constitutional flaws that enabled regional power elites to repress opposition and facilitated their ethnic mobilisation, but informs us only partially as to their motives for doing so. Increasing ethnic socioeconomic competition may explain the possibility for – perhaps even the fact of – ethnic conflict, but in itself, it does not satisfy our need to understand why ethnic conflict became so politicised, and then so polarised and intense.

Careful reading of the theories suggests that many of these factors are likely to have followed from or been heavily influenced by the structure of social cleavages, relating as it does the particular cleavage structures of ethnicity, federalism, party system and class, and affecting as it does the character and intensity of conflict. Similarly, democratic theory would lead us to expect most of the effects of structural variables upon democracy to be mediated through political culture and behaviour, and/or through changes in the effectiveness and popular legitimacy of democratic government.

Deeper examination of Nigeria's political development will suggest something more, however, something that was socially manifest at the time but that has been relatively neglected in historical and theoretical explanation. This is the analytic weight of class and state, and of the interaction between them. The intensity of the competition for access to' and control of the democratic state is not comprehensible without 'bringing the state back in', as Theda Skocpol (1982) puts it, to a central theoretical place in the explanation of political behaviour and development (see also Skocpol, 1979). In the rapid expansion of the Nigerian state and its growing domination over the economy and society lies an indispensable clue to the politicisation of ethnicity, the polarisation of conflict, and the desecration of the democratic process. These phenomena sprang from the linkage between class and state in modern Africa – the fact that 'dominant-class formation is a consequence of the exercise of [state] power' (Sklar, 1979: 536). The process of class formation, in turn, demands to be understood in its context of economic dependence, extreme poverty and underdevelopment, and an incipient revolution of expectations.

We have then at the core of our story these factors: *ethnicity*, in an ethnically plural and deeply divided society; *class* formation, in a dependent and extremely underdeveloped economy; a rapidly expanding *state*, in a society with scant alternative sources of modern resources and rewards; and an electoral *democracy*, requiring mass political mobilisation for the capture of state power. It is in the distinctive interaction between these four factors that the failure of Nigeria's first attempt at liberal democracy will be explained.

THE METHOD OF HISTORICAL ANALYSIS

How are the causes of democratic failure in Nigeria to be discerned, and their relative importance determined? Within the methodological tradition of historical sociology, this study employs a kind of hypothesis-testing strategy, or what Skocpol (1984) calls the 'analysis of causal regularities in history.' Rather than try to use the Nigerian experience to demonstrate a particular theoretical model – at the risk of 'tailoring historical presentations to fit a preconceived theory' (Skocpol, 1984: 366) – or simply employ general concepts to interpret this historical experience – at the expense of advancing theoretical understanding that might help explain the fate of other attempts at democratic government – I sift through historical events and pressures to analyse the role of specific variables and the salience and validity of specific hypotheses reviewed above. While the analysis retains some of the historical richness, and sensitivity to human intention and cultural distinctiveness, of the interpretive approach, it searches for general causal processes to a degree that the latter would not.

The specific strategy employed in this search is to stimulate the method of comparative case study analysis, or what George (1979a) has called 'structured, focused comparison'. Since the stability of democracy is seen closely to depend on its capacity to resolve crises and conflicts effectively, it makes sense to focus on the major instances of political conflict and crisis, tracing their causes, their outcomes, their consequences and their cumulative patterns over time. This assumes that the causes of democratic failure are largely to be found among the causes of particular crises and their outcomes. And to the extent that the same causal factors repeatedly emerge beneath the crises that diminished democratic stability, these factors would have a compelling claim to overall causal significance.

I begin by selecting the major crises and conflicts of post-Independence Nigerian politics: the most intensely contested issues and conflicts, tapping the nation's deepest divisions and posing the stiffest challenges to democratic institutions. Five such conflicts stand out: the 1962 split in the Action Group (Chapter 4), the bitter 1963–64 dispute over the census (Chapter 5), the 1964 General Strike (Chapter 6), the 1964 Federal Election (Chapter 7) and the final confrontation surrounding the 1965 Western Regional Election (Chapter 8). Other conflicts and lines of tension running across these are explored, but these five 'sub-cases' constitute the historical substance for the formal, event-centred analysis.

The next step is to 'formulate the data requirements', the general questions that will be asked of each case in the controlled comparison (George, 1979a). First, the *line of cleavage* and the *composition* of the competing *cleavage groups* are identified. Second, the *outcome* of each major conflict is established – whether it was resolved in a manner accepted as minimally fair and legitimate by all major groups, indeed, whether it was resolved at all in the sense of ceasing to be a current of political tension and enmity. This information is important for assessing the *effect of the outcome* on the stability and democraticness of the regime. Such an endeavour, when we already know the regime's ultimate fate, risks degenerating into *post-hoc* justifications. Certain assumptions must therefore be made explicit from the start. First, I assume that if the conflict is not resolved in a manner viewed as minimally legitimate and fair by each major competitor, its effect on democratic stability will be negative. Any outcome that insures the recurrence of the dispute with equal or greater passion will undermine democratic stability, as will an outcome that resolves the conflict only by defeating one group so massively as to alienate it from the democratic process. More generally, any crisis outcome that erodes the legitimacy of the regime among any significant segment of the population will be considered negative in its effect on democratic stability. Because high levels of civil violence reflect a failure of regime performance (in maintaining order), and often as well an alienation from the democratic process, they too will be taken as an indicator of negative effect. Finally (for obvious definitional reasons), when a crisis has the effect of eroding the democraticness of the regime, such as the level of civil and political liberty, its effect is negative.

The fourth and most important question concerns the *causes of the crisis* and of its outcome. This involves tracing causal contributions and sequences through the standard procedures of historical inquiry, and seeking to uncover the structural opportunities and constraints that motivated the historically specific choices of individual leaders and bounded their decisional latitude. This endeavour remains especially alert to the possible involvement of prominent theoretical variables. And it requires as well some determination of the priority or relative weight of the causes identified. Useful here is a kind of 'mental experiment' which asks whether the outcome of a particular crisis or conflict would have been different had the state of a given factor been different (George, 1979b).

Finally, the analysis of each crisis seeks to establish any *feedback effects* it may have had on social or political conditions, through which it may have shaped the nature and outcome of subsequent crises. To what extent might a crisis have served as a (positive or negative) 'learning experience' for political elites and participants, altering their beliefs, attitudes, and styles of advocacy, or even the social and political structures framing their competition?

All of these analytic concerns will be addressed in the study of each crisis. The conclusion will then assess the pattern across crises, identifying those factors that exerted the most consistently destabilising effects, and searching the cumulative pattern of conflict for additional explanatory factors. Here, the succession and cumulation of cleavages over time will be analysed. If the same lines of cleavage are invoked in successive conflicts, the cumulative impact on democratic stability may be more destructive than would be apparent from the study of any single conflict, just as the repeated defeat of the same cleavage group may more profoundly undermine democratic legitimacy.

Needless to say, the integrity and reliability of the historical analysis depends on a fair and careful tracing of the development and outcome of each crisis. Hopefully the extensive consultation of existing historical treatments of the subject (so widely varying in intellectual and political orientations) has diminished any temptation to shape or select the historical evidence to fit a given theory. Still, it must be recognised that the reliance on secondary materials for the bulk of the evidence makes this study a captive, to some extent, of the empirical limits of previous ones. The analysis also requires a clear determination of where Nigeria stood with respect to important theoretical variables when her democratic government was formally launched at Independence in 1960. This review is the task of Chapter 3, but it in turn must be informed by the historical origins and development of these factors, to which we now turn.

2 The Origins of Crisis

'Seek ye the kingdom of politics and all else shall be added onto you.' – Dr Kwame Nkrumah (quoted in Wraith and Simpkins, 1963: 161).

THE BALANCE OF CULTURAL GROUPS

Nothing can be understood about Nigeria until its pattern of ethnic diversity is delineated. Within the boundaries drawn by the British are a staggering variety of ethnic groups, as revealed by the presence of some 248 distinct languages (Coleman, 1958: 15). Many of these linguistic groups are tiny and politically insignificant. But just three comprise roughly two-thirds of the population: the Hausa-Fulani, the Yoruba, and the Igbo (Table 2.1). In this respect, Nigeria can be classified as having (in Horowitz's terms) a relatively 'centralised' ethnic structure.

The Hausa and Fulani are often grouped together because the Fulani, as they conquered the Hausa (first gradually through infiltration over centuries, then decisively in an Islamic holy war (*jihad*) beginning in 1804), adopted the Hausa language and culture and intermarried with them to such an extent that the two groups have become difficult to distinguish (see Coleman, 1958: 21; see also Paden, 1973: 22–3). In fact, 'Hausa' is probably best understood as a linguistic category encompassing 'the entire settled Moslem, Hausa-speaking population' (Smith, 1955: 3; quoted in Sklar, 1963: 6; Smith, 1959: 240). Closely related to the Hausa-Fulani are the Nupe, whom the Fulani also conquered and became absorbed by, and the Kanuri, whose ancient kingdom of Bornu successfully resisted Fulani conquest. Both of these groups shared with the Hausa-Fulani the two cultural elements that most sharply distinguished them from the Igbo and to a lesser extent from the Yoruba: a deep and diffuse faith in Islam, and a tradition of large-scale rule through centralised authoritarian states.

Though not as tightly organised as the Hausa-Fulani emirates, and never united in a single state, the Yoruba were also grouped into large-scale kingdoms. Militarily developed, these kingdoms arrested

Table 2.1   Distributions of Nigerian ethnic groups 1952–3, and 1963*

Group	Percent of population 1952–53	1963
Hausa	18.2 ⎫ 28.1	29.5
Fulani	9.9 ⎭	
Kanuri	4.2	4.1
Tiv	2.5	2.5
Nupe	1.1	1.2
Yoruba	16.6	20.3
Edo	1.5	1.7
Igbo	17.9	16.6
Ibibio-Efik	2.7	3.6
Ijaw	1.1	2.0
Total: Hausa-Fulani, Yoruba and Igbo	62.6	66.4

Source: Van de Walle (1970)

*The census has been a subject of continuing scholarly debate and political conflict in Nigeria for three decades, and hence no set of figures can be accepted as precise. Because the 1963 census was ensnarled in intense controversy (Chapter 5), the 1952–53 figures, compiled by the more neutral colonial administration in a less politically charged atmosphere, may represent more accurately the demographic balance of peoples.

the expansionist southward drive of the Fulani empire. Furthermore, the Yoruba shared a long, common history and such cultural bonds as 'belief in a common origin, . . . widespread intermarriage within the tribe, and the possession of Pan-Yoruba *orishas* (tribal deities)' (Coleman, 1958: 25). But this common history was in part one of intense warfare between the kingdoms (Ajayi and Smith, 1964), and their common language and identity 'resulted largely from the influence of the Anglican mission in Abeokuta in the nineteenth century' (Wallerstein, 1963: 666).

In this enterprise, of constructing a larger-scale identity, the Igbos came the furthest and the fastest, while starting the latest. Historically fragmented 'into 30 subtribes, 69 clans, and some 500 fairly autonomous villages or village groups' (Coleman, 1958: 30), the Igbos nevertheless manifested fundamental unities in religion, culture, and political and economic organisation which provided 'the basis for the later emergence of a Pan-Igbo consciousness' (Coleman, 1958: 31).

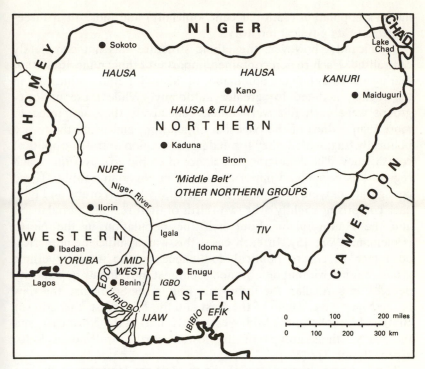

Map 2.1   Nigeria: ethnic groups and four regions

The predominance of the three major ethnic groups is amplified by their regional concentration in the country – the Hausa-Fulani in the North, the Igbo in the East, and the Yoruba in the West (see Map 2.1). The sharp differences in traditional culture and social structure between these three groups gave their numerical preponderance political significance. Still further was the political significance of this ethnic structure heightened by the British division of Nigeria into three regions whose boundaries conformed with the pattern of ethnic concentration. This regional structure gave the three major ethnic groups (and their political cultures and aspirations) dominant political roles in each of their regions, substantially exaggerating the centralised character of the ethnic structure. The regional distribution of the population thus itself became an important dimension of the ethnic balance of power, and this distribution was much more skewed. While the Eastern and Western regions were roughly equal in size (with 25.6 and 20.5 per cent of the population at Independence), the Northern Region contained an absolute majority of the nation's population (53.8 per cent, officially) and more than three-quarters of its physical territory. Significantly, however, the ethnic structure was not completely centralised. Each region contained important ethnic minorities who, fearing and resenting the dominance of the major ethnic minorities in the region, agitated for greater autonomy. While these minority groups were each relatively small, collectively they amounted to more than a third of the Nigerian population, and while they were politically fragmented, they formed in each region a strategic political constituency. The demographic balance of ethnic groups *within* each region thus became an important factor in Nigerian politics. These configurations were even more centralised, with the Yoruba and Igbo each comprising slightly over two-thirds of their regional populations and the Hausa-Fulani about half the population in the North (Coleman, 1958: 15). In each case, this was a sufficient numerical advantage to ensure political dominance by the majority ethnic group, but not without determined separatist movements by minority peoples: in particular, the Ibibio and Efik in the Southeast, the Ijaw in the Niger River Delta of the East and the Mid-West, the Edo (or Bini) and Urhobo of the Mid-West, the Kanuri in the Northeast, and the many ethnic groups of the lower North, or 'Middle Belt', especially the Tiv (Map 2.1).

This last area, home to roughly a third of the North's population, contained most of the more than two hundred linguistic groups in the North. So ethnically fragmented was the Middle Belt that its largest group, the Tiv, accounted for less than five per cent of the Region's population. Other significant groups included the Igbirra, Idoma, Igala, and Birom, while many smaller groups numbered in the thousands or even hundreds (Dudley, 1968: 57). These peoples shared, by and large, a common heritage of resistance to the Muslim religion and authoritarian state structure – not to mention the slave raids – of the Fulani (Post, 1963: 78). In resisting Yoruba political dominance, the Edo people manifested a similar determination for autonomy, but this was based on pride in a glorious past of artistic achievement and state-building (the Kingdom of Benin), while the cultural resistance of the Ibibio and Efik to Igbo domination grew from their common desire 'to restore the glories of the Calabar commercial empire' (Minorities Commission, 1958: 7) and to recover their initial advantage in Western education (from early colonial rule).

Religion further divided the peoples of Nigeria, but religious cleavage was generally less significant than ethnicity and region. Where religion was a factor in social and political conflict, it typically reflected broader cultural conflict, as in the Middle Belt, which contained 'vigorous concentrations of Christianity among groups of resolute animists' (Kirk-Greene, 1967: 6). In the East, Islam was virtually absent while Christianity claimed a high proportion of the population, especially among Igbos. Where religion might have functioned to crosscut ethnicity, among the Yoruba – who were fairly evenly split between Christianity and Islam – it failed to do so, because Islam took a different, less encompassing form in the South. As a result, 'Hausa and Yoruba pray at different mosques, and Islam does not function as a crosscutting interethnic solidarity structure' (Young, 1976: 280).

Within the Northern Region, Islam provided an overarching, transethnic identity throughout the upper North – and hence an important cultural bond for formation of a broader, more modern dominant class – but it also encompassed sectarian cleavage. While most of the Jihad leaders and their descendants among the nineteenth-century Fulani ruling class were affiliated with the Qadiriyya brotherhood, Tijanniya became the dominant Muslim brotherhood in Kano and a means for the assertion of Kano Emirate's religious and political independence from Sokoto. This conflict came to a head after 1954 when Emir Sanusi of Kano emerged 'as the spiritual leader of Reformed Tijaniyya in Nigeria' (Paden, 1973: 68–9). Although the development of Tijaniyya in Kano began as an ethnic (Hausa) phenomenon, it later incorporated Mallams (Islamic teachers) of other ethnic groups and became a force for integration across ethnic and class boundaries (Paden, 1973: 73–124). In the twentieth century, Reformed Qadiriyya similarly developed 'a transethnic base of authority and community' and shifted from an elite to a mass base. During the First Republic, there also emerged a highly inclusive Islamic movement, Usmaniyya (led by the Northern Premier, Ahmadu Bello), which 'came to represent a transethnic, transbrotherhood basis for northern regionalism' (Paden, 1973: 146–60, 179–89).

THE COLONIAL LEGACY

When the British granted Nigeria independence in 1960, they left behind a paradoxical legacy of colonial rule. On the one hand, the

Nigerian nation was wholly a colonial construction. The British not only welded these vastly different peoples and regions into a single political entity but left behind the physical infrastructure for their integration – roads, railway lines, harbours, telephone and telegraph systems, and a common currency (Coleman, 1958: 54–6). But in creating Nigeria, the British also fostered large-scale ethnic consciousness and conflict. Like other European colonial powers, the British carved arbitrary and artificial boundaries around their two Nigerian protectorates, merging peoples with few or no common cultural and political bonds. Even as leading Nigerian nationalists saw it, 'Nigeria is not a nation. It is a mere geographical expression' (Awolowo, 1947: 47–8).

While the British established over Nigeria a common political authority, transportation grid, and monetary system, they did not rule it as a single nation. In 1900, separate protectorates were proclaimed for Northern and Southern Nigeria, and a Native Authority System was constructed to rule indirectly in the North through traditional authorities. Even after formal amalgamation in 1914, the British continued to rule Nigeria, in effect, as two countries. In the South, Western education and religion were vigorously promoted and English was employed as the language of administration. Elective representation was introduced there 25 years before it would appear in the North. By contrast, British officials administered the North through the Hausa language and, seeking to preserve that region's social structure and institutions, effectively sealed off the North, especially the Muslim emirates, from Western influences, even in the person of Southern Nigerians (Dudley, 1968: 18–20). Those Southerners who migrated to the North were forced to live in segregated housing and to educate their children in separate schools, and were prevented from acquiring freehold title to land (Nnoli, 1978: 115; Coleman, 1958: 59, 137). Northern Muslims were forbidden on both religious and administrative grounds to associate with Southerners, whom they were taught to regard as 'pagans' and 'infidels' (Zungur in Paden, 1973: 292). As a crucial component of this policy, Christian missionaries were forbidden in the emirates and Western education was severely restricted, in order to forestall the emergence of what Governor Lugard termed the 'utter disrespect for British and native ideals alike' that was beginning to be seen in the South (quoted in Coleman, 1958: 137).

This separate administration of North and South not only

profoundly hindered the development of a common national identity but also generated an immense development gap. By 1947, the North, with over half the population of the country, accounted for only 2.5 per cent of the primary school enrolment (Coleman, 1958: 134). While the elected regional governments in the West and East embarked upon crash programmes to expand primary education in the 1950s, the North expanded much more deliberately, leaving it at Independence with less than 10 per cent of the nation's primary school enrolments and less than 5 per cent of secondary enrolments (Dudley, 1968: 281). 'As late as 1951 the 16 million people of the North could point to only one of their number who obtained a full university degree – and he was a Zaria Fulani convert to Christianity' (Coleman, 1958: 139). By 1960, only 57 of the more than one thousand students at University College, Ibadan, came from the North (Ogunsheye, 1965: 129).

The consequences of this educational gap were far-reaching. Literacy in English script, a prerequisite for the clerkships opening up in the public and private sectors, was attained by 16 per cent of the population (aged seven and above) in the East and 18 per cent in the West, compared to only 2 per cent in the North and 1.4 per cent in the Muslim upper North (Coleman, 1968: 133). Because of this huge disparity, and the migration of more highly educated Igbos to Northern cities, Northerners were poorly positioned to benefit from the move toward Nigerianisation of the Civil Service that began in 1948. In subsequent years, the predominance of Southern Nigerians in promotions stirred Northern apprehension that Southerners would come to dominate the Civil Service, even in their own region. These fears were well founded. At Independence, there were only 29 Northerners in the Federal administration and higher executive posts – barely one per cent of all Nigerian officials. Northern representation among Nigerian Police and Army officers was somewhat greater – 5 per cent and 14 per cent, respectively – but still slight (Miners, 1971: 54). Even within the Northern Regional bureaucracy, most of the Senior Civil Servants and post-primary teachers were expatriates.

The North trailed far behind in other dimensions of development as well. Its *per capita* income for 1952 was estimated to be half as large as the West's (Coleman, 1958: 66), and its rate of urbanisation was less than half that in the South (Coleman, 1958: 76). Though the North's *per capita* income was estimated to have drawn even with that in the East, and to 70 per cent of that in the West by 1960

(Coleman, 1962: 48), it still accounted for only 29 per cent of the total wage employment in the country and (by early 1962) for far less than a quarter of the more than one thousand factories in Nigeria (Dudley, 1968: 279–80).

Throughout Africa, the encouragement, even creation, of ethnic loyalty and consciousness was a leading feature of British colonial rule (Mazrui, 1983). Among the fragmented groups of the East and Middle Belt, the British induced federations of successively larger scale. Where larger-scale political organisations already existed, among the Hausa-Fulani and the Yoruba, British policy sought to draw the traditional rulers together to develop 'a wider regional approach' and regional consciousness (Coleman, 1958: 52; Sharwood-Smith, 1969: 119). Beyond this, 'the system of native administration was designed to foster love for and loyalty to tribe' (Coleman, 1958: 210), at the intended expense, Nigerian nationalists increasingly came to believe, of allegiance to a Nigerian nation.

Given this thrust of British policy, it was not surprising that when nationalism began to develop in Nigeria, it largely took the form of separate ethnic nationalisms. The 1939 division of the Southern provinces into Western and Eastern Regions (and the Colony of Lagos) accelerated this trend. These regions roughly coincided with Yoruba-Igbo ethnic boundaries, and after 1946 'every effort was made to encourage "regional thinking"' (Coleman, 1958: 323).

Colonial rule also failed to develop institutions that could have integrated Nigeria around common cultural, social and political symbols and structures. In education, young men from the North were deliberately kept from contact with Southern boys, not only through segregation in the North but through absence of any truly national higher schools. The colonial government 'consistently treated education as a low-priority item' (Coleman, 1958: 125); by 1939, only 12 per cent of the school-age children were receiving any instruction (Coleman, 1958: 125–7). Moreover, the curriculum contained little to foster national consciousness and allegiance. Colonial education was structured for the limited purpose of producing the clerks and petty bureaucrats needed to help administer the colony. Missionaries had as their main purpose the evangelisation of the African. Central to both objectives were a literary education in the English language, and religious and moral training aimed at building 'respect for authority and good citizenship' (Peshkin, 1971: 436; Coleman, 1958: 129–31; Ogunsheye, 1965: 130). Even at the University level, the curriculum was lacking in

Nigerian content (Lewis, 1965: 111).

The colonial failure of national integration was also reflected in the pattern of economic penetration, which connected the nation in relatively superficial ways and only insofar as it served Britain's needs to extract the colony's raw materials and to market its own manufactured goods in exchange. Hence, colonial transportation lines ran from north to south, linking the interior centres with the coastal ports. The colonial economy thus became organised around three isolated regional enclaves devoted to long-distance trade in the products of cash cropping and/or mining (Nnoli, 1978: 124). This, along with the further regionalisation of economic activity and political power in the 1950s, split the entrepreneurial class along regional lines. Members of the emerging bourgeoisie specialised in production, transport and marketing of their region's cash crops and local sale of British manufactured goods. Their horizon was limited to their regional economy, which they came to view 'as their own preserve or empire, their sphere of influence' (Nnoli, 1978: 149). Ethnic integration among upwardly mobile Nigerians was further obstructed by the colonial state's preservation of traditional land tenure patterns, which made it 'difficult for members of an ethnic group to own and develop land outside of their ethnic enclave' (Ogbeide, 1985: 46). With the development of a national conscious-ness thus obstructed even among the emergent bourgeoisie, class could not become an effective crosscutting cleavage in Nigerian politics.

This deepening regionalism, and the manifest contradictions in the regional system (Sklar, 1965a), constituted the most damaging legacy of colonial rule. The colonial administration steadfastly resisted any further division of the existing three regions – rejecting minority-group demands for the security of their own regions, and southern warnings that a federal system in which one region had a population majority could not be stable. 'By preserving Northern Nigeria especially as an area of cultural authenticity and autonomy, with its own strong institutions, Britain inadvertently contributed to the forces which culminated in the Nigerian Civil War' (Mazrui, 1983: 28; see also Kirk-Greene, 1971: 7–8).

Sharwood-Smith (1969: 407) insists that the British had no choice but to maintain the North's decisive numerical advantage, as it was 'the sole defence against political and economic domination by the South.' But the socioeconomic disparities between North and South were themselves a product of colonial penetration and rule. And the preservation of the North's traditional ruling class, for which the maintenance of the region's integrity and national political dominance was essential, was at least as important a motive in British policy. It will be seen that the structure of class domination in the North was the crucial bulwark against radical change, not only in the North but in the country as a whole. Mazrui (1983: 28) has written:

> The colonial philosophy of indirect rule was in part a derivative of British domestic political culture, which distrusted rapid fundamental change and emphasized the virtues of gradualism. The same social forces and ideological considerations which have helped to perpetuate the monarchy and the House of Lords in Britain have also helped to preserve the power of [the] emirates of Northern Nigeria.

A final significant legacy of colonial rule was the development of a modern state that dwarfed all other organised elements of the economy and society. Through the establishment of statutory marketing boards as monopsony purchasers for all export crops, private investment in agriculture was discouraged and the colonial state gained direct control over the greatest source of cash revenue in the country. Rather than supporting agricultural development and farm income, marketing board funds became a primary source of state revenue and the leading factor in its expansion during the commodities boom of the 1950s (Bates, 1981: 12–13; Ake 1981b: 63–5; Ogbeide, 1985: 37–40). State control was also extended over all minerals and mineral exploitation in Nigeria. Indigenous mining activity was eliminated and state mining corporations were established for tin and coal, setting a precedent for petroleum later (Ogbeide, 1985: 42–4). Private enterprise was also discouraged and public corporations established in transportation (road, rail, sea and air). 'Similar monopolistic public corporations were established to cover other public utilities – electric power, gas, water, telephone, postal services, radio and telecommunication' (Ogbeide, 1985: 48).

Colonial rule established a pattern of state monopoly – along with active discouragement of private indigenous enterprise (Akeredolu-Ale, 1976) – that was to continue and intensify after Independence. As indigenous enterprise was unable 'to provide the initiative, leadership, or managerial and technological expertise needed to generate substantial modern-sector economic development, government assumed an increasingly active role in the directly productive sector of the economy' (Schatz, 1977: 5) and the parastatal sector mushroomed (Abernethy, 1983: 12–13). By 1964, 54 per cent of all wage earners were employed by some level of government in Nigeria. Most of the rest (38 per cent) were employed by foreign, mainly British, capital. In the statist, dependent economy that was the legacy of colonial rule, only eight per cent of wage earners were employed by private Nigerian companies (Chapter 6). As in other African countries impatient for economic growth, the capitalist orientation in Nigeria became 'deeply tinged with statism' (Young, 1982: 189).

THE POLITICAL CLASS

If a class is defined in the Marxian sense as a group of people who share a common relationship to the means of production, significant differences will be recognised between the structure of class dominance in the upper North – a steep and rigid hierarchy centred around a titled aristocracy which extracted surplus wealth from the peasantry through taxation and forced labour – and that in the South – where dominance was much looser and more recent, emerging out of modern commerce and the rapidly proliferating opportunities in the civil service and educated professions. Here I conceive of class both in the Marxian sense of relationship to the means of production and in the Weberian sense of income or consumptive power in relation to the market. A class may be considered socially dominant if it owns or controls the most productive assets, appropriates the bulk of the most valued consumption opportunities, and commands a sufficient monopoly over the means of coercion and legitimation to sustain politically this cumulative socioeconomic pre-eminence (c.f. Miliband, 1969; Domhoff, 1983). Necessarily, the members of such a class will 'have controlling positions in the dominant institutions of society' (Sklar, 1965a: 202). They will also have high degrees of class consciousness and social coherence – constituting in the Marxian sense a 'class-for-itself' – as this is a precondition for the class action necessary to consolidate and preserve class domination.

Defined as such, a national dominant class never existed in Nigeria before or during the First Republic, for those in controlling positions in the economy and society were never able to develop a trans-ethnic consciousness and coherence. Rather, class domination developed as a regional and ethnic phenomenon. Within each of Nigeria's three (later four) powerful regions – virtual societies unto themselves – dominant classes emerged, or in the case of the traditional aristocracy in the Muslim North, a dominant class incorporated new social elements to modernise and secure its position.

While the historical roots, cultural orientations and social bases of these dominant classes were sharply different, they were, increasingly, the products of a common process. As Richard L. Sklar has put it in a seminal formulation: 'class relations, at bottom, [were] determined by relations of power, not production' (1979: 537). Both the structure of class domination and individual class standing came to be determined by the relationship to the expanding state, which controlled not only the means of coercion and extraction but, increasingly, the means of production as well. As the colonial state extended and deepened its control over economic and social life, and as state control began to be opened to indigenous competition, personal income and modern occupational status, as well as the control and distribution of national wealth, became ever more dependent upon position in and access to the state. The state thus became the instrument for the formation and consolidation of class domination (Sklar, 1979).

In the two regions of Southern Nigeria, political office became the most reliable and desirable route to membership in the emerging dominant class – what Sklar (1963: 480–94) termed the 'new and rising class' – and government power became the primary means for the accumulation of personal wealth. These materialist, elitist values were new phenomena fostered by Western contact and colonial rule. Traditional cultures did not value the personal accumulation of material wealth, nor did ordinary people seek mobility through it, and traditional stratification systems had no ruling class or aristocracy – indeed, some peoples (such as the Igbo) had no rigid class distinctions of any kind (Smythe and Smythe, 1960: 69; Lloyd, 1960: 47; Uchendu, 1965). But with the penetration of Western education, administration, mass media and market relations, materialist values diffused rapidly throughout the population, and Western symbols of material wealth – modern cars, houses, clothes and consumer goods – became the mark of rising class status. Those whose contact with the West was deepest – the educated elite, and especially those 'trained abroad in acquisitive societies' – sought most eagerly to accumulate and lavishly display this wealth (Smythe and Smythe, 1960: 69). Indeed, the new Nigerian elite sought not only the splendid lifestyle of the British but the very government homes and social clubs they left behind, and the social distance they had maintained. As they accepted power from rulers who had never been responsible to the masses, 'the new elite accepted the same remoteness from the popular will as their natural and proper role' (Smythe and Smythe, 1960: 132).

Socioeconomic consolidation

In a dependent colonial economy where economic opportunity was severely constricted – where capital was scarce, indigenous entrepreneurship small in scale, private enterprise foreign-dominated and poverty pervasive and extreme – the achievement of this new status, and the accumulation of the wealth that marked it, came to depend to an extraordinary degree on political office, political connections and political corruption. The high social status of political and bureaucratic office was a direct legacy of colonial rule, under which the British incumbents had been the dominant class for half a century. And so were the princely material returns. Throughout the emergent political system, the salaries and perquisites of office quickly became, virtually in themselves, a guarantee of high class standing. A new university graduate began in the civil service at a salary twenty times the annual earnings of the average farmer (Abernethy 1969: 243). Legislators, ministers and high-ranking civil servants could expect to earn from seven to thirty times the pay of an ordinary government labourer, even without considering their car allowances, housing subsidies and other emoluments (Sklar and Whitaker, 1966: 112). And such official earnings were trivial relative to what could be amassed through favouritism to private business concerns and misappropriation of public funds. Moreover, given the scarcity of private resources and opportunities, aspiring entrants to the dominant class who did not hold formal office heavily depended on those who did. Political office could deliver or block the licenses, the contracts and the public loan and investment funds that could make a new enterprise or a quick fortune; the scholarships that could launch a bureaucratic career; the government positions and military commissions that offered a coveted livelihood and status. Significantly also, political and administrative office provided leverage with which to obtain favoured admission to elite schools for one's children and relations, giving them a competitive advantage for higher education and professional employment, and so shifting the basis of status attainment in Southern Nigeria away from achievement, toward ascription (Abernethy, 1969: 244–9). Hence, as class privilege was being consolidated it was also beginning to reproduce itself across generations.

The desire to achieve elite social status and to accumulate wealth – to obtain a place in the emergent dominant class – thus motivated a fierce hunger for political power. This was accentuated by the pervasive poverty from which all Nigerians were struggling to escape. These were, for the most part, 'first-generation educated and prosperous men, having emerged from very humble peasant and working-class stock and from the most grinding and dehumanising poverty', to which they could not 'with equanimity' contemplate returning (Osoba, 1977: 378). For the typical incumbent, defeat meant the loss not simply of political office but of the socioeconomic position he had achieved for himself and his family. That so much was at stake in every election – both the major channel of upward mobility and the primary insurance against downward mobility – explains much of the bruising intensity of election campaigns and the increasingly ruthless repression of political opposition during the life of the First Republic.

Nowhere did political repression become more ruthless and systematic than in the North (Post, 1963: 290–2; Schwarz, 1965: 106–7; Dent, 1966; Feinstein, 1973: 156–7), for there the stakes were even greater than the formation of a dominant class position. In the Muslim emirates of the North, electoral politics and socioeconomic change challenged the dominance of what Lubeck (1979: 193) has termed 'an integrated Muslim ruling class', which had developed over centuries. Power, wealth and status were rigidly ascribed from birth to a titled aristocracy, the *sarakuna*, which ruled in despotic fashion over the mass of commoners, the *talakawa*.[1] At the peak of state power were the Emirs, or kings. Validated by the religious authority of Islam and institutionalised through complex bureaucratic and judicial administrations and elaborate networks of clientage, the authority of the Emirs was enormous and deeply based (Smith, 1959; Dudley, 1968: 11, 49–50; Sharwood-Smith, 1969: 141). So long as their kingdoms were insulated from Western education and foreign ideas of democracy and egalitarianism, their feudalistic authority – and the entire, sharply graded structure of power and privilege which it protected – was stable.

A common interest in the stability of this system was the basis for the highly successful class alliance between British colonial administration and trading firms and the *sarakuna*, which, through Lugard's policy of 'indirect rule', secured and advanced each of their material interests in Northern Nigeria for more than half a century (Lubeck, 1979; Watts, 1983: 149–86). In exchange for rationalisation and reform of the emirates' state structure, and for subservience to British dominion, the British agreed to recognise and rule through the authority of the *sarakuna* and not to interfere in any way with the sanctity and predominance of Islam (Coleman, 1958: 50, 133–7; Dudley, 1968: 13–20; Sharwood-Smith, 1969: 45–6, 54). Indeed the position of Islam was strengthened, and, while eliminating some abuses, indirect rule actually 'reinforced the emir's power by eliminating traditional checks on centralised authority' and enhancing his technical means of coercion and domination (Lubeck, 1979: 199–201; also Dudley, 1968: 14–17; Paden, 1973: 230; Watts, 1983: 171; Ibrahim, 1983: 40–61). Indirect rule increased the emir's administrative power (designating him the sole Native Authority in his territory), his economic security (by making him the instrument of colonial tax collection), and his judicial authority (through new powers of appointment and new Emir courts). In so doing, it increased the social distance between the rulers and the ruled and made the emirs 'more and more autocratic in their attitude toward the mass of the people' (Dudley, 1968: 16).

Later, with the emergence of competitive politics, colonial administration went to special lengths to structure elections in the North to favour the party of the *sarakuna* against its radical opposition (Sklar, 1963: 30; Feinstein, 1973: 154)[2] and to coopt, intimidate, punish or otherwise neutralise radical leaders and activists (Feinstein, 1973: 90–1, 114–16, 119–20, 129). Indeed, the colonial bias in favour of the ruling-class party, the Northern Peoples' Congress, was active and thinly veiled. The NPC, wrote the former Lieutenant Governor of the Region, was 'more sober and mature' in its programme than the radical Northern Elements Progressive Union, most of whose leaders harboured an 'almost hysterical hatred' for the system of authority. Whereas the NPC sought 'to unite and reform', NEPU leaders sought 'to destroy and replace' – 'to overthrow the regime for their own ends'. Mobilising mainly 'market rabble' and 'semiliterates', NEPU, in this colonialist view, had a weak base of support, but its 'incitement to revolution . . . could have been dangerous' (Sharwood-Smith, 1969: 217–19, 223, 235). Not surprisingly, colonial officials were instrumental in identifying the future 'responsible' political leaders of the North and encouraging them to organise politically, and Sharwood-Smith himself developed unusually close relations with NPC leaders such as the eventual Northern Premier, Ahmadu

Bello, and especially the eventual Prime Minister, Abubakar Tafawa Balewa (Sharwood-Smith, 1969: 163, 191, 212, 313, 348, 363–5).

The transition to self-rule that began in 1951 fundamentally threatened the social dominance of the *sarakuna*, forcing it to choose between the economic modernisation and rapid promotion of Western education it had previously eschewed and the otherwise likely domination of the North by radical and culturally alien southerners. Given the stated intention of the latter to dismantle what they saw as a feudalistic and unjust social system in the North, and their political liaison with radical young *talakawa* in the North similarly pledged to sweeping reform, the traditional aristocracy found itself confronted with a choice between adaptation and extinction. It (and the British as well) had to control the pace of change in the North to preserve its social dominance, and to do this it had to control the emergent parliamentary state in the North. With a shrewdness and political skill never figured on by southern elites, a new generation of northern aristocrats, educated in British schools, used the instrument of a modern political party, the NPC, to modernise and so preserve the structure of class dominance.[3] By delimiting the traditional authority of the emirs and subordinating it to that of the modern state, they sought to reconstitute the social and economic dominance of the aristocracy on a modern foundation.

From the lower ranks of the *sarakuna* – the educated clerks and officials of the emirates' native administrations – and the highest rank of the *talakawa* – the wealthy merchants, or *attajirai* – the aristocracy drew into a political alliance the additional social segments it needed to reproduce and entrench its class dominance in Northern Nigeria (Coleman, 1958: 353–68; Sklar, 1963: 323–35, 502; Dudley, 1968: 134–52; Whitaker, 1970: 313–54). This critical effort was assisted not only by Islam, with its 'insistence . . . on the unity of all believers' (Whitaker, 1970: 387), but also by colonial institutions and officials. The educated leadership for this new class alliance was drawn from the small but remarkably cohesive alumni of the elite Katsina Teacher Training College – the only institution of its kind in the North. Trained for leadership roles, its graduates (drawn heavily but not exclusively from the aristocracy) would become Regional Premier and Federal Prime Minister, and also occupy a number of key ministerial and political posts at both levels (Sklar, 1963: 90 (n.11); Whitaker, 1965: 544; Sharwood-Smith, 1969: 189). In addition, colonial administration played a catalytic role in the incorporation of the *attajirai* into the dominant class, succeeding in persuading the Emir of Kano to appoint the leading Hausa merchant of that commercial capital, Alhassan dan Tata, to his council (Sharwood-Smith, 1969: 205–6).

Herein lay the fundamental difference between North and South. In all three regions, the ruling party functioned 'to foster the integration of dominant elites on a class basis' (Sklar, 1963: 335). But in the North, power was used to preserve the position of a traditional dominant class, which incorporated rising commercial and professional elements in a subordinate role. In the South, the ruling parties were engines of class formation, inaugurated and controlled by modern professional and business elites who enlisted the traditional rulers in a subordinate role (Coleman, 1958: 284–91, 327–52; Sklar, 1963: 353, 485–94; Post, 1963: 46–7).

What these two processes shared in common was a recognition that control of the state was the necessary foundation of class formation and consolidation. In each region, state power became the unifying force that drew educated professionals, businessmen and traditional elites into the party of the dominant ethnic group and welded these diverse elites into a dominant class. This was accomplished through the vast powers delegated to the regional governments by the 1954 constitution (Sklar, 1963). Perhaps the most valuable of these regional powers (and crucial at the local levels as well) was the commercial patronage so vital to the formation of private wealth and business control. Government construction contracts were much less instruments for construction *per se* than for enrichment of the officials who awarded them and the politically connected 'contractors' who received them (Schatz, 1977: 190–5). Purchases of all kinds by public corporations and government bodies were padded, inflated in cost and otherwise manipulated for private gain (Schatz, 1977: 208–9). Loan programmes fostered not genuine agricultural and industrial development but, through favouritism in awards, security conditions and repayment enforcement, the enrichment of the well-connected (Schatz, 1977: 231–2; Helleiner, 1964: 98–123).

The largest source of commercial patronage was the finance capital held by the agricultural marketing boards and statutory corporations of each region. These strategic funds were placed under the direction of trusted operatives of the ruling parties and dispensed, under criteria defying economic rationality, to party-connected businesses and banks. In the wealthiest region, the cocoa-rich West, a 1962 corruption inquiry traced a dizzying haemorrhage of public resources to the ruling Action Group and a small, interlocking circle of its top politicians and businessmen, whose machinations and sheer reckless-ness and incompetence essentially bankrupted the Western Region Marketing Board in only seven years of operation (Coker, 1962; Diamond, 1980: 556–82). This was not the only state entity so drained in the West but was certainly the most significant, for the regional marketing boards were expected to use the vast surpluses they accumulated from monopoly trade in commodity crops to support agricultural prices and foster economic development. As had happened in the Eastern Region five years previously (Foster-Sutton, 1957; Sklar, 1963: 161–85), government purchase of majority control (with Marketing Board funds) rescued the major indigenous bank – and the party leaders who owned it – when, despite massive previous government deposits, it was threatened with financial collapse (Coker, 1962: Vol. 1, Part 3). In the North as well, the ruling party's 'far-reaching' control of the Regional Marketing Board and Develop-ment Corporation was 'used to further the purposes of the NPC *and* the privileged maintenance of the traditional elite' (Whitaker, 1970: 388–90).[4]

Political consolidation

Control of the state was thus essential to the economic and social consolidation of class dominance – to the accumulation of wealth and ownership and to the social fusion of elites with common class interests and 'a growing sense of class consciousness' (Sklar, 1963: 480). But it was equally vital to its political consolidation. For the state afforded the means to maintain class dominance – to induce support for and punish opposition to the party of the dominant class in each region. In an emergent capitalist society, where bourgeois dominance was not secured by the breadth of economic control and thick network of legitimating institutions that mark advanced capitalist societies (Miliband, 1969), a rising class risked its tenuous position if it allowed the possibility of rule by a party it did not control. Even for the more deeply rooted structure of class dominance in the North, sweeping social and economic change made the prospect of political defeat dangerously threatening. The democratic state thus had to be controlled *directly* by the dominant class. And in order to secure state control through 'democratic' elections, nothing was more valuable than the state itself. The powers of incumbency thus took their place beside manipulation of ethnicity as the primary weapons of the regional ruling parties.

Each ruling party set about in the early 1950s to use the lever of state power – the control over patronage, coercion and chieftancy in particular – to consolidate its political base and to suppress those elements that resisted consolidation. Pervasive state control over the economy 'promoted a degree of dependence of the ... Nigerian "entrepreneur" on those who controlled government to an extent unknown to his historic counterpart in Western societies' (Whitaker, 1970: 334). Rank favouritism in the award of loans, contracts, bank credits, positions on public boards and corporations, and licenses to trade commodity crops gave rise in each region to a 'privileged group' of entrepreneurs who came upon sudden and fantastic success and who, in return, 'were expected to contribute substantially to party funds, use their wealth and influence to mobilise support for their parties in their various localities, and maintain unflinching loyalty to party leadership' (Osoba, 1977: 370; Sklar, 1963: 501).

In the North, such vast patronage was the primary instrument for inducting new social strata into the expanding class alliance of the Muslim aristocracy and its party, the NPC. This instrument was focused on two critical strata: the *attajirai* and the traditional elites of Northern minority groups outside the emirates. The *attajirai* were crucial to the NPC not only because their wealth was a needed source of party finance, but because, as Hausas, they were ideal candidates to turn back the radical challenge of the NEPU, whose electoral strategy was to ignite ethnic resentment among the Hausa *talakawa* against the 'Fulani' ruling class (Whitaker, 1970: 333). The ethnic minorities around the perimeter of the emirates were crucial because, while the NPC could control the Regional Government without their political support, it could not control the Federal Parliament, which it needed to do to ensure against any federal assault on the social structure of the North or the regional unity and autonomy that facilitated its preservation. Political and commercial patronage forged the horizontal integration of these elites into the dominant party under its banner of regional unity: 'One North, one people, irrespective of religion, rank, or tribe' (Sklar, 1963: 338–49).

Patronage was similarly used to induce the electoral support of whole communities, which were explicitly warned during election campaigns that the provision of amenities depended on support of the ruling party. Even in federal elections, the ruling regional parties heavily exploited their capacity to deliver the lifeblood of development – roads, water, electricity, schools, health care – and to deny them to constituencies which might by some 'stroke of misjudgment' cast their votes for a 'worthless [opposition] candidate' (quoted in Post, 1963: 393). For individuals, open support of the opposition could mean denial of whatever they might need from the expanding state: scholarships for their sons, loans for their farms, stalls in the markets, even their personal freedom (Dent, 1966; Post, 1963: 264). 'Patronage' was also dispensed during the election campaigns, from the formidable campaign treasuries corruptly amassed by the ruling parties.

In all three regions, albeit differently in each, the power to regulate and depose chiefs was used to consolidate political domination. In the Western Region, the Action Group embarked from the very start on a strategy of integrating the culturally important Yoruba chiefs into its emergent class alliance. It gave formal recognition of and deference to their honorary status in exchange for their political support, while severely punishing those who resisted (Sklar, 1963: 230–41). In the North, the new generation of aristocrats who vaulted into party leadership used the power of the modern state to effect needed reforms in local government and judicial administration, and did not hesitate to punish traditional rulers whose resistance to change appeared to threaten the interests of the dominant class as a whole (Whitaker, 1970: 279–82; Dudley, 1968: 211–17).[5] In the East, where chieftancy was not a significant tradition, the ruling National Council of Nigeria and the Cameroons (NCNC) yielded in 1959 to minority demands for a House of Chiefs, at least partly 'to use the institution for partisan advantage, as in the North and West' (Sklar, 1963: 446).

The power of the state was also used to entice ethnic and radical (usually young) opposition politicians to 'cross the carpet' in the regional legislatures and otherwise decamp to the ruling party. As 'many of the radicals acquired attitudes and interests akin to those of a privileged class' (Sklar, 1963: 481), they were gradually co-opted. Those who resisted were repressed. During the 1950s, and especially after Independence, control over the judiciary (in the North), the local police (in the North and West), and tax assessment were used to intimidate and thwart political opposition. Opposition candidates and supporters were gaoled on trumped-up charges, while campaign rallies and processions were denied permits or banned by new regulations (Post, 1963: 66–71; Dent, 1966; Schwarz, 1965: 106; Feinstein, 1973: 156–7, 208–9). When massive repression and profligate patronage became insufficient to assure the election of an unpopular ruling party (as they did in the West in 1965), there was always the final instrument of wholesale electoral fraud.

Class action and ethnic conflict

The abuse of public responsibilities and resources for personal enrichment was not the random expression of individual greed; it was the deliberate, systematic effort of an emerging dominant class to accumulate wealth and to establish control over the means of production, at public expense. Given the paucity of other means for accumulation, and the costs of maintaining and enlarging politically crucial clientage networks, such political corruption was indispensable to the proces of class formation (Diamond 1984b). Similarly, the manipulation of state power by each regional party to entrench its rule must be seen in a larger context than the mere hunger for power. These processes of 'enrichment' and 'entrenchment' (Schatz, 1977) were the primary forms of class action, where this is defined as 'collective action ... to increase or reduce social inequality and domination, or to strengthen or weaken the means whereby the domination of a privileged stratum is maintained' (Sklar, 1979: 547). Because state power was the instrument of these processes, the resulting social formation has been given the name 'political class' (Sklar, 1965a: 203–4).[6] The term reflects the predominance of politicians among the emergent dominant class (one survey showing more than two-thirds of the nation's 'top elite' to hold elected or appointed government office (Smythe and Smythe, 1960: 78–9)), but its analytic logic derives precisely from the extent to which members who were not formally in politics or governments also owed their class position to relations of power.

If control of the state was the basis of class formation and consolidation, then dominant-class elements had to control the state at any price. In a democratic polity, this meant winning elections, and in a multi-ethnic society that was modernising but still largely illiterate, where expectations were growing faster than resources, no electoral strategy seemed more assured of success than the manipulation of ethnic pride and prejudice.[7] From the first significant elections in 1951 to the final, fraudulent and brutal confrontations in 1964 and 1965, the regional political classes used ethnicity as an electoral weapon against each other and against lower-class challengers from below. Prime Minister Tafawa Balewa himself conceded this when he wrote, 'it seems to me the greatest offenders in this direction are not the British officials but Nigerian politicians who, in order to gain advantage over their political adversaries, would exercise no scruples in fanning the fires of tribal jealousies and suspicion' (Balewa, 1961: xi).

In doing so, they were not manufacturing ethnicity out of whole cloth but rather, exploiting a powerful tendency for politics in plural societies to be perceived and expressed in ethnic or even communal terms (Melson and Wolpe, 1971), 'communal' here meaning not simply cultural identity but a sacred sense of community based on 'an integrated system of value' (Sklar, 1963: 474–6).[8] From the low levels of education, national integration and economic development, and the consequent absence of effective functional crosspressures, it naturally followed that the focus of politics would be the community, or what Ferdinand Tonnies termed *Gemeinschaft* in his classic distinction from the modern society or association, *Gesellschaft*. In contrast to the rational voluntary and deliberate character of associational participation, communal participation tapped 'a unified moral universe' of 'political, spiritual and cultural values', and so tended to view political opposition from within the community 'with moral indignation and to punish it as antisocial conduct' (Sklar, 1963: 474–6). Especially in the rural areas, where objective information was scarce and group pressure strong, individual choice based on ideology or economic interest was unheard of: 'for a man to support a political party different from the one supported by the rest of the community amounted almost to a repudiation of his own people' (Post, 1963: 396). For somewhat different reasons, ethnicity was also a naturally powerful force in the cities and towns, where ethnic consciousness and organisation fulfilled the psychological needs for identity and community among the swelling numbers of migrants to a strange milieu; the social needs for welfare, credit, security and support in a context of bewildering scale and rapid change; and the politico-economic need for mutual assistance in competition for the proliferating but scarce fruits of a modernising economy and an expanding state (Wallerstein, 1964; Cohen, 1969; Melson and Wolpe, 1971; Baker, 1974; Wolpe, 1974; Young, 1976; Markovitz, 1977: 112; Nnoli, 1978: 31–2). Thus, be it at the level of a village, an urban ward, a town, a clan, or a whole ethnic nation, it was through the familiar imagery of ethnic identity that politicians and opinion leaders interpreted regional and national political struggle.

Major party newspapers and leaders never failed to keep local elites and candidates amply supplied with ethnic accusations and suspicions, however hysterical and malicious. The Action Group would ban Islam in the North. The NPC would force it upon the South. The NCNC would stack the entire bureaucracy with Igbos. Far-fetched in the extreme, such tactics nevertheless successfully transformed people's basest prejudices and wildest fears into resounding electoral mandates. The fact that 'political constituencies were geographical in nature and ethnically homogeneous' (Nnoli, 1978: 152; see also Melson and Wolpe, 1971: 13) and the tendency for opposition candidates to be nominees of parties associated with 'foreign' ethnic groups, further heightened the utility of 'tribalism' as an electoral vehicle for the entrenchment of each region's political class.

Thus, in an economy where state power was the essential instrument of class formation and consolidation, in a polity where mass electoral mobilisation was necessary for the acquisition and retention of state power, and in a society where different ethnic groups hotly competed for scarce resources and rewards, with scant crosscutting solidarities or national ties to moderate that competition, 'tribalism' became the natural reflex and indispensable vehicle of the rising class. By whipping up communal fears and suspicions, by casting each election as a threat to the sacred values and even the survival of the ethnic community – by establishing 'tribalism' as the ideology of politics (Mafeje, 1971: 258–9) – the politicians and business allies of each regional party were able to entrench themselves in power.

In two other senses as well, this political manipulation and magnification of ethnic consciousness sprang from the process of class formation. First, it functioned as 'a mask for class privilege' (Sklar, 1967: 6) and as 'one of the major antidotes against the development of [lower] class consciousness' (Nnoli, 1979: 154; c.f. Mafeje, 1971: 259). The contrasts between the wealth that the political class[9] was rapidly accumulating and flaunting and the poverty that the masses were failing to escape was becoming increasingly stark. While the wealth of the *nouveaux riches* was at first a matter of pride for their communities, this 'pride in Nigerian achievement gave way to resentment and to questions about how certain forms of wealth had been built up' (O'Connell, 1966: 134). Disillusionment with the political class became especially acute among its own junior and marginal elements, who found their progress in the civil service and other modern institutions blocked by the large number of not-very-much-older (but often less qualified) Nigerians rapidly promoted during decolonisation, and whose ideals were deeply offended by the mounting greed, corruption, and inefficiency. The political class had to fend off the challenge from this increasingly restive and outspoken counter-elite. In particular, it had to keep radical criticisms and class-based appeals from infecting and mobilising the mass. By distributing patronage to their ethnic communities, the members of the political class built support among the 'primordial public' and so won its toleration for corruption against the 'civic public' (Ekeh, 1975). At the same time, 'tribalism' diverted attention from dominant-class action and so precluded class-based mobilisation against it.

Second, tribalism became an instrument of competition within the emerging dominant class for the limited spoils of the developing state. As suggested by their aggressive forays into each other's political 'turf' (a strategy eschewed only by the NPC, and progressively less so after Independence), the political classes were deeply divided by ethnicity and region. Despite their common interest in using the state to consolidate their class dominance, they could not agree on a sharing out of the national spoils, in part because demand for the goods of the modern state was increasing much faster than supply. Bitterly and repeatedly they contested for control of the Federal Government and its resources, and, in the case of the two major southern parties, for control of the other regions as well, since their own regions were insufficient bases for federal power. Increasingly, ethnic segments of the political classes also fought for control of major social and economic institutions.

It was the leaders of these political classes who organised the competition for scarce resources and opportunities along ethnic lines. As development created new resources of class formation, the new generation of educated elites modernised and familiarised the languages, cultures and histories of their peoples so as to transform 'latent ethnicity into manifest nationalism' that could be mobilised for competitive advantage (Young, 1976: 46). Through the ethnic unions they formed, in particular the Igbo State Union and the (Yoruba) *Egbe Omo Oduduwa*, they sought to create and historically justify a larger ethnic consciousness (Ekeh, 1975: 105; Melson and Wolpe, 1971: 23). Their efforts succeeded in pushing out ethnic boundaries to encompass a wider circle of commonality that still contained the irreducible core of cultural unity – a common language of communication and understanding. It was around this cultural core that people rallied for mutual assistance in the competition for wealth and power, and it was precisely the real cultural content of ethnicity that made it 'possible for class actions to be successfully dressed in ethnic garb' (Nnoli, 1978: 20). Similarly, it was the real emotional force of cultural attachments that so disposed them to erupt in conflict and made such conflict so difficult to manage. Nevertheless, the roots of conflict lay not in cultural dissonance but in cultural similarity – in the common value placed on the fruits of economic growth and state expansion. At the federal level in particular, elites of different ethnic groups sought the same material and psychic rewards, the same positions of power, prestige, security and challenge. Their competitive mass mobilisation and their resulting political conflicts appeared ethnic and regional in character. But what catalysed these tensions into conflict was not 'tribalism'. It was class action.

Fundamentally, it was this class action that destroyed the democratic prospect in Nigeria. The desperately instrumental view of politics it produced allowed no respect or tolerance to be accorded political opposition, and no stone to be unturned in the pursuit of victory. Politics became a zero-sum game without rules or boundaries. Constitutional guarantees were trampled and ethnic and regional insecurities heightened in a vicious cycle of tribalism, violence and repression. This cycle sharply accelerated after Independence when the one arbiter of competition with any claim to neutrality withdrew from the scene, giving rise to a succession of fierce political crises that helped to erode the legitimacy of the regime. But by then, the lines of political cleavage and roots of political crisis had already been sharply exposed in a decade of intense, shifting political conflicts.

THE EMERGENCE OF POLITICAL CONFLICT

At one level of analysis, political conflict in Nigeria during the 1950s was largely the product of the convergence of ethnic, regional and political cleavage. All of the major conflicts of the decade tapped at least one of these cleavages directly, and inevitably involved the other two in some form. But conflicts that appeard sectional were significantly rooted in class action. For the most part, these conflicts were dominant-class conflicts, even when they mobilised a mass base. They sprang from the struggle among the political classes to control the narrow resource base of an underdeveloped economy and state, a struggle which, as it became 'tribalised', ultimately infected the whole of political and social life in Nigeria.

Igbo *v.* Yoruba

The first major ethnic conflict among emergent dominant-class elements grew out of the nationalist movement. The late 1930s and 1940s witnessed a sweeping movement for collective improvement among the Igbo people, both in Igboland and in the multi-ethnic towns 'abroad', Lagos in particular. Through amazingly rapid adoption of Western education and Christian religion and determined ethnic organisation, the Igbos closed by 1950 a substantial early Yoruba advantage in Western education and employment (Coleman, 1958: 332–43). This sweeping Igbo advance put them in competition with the Yoruba for the educational, economic and political opportunities that were opening up to Nigerians. Alarmed by this challenge, the Yoruba elite organised in defence of its privileged position, and there ensued in the 1940s a struggle for socioeconomic power between the Yoruba and Igbo 'new men' that permanently split the nationalist movement along largely ethnic lines (Coleman, 1958: 343–52).

The competition peaked in 1948 when the rivalry between the two nationalist organisations erupted in a war of words between their newspapers. Though the Igbo-led NCNC had sought with some success to construct a multi-ethnic base, the press war featured an ugly outpouring of ethnic hatred that came close to exploding into mass violence that summer (Coleman, 1958: 346). The bitter confrontation permanently politicised Yoruba and Igbo cultural organisations (Sklar, 1963: 70) and sowed an ethnic political tension that was never successfully bridged. It sprang from years of competition within the rising elite for the limited resources of class formation – newspaper circulation, organisational membership, popular (especially youth) political support, bureaucratic position, local elective office and leadership positions in the trade unions and nationalist movement.

The onset of party competition

Embittered by another outburst of press warfare and continuing streams of mutual vilification, entrenched by successive failures of half-hearted attempts at reconciliation, this Yoruba-Igbo cleavage could not but assume a formal political character with the preparation for full-scale electoral politics during the constitutional review of 1949–50. This brought multiple conflicts not only between Yoruba and Igbo but between Northern and Southern political leaders over the distribution of power and revenue between the regions they expected to control. As the first regional elections approached in 1951, openly regionalist parties were formed in the West and North out of existing cultural organisations, for the express purpose of winning political control of those regions against challenge of the better organised and more broadly based NCNC.

The regional character of each party was reflected in its leadership. To many Yoruba elite, the Igbo challenge was personified in the NCNC national leader, Dr Nnamdi Azikiwe, who had built a vast commercial and journalistic empire since returning to Nigeria in 1937 from study in the US and journalism in Ghana. As he forged to the leadership of the nationalist movement, Dr Azikiwe had become a symbol of cultural pride for the Igbo people. His solid political base among them, reflected in an increasingly close association between the pan-Igbo ethnic movement and the NCNC nationalist campaign, along with his aggressive personal style, heightened Yoruba apprehensions of a 'growing threat of Igbo domination' (Coleman, 1958: 341–2), and inspired a young Yoruba barrister, upon his return to Nigeria in 1946 from study in London, to organise a pan-Yoruba cultural society, the *Egbe Omo Oduduwa*. Early in 1950, this gifted and ambitious lawyer, Obafemi Awolowo, used this cultural base to organise a new political party, the Action Group, for the explicit purpose of winning control of the Western Region the following year.

At the same time, the aggressive mobilisation of these and other Southern groups stirred a 'political awakening' in the North, led by a new generation of Northern elites (predominantly aristocratic) whose exposure to Western education had bred reformist inclinations and who had become alarmed to discover the massive disadvantage of their region and peoples in every aspect of modernisation. While some of these young elites were of relatively humble birth, such as Mallam Abubakar Tafawa Balewa (one of the first northerners to receive higher education in London), their leader, Alhaji Ahmadu Bello, epitomised the traditional oligarchy. A direct, lineal descendent of Shehu Usman Dan Fodio (the leader of the 1804 Jihad and founder of the Sokoto Caliphate), he held a major traditional title, Sardauna of Sokoto, and aspired to the pre-eminent traditional office in the North, Sultan of Sokoto. But as a shrewd, Western-educated defender of the traditional system he understood acutely the need to adapt it to the forces of modernisation. This required educating the Northern elite in Western schools and reforming the traditional systems of local government and justice, even to the extent of punishing traditional rulers whose resistance to change 'might be prejudicial to the interests of the whole' (Whitaker, 1970: 352). But, first and foremost, it required a modern political party to secure control of the new government to be elected in the North. Stunned by victories of the radical NEPU opposition in the early rounds of the 1951 elections, conservative and moderate Northern elites hastily revived their sagging cultural organisation, the Northern Peoples' Congress, and transformed it into a political party – just in time to win a sweeping victory in the final stage of the voting (Whitaker, 1970: 361–2).

With the 1951 victories of the NPC, the AG and the NCNC in their home regions, a rough identity was established between region, ethnicity and party, which heightened over the course of the decade. Each cleavage contributed a distinctive dimension of strain to the resulting conflicts. The huge disparity in development level moved Northern leaders to demand resources to catch up, while Southern leaders argued for investment in demonstrated progress and bureaucratic placement strictly by merit. Social and political tension inhered in the enormous cultural distance between North and South, as reflected in their vastly different structures of authority and status, and in the fact that 'the Christian South was looking toward England and Western Europe' while 'the Islamic North fixed its gaze on Mecca' (Davies, 1961: 92). But these groups were not without cultural similarities as well (Nnoli, 1978: 110–12), and cultural distance did not keep ethnic group leaders from forming all manner of alliances when it served their interests to do so. It was the intersection of cultural and regional tensions with the emergent class structure that fixed party competition around these sectional tensions and thereby inflamed them.

North *v.* South

The close interaction between sectional conflict and class structure is illustrated even (perhaps especially) by those conflicts which appeared most purely ethnic, such as the tragic Kano riot of 1953. Early in 1953, a bitter political confrontation erupted in the Central House of Representatives with the introduction of a motion calling for self-government for Nigeria in 1956. This date, to which both Southern parties had committed themselves in their competition for nationalist leadership, was bitterly opposed by Northern politicians, who feared that self-government would mean government by Southerners unless postponed until the North 'caught up' in education, training and political expertise, and freed itself from Southern control of its bureaucracy, commerce and transportation system. When Northern politicians blocked the motion, they were insulted and abused by street crowds in Lagos and subsequently by the Southern press. This press condemnation escalated when, upon their return to the North, they announced a programme for the virtual secession of their region from Nigeria. As the war of rhetoric was peaking, the two Southern parties sent delegations to the North to campaign directly for self-government. The arrival of one such delegation in Kano sparked four days of rioting in that city's Sabon Gari (strangers' quarters) that left more than 200 people injured and 36 dead (21 of them Igbos) (Coleman, 1958: 398–9). A massacre of hundreds of Igbos was only narrowly averted (Sharwood-Smith, 1969: 263–75).

The 1953 Kano riot was an event of great historical significance. Though not the first instance of interethnic violence in the North, it was the bloodiest, and foreshadowed an even more traumatic confrontation in Kano thirteen years later that would accelerate the slide to civil war. Like the 1966 clash, the 1953 riot was essentially an outpouring of resentment by the indigenous Hausa population against the escalating pre-emption of commercial opportunities, modern education and modern clerical and semi-skilled jobs by Igbo migrants to the city (Paden, 1971: 124–31). This mass-based social and economic competition, rubbing against sharply visible cultural differences, generated the necessary preconditions for violent ethnic conflict. But, as in 1966, these palpable tensions exploded only in a climate of national crisis created by competing political leaders, who depicted the timing of self-government as an issue involving consummate cultural interests. This was not simply cynical manipulation. Southern leaders sincerely saw the North as feudal and backward and 'were growing weary of recurrent threats of northern secession' (Coleman, 1958: 401). And Northern leaders, both the reigning traditional rulers and the new Western-educated generation, perceived the prospect of Southern domination as a threat to cherished cultural values and their people's socioeconomic interests. But their attachment to Islamic values could not be separated from their commitment to the structure of power and privilege which those values legitimated. Nor could their concern for their people's progress be divorced from their anxiety over the threat of Southern penetration to their own careers. The fuse for mass violence in Kano was conflict between the regional political classes over not simply cultural and regional but also class interests. At stake was control over the basic instrument of class formation – the modern state.

The dominance of the traditional ruling class in the North was endangered perhaps most imminently by the alarming advance of Southerners in the Northern bureaucracy, which threatened not only to frustrate the policies of the new Northern Regional Government, but to undermine the entire Native Authority System as well. Fearing that Southerners would seize control of the Northern Public Service as it hurried to 'Nigerianise' in the final years of colonial rule, the Northern Government resolved to give qualified Northerners explicit preference over Southerners in hiring, while the traditional leadership, which had hitherto shunned Western education and training as a threat to the emirate class structure, now embraced them as essential for its preservation (Nicholson, 1966: 171–3; Whitaker, 1970: 401–2).

This regionalist strategy accelerated with the division of the unitary Public Service into regional branches in 1954. While the Eastern and Western Regions raced to 'indigenise' their bureaucracies, the North sought 'Northernisation'. Expatriates were actually preferred to Southerners when no qualified Northerner was available, while Southerners were frozen, driven out, and permanently excluded from the Northern Public Service (Nicholson, 1966: 174; Dudley, 1968: 220). While engendering bitter Southern resentment, this policy worked almost precisely as intended: purging the bureaucracy of all but one Southerner by 1959; raising its proportion of Northerners from almost nothing to one-half in 1961; heavily disposing it toward manipulation and domination by the ruling NPC, and so further concentrating administrative and political power in the narrow, dominant class of the North (Dudley, 1968: 220–1).

The character of Northernisation as the confluence of ethnic and class action was apparent in its other ramifications as well. Northern businessmen used their growing prominence in the NPC to press for provisions excluding Southerners from government contracts, retail trade and ownership of land (Sklar, 1963: 328; Dudley, 1968: 232; Nnoli, 1978: 194). By 1958 Northern Premier Ahmadu Bello was boldly declaring that the goal of Northernisation was to have

'Northerners gain control of everything in the country' (Dudley, 1968: 220). In fact, the political instability of the time stemmed significantly from this determination of the Northern ruling class to establish firm control over the federal state and its resources, and so to secure its dominance over the political classes of the Eastern and Western regions.

Regional rivalry

From its base of political power in the regional government, the emergent dominant class in each region competed with the other two for the resources and opportunities of class formation. Both the Eastern and Western Regions as well hurried to indigenise their public services, bringing home large numbers of civil servants from around the country. Though neither region formally assumed the radical exclusionist policy of the North, both achieved it in practice (Kingsley, 1963: 305).

Regional rivalry was apparent as early as the 1950 Constitutional Conference, where the NCNC opposed a proposal to incorporate Lagos into the Western Region and leaders of each region contested the formula for revenue allocation. The former issue was finally settled in 1953, when the Secretary of State for the Colonies decided in favour of a federalised capital separated from the West, but not before the Action Group had threatened 'to lead the West in a secession out of the federation' over the issue (Nnoli, 1978: 160). The formula for revenue allocation, by contrast, was never permanently settled. With their region's population vastly exceeding its wealth, Northern delegates to both the 1950 and 1953 constitutional conferences pressed for distribution on a per capita basis. Those from the cocoa-rich West called for allocation of all revenues to the region of derivation, while delegates from the East 'pleaded on behalf of the principle of need' (Nnoli, 1978: 203). A complex compromise in 1950 gave way to an emphasis on derivation after 1953 that clearly favoured the West, but this only deepened the political rivalry between the West and the poorer East and North. A new compromise was fashioned in 1957 as independence approached and the West's cocoa exports slumped (Coleman, 1958: 375–6), but the issue would resurface with new force as the balance of economic advantage in the Federation shifted (Chapter 5).

For both the class structure and the pattern of political conflict, the key decision at the 1953 Conference was the scrapping of the unitary state structure for a genuinely federal system. This gave the Northern ruling class the autonomy it sought to protect its position against the threat from the South, and gave the rising elites of each region the political and economic resources of class formation. With the establishment in 1954 of regional premiers, cabinets, legislatures, judicial systems, public services, marketing boards and development corporations, the regions became the chief centres of political power in Nigeria, and their struggle for socioeconomic resources came to dominate Nigerian politics.

The three ruling parties developed similar competitive strategies in this struggle. Beginning with intensive mobilisation of the ethnic homeland to ensure its monolithic electoral support, they then reached out to the region's ethnic minorities and used regional power to consolidate total control of the regional government. This regional hegemony was, in turn, a precondition for effective national competition. Ethnic minorities in the other regions were incited to oppose their government and demand separate regions, which would presumably support the party that had championed their cause. With this added support, each party hoped to win parliamentary control of the Federal Government, or at least to share control in coalition with another party. This was crucial to the ultimate aim of the strategy: capturing for the region and its political class the maximum feasible share of federal resources (Nnoli, 1978: 159–60).

Minorities and majorities

A different ethnic cleavage in Nigeria found the various ethnic minority groups rising in opposition to the dominance of the major group in each region. The political organisation of ethnic minorities gathered momentum in the twilight of colonial rule, fed by mounting apprehension of political repression, socioeconomic discrimination, even cultural extinction by the majority groups when they took unfettered control of regional governments after Independence. Seeking for their people safeguards against such abuse, and for themselves power and its material fruits, minority-group politicians spawned movements for separate states that, if successful, would have totally transformed the existing regional structure.

By the time of the 1957 Constitutional Conference, minority-group demands for separate states had become the most explosive issue in Nigerian politics. Elites of Ibibio, Efik, Ijaw and other non-Igbo ethnic minority groups in the southeastern corner of Nigeria were demanding that the Calabar, Ogoja and Rivers provinces be made a separate state (or even three states). Similarly, the Edo-speaking people of Benin province were seeking a Mid-West state separate from the West, while NCNC-allied leaders of the Yoruba Muslim population (who were dispersed in location but centred politically in Ibadan) began to petition for a Central Yoruba State that would excise Ibadan and Oyo provinces from the West. In the North, the NPC faced three separatist movements: by Yorubas in Kabba and Ilorin provinces to merge with the contiguous Western Region, by leaders of northeastern minorities (especially the Kanuri) for a state comprising Bornu and adjacent provinces, and – most significantly in number and territorial scope – by the predominantly non-Muslim ethnic groups in the provinces south of the emirates for a 'Middle Belt State'. While the Action Group and NCNC vigorously supported the separatist demands of minorities outside their own regions – parlaying these stances into significant electoral inroads – the NPC viewed statehood demands in the South with relative indifference and strenuously opposed them in the North.

As with the majority groups, the cultural mobilisation of the ethnic minorities sprang from the intricate and volatile interaction between ethnicity and class. The chemistry of minority political ferment involved two familiar components: mass-based socioeconomic competition, grounded in real cultural attachments, and elite mobilisation of these attachments for class ends.

Once again in Nigeria, ethnic consciousness and organisation was stimulated by the expansion of the state and its social and economic activity, and by the expectation of still more rapid expansion after Independence. As detailed by a colonial Commission of inquiry, minority fears and grievances centred around obtaining a 'fair' share of the rewards of an expanding economy and state: contracts, loans, scholarships, processing plants, water supplies, street lights, schools, hydroelectric projects (Commission, 1958). Minority demands for separate states were based on the belief – actively fanned by their leaders – that they were being cheated in the distribution of these resources by the regional governments, and that the existing modest restraints on this oppression would evaporate with the departure of the British. The root of ethnic mobilisation in the competition for scarce resources was strikingly manifested in the extent to which communal groups fell back upon ethnicity to rationalise their setbacks. Time and again the Commission heard that businessmen could not obtain the contracts, farmers the loans, graduates the appointments and towns the amenities that others were getting because the others were of the regions' majority ethnic group and they were not (Commission, 1958: 13–14, 17–19, 30, 39–43).

It was not simply by default of other lines of cleavage that socioeconomic competition was organised and perceived through the prism of ethnicity. The political mobilisation and statehood demands of the minorities also reflected deep emotional attachment to their distinctive group values, symbols, languages, ways of life and historical traditions, and genuine fear that these would be suppressed or obliterated. This cultural content of ethnicity paralleled that of the majority groups, to the extent that where minority cultural fears were most pronounced, in the Northern Region, they closely resembled the chief cultural fear of both the Yoruba and the Igbo – that the Islamic aristocracy would seek to impose on them its authoritarian traditions. In every region, the fear of intimidation and repression was real enough for the Commission to recommend as protection for minorities continued federal control of the police. But it flatly opposed creation of any new states, as the colonial administration had explicitly hoped it would (Commission, 1958: iii, 16–17, 45–6, 88).

If minority ethnic mobilisation was based in anxiety and conflict at the mass level, the perceptions of conflicting interests were nevertheless heightened (if not largely generated), and their transformation into political movements was achieved, by minority-group leaders with personal interests. Gifted and ambitious individuals of every ethnicity coveted political office for its sheer power, its salary and perquisites, the status it conferred as 'big men' in their communities, and the vast wealth that could be accumulated in it through enterprising manipulation of the public trust. Just as shrewdly as the politicians of the ethnic majorities, minority-group politicians understood the relationship between class formation and state power, and the importance not simply of holding political office but of controlling the primary accumulations of public capital in the Regional Marketing Boards and Development Corporations. This was one reason why their movements demanded separate states; separate states would have separate marketing boards and corporations and governments, which their own parties would control.

Just as much as their Yoruba, Igbo and Hausa-Fulani competitors, minority-group politicians found in ethnicity the surest vehicle for their political ambitions. Thus they not only cast their electoral appeals quite blatantly in ethnic terms, but they organised ethnic political parties to fix the identity between their personal cause and their people's. At times this required substantial cultural entrepreneurship to mould latent corporate feelings into a coherent identity that could be embodied in a political party, which the politician could then ride to power. The Minorities Commission observed:

> It can hardly be said too often that at the moment there is a general struggle for power in Nigeria and that any group with a corporate feeling can be the vehicle by which a politician reaches power; there is therefore a tendency on the part of the ambitious to work up party feeling where it was hardly formulated before (Commission, 158: 26).

The description could also have been applied to the birth in ethnic consciousness of the AG in the West and the NPC in the North, and to the increasingly close association between the NCNC and the Igbo State Union, but nowhere was it more graphically reflected than in the dizzying fluidity of minority politics: the formation and dissolution of parties and alliances, the movement in and out of them of young politicians, searching for vehicles for their political advancement, settling on ethnicity as their paramount instrument for rallying mass support (Commission, 1958; Sklar, 1963: 119–24, 245–55, 296–302, 339–54; Post, 1963: 78–98). In the indefatigable manoeuvring of these minority entrants into the rising class may be found the most vivid expression of the relationship between ethnicity, class action and democratic politics.

Electoral competition

By 1959, Nigeria had conducted, in the space of eight years, three elections in the Eastern Region, two each in the North and West, and one (in 1954) in the Federation as a whole. Electoral competition had evolved into a three-way struggle between the NCNC, the Action Group and the NPC, each of which captured regional power in 1951 and recaptured it more decisively in subsequent regional elections. The electoral campaigns of both the major and minor parties were waged, overwhelmingly, around sectional issues. This could not have been otherwise, because the parties were organised on the basis of ethnic and regional solidarity, bridging and disguising emergent class distinctions. However, where class distinctions were deeply rooted, in the northern emirates, a very different kind of party opposition emerged.

Unlike the anti-establishment parties in the East and West (and the lower North as well), the Northern Elements Progressive Union challenged the Region's dominant party on a class basis and attempted to mobilise support among the core ethnic group of the Region, the Hausa. Founded in 1950 by a group of educated, mostly *Habe* (Hausa, non-Fulani) commoners, NEPU's

> declaration of principles proclaimed the existence of a 'class struggle between the members of the vicious circle of Native Administrations on the one hand and the ordinary *talakawa* on the other', and announced that NEPU was to be dedicated to the 'emancipation of the *talakawa* from domination by these privileged few' through 'reform of the present autocratic political institutions' (Whitaker, 1970: 358–9).

Throughout the 1950s, NEPU not only campaigned politically on these principles but also enlightened illiterate and exploited peasants and encouraged them to assert their rights (Whitaker, 1970: 380). By contrast, the NPC campaigned for the preservation of traditional institutions and values.

Like the NPC, NEPU sought to legitimate its cause through identification in various ways with Islam (Whitaker, 1970: 394–7, 413–14). The party's charismatic President, Mallam Aminu Kano, was admired not only as a political reformer but 'as a modernist and progressive in Islam' of deep religious faith and knowledge (Sklar, 1963: 372). Stressing the centrality of social justice in Islam, Mallam Aminu (himself a Fulani from a long line of Islamic teachers and judges) and other NEPU leaders gave their party's ideological protest a strong religious basis while also appealing to latent anti-Fulani feeling in attacking the oppression and corruption of the emirate system (Paden, 1974: 273–91, 298–305; Whitaker, 1970: 329–31, 381–4; 393–4; Feinstein, 1973).

This class-based and religiously infused political message, directed squarely at the Region's largest ethnic group, represented a challenge for the NPC wholly unlike that faced by its counterparts in the East and West. Partly for this reason, the NPC was by far the most inward-looking of the three major parties, and the most obsessed with regional unity and security. This orientation continued through the final and most decisive electoral contest under colonial rule, the Federal Election of 1959, to choose the government of a soon-to-be independent Nigeria. As it had throughout the decade, the NPC confined its campaign to the Northern Region, a strategy that probably appeared not only necessary to secure the emirates against the radical challenge, but also sufficient to capture Federal power, given that the North had a majority of the Federal House seats and that the NPC had been regularly winning more than 80 per cent of the Northern constituencies in previous elections.

The two major southern parties were compelled to pursue much more national strategies. The NCNC, still the most broadly based party, had seriously contested the Western Region throughout the decade. Narrowly defeated by the AG in 1951, it won a thin majority of Western seats in the 1954 Federal Election but lost political dominance for good in the regional election of 1956. While the NCNC twice renewed its regional dominance in the Eastern elections of 1953 and 1957 (by using political crises to rally Igbo communal solidarity), the AG began to press vigorous challenges in the minority areas of the East and North. On the strength of close alliances with the ethnic minority parties in the areas, it became the chief opposition to the NCNC in the East and to the NPC in the North. The AG hoped to capture Federal power in 1959 by extending these inroads into the Hausa-Fulani heartland, where it launched a high-powered and well financed, but spectacularly inept and naive campaign to rally the *talakawa* to overthrow the traditional aristocracy at the polls. By contrast, the NCNC pinned its hoped in the North on its alliance (since 1953) with NEPU, which stood a better, if somewhat limited, chance of breaking the NPC's electoral lockhold on the emirates.

The more culturally alien and threatening character of the Action Group – with its strident denunciations of the institutions and culture of the emirates – led the NPC to look to the NCNC as a potential coalition partner, despite the latter's alliance with NEPU. When the election results left the NPC nine votes short of a parliamentary majority, it invited the NCNC to join a government headed by Abubakar Tafawa Balewa, NPC leader in the Federal Parliament. Resenting the AG's intrusion into Eastern minority areas and support for statehood demands there, harbouring the cumulative suspicion and animosity of two decades of bitter ethnic and political conflict with the Action Group, and fearing national disintegration, perhaps even Northern secession, in the event of an all-Southern Federal coalition, the NCNC accepted the invitation (Post, 1963: 423–5; Azikiwe, 1961: 205–6).

More significant perhaps even than the outcome was the tone of the 1959 election. Crudely, at times hysterically, candidates heaped personal and ethnic abuse upon one another. The NCNC and the NPC were 'exhibiting dictatorial tendencies of the hitlerite or nasserite type', the Action Group leader warned (Awolowo, 1959: 256), while the NCNC President condemned the Action Group as 'godless worshippers' and 'enemies of democracy' (Azikiwe, 1959: 15, 24–25, 37). Such vituperative rhetoric had marked electoral competition throughout the decade, particularly that between the AG and the NCNC, whose leaders and candidates routinely vilified their counterparts as 'jelly-fishes in human form', traitors to the nationalist cause, incipient fascists, crooks, liars, hypocrites, 'semi-literates' and so forth (Azikiwe, 1959: 15, 172–78; Agunbiade-Bamishe, 1954: 9–10, 12; Action Group, 1954: 3; Awolowo, 1959: 25–6).

Such abusive rhetoric and the malicious incitement of ethnic prejudice completely overshadowed the substantive plane of the campaign, in which the Action Group's pledge dramatically to expand social welfare services, and the NCNC's somewhat less detailed and sweeping echo of this appeal, contrasted with the NPC's more modest and conservative platform. More ominously, the fanatical and tribalistic tone of the 1959 campaign (and the entire political decade) had dangerous behavioural consequences. In a context in which so much was at stake in an election and in which the largely rural and illiterate electorate lacked the sophistication and breadth of exposure to dismiss the fantastic charges as mere rhetorical excess, venomous rhetoric bred violence and repression. The latter was most prevalent in the North, where the NPC used its control of traditional systems of administration and justice to obstruct, harass and punish opposition candidates and their supporters. This, too, intensified in 1959, as widespread denial of campaign permits, harassment of rallies and false imprisonment of candidates and campaigners brought the NCNC–NEPU alliance and the AG together in heated condemnation of the NPC (Post, 1963: 290–2; Schwarz, 1965: 106; Feinstein, 1973: 186).

Regional power was also deployed with a heavy hand against electoral opposition in the West and to some extent the East in 1959 (Post, 1963: 276–89), but, perhaps because electoral outcomes were not as much secured through institutional repression in the South, the campaigns there were much more violent. From the inception of electoral competition in 1951, parties fielded bands of thugs to disrupt, intimidate, and attack the opposition. Injuries in the hundreds were not uncommon, and in the East, 'election campaigns

... were exceedingly tough, with cars burnt, semi-riots where the campaign teams converged, and politicians declaring that their lives were in danger' (Mackintosh, 1966: 525). During the 1959 campaign, such violence spread throughout the North as well, frequently victimising Southern and NEPU campaigners, and exploding among the Tiv in reaction against the harsh repression of their party, the United Middle Belt Congress (Dent, 1966: 486).

THE PATTERN OF CONFLICT

National political conflict arose in Nigeria during the final three decades of colonial rule, when political and economic resources expanded rapidly, along with a new class of professionals and businessmen who eagerly sought them. It was hardly unusual that these new elites should have organised to compete for the new possibilities of wealth and power. Nor was vigorous competition in itself a bad omen for democracy; competition is, after all, the stuff of democratic politics. Indeed, it could be taken as a healthy sign that the competition was waged through politics rather than through violent confrontation, though this was all too evident as well.

What portended trouble for democracy in Nigeria was not the fact of competition but its motivations, its tone and its structural patterns. From the very beginning, competition was organised along ethnic lines. Given the social structure, this was natural and probably inevitable. What was dangerous was the interaction of this reality with the emergent class structure – which pushed rising elites to manipulate ethnic cleavage for advantage in the twin processes of political competition and class formation – and its interaction with the political structures. The latter was not wholly inevitable. The three-region structure was a colonial construction and the British insisted to the end on preserving it despite the clear warnings and manifest evidence of its flaws. This produced the peculiar coincidence of region and ethnicity observed during the final decade – one which reified the tripartite ethnic division, forged a volatile contradiction between the political power of the one and the socioeconomic pre-eminence of the other two, and fostered deep, reciprocal distrust and insecurity not only between the three major groups but between these and the numerous minority groups as well. From this system of regional dominance and ethnoregional insecurity could only follow the organisation of political parties along ethnic and regional lines, completing the structural convergence of major cleavages.

While class cross-cut the accumulated cleavages of ethnicity, region and party, it did not do so in a way that might have complicated the pattern of conflict and so relieved some of its gathering intensity. In part this was because the limited resources of class formation made it difficult for the emerging dominant class to be a trans-ethnic class. In part it was because the cross-cutting occurred only at the level of one class – the emergent, Western-educated bourgeoisie. The ordinary Nigerian remained locked in primordial, agrarian social networks, unreceptive to mobilisation on the basis of functional and class solidarities, and in any case such mass-based organisations were virtually nonexistent.

The ethnic and regional competition that followed in the 1940s and '50s closely paralleled the growth of the Nigerian economy and state. With each new step in the devolution of power from coloniser to colonised, with each increase in the resources under the domain of indigenous authority, ethnic competition widened to encompass the larger possibilities of power and wealth: from the first movement toward Nigerianisation of the public service, in 1948; in the anticipation of elected, 'semi-responsible' government during the 1948–50 constitutional review; with the introduction of elected regional governments in 1951; from the dramatic expansion of regional powers and revenues in 1954. Equally revealing were the issues over which ethnic groups and regions competed: the allocation of national revenue, the distribution of seats in the federal legislature, the regional structure of government, the status of Lagos, the timing of self-government, bureaucratic position and control – all involved the distribution of resources and rewards either directly or indirectly, through the distribution of national political power.

Because this political competition was at once both class and sectional in character – with members of the rising class seeking resources for their ethnic communities and wealth, prestige and power for themselves – and because it was the primary vehicle for the attainment of both individual (class) and community aspirations, political competition became desperate and frenzied. Even more than the campaign thuggery and repression, the calculated and malicious manipulation of ethnic consciousness was the most dangerous byproduct of this desperation. In the multi-ethnic cities (of the North in particular), the salience of ethnicity was already manifest in the visible and growing prominence of Igbo clerks, and other 'foreign' civil servants and traders. In such circumstances ethnic political conflict within the rising class could quickly catalyse mass ethnic conflict. In the countryside, the signs of ethnic threat were less immediate and tangible, but could be generated by national political conflict. While it may have been difficult for the peasants and traders of Igboland to fully understand the danger entailed in the North's population and parliamentary majority, they were made aware of these other ethnic groups, they were increasingly aware of their own poverty, and surely they understood their politicians' warnings that more for those other people would mean less for them. A visceral chord was struck within them by the appeals for ethnic solidarity which permeated all of their political messages – from the village branch of their tribal union, from their candidates for political office, from their regional and national leaders. Political conflict between the regional political classes set the context and shaped the framework for mass ethnic solidarity and conflict.

Thus, it was significant that national politics settled in the 1950s into a pattern of regular conflict between parties that were based upon the hard-core support of a single ethnic group and the control of a single region. Coalitions were made to gain advantage in the competition, but always they carried the fragility of any coalition in a three-player game, and invariably they fractured at the peak of crisis. In the end, each regional party set out to defeat the other two by sweeping their own regions and forging alliances with the minority parties of other regions.

The ethnic minorities thus became the pivotal destabilising element in an inherently unstable tripolar balance of power. In one sense minority political mobilisation was a potentially healthy development, as it widened the focus of politics beyond the three major ethnic groups and so offered the potential for generating a more fluid and complicated pattern of cleavage. Indeed, the pattern *was* complicated to some extent, as two of the major parties reached out beyond their home regions for political support. But this only heightened insecurity and distrust between the ethnic majorities. Each of the ruling regional parties drew deep anxiety from the political insurgency of its minority groups and the exploitation of this unrest by its major competitors.

As it congealed during the 1950s, the pattern of conflict found regional, ethnic and/or political formations contesting every new dimension of wealth and power. If it was not known on exactly what basis the next conflict would be waged, there was little doubt that it would fall upon one of these three lines of cleavage and somehow invoke the other two. As a result, party, region and ethnicity converged into a single broad channel of division, in which conflict became regular, incessant and obsessed. The political conflicts of the 1950s placed a heavy and continuous strain upon this broad line of cleavage. Cleavages converged not only within conflicts, at moments in time, but also across time.

However, over time, the coincidence of cleavages was far less perfect, and the load upon the polity at least somewhat less intense, than might have been expected. For one, successive conflicts tapped different elements of cleavage within one broad channel. If party, region and ethnicity heavily overlapped, still they were not identical, and the fact that conflict was joined at one moment primarily between parties, at another on the basis of regional interests, and a moment later through ethnic identity and associations, provided at least a small measure of relief. Secondly, the configurations of opposing actors were fluid. Igbo and Yoruba elites competed for position in the 1940s, but with the 'Northern awakening', elite interests were pressed on the basis of North *vs.* South. Beginning in 1951, each party fought for total control of its base region, but the NCNC, with appreciable Yoruba support, almost won control of the Western Region, and then briefly surged past the AG there in 1954. In 1953, Northern and Southern politicians bitterly divided over the timing of self-government, only for the AG and NCNC to split bitterly a few months later over the status of Lagos. The Kano Riot that same year exposed as well a deep Hausa-Igbo tension, which helped inspire the concerted purge of Southerners from the Northern bureaucracy and economy. And yet, this running tension did not keep leaders of the Northern and Eastern governments from teaming up against the West on revenue allocation nor from joining in a coalition government after the 1959 elections. Indeed, from 1957 to 1959, all three parties participated in a consociational-type coalition government (headed by Tafawa Balewa). Hence, the succession of issues over time threw the various interests against each other in a shifting rather than cumulative pattern. Finally, there was continuous variation in outcomes over the decade. No one party or group always won or always lost; each enjoyed victory and suffered defeat, and was now and then coaxed or coerced into a compromise by the British.

While not actually cross-pressuring political actors, these *longitudinally* cross-cutting factors reduced the intensity of conflict and facilitated accommodation and reconciliation when any particular cleavage threatened a conflagration. So long as the system avoided a permanent configuration of forces and a predictable and consistent victor in every conflict, there was reasonable hope for preventing conflict from polarising to the point of bringing down the constitutional system. But even so, the intensity of conflict had reached a dangerous level by the end of the decade. Mutual tolerance, trust, restraint and respect all waned through the successive electoral struggles and intervening conflicts. By the time of the 1959 election, the 'rules of the game' had been badly trampled by the 'inability to see an election in any terms except those of a battle' (Post, 1963: 299). This inability followed from the rapid expansion of the state in an underdeveloped economy and culturally plural society, in which the developmental future of communities and the class standing of rising elites were almost completely at stake in each election.

In 1959, the impartial 'steel frame' of colonial administration was able to compel some compliance with the rules of democratic competition and to maintain some semblance of order and freedom. But Nigeria had yet to face the test of administering its own national election. When that test came in 1964, it would prove to be the last great gasp of the First Republic.

3 Conspiracy of Optimism: Nigeria at Independence

'Parliamentary government has been attempted in Nigeria and we have proved more than equal to the task. . . .

What remains for us to do now is to dedicate our lives anew to the fascinating task of nation-building. The past is gone with all its bitterness and rancour and recriminations. The future is before us and great events await the leadership of the wise and brave.' – His Excellency Dr Nnamdi Azikiwe, Governor-General, Federation of Nigeria, Inaugural Address, 16 November 1960 (Azikiwe, 1960: 7, 14)

'It is imperative . . . that the parties in power for the time being should . . . faithfully adhere to the principles and practice of liberal democracy. If by any unfortunate mischance or deliberate premeditation, democracy and the rule of law were murdered, stifled or suppressed, reason and moderation would of necessity cease to rule the hearts of many a well-meaning and devoted Nigerian.' – Chief the Honorable Obafemi Awolowo, Presidential Address to the Seventh Congress of the Action Group, 19 September 1960

At the stroke of midnight, on 1 October 1960, the green and white flag of the Federation of Nigeria was raised for the first time. In an atmosphere remarkable for its subdued character and 'quiet constitutional dignity,' Nigeria was formally granted its independence. The ceremonies and speeches emphasised nothing so much as continuity. Paying 'tribute to the manner in which successive British governments have gradually transferred the burden of responsiblity to our shoulders', the Prime Minister of this most populous African nation expressed the quiet optimism and sobriety with which Nigerians accepted their birth as a nation (Balewa, 1964: 60).

For a moment at least, the bitter divisions of the preceding decades were submerged in the glow of nationalist pride. In this expansive mood, Dr Nnamdi Azikiwe took the occasion of his inauguration as Governor-General to appeal to his former rivals to join with him to 'bind the nation's wound and heal the breaches of the past' (Azikiwe, 1960: 15). The tone of optimism and hope was echoed as well by

64

foreigners, especially the British, who took considerable pride in leaving behind a functioning parliamentary democracy.

But if the British and most Nigerians chose to believe that the bitterness and rancour of the past had been overcome with the achievement of nationhood, and if foreign observers knew too little of Nigeria to appreciate the depth of these divisions, there were a few who saw real dangers. Even as the Independence ceremonies were being prepared, and government leaders were speaking magnanimously of a new beginning in Nigerian politics, the Action Group leader was warning his party of threats to its constitutional rule in the Western Region and to its survival as the Federal Opposition, threats that could mean the end of democracy in Nigeria. The continuing enmity and distrust between the Action Group and the two parties of the ruling coalition, the continuing agitation of minority groups for separate states (which the Action Group championed), the high expectations of an impoverished population for rapid economic progress, and the wide and growing gulf between the people and the venal political class, suggested to some that 'the optimism of 1960 was justified only in the sense that without optimism there is no hope' (Oyinbo, 1971: 9).

As we have seen (Chapter 2), the structure of social cleavages, the traditional and emergent structures of class domination, the contradictions of colonial rule, and the evolving pattern and character of political conflict did not augur well for the future of liberal democracy. It will be seen that the cultural, political, and economic conditions in Nigeria at Independence were also far from what theories of democracy would consider favourable terrain for an experiment in parliamentary government.

POLITICAL CULTURE

The repression, violence and fanaticism of political competition in the 1950s signified – despite elite protestations to the contrary – a weak commitment to democratic values in Nigeria. The election campaigns during the last decade of colonial rule revealed a shallow disposition among political elites to tolerate opposition when they had the power to discourage and repress it. But these anti-democratic tendencies in political behaviour can be traced only partially to the traditional political cultures of Nigeria's main ethnic groups. While the cultural lineage is apparent in the case of the Muslim emirates of the North, it is hardly so for many other Nigerian ethnic groups. Rather, 'dissimilar political cultures – parademocratic versus monarchical versus theoractic-autocratic – were juxtaposed within the state of Nigeria' (Olorunsola, 1972: 1). The inheritance from traditional cultures was thus too variegated to have enabled any certain predictions about the character of modern politics in Nigeria.

What could have been predicted well in advance of the inauguration of large-scale political competition in 1951 was that the Northern Region, in particular the emirates of the upper North, would present the stiffest challenge to the institutionalisation of democratic competition and its attendant political rights. The structure of emirate power was despotic and highly centralised, endowing the emir with nearly absolute political and religious authority. This authority was dynastic in origin, flowing from the highest circle of an elaborate and finely graded social aristocracy. The emir appointed the administrative elite, conferred aristocratic titles, and directly or indirectly, controlled all offices down to the village chief and ward head (Dudley, 1968: 49–54). He also derived judicial power through appointment of the Alkali judges (who interpreted Koranic law) and economic power in the authority to impose taxes, tolls and licence fees (Schwarz, 1965: 30–1). His scope of authority was immense precisely because it was theocratic, resting on a deep religious foundation: the duty of Muslim government 'to command the good and forbid the evil' by the law of the Koran (Low, 1972: 26). As the 'sole interpreter of divine legislation', as manifested in the scriptural writings, an emir could effectively exercise enormous legislative power as well (Paden, 1973: 229). Indeed, the scope of his authority and the basis of its legitimacy was reflected in the expression, 'the emir is the shadow of God' (Paden, 1973: 35).

The severely hierarchical nature of authority in the emirates pervaded all levels of society through chains of feudalistic clientage relations. Commoners obtained protection, and if they were destitute, means of subsistence, in exchange for service and allegiance to a single lord, who, in turn, paid obeisance to a figure of higher aristocratic rank. Typically, 'a clearly defined hierarchical edifice' linked all government officials as both patrons and clients 'in a chain of command along which orders, requests and intelligence could move in culturally familiar ways' (Low, 1972: 17). In the emirate capitals, fiefholders were clients of the emir and were, in turn, 'patrons of subordinate agents through whom they administered and exploited the subject communities within their jurisdictions' (Sklar,

1963: 9). This pyramid of clientage relations was the political expression of a similarly steep and finely graded status hierarchy, which tended to be reproduced over generations.

The clear definition, religious foundation, and extreme hierarchy of these social and political structures led the common man to an unquestioning acceptance of his place. Social mobility was infrequent and mass political protest was unheard of. Almost absolute power produced 'an almost equally absolute duty of obedience on the part of the mass of the citizens, a duty which was in no way abated by Islam, which enjoins on its members a seemingly unconditional subservience to the ruler' (Dudley, 1968: 56). This extraordinary emphasis on obedience to authority was not unique to the Hausa-Fulani emirates; it was, as well, 'the most highly valued and most important behaviour known to the Kanuri of Bornu' (Cohen, 1966: 130–1). And, as we have seen, the authoritarian character of the emirates was deepened by colonial indirect rule.

The minority peoples of the Middle Belt lacked the centralised and hierarchical state structures of the emirates, and their political cultures presented a striking contrast with the Hausa-Fulani. With their tradition of a radically dispersed and unstable structure of political power (Bohannan, 1965: 533), the Tiv steadfastly resisted British attempts to concentrate power in the hands of any individual. Given the absence of chiefs, disputes were settled in the open among a general gathering of community elders. Other peoples, such as the Idoma and the Birom, were similarly acephalous and egalitarian, sharing with the Tiv a fragmentation of political power, a lack of role differentiation, a lack of hierarchy in social structure, and as a result, a greater receptiveness to change (Dudley, 1968: 57–65). But because the Hausa-Fulani were numerically dominant in the Northern region, and because the youth of the emirate aristocracy were groomed for public office by the colonial administration, the authoritarian culture of the emirates came to shape political behaviour in the North (and to a significant degree, in the nation) when self-rule came.

Southern cultural traditions as well were much more democratic and less hierarchical in their orientation to authority than the Islamic culture of the North. The Igbo, in particular, were noted for their dispersed system of power, extensive popular participation, egalitarian social relations, and deprecation of hierarchy (Uchendu, 1965; Ottenberg, 1959; Sklar, 1963; Olisa, 1971; Olorunsola, 1972; Njaka, 1974). The self-assertiveness, individualism and achievement orientation of the Igbo functioned to prevent the concentration of authority in a single member of the community (Ottenberg, 1959: 136–9; Njaka, 1974: 66). Like the Tiv but unlike the Yoruba and the peoples of the upper North, the Igbos had no political kingdoms, nor even a central government. Each Igbo village was an autonomous 'exercise in direct democracy' (Uchendu, 1965: 41). Legislative functions inhered in an *ad hoc* assembly of all adult males, in which each individual was afforded a hearing, and issues were discussed until a consensus was reached. The right of the individual to participate and express his opinion was cherished, and political education was encouraged at an early age to prepare for this. While loyalty to community and belongingness to group were valued, the Igbo stressed equality of rights for all individuals, attainment of leadership and status through achievement rather than ascription, and self-regulation rather than external control (Njaka, 1974: 50–67).

Authority relations in the Yoruba kingdoms were more hierarchical than in the Igbo villages but significantly more democratic than in the Northern emirates. While these large and relatively centralised Yoruba states were independent, they shared important common features. Most crucially, the Yoruba monarchies were constitutional rather than despotic, limited in power by customs and by a subordinate council of chiefs, which held some legislative and judicial authority and could remove an *oba* who abused his powers. Though the *oba* was a sacred ruler, infused with some of the divine authority enjoyed by the emirs, he was democratically elected by chiefs representing the non-royal lineages, the equivalent in Hausa-Fulani society of the commoner class (Lloyd, 1960: 233, 237). Unlike the Hausa-Fulani emirates, Yoruba society lacked a ruling class or aristocracy. The royal lineage was limited in wealth, size, and power, and personal achievement and popularity were important criteria in the selection of chiefs in the non-royal lineages (Lloyd, 1974: 47). While the *oba* stood at the apex of a complex, centralised and hierarchical government (Lloyd, 1960: 229), he was less removed from his people than the emirs of the North, and his authority was not significantly feared by them (Sklar, 1966: 122). However, mistaking the Yoruba monarchies for the absolutist structures of the North, the British attempted to institute indirect rule in the West as well. As they 'converted the constitutional kings into autocratic agents of the colonial administration and transformed the Yoruba states into untraditional despotisms', the colonial rulers reaped much bitter resentment from the Yoruba (Sklar, 1966: 122).

The differences in social organisation and authority relations gave rise to related differences in political culture. Tolerance of opposition was antithetical to the autocratic political style of the North. Freedom of speech, of association and of the press was comparatively scant throughout the emirates and criticism was stifled (Coleman, 1958: 139, 357). The patterns of clientage and deference to authority, the immense concentration of power in the emir and the threat of victimisation by him, 'tended to inhibit any opposition to him, even from within the ranks of the ruling stratum' (Sklar and Whitaker, 1966: 12). By contrast, the south had cultural traditions of opposition emanating from the wider dispersion of authority: a certain respect among the Yoruba for rights of criticism and opposition, stemming from the limits on monarchical power, and more vigorous and institutionalised channels for dissent among the Igbo as part of the process of village government. This stronger tradition of opposition and tolerance in the South also found expression in an outspoken free press.

Again, because power in the Northern emirates was organised along absolutist lines, there was no need for compromise between opposing forces and hence no tradition of political bargaining and accommodation, except perhaps within the narrow aristocratic circles of kingmakers. Among the Igbo, by contrast, negotiation was a highly valued art and pervaded all forms of social exchange, including political life (Njaka, 1974; Uchendu, 1965). Among the Yoruba, the regulation of conflict rested largely with the *oba*, whose capacity to arbitrate successfully between competing chiefs and other factions was among the chief criteria of his selection (Lloyd, 1974: 47).

The variation across the three regions in political tolerance and repression during the 1950s reveals some significant legacy from the traditional cultures. Obviously, the difficulty in mobilising political opposition in the Northern Region was heavily rooted in the authoritarian values and structures of emirate society and the pervasive and deeply ingrained submissiveness to authority among its people (still scarcely touched by Western education). Official repression was more limited in scope and degree in the South. But in the South – even in the traditionally democratic East – groups of zealous party 'strong-arm' men intimidated and physically punished opposition. In each region, the heavy hand of government power accelerated the drift to one-party rule. Moreover, the abusive and fanatical tone of political competition fell far short of the 'civic' culture. As a matter not only of philosophical values but nationalist pride, political leaders such as Balewa, Azikiwe and Awolowo professed a deep personal commitment to democratic institutions and a sincere aspiration for their success (e.g., Balewa, 1961: x; Azikiwe, 1960: 85; Awolowo, 1960: 302–3). But survey data and subjective observations of the political elite suggest that this commitment did not extend deeply below the top level of political leadership (Free, 1964: 49; Schwarz, 1965: 190; Bretton, 1962: 17; Doob, 1965: 365–7).

At the mass level, the commitment to modern, parliamentary institutions was ambivalent and lacked deep roots. On the one hand, there was, in Sklar's words, a strong ' communal basis of democracy' in Nigeria. In the South in particular, the new men of the political class were expected to be responsive to communal aspirations for social welfare programmes: if the *arrivé* 'is too aloof or umindful of customary obligations,' Sklar observed (1963: 503), 'he may lose both his chance of election and communal prestige.' Indeed, 'the assiduity with which members of the political elite ... [kept] their ears to the ground and [sought] to justify public politics to their constituents' suggested the vitality of communal pressure and called into question the hypothesis of a great gulf between elite and mass (Sklar, 1963: 504; also Peil, 1976: 4). Despite the very low levels of literacy and education, attitudinal surveys found a population deeply interested in public affairs, actively seeking information – through newspapers, radio and word of mouth – and much better informed than would have been predicted by the level of social development (Free, 1964; Mackintosh, 1966). These and later surveys showed the Nigerian people to 'have a shrewd understanding of their political needs and how to fill them,' and 'to be actively concerned about their political system and eager participants in it' (Peil, 1976: 3, 6).

On the other hand, the 'interest in things political' was too great, the 'concern with power and the resources available to those in power' was 'too intense and too widespread' (Peil, 1976: 15, 185; also, Dent, 1966: 473) to allow for compromise, much less defeat. Rather, the obsession with power infused the struggle for it with the aura of 'winner takes all'. And the high levels of participation (in particular, huge voter turnouts, reaching nearly 80 per cent in 1959) were largely the product of intensive elite mobilisation, amidst apocalyptic warnings of group danger. Such mobilised electoral participation bore little resemblance to participation in the traditional village and clan politics, and may explain why the traditions of

Nigeria's democratic cultures for tolerance of opposing views and pursuit of negotiated consensus did so little to restrain the brutal intensity of modern politics. Moreover, democratic beliefs and practices prevailed not among the groups with large, complex political systems but in small communities that enjoyed high levels of cultural consensus, solidarity, and trust. And even among the highly individualistic and participatory Igbo, opposition took the form not of the structured and sustained contestation of parliamentary democracy but of the continual thrashing out of a communal consensus (Oyinbo, 1971: 11–12).

Nigeria thus began its experiment in independent democratic government with little understanding of the institutional role of political opposition in a large-scale competitive democracy. To the extent that the top political elite had such an appreciation, it tended to be overwhelmed by the antidemocratic culture of the emirates, the insecurity and distrust fostered by the federal system, the competition between ethnic groups, and, not least, the huge electoral stakes generated by a swelling state, to which everyone was looking for a better life.

Detached from the familiar frames of reference of traditional political life, mobilised by urgent appeals to ethnic security, unaware of the complex of issues beyond immediate communal needs and fears, the average Nigerian would seem to have lacked a compelling commitment to the system of political competition in place at Independence. His overriding commitment was to the tangible progress he expected it to deliver, and upon this his judgement of the system would rest.

POLITICAL STRUCTURE

Constitutionally, Nigeria had a federal structure at Independence, but it was a structure fraught with tensions and contradictions. The number, size, and boundaries of the Regions gave rise to several interrelated difficulties. As noted in Chapter 2, the federal structure encompassed an explosive contradiction between socioeconomic and political dominance (Sklar, 1965a), which fed a reciprocal insecurity between North and South. Northern leaders felt they needed the protection of their own Region, with control over local government, chieftaincy affairs, the judiciary, and the public service, if they were to preserve their culture and social structure against the winds of radical change sweeping up from the South (Whitaker, 1970: 402). And they were determined to preserve their Region's population (and hence political) majority in the Federation, in order to stave off any Southern attack on the guarantees of regional security and to capture the largest share of federal development resources. Southern political leaders clearly perceived the NPC's determination to dominate the Federation and, they felt, to usurp resources and positions that rightfully belonged to Southerners. As the Federal Government's economic power and initiative expanded, the prospect of this dominance became steadily more disturbing. More than any sympathy for the plight of the minorities, it was this fear of Northern domination of the Federation that motivated NCNC and especially Action Group leaders to demand the creation of more states before Independence. Much of the post-Independence political turmoil can be traced to 'the failure of the British to sympathise at any stage with the Southern fears that a country in which one region was larger than all the others together was exposed to undue strain' (O'Connell, 1967: 159).

The Federal structure was unstable in related senses as well. By creating regions around each of the three major ethnic groups, and only them, it heightened the centralised character of the ethnic structure and so reduced its fluidity, in part by diminishing the potential mediating role of the ethnic minorities. In fact, it left minority groups exposed and vulnerable, fearing for their security at the hands of the dominant group in the region. It also brought regional and ethnic cleavages into broad coincidence, giving rise to regional parties and making the resulting competition more intense. In facilitating the rise of one-party dominant regions, the federal system fostered a more complete coincidence of the party cleavage with the other two.

To some degree, however, the federal system did decentralise government power. It did not do so to the extent of insuring against devastating conflict at the centre – no constitution could have devolved that much authority to the regions without crippling the sacred mission of the central state to generate economic development. In fact, the exigencies of national development in a world of powerful nation-states figured to keep expanding the arena of federal control. But the regions were given substantial autonomy over their internal affairs, including not only their own public services, judicial systems, marketing boards, and development corporations, but 'residual powers over a wide range of subjects which affected most directly the everyday life of the people – like local government, land use, education, and health' (Arikpo, 1967: 86). In addition, the Northern and Western Regions were allowed to maintain their local police forces, and each region retained control over chieftaincy. To finance these responsibilities, the regions' share of total government revenue rose from one-fifth to one-third after 1954 (Phillips, 1971: 396). The Constitution also contained a number of provisions to protect regional interests at the Federal level, such as equal representation in the Senate and on Federal boards and commissions concerning the police, the judiciary, development planning and so on.

Four factors converged to make regional power an object of such intense pursuit: the extraordinary proportion of total social and economic resources mediated by the state, the subordination of so wide a scope of state functions to political party control, the substantial regionalisation of state power in 1954, and the small number of regions, which allowed few opportunities for the capture of sub-central power and so made each particular opportunity enormous in its potential rewards. These factors produced an enormous volume of financial and coercive resources at the command of the ruling party in each region.

The presence of so few regions was thus, in itself, a serious flaw. In a plural society like Nigeria's, a federal system must insulate both regional politics from the centre and federal politics from the regions. Not only did regions need the security of knowing they would be truly autonomous in their own affairs, but the underdeveloped and deeply divided federal arena needed the relief of distance from the internal conflicts of the regions, so as to conserve its limited capacity for conflict resolution. But in a Federation where even the smallest region elected a quarter of the House and a third of the Senate, intraregional conflict had of necessity to be of interest to competing political parties at the centre. To this motive for intervention the Constitution added a mechanism as well, emergency rule in a region by the centre, which the Northern party, in coalition with one of the two Southern parties, could employ against the other (see below).

Though the Constitution was theoretically designed to prevent it, it was also possible for two regions to gang up upon a third in the process of constitutional amendment. All constitutional amendments required the assent of two-thirds of all the members of each Federal House. In addition, amendment of 'entrenched' provisions – concerning such pivotal issues as the division of powers, parliamentary representation, allocation of revenue, fundamental human rights, and control over the judiciary and police – required the assent of simple majorities of both houses in a majority of the regions (Sklar and Whitaker, 1966: 61–2). Hence, even entrenched provisions could be amended over the strenuous and unanimous objections of one Southern region. Creation of a new region required these same legislative votes, plus a 60 per cent majority of the proposed region's voters in special plebiscite. With this, a piece of a region could be severed, fundamentally altering its power position in the Federation. These provisions did little to restrain the legislative power of a coalition such as that which came together following the 1959 election.

Thus, while the regions had substantial power, they had too little truly secure autonomy. Given the existence of ethnic minorities with whom the competing parties sought alliance, the necessity of the two Southern parties to win numerous seats outside their regions, the preceding decades of acrimonious conflict between the regions, the deep contradiction between their relative political and economic power, and the capacity of a federal coalition to establish emergency rule in a region, any serious political conflict within a region was likely to spill over into the federal arena and compel extra-regional forces to take sides.

NATIONAL UNITY AND IDENTITY

The decades preceding Nigerian Independence had featured conflict within the nationalist movement far more intense than anything it had waged against British colonial rule. The artificial nature of the country, the absence of any colonial effort to inculcate a sense of nationhood, in fact the deliberate encouragement of regional identities and separation, further worked against the development of a sense of national unity and identity. By Independence, the challenge of integrating Nigeria around a common, overarching sense of nationhood still remained. So also did many of the major issues of the previous decade: minority demands for new states, the AG's determination to break the monolithic power of the North, and the North's endeavour to redress its socioeconomic disadvantage, which was beginning to produce 'a considerable number of Northern recruits' in the upper ranks of the Federal Civil Service 'who would not qualify by normal standards' (B. Williams, 1960: 4).

However, there were also positive developments as Independence approached. With the acceptance of the Raisman Commission formula at the 1958 Constitutional Conference, an enduring compromise seemed finally to have been reached on the vexing issue of revenue allocation. Out of the NPC-NCNC coalition (rooted though it was in a temporary coincidence of political interests) was emerging a growing spirit of cooperation between Igbo and Northern Muslim political leaders. Cole (1962: 47–62) found hope as well in the use of English as a national *lingua franca*; the increasing acceptance of common legal forms, as evidenced by the new Penal Code in the North; growing economic interdependence, fostered by central control of the transport system; the spread of organisations, such as schools and trade unions, bringing together people of different ethnic origin, and the growing talk among Nigerian political leaders not of secession but of unity, and the common cultural and psychological roots of Nigerian nationhood. In this spirit of national pride and hope, the nation's ethnic diversity was seen as 'a source of strength and stability' in a democracy, rather than weakness, because 'ethnic differences offer a foundation for healthy rivalry in social development and progress' (Davies, 1961: 125; also Herring, 1962: 249–50).

At the mass level, the 1962 survey of Hadley Cantril and Lloyd Free revealed a greater sense of nationhood than might have been expected and also – in the context of the Western Regional crisis – widespread and grave concern over the unity and political stability of the nation.[1] The popular sense of nationhood was reflected in the great pride that Nigerians expressed in their nation and in their widespread anticipation of its future progress. Three-quarters of the Nigerians surveyed judged Nigeria to have made progress in the last five years, while two-thirds expected progress in the coming five years (Cantril, 1965: 79).[2] The mean increase of 2.2 steps from past to present in national ratings (i.e., the judgement of past progress) was among the highest observed in any nation, as was the increase of 2 steps from present to future standing (Cantril, 1965: 185–7). What is more, 'the fact that only sixteen per cent were unable to rate the present national standing of Nigeria suggested that most Nigerians had – or thought they had – at least some concept of the nationhood of Nigeria' (Free, 1964: 54).

Even in the widespread concern over the disunity in the nation, Free found evidence of a genuine national identity and commitment.

If there were no such identity, he reasoned, Nigeria's internal conflicts would not so frequently have been at the centre of people's hopes and fears (Free, 1964: 64). More than half of both the public and the legislators surveyed expressed a hope for national unity or political stability, while this concern was listed in some way among the fears of even larger proportions of the two samples (Free, 1964: 59). The 20 per cent of the Nigerian public worrying specifically about national unity was twice as large as the figure for any of the other twelve nations surveyed.

Among the Nigerian comments on this problem, two themes stand out. First was the Southern fear of Northern domination as the greatest threat to national unity:

> As things are, it appears Nigeria will be governed all her life by Northerners who were once the most backward people in civilization. If we allow Northerners to govern us, then in about ten years from now Nigeria will only be regarded as Northern land – and thus all our birthrights sold to the backward set of people.
>
> I fear our being controlled by a dictatorial type of government such as can be seen in all the Muslim countries today. We shall all be subject to control by feudal lords who rule by Muslim decree.... This means we shall be ruled by whatever the Koran says (Free, 1964: 61).

Second was the frequent attribution of responsibility for the disunity to the political parties and politicians:

> My fear about Nigeria is very great now. I don't know what will be the end of the crisis.... There is no peace all over the country. This is the result of the selfishness of some of our political leaders.
>
> [My greatest fear for the country is] disunity among tribes as a result of clamor for power by greedy politicians (Free, 1964: 60).

Such comments echo the opinion of the Prime Minister that Nigeria's politicians were the worst threat to its unity, and that, 'If the leaders are willing to foster national unity, the common man will respond' (Balewa, 1961: xii). The biggest obstacle to national unity was not the average Nigerian's primordial attachment to his communal group but 'the clamour for power by politicians'. Implicit in the Prime Minister's aspiration for more responsible and nationally oriented political leadership lay also a prophetic warning.

REGIME EFFECTIVENESS AND LEGITIMACY

The parliamentary regime that accepted full sovereignty for Nigeria began with a large measure of popular goodwill. The achievement of independence had been cause for a restrained but genuine outpouring of nationalist pride and optimism – pride, in part that Nigeria was a working democracy at the very time that African nations were being described by some Western observers as too underdeveloped or culturally primitive to sustain a democratic form of government.

Partly as a matter of pride, there was a sense among elites that democracy was a legitimate form of government for Nigeria, that it represented a challenge that Nigeria could and would successfully meet. The broad participation of elected representatives from all three Regions in the various stages of constitutional drafting further enhanced the legitimacy of the democratic system. For most politically aware Nigerians, this was not a form of government simply imposed from the outside but one which leaders of each of the major regional and ethnic groups had helped shape. The close association of Yoruba chiefs in the West and native Authorities in the North with the elected governments of those Regions added some aura of traditional legitimacy.

The legitimacy of the regime was shallow, however, and depended heavily on the future pace and spread of socioeconomic development. The support of the people was not for democracy in the abstract, as a set of sacred principles and values, but for what the system could produce for them. This was no different from the instrumental view of most politicians, whose support for democratic institutions depended on the rewards they derived from them, and who were already beginning to warp the institutions in pursuit of the rewards. The resulting corruption and repression not only reflected the shallowness of elite commitment to the democratic system, but were beginning to erode popular belief in its legitimacy.

To the extent that the legitimacy of the system was actively doubted in 1960, these doubts appear to have concentrated among younger intellectuals, professionals, bureaucrats, and trade-union activists (as well as college students) who, largely omitted in the allocation of power, income, and prestige, represented an embryonic challenge to the political order (Bretton, 1962: 49). A narrow but vociferous minority of these, symbolised by the Dynamic Party leader, Dr Chike Obi, viewed democracy as inherently unable to meet the challenge of development and favoured instead, a kind of

benevolent, inspirational dictatorship to mobilise the nation's resources (Wallerstein, 1962; Schwarz, 1965: 150). They shared with
the more moderate, numerous and democratically inclined 'counter-
elite' a deep concern over the corruption and 'squandermania' of the
political class. This larger group of intellectuals and political activists
hoped to eliminate these ills and turn the country toward socialist
development policies through the democratic process. The failing
they saw, as expressed by the radical leader of the NCNC Youth
Association, Mokwugo Okoye, was not in the democratic system
itself, but in its current crop of political leaders. Only new political
leaders, 'committed to high standards of integrity and austerity in
place of acquisitiveness and exhibitionism,' could root out the
corruption, foreign exploitation, and apathy and haphazardness in
development planning that obstructed rapid and broad-based development (Okoye, 1961).

Such radical criticism was clearly gaining momentum as Nigeria
achieved its independence. Organisationally, the left was in ferment,
and while several groups came and went during 1960 and 1961, one –
the Nigerian Youth Congress, led by Dr Tunji Otegbeye –
immediately began to attract a large following, especially among
NCNC youth. Like the other radical groups that were being formed,
the NYC railed against corruption and proclaimed socialist and pan-
Africanist ideals. But unlike most of the other groups, the NYC
began to construct a political base, establishing branches in most
Southern towns and some in the North as well (Post, 1962: 529).
Behind Dr Obi's impassioned attacks on the venality and extravagance of leading politicians, the Dynamic party also grew, winning
five seats in the Eastern House in 1961 and a significant following
among youth of the Region.

These radical political groups, especially the NYC, benefited from
the growing activism and restlessness of Nigerian university students,
many of whom were attracted by the new brand of radical African
nationalism espoused by Patrice Lumumba. The news of his murder
in February 1961 brought 'the first serious anti-European riots in
Nigeria,' following which public meetings in the capital were banned
for a time (Post, 1962: 528). A few months earlier, university students
had staged angry riots and demonstrations against the Anglo-
Nigerian Defense Agreement, which the Balewa Government finally
felt compelled to abrogate (by mutual consent) in January 1962.

The two Southern parties were pressed to respond to this radical
ferment, and did so in different ways. The NCNC took some cosmetic

steps to identify with the growing reformist sentiment, endorsing at its January 1962 convention calls for a ten per cent reduction in the salaries of major government officials and the adoption of a programme of 'Pragmatic Socialism' (Post and Vickers, 1973: 74–5). But fundamentally, its response was hostile. Members of the party's activist youth wing, the Zikist Movement, were ordered by NCNC President Dr Michael Okpara to resign from the NYC. Party discipline was emphasised (Okpara, 1962: 20) and sanctions were imposed on those who persisted in an independent course.

It thus remained for the opposition party to capitalise on the growing disaffection with the status quo. Determined to lift the Action Group to a national majority in the next Federal election, Chief Awolowo began to embark boldly on a much more radical course. In September 1960, the AG's Federal Executive Council adopted a programme of Democratic Socialism that pledged to 'get rid of the dead-weight of feudalism, aristocracy, and privilege' by constraining foreign investment, expanding state enterprises, and emphasising the needs of peasants, wage-earners, and small business-men in the formulation of development priorities (Action Group, 1960). Throughout 1961, Chief Awolowo moved further to the left, introducing a bill in Parliament to nationalise basic industries (Wallerstein, 1962: 17), condemning what he charged was the growing domination of Nigeria's economy by Western, imperialist interests, and escalating his criticism of Nigeria's pro-Western foreign policy (Sklar, 1966: 130). Increasingly, he surrounded himself with younger men from the more radical and intellectual ranks of the party.[3]

While the radical perspective had not yet mobilised a major national constituency at Independence, it understood the primacy and urgency of the common Nigerian's aspiration for socioeconomic development. The breadth of Nigerian desires for economic improve-ment was virtually without parallel in the Cantril and Free study. Only one nation had a higher proportion of its population expressing economic hopes and fears both for their personal future and their nation's (Cantril, 1965: 163–74). Most of Nigerians' hopes (69 per cent in all) and fears (60 per cent) specifically involved improvement or adequacy in the standard of living. By contrast, in India, Brazil and Cuba no more than 40 per cent of the people expressed such a hope about their standard of living. The aspiration for a better standard of living had penetrated throughout every region and social group in Nigeria, and was even higher among the less privileged groups – those with less education, lower socioeconomic standing, rural and/or Northern residence (Free, 1964: 26–7). While the general concern for material improvement was the most frequent aspiration, the second and third most common personal hopes – good health and education for their children – also depended on economic development. Free (1964: 40) thus concluded that 'the revolution in rising expectations has taken hold with a vengeance in Nigeria in ways that have political meaning at the national level'.

This political meaning is seen even more vividly in the aspirations Nigerians expressed for their nation. Greater national prosperity or economic development was mentioned in some way by 60 per cent of the Nigerians interviewed. Five specific public sectors – education, public health, agriculture, employment, and modern amenities – were each mentioned as an aspiration for improvement by at least 30 per cent of the sample. 'Very much higher than customary' were the percentages of Nigerians who considered these 'national problems' (Free, 1964: 38). Contrary to their expectation that 'the Nigerian government might be under minimal public pressures in such respects' because of the low educational level of the public, Free and his colleagues found, 'The list of problems considered national, about which the Nigerian people implicitly expect the government to act, is the most extensive we have encountered in our studies to date' (Free, 1964: 37–8). This was further seen in the strong correlations (the strongest of any nation surveyed) between the ratings Nigerians gave their personal standing and those they gave their nation. These correlations suggest the degree to which a people identify their own lives and fortunes with those of their country (Free, 1964: 70). The uncommonly close association in Nigeria implied a 'special risk': that if a collective sense of disillusionment about the nation developed, it could spill over into personal 'frustration, pessimism and despair', disposing people toward extremist politics (1964: 70–1).

The survey revealed a new nation with extraordinary expectations for the future. Only two of the twelve national samples showed higher mean expectations for improvement in personal and national standing (Cantril, 1965: 187). Two-thirds of the Nigerians interviewed, and 92 per cent of those able to rate both their present and future personal standing, expected to be doing better in five years; almost no one expected to be doing worse (Cantril, 1965: 79). Similar percentages were registered for national standing. At times, these expectations were ludicrously unrealistic, such as the belief that, 'In ten years, Nigeria will be one of the leading countries in industry,' or 'one of the wealthiest countries in the world' (Free, 1964: 67–8). Overall, the responses portrayed Nigerians 'as a people bubbling with aspirations both for themselves and for the country as a whole' (Cantril, 1965: 81).

These high aspirations for progress and equally high expectations for their realisation implied a precarious situation for the new regime. To an unprecedented degree, Nigerians believed their new government responsible for the rapid social and economic development they desired.[4] Failure to distribute widely these tangible improvements in the standard of living figured to produce not simply frustration and extremism (and probably heightened ethnic conflict) but a precipitous loss of legitimacy for the democratic regime. Indeed, in the East and West, Free's data uncovered significant currents of popular disaffection. Large proportions of Southern Nigerians – 37 per cent in the West and 45 per cent in the East, compared to only 8 per cent in the North – listed among their national worries and fears social injustice or inequality.

Coupled with the increasing political momentum for radical alternatives, especially among the young and the better educated, the data from the two surveys indicate an incipient and potentially potent challenge to the legitimacy of the parliamentary system. Especially ominous was the apparent growing disenchantment in the Army, about which Wallerstein (1962: 18) observed: 'Army grumbling about the incompetence and venality of civilian politicians cannot be taken lightly, since similar grievances have led to military take-overs in a number of newly independent countries'. Similarly, only eight per cent in the North, but 26 per cent in the East and the West, worried about corruption in government.[5] The 23 per cent of the overall sample worrying about social injustice was seen as 'alarming' – 'by far the highest such figure we have ever encountered in our studies' (Free, 1964: 46), and often contained strong political overtones, as in the fear expressed by a respondent that 'There will be worsened political oppression and continued exploitation of the underprivileged ones by the ruling class' (Free, 1964: 46).

Such comments suggest that many of those concerned about social injustice seriously questioned the legitimacy of the regime. Such doubts, were surely also prevalent among the 16 per cent of the national sample who listed corruption in government among their national worries. Unfortunately, we cannot know what portions of the 20 per cent who worried about 'disunity among the people or the leaders' or the 51 per cent worrying about political instability and chaos (Free, 1964: 43) similarly doubted the entitlement of the regime to their support. But the frequency and intensity of these concerns indicate that the popular legitimacy of the democratic regime, never deeply rooted, was beginning visibly to erode just two years after Independence.

Similar undercurrents of disaffection were uncovered by John P. Mackintosh in a more limited survey in 1961 of voters in three urban constituencies: Enugu (in the East), Zaria Central (North) and Ibadan Central (West). As in the Cantril and Free survey, the Southern respondents in particular expressed a disturbing level of concern about the conduct and character of the politicians. In Enugu, one-fifth of the respondents voiced criticism of the ruling NCNC, 'their remarks ranging from the definite accusation that the leaders were corrupt, that they were interested only in themselves or that their salaries were too high, down to the milder comment that the party had deteriorated since the days of Dr Azikiwe's leadership' (Mackintosh, 1966: 308). The motive for this cynicism was not any preference for the Action Group, nor was it simply disagreement with NCNC policies. It was a growing sense that the politicians were not serving the public interest, a sense expressed in one way or another by roughly a third of the Enugu sample. Similarly in the Ibadan constituency, about a quarter of the sample criticised their party leaders for being selfish, too rich and so on (Mackintosh, 1966: 353).

Even with honest and dedicated government, the challenge of meeting popular expectations for development faced a number of obstacles. There was, to begin with, a narrow base of indigenous administrative talent, evident in the large proportion of senior Federal and Northern civil service positions still filled by expatriates, few of whom planned to stay indefinitely (Howe, 1960: 2). Nigeria thus faced the need to produce highly skilled administrators more rapidly than was perhaps possible.

On the other hand, the rapid educational expansion in the South was producing by 1960 a growing surplus of applicants for the lower and middle ranks of the bureaucracy and modern economy. By December of 1960, the Western Region alone had over 180 000 young people leaving primary school (the first graduates under the Region's universal primary education scheme). While some would continue on to secondary school, most (more than twice the number of the previous year) would seek employment in the modern, non-agricultural wage sector (Callaway, 1962: 221). The satisfaction of their expectations required a rate of growth in the modern sector almost beyond comprehension for an economy in which the agricultural sector still employed more than three-quarters of the labour force. Tens of thousands were finding no work. Abhorring the thought of returning to the farm, most of them were left to roam on the fringes of the cash economy, barely subsisting (Callaway, 1962: 222–4). Already at Independence, frustration was brewing.

With more school leavers coming on the job market each year, the problem promised to get much worse. Industrial expansion was unlikely even to begin to fill the gap, because most of the industries being built (cement, textiles, glass, aluminum products, and oil refining) were highly capital-intensive, and because capital was scarce in an economy where internal savings were meagre and taxation haphazard and incompetent (Callaway, 1962: 225). What domestic capital could be mobilised was substantially dissipated by 'the spreading virus' of corruption and the enormous salaries at the bloated higher ranks of government and administration (Herring, 1962: 5). Furthermore, there were few large-scale Nigerian entrepreneurs, and small businesses – which had the greatest potential for rapidly expanding markets and employment opportunities – received little in the way of government assistance (Callaway, 1962: 236).

The central economic problems faced by Nigeria at Independence were that the agricultural sector was largely ignored by political leaders in their obsession with all things modern, and that growth would require a level of discipline, savings, and sacrifice that the people seemed little disposed to endure and that the politicians had no intention of proposing in a political system that demanded immediate and tangible improvements. Considering as well the heavily adverse balance of trade, caused by declining world prices for cocoa and other export crops, and the huge costs of universal primary education in the West and East, the prospect for rapid (and broadly distributed) growth was hardly promising in 1960. Instead, the likelihood was that mass expectations for a better life would not be quickly met.

THE FRAGILITY OF DEMOCRACY

As for the nature of the political system at Independence, it was certainly a democracy in its constitutional structure. Legislative power was vested in an elected Parliament, consisting of a powerful lower chamber, the House of Representatives, which elected the Prime Minister and was responsible for the laws and finances of the Federation, and a Senate that resembled the British House of Lords in its inability to do more than delay ordinary legislation. Genuine power was exercised by the Senate on two matters of gravity, however, the declaration of an emergency and the amendment of the Constitution. Executive power was vested in a Council of Ministers (or Cabinet), headed by a Prime Minister who was to be appointed by the Governor-General upon demonstrating majority support in the Lower House. The Governor-General exercised the largely ceremonial functions of the British monarchy (which were assumed by the office of President when Nigeria became a republic on 1 October 1963). Judicial power was vested in an independent court system, including a Federal Supreme Court with power to decide cases involving the Federal Constitution, federal legislation, regional constitutions and regional statutory law (Odumosu, 1963: 193–7; Schwarz, 1965: 196–211).

Nigeria thus had at Independence the basic structure of Westminster parliamentary democracy. Power was distributed between three branches of government. Regular political competition followed from the requirement that Parliament be dissolved no later than five years after its first sitting. Extensive participation was assured through direct election of the House of Representatives (from constituencies of roughly equal population). Adult suffrage and eligibility for elective office were less than universal only in the Northern Region, where they were restricted to males. And political and civil rights were formally guaranteed in the Constitution's detailed chapter on Fundamental Rights.

There were also other democratic features of the political landscape. A number of political parties contested for political power. Their contestation was flawed in many important ways, but still it existed. In addition, though plagued by zealous partisanship, inexperience, irresponsibility, and economic and political pressure from parties and governments that detested criticism (Ogunade, 1981: 165–218), the Nigerian press did display some of the vitality and independence required of the press in a democratic society. It was regarded at the time by many outside observers as:

the most potent institution supporting democratic freedom in Nigeria. There is a tradition of hard-hitting, fearless, and independent journalism which has carried over from the colonial days when the press was the spearhead of nationalism. Though most papers are intensely partisan, they have several times agreed with each other and opposed the authorities who sought to restrict freedom – of the press or individuals (Schwarz, 1965: 163; also Herring, 1962: 261).

While the independence of most newspapers was compromised in their ownership by a regional government or political party, and while the exposed position of the foreign-owned papers and foreign journalists inevitably dampened their enthusiasm for criticising the government (Bretton, 1962: 99–103), the pluralism and criticism encompassed by the Nigerian press as a whole represented a significant degree of freedom in society.

On other dimensions of democratic performance, Nigeria fell much wider of the mark. Loopholes in the Constitution facilitated abuse. Among the 'fundamental human rights', the right to personal liberty and a fair trial appeared to proscribe the kind of preventive detention legislation then appearing in other developing countries, while the freedoms of belief, expression, movement, and association were designed to guarantee the security and meaningfulness of political opposition. But each provision carried a qualification excepting laws that were 'reasonably justifiable in a democratic society' in the interest of national defence, public order and so on. These extensive exceptions not only diluted the potential effectiveness of the Fundamental Rights as an educative instrument for Nigerians, but made it easier for Parliament to restrict political freedom and more likely that a court would uphold it (Schwarz, 1965: 182–3).[6]

More serious than these exceptions was the constitutional provision for declaration of emergency, during which exceptions to the basic freedoms were further widened (Constitution, Chapter III, Section 28). A 'period of emergency' was defined to exist when the Federation was at war, or when each House had declared by two-thirds vote that democratic institutions were threatened by subversion, or when each House declared by simple majority vote 'that a state of public emergency exists' (Constitution, Chapter IV, Section 65). In addition, the Constitution gave Parliament the power, by a two-thirds vote of each House, to take over the lawmaking functions of any regional government found to be exercising its authority 'to impede or prejudice the executive authority of the federation or to endanger the continuance of federal government in Nigeria', or to be failing to maintain the constitution of the Region (Constitution, Chapter IV, Sections 66 and 80). These constitutional provisions – especially the broad and ambiguous language of Section 65 on 'states of emergency' – raised ominous possibilities for the eclipse of political liberties or the displacement of a region's government, even by a simple majority vote in Parliament. In a system where parliamentary opposition was regionally based, this created enormous potential for intimidation of the opposition to a ruling coalition.

Indeed, Section 65 became the subject of perhaps the first serious political controversy in the new nation, shortly after Independence. In sharp exchanges in the press and parliament, Action Group leaders strongly challenged alleged interpretations by Federal Attorney General Elias and Eastern Premier Okpara that Section 65 gave the Federal Government power to dissolve a Regional Legislature. Only an assurance by Prime Minister Balewa of the autonomy of each government in the Federation quieted the brief but bitter controversy. Several months later, Parliament enacted (with little opposition) an Emergency Powers Act, empowering the Government during a declared emergency to make regulations for the arrest and detention of persons, the 'entering and search of premises', and the 'requisition of property or undertakings' (Cole, 1962: 80–1).

Still much more troubling questions were raised by the actual performance of the regime. Even under the impartial oversight of the British, the 1959 Federal Election had seriously abridged the rights of political oppositions to articulate their positions and compete for power. In all three regions, but especially in the North, regional power – control over chieftaincy and local government councils, harassment by tax-assessment committees, customary courts and local government police, and the multiple channels of economic and political patronage – was being applied with increasing vigour to repress and intimidate opposition. Structural reforms were implemented, but they made little difference. Just as the modernisation of the Native Administrations in the 1950s failed to restrain their repressive power, so the introduction of a new Penal Code in 1960 similarly failed to alter the basic position that 'in the North the freedoms normally regarded as essential if a two-party system is to work simply do not exist' (Mackintosh, 1966: 538). And regional government power to reconstitute a local government body (in the North and East) or (in all three Regions) to dissolve it altogether was being used with increasing frequency to eliminate local centres of opposition. 'Thus, in one week in the West in 1960, NCNC-controlled councils in Ilesa, Ijesha, and Benin were dissolved', while the Northern government dissolved opposition controlled councils in Ilorin and Jos (Schwarz, 1965: 157).

Genuine political competition was in the process of becoming constricted to the Federal arena, as one-party states were emerging in each region. These trends, fundamentally inconsistent with liberal democracy, were advanced in the regional elections of 1960 and 1961, during which each ruling party significantly consolidated its regional dominance. In the Western Regional election of August 1960, the Action Group won 54 per cent of the vote and 63 per cent of the seats – less sweeping a victory than those typically enjoyed by its two rivals in their home regions, but nevertheless a stronger showing than any previously by the AG. Aggressively manipulating the levers of regional power, the AG improved its fortunes not only in the Yoruba constituencies but in the minority constituencies of the Mid-West, where it took half the seats (as compared to 20 per cent in the regional election of 1956). As centres of opposition gradually and often bitterly came to terms with the growing political dominance of the AG (and the unhappy consequences of resisting it), the NCNC was clearly fading as an opposition force, taking barely a quarter of the seats in 1960 (compared to two-fifths in 1956). In the following year and a half, the atrophy continued, as the NCNC was humiliated and crushed in balloting for the Ibadan District Council, and six of the 33 NCNC members of the Western House 'crossed the carpet' and joined the Action Group. 'By 1961 even the leaders of the NCNC in the West were commenting privately that their party was dying' (Mackintosh, 1966: 514).

The trend was even more striking in the last of the three regional elections, that in the East in November 1961. There the Action Group and its minority-party ally saw their legislative strength in the Eastern House cut in half, to barely ten per cent. As happened in the Northern election six months earlier, the AG was badly hurt in the East by the sharp decline around the nation of ethnic minority parties after 1959 (Mackintosh, 1966: 527). In the wake of the AG's massive defeat that year, and the consequent evaporation of any real prospect of federal action to create more states, these parties lost their main reason for existence, and the AG its core strategy for building a parliamentary majority. Although the loss of twenty seats to independent candidates and five to the Dynamic Party indicated disaffection within Igboland, the NCNC still won almost three-quarters of the seats outright, and retained the allegiance of most of the independents. With these NCNC dissidents resolutely resisting AG overtures, the NCNC effectively controlled 85 per cent of the seats in the Eastern House (and three-quarters of those from the minority areas).

By far the most significant election, however, was that in the North, where the NPC won 69 per cent of the popular vote and a stunning 94 per cent of the seats in the Northern House. Despite another ambitious Northern campaign, the AG suffered an even more disastrous setback than in 1959, capturing only five per cent of the seats (as compared to 14 per cent in 1959). The NEPU, largely abandoned by its NCNC ally (now reluctant to offend the NPC), and its radical image tarnished by the appointment of Mallam Aminu Kano as a Government Whip in the Federal parliamentary coalition, was still more devastated, winning only a single seat. In the space of just seventeen months, 'the Action Group had lost control of sixteen of twenty-five constituencies it had won in 1959, and the NEPU had lost five out of six' (Post and Vickers, 1973: 65). Moreover, this monolithic control appeared to augur NPC hegemony in the North for a very long time to come, as it was achieved with less manifest intimidation and harassment and more institutional depth and vigour in the NPC, which was now sinking extensive roots through village and hamlet branches and Youth Organisations. Several minority parties in the North began to wither and disappear, while most of the NEPU–NCNC chapters outside Kano died away, and the NEPU was further wracked by a bitter internal division. Only in the Tiv division did opposition to the NPC remain steadfast, even as it became the object of escalating political repression. Tiv resistance exploded in early 1960 in riots that required the calling in of the Army, and again that September in the burning of some 30 000 homes of NPC functionaries in the division. In the 1961 election, the United Middle Belt Congress, in alliance with the AG, swept all the Tiv constituencies with massive victories, and UMBC leader J. S. Tarka scored the highest majority of any candidate in Nigeria that year (Dent, 1966).

In the course of each regional election, then, the opposition was shattered, demoralised and effectively neutralised as a meaningful force. And given the scope of regional power, the process was self-reinforcing, sharply diminishing the prospects for serious opposition in future elections. The regional elections thus completed a decade-long trend toward a hybrid political structure: a multi-party federal system composed essentially of one-party states.

This trend carried two negative implications for the democratic prospect in Nigeria. First, it implied an escalating insecurity and instability in the Federal system. If the NPC duplicated its massive victory in the next Federal election – and there was no reason to doubt that it would – it would win an outright majority of the Federal House of Representatives, and thus the opportunity to form a government unilaterally. Indeed, by mid-1961 it had already (barely) assembled such a majority. This was exactly the prospect that had most distressed Southern politicians over the past decade. Now it seemed all but impossible to avoid – unless the 1962 census were to reveal a substantial change in the regional distribution of the population. In the wake of its May 1961 landslide, the NPC was already waxing more confident and aggressive.

The second distressing implication was the further erosion of both the reality and the concept of political opposition. The continuing and in many areas escalating intimidation and repression of opposition exposed again the shallow commitment of the regional political classes to democratic norms of fair play. Although the national political scene was relatively calm and civil during 1960 and 1961, the ruling parties seemed to be showing, with the departure of the British, even less restraint and respect for political opposition. Virtually everywhere, it was being not only defeated but cowed, humiliated and silenced. And being crushed as well were the hopes of both the AG and NCNC to build national political bases across regions and tribes.

Organised opposition, as Chief Awolowo so eloquently expressed it shortly before Independence, is 'the soul of democracy'.[7] The escalating repression and harassment it was encountering in the three regions, and the threat it faced at the centre, make it difficult to classify Nigeria in 1960 as a genuine democracy. It had a quasi-democratic regime, and was struggling to establish and institutionalise liberal democratic government. The elements were there – a democratic constitution, a multiparty system with competitive elections, a relatively vigorous press – but they were under assault, and the outcome of the experiment was in doubt.

CONSPIRACY OF OPTIMISM: EXPECTATIONS FOR NIGERIAN DEMOCRACY

Expectations for Nigerian democracy at Independence were generally high, both among Nigerian politicians and world leaders and observers. While doubts abounded in the First World about the capacity for democratic self-government in the Third World – fuelled by the collapse in quick succession of democratically elected governments in Burma, Pakistan, and Sudan and the drift to one-party rule in Ghana – the prevailing sense was that if there was hope for democracy anywhere in Africa it was in Nigeria (e.g., D. Williams, 1960; Taylor, 1960). The typical optimism of 'the superficial foreign observer' at the time has been summarised by Miners (1971: 4):

> In the case of Nigeria in 1960, the new state's future stability seemed assured not only by the apparent weakness of the armed forces . . . but also because of its peculiarly peaceful advance to Independence. The 'struggle for freedom' had been remarkably free of violence, even by comparison with Ghana. None of Nigeria's leading nationalists went to prison. . . . No country, it might have seemed, could be set for a more harmonious passage after Independence.

Common among Nigerian leaders and British officials was a feeling that the worst national divisions had been laid to rest, that the last decade had already demonstrated the viability of democracy in Nigeria. In part, this optimism may have grown out of an impatience to get on with the final transfer of power, which was lagging behind the independence dates of Ghana and other Third World nations. With the British viewing their mission as essentially discharged and the various Nigerian parties all eager for Independence, 'nobody was prepared to . . . [seek] an extension of colonial rule in order to sort out more domestic problems' (Oyinbo, 1971: 8).

> Thus it suited neither the departing British nor the Nigerian elite to whom they transferred power to examine too closely the defects in the structure handed over and the problems its maintenance would entail. Both parties to the settlement had cause to know that it might have been very much worse, and there were in any case ample grounds for optimism. But it was an optimism which tended to dull the sensitiveness to reality. . . . Many problems were shelved rather than solved in the euphoria . . . . So long as the British were present they acted as a referee for whom an indigenous substitute could never be found, obscuring the inevitable power struggle which alone would produce political equilibrium.

Neither the British nor the Nigerians fully realized how vital the British presence was to the operation of a system which contained gross imbalances, was rooted in an alien culture, and the product of another nation's history (Oyinbo, 1971: 9).

Perhaps nothing so clouded the future of Nigerian democracy as these 'gross imbalances' in its federal system, of which Chief Awolowo repeatedly and stridently appealed for resolution before Independence, even on the very eve of it. Given the previous decade of conflict, the structural strains, and the absence of any deeply institutionalised or widely shared respect for basic democratic rights, his apprehension that the Opposition he led in Parliament might be suppressed and even crushed after Independence was neither wild nor unfounded. Indeed, events would soon reveal the remarkable prescience of his warnings:

Several threats have of late been issued by spokesmen of the Federal Government . . . It has been said that, after independence, if the Western Region Government does not behave itself it will be dissolved, and that the Action Group is an evil party which does not deserve to live in a free Nigeria . . . .

I have a shrewd guess that some leaders and members of the parties in coalition at the federal level are planning to incite turmoil and violence in the Western Region with a view to spiting and discrediting the Action Group . . . .

Recent trends . . . indicate that the parties in power at the Centre have not yet succeeded in attuning themselves to the activities of an opposition, and it is not unlikely that they have been wondering whether one should be allowed to exist at all after independence. . . .

Any flagrant departure from, or violation, or discriminatory and spiteful amendment, of the provisions of our Constitution would only land all of us in a desert of bitter strife (Awolowo, 1960b: 5,6,7,8).

Equally profound was the challenge of satisfying popular expectations for improved standards of living, on which the legitimacy of the regime most immediately and directly depended. As one American scholar observed, 'If minimum goals either on a regional or on a national basis are not attained, then the claims to legitimacy by proponents of democratic ways will be subjected to counterclaims by what may appear to be more efficient managers of material and manpower resources' (Bretton, 1962: 54).

Some speculated at the time, particularly in the wake of the military coup in Sudan, that the military in Nigeria might assert these counterclaims and end the democratic experiment in Nigeria. Many dismissed the prospect as impossible for a nation of thirty-five million people with an army of only 7500. Addressing in 1959 the question, 'Can it happen here?', Ayo Ogunsheye, Director of the Extra-Mural Department of the University of Ibadan, offered as incisive an analysis as will be found:

> We can answer indirectly by asking, 'Why did the military intervene [in Sudan]?' At the risk of over simplification, because the civilians did not deliver the goods. The people expected good government and higher standards of living; instead they got inefficiency and corruption. Without suggesting that the Army can do better than the politicians, the lesson is clear. If we do not want people to lose faith in parliamentary democracy we must insure that it does not become a farce (quoted in Miners, 1971: 247).

4 Crisis and Conflict in the Western Region, 1962–63

'I am in a confused state because I think something has started today, something has begun today which is going to go much further than most of us here imagine.'—Chief Anthony Enahoro, Action Group Member, in parliamentary debate over the motion to declare a State of Emergency in the Western Region, 29 May 1962 (quoted in Balewa, 1964: 128)

'I solemnly assure you that the powers we shall soon be forced to assume will be exercised in as humane and democratic a manner as the circumstances will permit, and that, as soon as reasonably may be, the Federal Government will actively promote ... an early return to the normal processes of democracy.'—Prime Minister Alhaji Sir Abubakar Tafawa Balewa, in the same debate, 29 May 1962 (Balewa, 1964: 132)

ORIGINS OF THE CRISIS

During 1960 and 1961, fundamental tensions in the Action Group had begun to crystallise and then to surface. To a significant degree, the brewing crisis stemmed from the staggering defeat of the Action Group in the 1959 Federal Elections, which left Chief Awolowo stranded in opposition at the centre without a firm base of power resources and at the same time compelled him to devise a fresh strategy for building a national political majority. Defeat led him to more strident opposition, while convincing his party's more conservative businessmen and traditional rulers of the futility of political pursuits beyond their own region. Increasingly, the party found itself sharply divided over ideology, political strategy and party control between the rival factions of Party Leader Obafemi Awolowo and Regional Premier Samuel Ladoke Akintola.

As Chief Awolowo positioned the Action Group in increasingly explicit advocacy of socialist development policies and radical ideological themes, many of the Yoruba businessmen and merchants at the party's financial core became nervous (as did conservatives and business interests in the other two parties). Their concerns were intensified by the meeting of the AG's Federal Executive Council on 18 December 1961, when the radical intellectuals on Awolowo's National Reconstruction Committee submitted their policy proposals elaborating the party doctrine of Democratic Socialism. While the Committee's paper on economic measures was accepted, its 'paper on austerity measures, deploring the extravagant financial benefits extended at public expense to governmental ministers and civil servants, appears to have occasioned bitter debate; a few party leaders are reported to have alleged that Awolowo had fallen into the hands of the "communists" ' (Sklar, 1966: 130). Chief Akintola took this as a direct personal attack, and party conservatives no doubt saw it as distressing confirmation of their fears that Awolowo meant to dismantle the structure of class privilege; together they succeeded in referring it out to a committee of civil servants. Even more intense opposition was summoned against the general ideological statement submitted by the committee, which was referred out to the Regional Executive Committees of the party. As the Action Group approached its 1962 Annual Congress, scheduled for February in Jos, a crucial showdown loomed between the radical and conservative factions.

Coinciding with these ideological divisions was a widening gulf within the party over its future political strategy. In articulating a radical socialist programme, Chief Awolowo sought to redesign, rather than abandon, the 'federalist' political strategy that had been blown apart in the elections of the previous two years. Awolowo realised that alignment with the nation's ethnic minorities and Northern commoners would not suffice. As he sought to capture the growing disenchantment with the political class, he also quietly pursued a progressive coalition with the NCNC to oppose the 'reactionary' NPC, proposing Dr Azikiwe as titular leader (Sklar, 1966: 130). The NCNC had other ideas for its long-time Southern enemy, however, and nothing came of the overtures. Meanwhile, the more conservative and pragmatic faction of the AG, led by Premier Akintola, had determined that continued pursuit of national power was hopeless and decided instead upon a 'regionalist' strategy. This school of thought favoured a grand alliance between the three major Parties – a kind of status quo consociationalism – that would recognise each region as the preserve of its ruling party and divide up the spoils of Federal power between them. This was unacceptable not only to the young radicals, who were determined to overthrow the 'feudal oligarchy' in the North and the entire structure of privilege in the country, but also to the Action Group leaders (mainly from ethnic minorities) in the North and East, whom it would essentially abandon. Thus, as the Awolowo faction was trying to woo the NCNC into a nationwide progressive coalition against the NPC, the Akintola faction sought an agreement with the NPC that would preserve the political status quo and secure for the Western Region and its political class a greater share of Federal wealth and power (Sklar, 1966: 128; Post and Vickers, 1973: 76).

Intensifying personal rivalry between Chief Awolowo and Chief Akintola aggravated these substantive schisms. Though close political associates for more than twelve years, Chief Akintola did not take well to Chief Awolowo's effort to retain control over policies and appointments in the Western Region after he left the premiership to lead the Federal Opposition. A proud and ambitious politician, the new Premier bitterly resented Chief Awolowo's 'insatiable desire to run the government of which I am head from outside the cabinet' (quoted in Osuntokun, 1982: 133). Yet Awolowo, shut off from a base of revenue and patronage, needed to retain control in the West to preserve not only his pride but his party dominance. If Akintola established himself as the primary source of patronage and influence in the Action Group, he might someday wrest control of the party from Awolowo (Mackintosh, 1966: 441). Waged behind the scenes at first, this personal rivalry sharpened and became increasingly public during 1961 as the financial position of the region deteriorated.[1]

The financial crisis stemmed in part from Premier Akintola's decisions, in preparation for the 1960 Regional election, to cut the tax rate by more than half and to exempt women completely. Chief Awolowo opposed these decisions on the grounds that the Region could not afford the £5 million loss of annual revenue. Awolowo appeared to have been proven correct early in 1961 when world cocoa prices fell and the Region was unable to continue subsidising the price of that commodity, though the financial squeeze was also occasioned by the heavy drain on Marketing Board resources by the Action Group and its business network (Osuntokun, 1982: 134). In January 1961 and again in August, Chief Akintola announced reductions in the government-set price of cocoa, consulting neither Chief Awolowo nor the Minister of Agriculture, Chief G. Akin-Deko, a close friend of Awolowo (Mackintosh, 1966: 441–2).

As the new Premier continued to formulate Regional policies without benefit of consultation and instruction from the Party Leader, their division began to seep into the Action Group press, still firmly controlled by Awolowo. Late in 1961 'it became evident that the party leaders close to Chief Awolowo and the newspapers under his influence were trying to force the Western Region Government to adopt austerity measures and to cut Ministers' salaries and car allowances' (Mackintosh, 1966: 442). When Premier Akintola chose instead to reduce government grants to secondary schools (meaning higher student fees), the AG press accused him of contradicting the Party programme and scandalously favouring the high living of Ministers and civil servants over the public welfare. As a result of this vigorous press assault, the government withdrew its cuts in school grants and announced austerity measures (Mackintosh, 1966: 422).

The increasingly strident and radical pitch of Awolowo's political message thrust him squarely in conflict not only with the conservatives in his own party but with those in the Federal Coalition, who needed no further reason for wanting badly to be rid of Awolowo and his audacious party. His attacks on Nigeria's pro-Western foreign policy hit the ruling coalition in an area where it was politically vulnerable. Similarly, it was feared that Chief Awolowo's condemnation of 'neocolonialism' and the Action Group's call for nationalisation of 'vital' industries would drive away foreign capital and might only be a prelude to nationalisation of Nigerian enterprises, in which many key politicians and supporters of the ruling parties had a large personal stake (Schwarz, 1965: 120–1).

But these concerns were modest relative to the issues on which the Federal Coalition was most vulnerable and sensitive – corruption in government and social injustice in the North. The AG attacks on NPC policies in the North were a continuation of its irreverent and bitterly resented themes in the 1959 campaign. NPC leaders held the AG, in alliance with the UMBC, responsible for the rioting in Tivland and remained bitter as well over the AG's attempt to get the Northern Cameroons to delay joining Nigeria and hence the Northern Region in early 1961. Most of all, NPC leaders feared and opposed the Action Group proposal to break up the Northern Region – and so, to unravel the NPC's national political dominance as well as its social dominance in the Upper North. The sharpening AG focus on government corruption, extravagance, and high salaries seriously threatened the political classes of each region. This campaign challenged fundamentally what Post and Vickers (1973) have termed 'The System of Rewards', which was the essential machinery for formation of class dominance in Nigeria.

There were other compelling reasons the two Coalition parties might have had for wanting to neutralise or destroy their common antagonist. In each of their home regions, Chief Awolowo's strategy continued to stress a direct AG challenge to their dominance. With leaders of both parties, including the more accommodating Prime Minister Balewa, he had a long record of personal antagonism. His strident atacks on Federal policies convinced the Prime Minister that he was a threat to national unity (Mackintosh, 1966: 656). His party's deft and forceful use of regional power to consolidate its grip on the West (not to mention the entire decade of vituperative political conflict) had embittered the NCNC and moved its President, Eastern Premier Michael Okpara, bluntly to threaten retaliation.[2] Moreover, Awolowo was beginning to consolidate a firm base of support among the nation's educated youth, coveted by the progressive wing of the NCNC, which may have resented the Action Group for stealing its thunder (Schwarz, 1965: 123). Some thought he had the potential, especially with the increasing tensions inside the NEPU, to unite the *talakawa* of the Upper North and the pagans of the Middle Belt in the one coalition that Northern leaders feared the most.[3] And his demise in the West promised tangible political gains for both parties, including the possibility of complete control of Southern Nigeria for the NCNC.

Thus, both the NPC and the NCNC had powerful and abundant motives for wanting to eliminate the Action Group – and Chief Awolowo in particular – as an effective opposition force, and both parties appear to have harboured this desire. The tacit NCNC–NPC alliance in the 1959 Federal election; the rumours and charges of Federal Government plans to use its emergency powers in the West; Dr Okpara's hasty return from a European tour in August 1961 to call for a State of Emergency in the West (because of political violence in the Mid-West); the vote in April 1961 (later overturned by the Supreme Court) to create a new Region in the Mid-West but not in other areas of minority agitation; and the abortive Federal Government effort in October 1961 (also blocked by the Supreme Court) to investigate the AG's National Bank in the hope of exposing a financial scandal suggest a continuing search for some pretext to discredit, cripple, or destroy the Action Group.

THE OPEN FRACTURE: THE JOS CONGRESS AND ITS AFTERMATH

As the Action Group Congress opened on 2 February 1962, Chief Awolowo wasted no time in drawing the issues sharply in his Presidential address. Calling on his party to acknowledge 'openly for once' the existence of 'real and dangerous contradictions' within the party that would have to be resolved – in particular 'a growing disaffection between privileged and non-privileged classes (so-called) within the party' – he proceeded to reaffirm forcefully his positions on the continuation of active opposition in the North and East, the undesirability of joining the NPC–NCNC coalition in a National Government, the continuing demand for the creation of new states, and the AG platform of democratic socialism (Sklar, 1966: 130–1).

Premier Akintola had taken leave of the Congress on its eve to greet the Northern Premier, the Sardauna of Sokoto, on his long-planned official visit to the West. He returned on the second day to learn that news and pictures of his meetings with the Sardauna had brought a stream of open condemnations from Awolowo supporters on the floor (Uwanaka, 1964: 54). Having realised the previous evening that they were badly outnumbered, Chief Akintola, his close associate Chief Ayotunde Rosiji, the AG Federal Secretary, and six of their leading supporters withdrew from the Congress on 4 February and returned to Ibadan (Sklar, 1966: 131; Mackintosh, 1966: 445).

With their departure, the victory of the Awolowo faction, already assured, became a rout. In a series of motions orchestrated by the National President, critical changes were effected in the party's leadership and structure. The report of the absent Federal Secretary, noting the AG's electoral setbacks in the North and East and stressing the consolidation of regional power by each major party, was emphatically rejected. The Constitution of the Action Group was then amended to weaken the position of the Western Premier in the Federal Executive Committee, to strengthen the Federal President's control over this and a new committee, and to provide for the removal of a parliamentary leader by the body which elected him (Sklar, 1966: 131; Mackintosh, 1966: 445). On the fourth day of the Congress, the Awolowo faction scored a clean sweep of the elections for major party offices (Uwanaka, 1964: 54–5; Osuntokun, 1982: 128).

The provision for removal of a parliamentary leader portended a move to oust Premier Akintola from office. In fact, this appears to be what Chief Awolowo had in mind when, soon after the Congress, he summoned a meeting of the body that had appointed Chief Akintola as the Western Parliamentary Leader (and had thus made him Premier). Before the meeting occurred, however, the elders of the party intervened. Led by Dr Akinola Maja, 'Father of the Party' and President of the *Egbe Omo Oduduwa*, and Sir Adesoji Aderemi II, Governor of the Western Region and esteemed Oni (Oba) of Ife, the elders convened a meeting of some 100 members of the Action Group 'old guard' on 9 February in the hope of reconciling the two warring party leaders. After a bitter exchange of accusations by Akintola and Awolowo, the dispute was referred to a more select body of elders. Again the outcome was inconclusive, though this time Chief Awolowo was asked to accept his Deputy's denial that he alleged Awolowo was planning a *coup d'etat*, 'and after Chief Akintola had promised to consult the party executives on major questions, it was announced that the rift was closed'. Perhaps sensing that the shrewed Akintola still had cards of his own to play, and that the members of the Western House of Assembly, not eager to risk having to stand for election again so soon, would 'hesitate before casting aside the Premier', Awolowo apparently resolved 'to give his Deputy one more chance' (Mackintosh, 1966: 445–6).

Parliamentary developments in March and April of 1962 gave the appearance of renewed party unity. But in fact, there was little respite from the struggle. The newly elected Federal Secretary (Eastern socialist Samuel Ikoku), quickly moved to tighten central control over the local branches. Premier Akintola countered by demoting, removing, or threatening to remove Awolowo's supporters on Regional boards, and by moving ahead on his announced intention to reshuffle the million-pound Western Nigeria Development Corporation, then controlled by Chief Awolowo through his political secretary, Alfred Rewane. Contending that such a move would violate the terms of their reconciliation, Awolowo in turn threatened to force a major reshuffle of the Western Regional cabinet. As the Premier toured his strongholds and enlisted support, Chief Awolowo responded with a political tour of his own. 'Matters reached a climax in May when the National President announced that he would tour Oshun [Akintola's home] and was warned by local chiefs and politicians to keep out of his rival's territory' (Mackintosh, 166: 446; also Sklar, 1966: 133; Worrall, 1965: 101).

With the supporters of each faction now actively mobilised and the press 'in full cry', party leaders made a final attempt to save the situation, appointing a peace committee under the esteemed Action Group lawyer Chief Rotimi Williams. At its meeting on 16 May, a tentative compromise was drafted for submission to a Joint Meeting of the AG Mid-Western and Western Executive Committees on 19 May. But the Awolowo faction was in no mood for further compromise. Accusing Akintola of 'maladministration, anti-party activities and gross indiscipline', and raising, point by point, the full array of their differences over party ideology, regional policies and appointments and national strategy, Chief Awolowo now pressed for a decisive conclusion to the conflict (Sklar, 196: 134). Ignoring Premier Akintola's reply, the Joint Meeting unanimously resolved to find him guilty of all charges. Then, unmoved by Akintola's reluctant full apology to the party, it voted (81 to 29) to demand his resignation as Premier and Deputy Leader. Chief Akintola refused, vowing a fight to the finish. On the following day (20 May), the AG Federal Executive Council unanimously endorsed the two resolutions, and, meeting jointly with the AG's parliamentary councils, deposed Chief Akintola as Deputy Leader and called upon the Governor to remove him as Premier (Sklar, 1966: 133–4; Mackintosh, 1966: 446–7; NYC, 1962: 2).

Events were now accelerating to a furious pace. Premier Akintola countered by asking the Governor to dissolve the Western House of Assembly. Sir Adesoji, noting that an election had been held only two years previously and fearing the chaos that might result from a new one, refused Akintola's request (Osuntokun, 1982: 137). Similarly, on more questionable grounds constitutionally, the Speaker refused Akintola's request for a meeting of the House on 23 May to consider a motion of confidence in his government. Leaders of the Awolowo faction had already begun bringing loyal members of the Western House from their constituencies to Ibadan to sign a petition asking the Governor to dismiss the Premier. On 21 May the petition was presented, with the signatures of 66 members (of an AG block of 84 and a total membership of 117). Meeting that same day as the Parliamentary Council, these 66 members elected Alhaji O. S. Adegbenro, Minister of Local Government, as leader in place of Chief Akintola. The Governor preferred to wait for a House vote of no confidence, but the Awolowo faction was determined to have a new Premier before the House met, and the Governor, a long-term supporter and beneficiary of Awolowo's party, had little choice but to accept the petition and dismiss Akintola as Premier on the evening of 21 May. Immediately thereafter, Alhaji Adegbenro was sworn in to replace him, while Chief Akintola requested the Ibadan High Court to invalidate the Governor's action and petitioned the Prime Minister and the Queen to remove Governor Aderemi from office. The next day, as the civil service was recognising Alhaji Adegbenro as the new Premier, Chief Akintola forced his way back into his office (Mackintosh, 1966: 447–8; Sklar, 1966: 134). Newspapers announced in banner headlines Akintola's refusal to go, and the Sardauna issued a statement supporting him (Osuntokun, 1982: 143).

These were not the only steps Chief Akintola was taking to hold on to power. The Speaker had granted Alhaji Adegbenro's request for a meeting of the House of Assembly on 25 May. As the date approached, it became 'widely known that since the Akintola faction were in a minority, they intended to disrupt the meeting of the House in order to try to prevent Alhaji Adegbenro receiving a formal vote of confidence as Premier' (Mackintosh, 1966: 448).

THE CRISIS OF 25 MAY AND FEDERAL INTERVENTION

Few events during the First Republic generated more controversy than the meeting of the Western House of Assembly on 25 May 1962. What is beyond dispute is that soon after it opened the session degenerated into such total physical disorder that business could not be conducted. The weight of the evidence indicates that the disorder was carefully orchestrated by the Akintola faction to prevent the confirmation of Adegbenro as Premier and possibly to invoke the very State of Emergency that was subsequently declared (Schwarz, 1965: 135). The definitive account is that of John P. Mackintosh, a British political scientist who was then Senior Lecturer at the University of Ibadan:

> The House of Assembly met at 9 a.m. and after prayers, as Chief Odebiyi rose to move the first motion, Mr E. O. Oke, a supporter of Chief Akintola, jumped on the table shouting 'There is fire on the mountain'. He proceeded to fling chairs about the chamber. Mr E. Ebubedike, also a supporter of Chief Akintola, seized the mace, attempted to club the Speaker with it but missed and broke the mace on the table. The supporters of Alhaji Adegbenro sat quiet as they had been instructed to do, with the exception of one member who was hit with a chair and retaliated. Mr Akinyemi

(NCNC) and Messrs Adigun and Adeniya (pro-Akintola) continued to throw chairs, the opposition joined in and there was such disorder that the Nigeria Police released tear gas and cleared the House. (Mackintosh, 1966: 448)[4]

With the complete breakdown of order in the Western House, the controversy turned on the action of the Nigerian police, who were ultimately responsible to the Prime Minister and had been instructed to recognise for the time being neither Adegbenro nor Akintola as Premier. Phoning the Prime Minister in Lagos, Awolowo and Adegbenro appealed to Sir Abubakar to permit police protection within the Assembly Chamber when the House next attempted to meet, while the Akintola faction warned him that a further meeting would only produce more trouble. The Prime Minister took a curious compromise stand. He acknowledged the right of the House to reassemble that day but refused to order police protection within the Chamber. If any party insisted on police protection, they were to be afforded it, but with the understanding that 'the Federal Government will not accept any decision reached as a result of such proceedings in the Chamber' and that if 'there should be [another] outbreak of violence or disorder, the Police have authority to clear the Chamber and lock it up' (quoted in Mackintosh, 1966: 449).

Within hours of the Prime Minister's statement, the Awolowo faction tried once more to hold a meeting of the Western House. Despite the presence of policemen beside and behind the Speaker's Chair, Akintola's AG supporters and NCNC allies once again disrupted the House. With furniture flying in all directions, the police once more released tear gas and cleared the House (Mackintosh, 196: 449). The Speaker considered a final attempt at a meeting the following morning, but when it became clear that the Akintola forces would disrupt this too, the idea was abandoned and the Chamber was locked.

Following the second outburst on 25 May, the Prime Minister announced that the Federal House would meet on 29 May and take action. Fearing what was by then widely assumed, and what Awolowo had warned against for two years – that the Federal Government would 'take over' government in the West – 'A delegation of Western chiefs and Obas visited the Prime Minister on the 27th in Lagos and asked for time so that the Westerners could settle matters among themselves. This had no effect' (Mackintosh, 1966: 450).

On 29 May Chief Awolowo's fear came to pass. A motion declaring that a state of Public Emergency existed in the Western Region was moved by the Prime Minister himself. With the unanimous backing of the NPC, the NCNC and the few AG members loyal to Akintola, the motion carried by votes of 209 to 36 in the House of Representatives and 32 to 7 in the Senate.[5] A number of regulations were also approved, removing the Governor, Premier, Ministers, and other top executive and legislative officials of the Western Region. In their place, the Prime Minister was to appoint an Administrator, to whom was delegated sweeping powers to appoint commissioners, to command the police and civil service, to promulgate orders, 'to imprison anyone spreading misleading reports, to prohibit public processions and meetings, to detail or restrict any person in the interests of public order, and to search premises without a warrant' (Mackintosh, 1966: 450; see also Odumosu, 1963: 283). To this exceptionally powerful position, Sir Abubakar appointed his close friend and Federal Minister of Health, Senator M. A. Majekodunmi, a distinguished Yoruba gynaecologist.

The subsequent six months of emergency rule featured harsh limitations on the relevant politicians, especially Chief Awolowo and his followers, intense legal wrangling over the controversial decisions in May, and escalating legal and political pressure on the Awolowo faction. Upon assuming power on 9 June, the Administrator restricted all of the leading politicians (and many secondary ones) to places outside Ibadan. But here even-handed administration ended. Within two months, virtually all restricted Akintola supporters were free while officers and organisers of the Awolowo Action Group remained restricted. For the month of June, all public meetings and processions were banned 'despite complete calm throughout the Region'. The following month, two leading AG journalists, Bisi Onabanjo and Lateef K. Jakande, 'were restricted to distant places in the Delta for what appeared to be normal journalistic criticism of the conduct of the Federal Government and Dr Majekodunmi'. On 9 August, the power of the emergency Administrator to punish and prohibit types of published material was further extended (Mackintosh, 1966: 451).

Meanwhile, suits and countersuits worked their way through the courts. Chief Akintola's suit against his dismissal as Premier was eventually upheld by the Federal Supreme Court. This was appealed to her Majesty's Privy Council by Chief Adegbenro, who also challenged the constitutionality of the Emergency Powers Act and the regulations and restrictions promulgated under it. Again Adegbenro lost in the Supreme Court, which declined to rule on the suspension of the Executive but found his restriction justifiable.

Pressure was also mounted on the Awolowo Action Group in the form of the 'Coker Commission of Inquiry into the Affairs of Certain Statutory Corporations in Western Nigeria'. The swift appointment of the Commission, chaired by Justice G. B. A. Coker, was widely seen to be motivated by the long-standing desire to discredit Action Group rule in the West. This became apparent in the course of the Commission's 92 days of often sensational public hearings between July and November of 1962, during which the Commissioners pursued with special zeal the pivotal role of Chief Awolowo and the central involvement of his chief allies.

There was probably little doubt that Awolowo was at the hub of an intricate financial network that diverted vast sums of public money to his party. Indeed, the overwhelming evidence presented to this effect 'created little surprise or shock among AG supporters' (Mackintosh, 1966: 453). The rank and file supported the party for the economic prosperity it had brought to the Region, and educated followers believed Awolowo and his party had laid more emphasis on personal honesty than had opposing parties (Mackintosh, 1966: 453). What betrayed the political motives of the Coker Inquiry and blunted the impact of its findings of massive corruption was the complete vindication of Chief Akintola, who had been Premier for more than two years and who appeared to be implicated at a number of crucial points in the investigation. Consistently accepting his denials (often at face value) the Commission fixed the blame squarely on Chief Awolowo:

> With respect to the two Premiers . . ., we conclude without a doubt that Chief Awolowo has failed to adhere to the standards of conduct which are required for persons holding such a post. We take the view that there is no evidence sufficient, in our view, to say the same of Chief Akintola and we absolve him on all grounds. (Coker, 1962: Vol. I, Ch. 1, p. 40).[6]

With the submission in December 1962 of the Coker Commission's Report exonerating Chief Akintola, the stage appeared set for his reinstatement as Premier. Early in the Emergency, Chief Akintola had organised his faction into a new party, which he later designated the United People's Party (UPP). By August, he had attracted a minority of AG members in the Federal Parliament, several key

Western political figures and the open backing of the NCNC (Idem, 1962: 10; Worrall, 1965: 103). As the increasingly blatant bias of the Emergency Administration began to foreshadow the shape of things to come, a growing trickle of defections from the Awolowo faction followed. By December, Awolowo's support in the Federal House and dwindled to 20 members (from the 36 who had opposed the Emergency resolution six months earlier and the 75 Opposition members elected in 1959), and the Prime Minister announced that he would no longer be recognised officially as Leader of the Opposition. Nevertheless, Chief Awolowo appeared to retain superior popularity in the Western Region.[7] This generated a dilemma for the NPC–NCNC coalition. While it had seemed to commit itself to elections and people widely expected them, it was also clearly committed to returning Akintola to power, which was not likely to be the outcome of a free and fair vote in the Region. In August and September, the leading barons of the coalition – Sir Abubakar, Dr Okpara, the Sardauna – began to back away from elections and to maintain that Chief Akintola was the legal Premier of the Region.

The coalition's reluctance to hold an election was no doubt heightened by the dramatic events of subsequent weeks. On 22 September 1962, the Federal police reported placing Chief Awolowo under house arrest in connection with an arms plot involving members of the Action Group. During the following week, homes were searched around the Region, quantities of arms and explosives were seized, and more than twenty other political figures were arrested. Virtually the entire leadership of Chief Awolowo's party was in custody or in refuge as the Prime Minister revealed to the stunned nation the existence of a secret army organisation. In November, charges of treasonable felony – including a conspiracy to stage a *coup d'etat* in Lagos in September – were filed against Chief Awolowo and thirty other persons.

Even after his arrest, Chief Awolowo demonstrated the continuing strength of his popular base, as the Action Group scored a solid victory in the Lagos Town Council elections on 16 October. Split in two by the turmoil of the preceding year, bereft of its national leaders and disadvantaged by the ruling coalition's control over patronage in the Federal capital, the AG still won 27 of the 42 seats, wresting control from the NCNC (*Africa Report*, November 1962: 23). The vote reflected not only strong support for Awolowo but gathering Yoruba resentment at the effort of the ruling coalition to destroy him and his party.

AFTERMATH: THE DESTRUCTION OF THE ACTION GROUP

On 1 January 1963, the Action Group received a double blow. Chief Akintola was reinstated as Premier, and the Report of the Coker Commission was formally released to the public. The restoration of Akintola was an especially sharp blow to AG fortunes, giving its former Deputy Leader the resources to assemble solid majority support in the Regional House. His effort to do so was substantially boosted by formation of a coalition government with the sizable NCNC parliamentary block. Chief Akintola's close association with the Western NCNC and its ambitious leader, Chief R. A. Fani-Kayode, had been apparent during the confrontation in the Western House the previous May and was reportedly formalised in an agreement in November 1962 (Worrall, 1965: 104). In exchange for NCNC support, Chief Akintola was required to support unconditionally the creation of a Mid-West Region, which he had previously bitterly opposed (Osuntokun, 1982: 151), and to give the NCNC a generous share of power in the West. Of the fourteen ministerial positions opened up by the dismissal of AG loyalists, eleven went to the NCNC, giving it as many portfolios as the UPP. Chief Fani-Kayode won the newly created post of Deputy Premier, and the Ministry of Local Government as well (*Africa Report*, February 1963).

Once returned to power, Chief Akintola wasted no time in consolidating his position, using all the old levers of regional power to cajole and induce local government councils, traditional rulers, and individual House members to join up (Mackintosh, 1966: 458–9). By the time the Western Regional House of Assembly reconvened on 8 April, Chief Akintola and his coalition partners were finally in command. The motion of confidence in his administration carried in the 122-seat House by a vote of 79-0, the remaining AG contingent having boycotted the session. The vote was a striking indication of how far the fortunes of the Action Group had fallen from before the crisis, when it commanded 82 votes, and from 25 May 1962, when it could still muster 66 votes for a new Premier.

These fortunes appeared to rebound suddenly on 28 May 1963, when the Judicial Committee of the Privy Council reversed the Supreme Court decision of the previous July declaring Akintola's removal invalid. Ruling finally on Alhaji Adegbenro's appeal, the

Judicial Committee confirmed the right of a Governor to remove a Premier from office if he no longer appeared to command majority support in the House. Effectively, this rendered Chief Akintola's government illegal, since his reinstatement without election had been justified on the basis of the Supreme Court ruling. Indeed, the Privy Council advised the Queen that Adegbenro was the rightful Premier of the Western Region (Schwarz, 1968: 150; Worrall, 1965: 104).

The news of the decision inspired a wave of rejoicing in Lagos and dozens of towns and villages in the West. But the celebration was short-lived. Anticipating the Judicial Committee's decision by one hour, the Regional Government hastily summoned a special session of the House and amended the Region's constitution – retroactive to October 1960 – requiring a no-confidence vote before a Premier's removal. The House then declared no confidence in Adegbenro as Premier and reaffirmed its confidence in Akintola. On 6 June the amendment was ratified at an emergency meeting of the Federal Parliament. (Appeals to the Privy Council were later abolished entirely) (Worrall, 1965: 104; Schwarz, 1968: 150; *Africa Report*, June 1963).

Throughout 1963, Chief Akintola continued to consolidate his power base and root out AG loyalists. He dismissed the Council of Ife University and packed it with his own supporters. University Staff who had formed a Council for Civil Liberties and criticised Akintola's new government were tried for sedition and pressured by University authorities. 'AG dominated councils were suspended in large batches and there were few aspects of social, political or commercial life in the Region where the change of masters was not felt' (Mackintosh, 1966: 459).

The entrenchment of the Akintola–Awolowo rift through this period was a source of deep concern to a wide spectrum of Yoruba leadership, which worried for its effect on the prospects of the Yoruba people. In mid-1963, negotiations took place between the AG and UPP, and then also the NCNC, but the attempt at reconciliation ended only in further recriminations (with NCNC participation in the coalition a key bone of contention).[8] With this failure, influential Yoruba personalities sympathetic to Chief Akintola formed a competitor to the *Egbe Omo Oduduwa*, the major Yoruba cultural organisation, which was still dominated by Awolowo loyalists (Sklar, 1966: 151).

The Coker Commission report

With the release of the Coker Report on 1 January 1963, the AG's enemies moved swiftly to capitalise on the Commission's findings of lurid scandal. That same day, Premier Okpara attacked the Action Group as 'a party of vandalism' which had 'no doubt raped the West' and 'milked the people of that region dry in the name of socialism', and two days later the NCNC called for disbandment of the Action Group 'in the interest of the public good' (both quoted in *Africa Report*, February 1963: 15). On 15 January, Premier Akintola announced that his government would take over certain AG-controlled properties and press for the repayment of all loans to the AG.

Such tangible steps did the real damage to the Action Group. While the propaganda campaign did little to erode its popular support, the party suffered substantially from the break-up of its network of commercial, financial, and personal connections. The Coker Report was instrumental primarily as a justification for this systematic destruction of the AG's political infrastructure. That such justification was felt necessary may be seen in the Akintola Government's harsh treatment of those who criticised or questioned the Coker Commission's conclusions. Several of the critics were charged with sedition (Worrall, 1965: 104, 107 no. 35).

The creation of the Mid-Western Region

The effort of the Federal Coalition partners to carve out of the West a new Mid-Western Region must be seen as part of their multip-ronged initiative to undermine their Western-based opposition. The Federal House vote of 22 March 1962 to create the Region followed party lines precisely and came as the AG was beginning to unravel in public view. Indeed, it was one of the few issues in the months before the Emergency that united the two Action Group factions.

Creation of the Mid-Western Region had for many years been a cherished objective of the NCNC, which repeatedly scored well among the area's predominantly ethnic minority voters, who felt victimized by the Yoruba-dominated AG government in the West. Indeed, two of the NCNC's most powerful figures, Federal Senate President Chief Dennis Osadebay and Federal Finance Minister Chief Festus Okotie-Eboh, were founders of the Mid-West State Movement in 1956. If a Mid-Western State was created, the NCNC seemed all but certain to control it. Creation of the Mid-West was thus another motive for humbling the Action Group, which, if it remained united and strong, figured to be able to continue to block the initiative (Schwarz, 1965: 131).

The drive to create the Mid-West tangibly benefited from the crisis in the West. As Abernethy (1964: 9) observed, the political vacuum left by the AG split 'provided the NCNC with a classic opportunity to press forward with its plans for the Mid-West. Hence, the despatch with which requisite legislative approval was obtained and the referendum prepared for 13 July 1963'. That referendum of the Mid-Western people endorsed the proposed Region in an incredible landslide. Fully 90 per cent of the total registered voters – and 98.8 per cent of those voting – voted for the new Region (with the demoralised Action Group now supporting the *fait accompli*).

Thus, on 14 August 1963, another step was taken in the demolition of the Action Group with the separation from the Western Region of its two Mid-Western provinces. Pending an election six months later, Chief Osadebay was sworn in at the helm of an interim Regional Administration, which included five NCNC representatives, three UPP, two AG, and two NPC (*Africa Report*, October 1963).

The treason trial

To this day, the treason trial of Chief Awolowo stands out as perhaps the most bizarre episode of this period in Nigerian history. The crucial questions of the case have eluded definitive historical settlement. The police discovered a cache of arms and ammunition in Lagos on 15 September 1962; what is not clear is whether the weapons were intended as a precautionary measure in the political climate of escalating violence and fear – as claimed by the defence – or as part of a plot to seize control of the national government by force – as claimed by the prosecution.

For eight months, between November 1962 and June 1963, these issues were contested in an extraordinarily complex trial riddled with contradictions in testimony and heavily coloured by the context of scathing political conflict in the West. With Awolowo on trial stood 24 co-defendants, most of them leading Action Group officers and activists. Of the remaining six formally charged in the treason plot, two turned Queen's evidence and had their charges dropped; three, including AG Federal Secretary Samuel Ikoku, took refuge in Ghana; and one, AG First Vice-President Anthony Enahoro, fled to

London, from where he was later extradited to stand trial separately. The evidence of these two trials has been searchingly reviewed elsewhere (see especially Sklar, 1966: 140–8; also Mackintosh, 1966: 453–6; Schwarz, 1968: 138–149). Even a very skeletal recapitulation suggests its highly problematic nature. Prominent among the uncertainties were the motives and veracity of the prosecution's key witnesses. Its principal witness, Dr Oladipo Maja, was a prosperous young Lagos medical doctor and militant AG partisan who described himself as very much to the left of Awolowo politically. Orginally, he had headed the list of accused, but the charges were withdrawn when he turned Queen's evidence. Dr Maja testified that Chief Awolowo had delegated him immediately after the Emergency was declared to purchase arms and ammunition in Ghana, and he claimed to have given Ikoku in Ghana half the money he was given while spending most of the rest on explosives in Nigeria. As Sklar (1966: 146) recounts, 'Maja testified as a confessed accomplice, and there is no doubt about his intention to commit a violation of the law. The question is whether or not he acted independently or as an agent of Chief Awolowo.'

Awolowo and Enahoro both claimed to have been apprehensive that Maja's self-initiated militant activities would implicate and harm the party. Alhaji Ibrahim Imam, one of the two Northern AG leaders to testify against Awolowo and Enahoro, confirmed that Awolowo warned him not to have anything to do with Maja, and indicated that Maja had, on his own initiative, offered Imam and Tiv leader Joseph Tarka arms and money. But, Imam testified, Awolowo told him the AG had its own plans to fight against the government from bases in Tiv country. Awolowo, in turn, charged that Imam and the other Northern AG witness had fabricated their story in consultation with the prosecution and that Imam had conspired with Maja independently to import arms.

In all, eighty witnesses testified, many filling in the picture of a planned *coup d'etat*. And then there was the physical evidence: two machine guns, 24 tear-gas pistols, several revolvers with some 3000 rounds of ammunition, 20 gas and automatic pistols, 50 cases of explosives, 48 special torchlights. In itself, it was ludicrous preparation for a full-scale *coup d'etat*, but neither was it easy to square 50 cases of explosives with the precautionary intentions claimed by defence attorneys.

The accused could point to a number of weaknesses in the prosecution case. Four of the minor witnesses broke down under defence cross-examination, and the credibility of virtually all of the major witnesses was much in doubt. Several leading witnesses, including three regional ministers, came from the Akintola faction (Osuntokun, 1982: 153). At least two witnesses (maybe more) escaped prosecution in exchange for their testimony. Others were notable for the frequency with which they had switched parties, and were alleged by the defence to have fabricated testimony in pursuit of political favour.

At the Appeal, the court rejected the conclusion that Chief Awolowo had tried to organise a coup, because it rested only on the testimony of accomplices whose evidence was inherently dubious. (On the charge of arms importation and possession, however, his conviction was sustained.) And four AG members who had been harshly sentenced had their convictions thrown out altogether on Appeal.

Further doubt was cast upon the proceedings by the atmosphere of heavy anti-AG bias in which it took place. Awolowo's choice of British counsel was refused entry into the country, as was Enahoro's. The judge who should have tried the case – an independent-minded man who had frustrated the Federal Government's original attempt to investigate the National Bank – was made an Acting Justice of the Supreme Court a few days before the treason case came up. And while rigorously attentive to correct legal procedure, the judge who did preside raised many eyebrows when, in dismissing the objection that three prosecution witnesses were biased against the AG as members of the UPP, he said: 'I must confess . . . that I do not know what the alphabet "UPP" stands for' (Schwarz, 1968: 146).

But most of all, the essence of the prosecution case was incredible: that so astute a politician as Obafemi Awolowo would believe he could seize power by force with such a puny arsenal,[9] or that the shrewd Enahoro would confidently assure Imam (as the latter alleged) that the coup would be bloodless since it would be supported by the Army – an Army in which Igbo officers figured most prominently.[10] Mackintosh (1966: 445) concludes that 'the charges of importing arms and of sending men for [military] training were proved'. But as to the charge that Awolowo was plotting a coup, Osuntokun (1982: 153) writes, 'it is just inconceivable that Awolowo could have planned to fight [a 9000-man army] with his own forces. What was more probable was that the Action Group had sent out men to be trained as party thugs so that if need be the party would be able to meet force with force when in confrontation with its enemies'. To the question of Awolowo's guilt, Stanley Diamond (1963: 25) similarly responded:

> Legally and formally – perhaps; at least a few of his lieutenants may have been, although the outlines of the plot seemed childish, fragile, even irrational. It is just as plausible to believe that paramilitary activity of Action Group members would have been designed to protect themselves and their allies against violence and harassment by well-organized NPC strongmen in the North, as was in fact pleaded; or a presentiment of trouble ahead may have led Awolowo to put his party on a more military footing. Preparations for a coup (if trouble at the Centre developed) may have been part of a vaguely defined plan – but it seems doubtful that they were seriously being considered.

In any case, scholarly assessments agree that the political element was the trial's most significant feature. Whether or not the charges were fabricated and the witnesses orchestrated, it was clear that Awolowo's political enemies had seized a timely opportunity to destroy him. The trial decimated the ranks of the AG leadership. Awolowo was sentenced to ten years in prison, Enahoro to fifteen. Ikoku was in exile. Of the major AG figures, only Tarka was acquitted on all charges (in all, only three of the 25 defendants were acquitted).

The trial was the final act in a long sequence of humiliating and embittering blows to Awolowo's huge Yoruba following. Schwarz (1968: 147) has concluded:

> Whatever its merits the trial did little to strengthen popular faith in Nigerian justice. The acknowledged contradictions and weaknesses in the evidence, the dubiousness of the motives of several key prosecution witnesses, and above all the inherent implausibility of a plot to capture Lagos with a few pistols, rifles and torches, with apparently no arrangements for winning power in the Regions, strengthened a widespread belief that Awolowo had somehow been betrayed, if not actually framed. A more moderate version of this belief is that Awolowo must have known about a plot ... but that he may well not have been as deeply implicated as the prosecution claimed. In any case, the background of violence and bribery in politics made his precise degree of guilt or innocence seem largely academic to many Nigerians.

ANALYSIS OF THE CRISIS

The cleavage groups

Historical understanding of the Western Regional crisis depends on a determination of just what the conflict was about. This is not a simple task; personal, ethnic, ideological, and strategic differences were densely intertwined. The conflict was at once between 'the old and new members, between those in government in the West and those ... outside, between intellectuals and practical politicians, between old age and youth, between plebians and patricians, non-Yoruba against Yoruba, Oyo Yoruba against other Yoruba' (Osuntokun, 1982: 129).

Personally, Awolowo and Akintola had become competitors since Awolowo's frustrating and unexpected relegation to opposition leader in Parliament. Ethnically, the conflict exposed a deep, latent animosity between Chief Awolowo's Ijebu Yoruba and Chief Akintola's Oyo Yoruba, rooted in the complex web of economic and military conflict between Yoruba sub-tribes in the nineteenth century (Osuntokun, 1982: 159). As a result of this ethnic tension, Ijebu Yorubas generally aligned behind Awolowo and Oyo Yorubas behind Akintola (Osuntokun, 1982: 139–40).

The most revealing clues to the character of the cleavage can be found in the alignments of key actors in the struggle. But these were not unambiguous. It appears that a number of esteemed party elders and traditional rulers viewed the conflict as essentially a personal struggle between Awolowo and Akintola – and between their economically active and strong-willed wives (Osuntokun, 1982: 116) – and resisted taking sides until the last possible moment. This may explain their repeated attempts at reconciliation and their apparent confidence that such reconciliation could be effected. That this confidence was naive, and their every healing effort quickly torn asunder, suggests that more fundamental issues were at stake. This is confirmed by the political character of the actors on each side of the conflict. While the sincerity of Awolowo's commitment to the programme of Democratic Socialism has been questioned, there is no doubting the radical orientation of many of the younger politicians and socialist intellectuals (such as Agunbiade-Bamishe) who had pressed the party leftward during the 1950s and on whom Awolowo came increasingly to rely after 1959.

Like those of Awolowo himself, the socialist convictions of

Anthony Enahoro were less radical and later in developing; yet, with both men, they had been developing steadily for a number of years. While Chief Awolowo's radical beliefs neatly fitted his chosen political strategy they also appeared to many expatriate observers sincere and deeply based (Sklar, 1963: 281, 1966: 128–9; Post and Vickers, 1973: 76; Schwarz, 1965: 121). Stanley Diamond (1963: 24) observed, 'If Awolowo's interests began in a struggle for power . . . his intimate knowledge of the disparities within Nigeria and of the effects on himself and his party of political compromise and cynicism turned him into a man who insisted that principle must be realized in action'.

If we may assume that Chief Awolowo had developed by 1962 a real moral and ideological commitment to a leftist programme, so it is also clear that Chief Akintola, and the businessmen and traditional leaders around him, felt strongly opposed to this programme and genuinely threatened by it. It was not simply an ideological repulsion from socialist principles *per se*. In fact, the programme of 'democratic socialism' adopted by the party in 1960 was surprisingly lean on specifics and even proposed 'that the Nigerian strata of the employer class be allowed to develop much further within certain limits' (Action Group, 1960: 6). While clashing strongly with the sentiment in that programme for nationalising foreign economic interests, and with its egalitarian, class-conscious tone, Chief Akintola and his allies were most disturbed by the avowed determination of the Awolowo faction to dismantle the system of rewards that had made politics in Nigeria such a lucrative and cherished calling. Thus, the intensification of this objective, with the call for sharp austerity measures on Western Region politicians, occasioned one of the most acrimonious debates between the two factions. That debate was one of many indications of the class component in the conflict.

On this dimension of ideology and class, the alignment of personalities in the conflict was not without anomalies. Personal and ethnic loyalties pulled many party members to one side or the other, especially those who had no strong stake in the ideological debate, such as S. O. Shonibare, Alfred Rewane, and S. O. Lanlehin, key operatives in Awolowo's intricate political–financial network. The attachment of such wealthy Yoruba businessmen to Awolowo might diminish an ideological interpretation of the conflict. But the serious radicals in the party were unanimously behind Awolowo, and of the defenders of wealth and tradition – the Obas, the industrialists, the merchants, the building contractors, the market women – those among this group who took a stand early on were solidly behind Akintola. These 'bigwigs' of the party 'had funded the Action Group in its formative days as a kind of investment', one which had paid off handsomely and, for some, tremendously. They 'could not understand how the same party could begin to espouse socialism' (Osuntokun, 1982: 123). Increasingly, as they were forced to choose they took Akintola's side. Post and Vickers (1973: 76) conclude:

> The loyalties and interests were themselves only part of what we have called the System of Rewards, and the fact that such bound certain people to Chief Awolowo rather than Chief S. L. Akintola . . . should not be allowed to disguise the fact that the conflict was essentially between those members of the party who wished to make a radical challenge to the System, and those conservatives who wished to entrench it.

Understood as a struggle over the structure of rewards, of class privileges and class formation, it is easy to see why the conflict became so intense. All three parties had been a loose amalgam of interests and beliefs. With his shift to a radical programme, Awolowo was asking a crucial segment of his party to turn against its own perceived interests: 'he relied upon a class-conscious regional power group to support a nationwide movement of the "have-nots"' (Sklar, 1965a: 206). At the same time, he was challenging the class interests of the political classes in the other two regions as well. In each of the three Regions and at the Centre, these conservative party forces held power and were committed to retaining the structure of salaries, favours, contracts, jobs, and honours that made power the essential instrument of class formation. Everywhere, smaller regions would mean smaller stocks of patronage and rewards for the existing ruling parties. And especially in the North, the conservatives' hold on power depended on the existing regional structure being maintained. A Middle Belt Region – which, free of systematic pressure and intimidation from the Northern Regional Government, figured to be ruled by a change-oriented party hostile to the NPC – would mean an end to the national dominance of the Northern aristocracy and might even undermine its control in the emirates (Diamond, 1964). This is why regionalism went hand in hand with conservatism in the conflict, while Awolowo's anti-regionalist strategy fitted logically with his radical challenge to the status quo (Sklar, 1966: 129).

Chief Awolowo understood sufficiently the weakness of his new position to seek a rapprochement with his old foe, Dr Azikiwe. His vision was a party realignment that would unite progressive Southern elements against the NPC (Sklar, 1966: 130). Eventually, the realignment would come, but only under circumstances in which both parties were fighting to stay alive. At the time, the NCNC had too much to gain from sharing power at the Centre. With their coalition partners, NCNC leaders sought to cripple the Action Group and 'to place in power in the West individuals who would be content to limit themselves to that sphere . . ., and thus [to] consolidate and stabilise their control of the system' (Post and Vickers, 1973: 78).

Thus the central cleavage in the Western Regional crisis concerned the very character of the sociopolitical system in Nigeria. Those allied with Chief Akintola wanted to preserve it roughly as it was. Those allied with Chief Awolowo wanted to change it fundamentally – to eliminate its dominance by narrow and conservative political classes and to transform the Regional structure which supported that dominance. This is indicated by the alignment of key political actors in the crisis, as depicted in Table 4.1.

The first entries in the table have been discussed. As for the second group, AG incumbents of public office, while Chief Akintola by no means commanded the support of all the ministers and key appointees, these were about the only officeholders who lined up behind him. He had few supporters among AG members in the Western House; indeed, his biggest block of House support before the Emergency was probably the NCNC contingent, with which he formally allied when he resumed power. Group three indicates the coincidence of ideology and strategy in the conflict. Awolowo's command of AG leaders and allies in the East and North was thorough, given Akintola's intention to cut off these arms of the party. Akintola had the strong tacit support of the NPC–NCNC Federal Coalition and especially the NPC leaders, an alliance facilitated by his warm personal relations with the Sardauna and the Prime Minister, his fluent command of two Northern languages (Hausa and Nupe), and a shared recognition between Northern and Yoruba conservative leaders of important cultural similarities between their two people (Osuntokun, 1982: 112, 114, 146–8).

Among the most interesting alignments in the crisis was the support given Chief Awolowo by radical elements within the NCNC, who were won over to Chief Awolowo's idea of a 'progressive' alliance. 'During the Western emergency, a few prominent members of the NCNC had pressed for unity with the Action Group and the NCNC even extended some financial assistance to help the Action

Table 4.1   Alignment of key political actors in Western Regional crisis

Chief Awolowo	Chief Akintola
1. Action Group radicals, intellectuals, students (e.g., O. Agunbiade-Bamishe, S. G. Ikoku, Nigerian Youth Congress)	1. Action Group conservatives, businessmen, market women, Obas
2. Action Group members of Federal House of Representatives (Anthony Enahoro) Certain key Western Regional officials (Alfred Rewane) Most Action Group members of Western House	2. Certain key Western Regional Ministers and officials Ministers: (Chief Adayi–Trade) (Chief Adigun–Land) (Dr Omitowoju–Chieftaincy) NCNC members of Western House (Chief R. A. Fani-Kayode)
3. Action Group leaders and activists in North and East (J. S. Tarka–Tiv UMBC–AG) (Ibrahim Imam–Bornu UMBC–AG, Leader, opposition, Northern House) (S. G. Ikoku–Leader, opposition, Eastern House) Radical elements, NCNC	3. NPC–NCNC Federal Coalition – Federal Parliament & Cabinet (Prime Minister Tafawa Balewa–NPC) (Chief Dennis Osadebay–NCNC) (Chief Festus Okotie-Eboh–NCNC) – Northern Regional Government (Premier Sir Ahmadu Bello) – Eastern Regional Government (Premier Michael Okpara)
4. Ijebu (and non-Oyo) Yorubas	4. Oyo Yorubas

Group meet its political expenses' (Sklar, 1966: 150). The gesture was reciprocated in October 1962 when the AG, having defeated the NCNC in the Lagos City Council elections, offered to retain the NCNC chairman of the Council. The NCNC 'appreciatively declined' this offer, but accepted 'a generous allocation of committee assignments' (Sklar, 1966: 150).

The outcome

There can be no doubt about the outcome of the conflict. The breadth and magnitude of the defeat inflicted upon Chief Awolowo and his AG supporters by the NPC and the NCNC was simply staggering. Not only did the Awolowo Action Group lose the power struggle in the West, it was also administered a string of other humiliations that destroyed it as an effective opposition force.

As depicted in Table 4.2, the Awolowo faction had the upper hand, and appeared to have won the conflict, when the Federal Government intervened on 29 May. After this, the dominant faction of the Action Group won not a single major skirmish or contest within the overall conflict. It suffered through six months of increasingly biased administration during the Emergency. The very fact of the Emergency was a heavy (though not unexpected) blow, coming at the moment of the Awolowo faction's triumph over the Akintola wing. If there were doubts about the purpose of the Federal Government intervention, these were eliminated when Akintola was reinstated without the election that had been promised. This was the first of four major defeats for the Action Group.

The second defeat was the Coker Commission Report, the ultimate effect of which was to scuttle the elaborate financial network that had been so important to the Action Group's political vitality. The political motives of the Commission – as indicated by the previous NCNC–NPC attempts to investigate the AG's National Bank, the heavy reliance on the Coker findings to justify Akintola's reinstatement, and the swiftness with which the NCNC seized upon the Report to condemn the AG – clearly place it as a part of the larger assault on the Action Group.

Equally motivated by political considerations was the creation of the Mid-West Region, which both the NPC and NCNC hoped to dominate politically, and which, by diminishing the AG's regional political base, reduced any future political threat it might pose. This was the third defeat for Awolowo's party.

Finally, the treason trials, like the above three issues, were a part of the political struggle and may well have been manipulated in their prosecution for political ends. Indeed, 'in the general trajectory of Nigerian politics since 1959', the treason trials seemed to 'have an aura of inevitability – whether or not Awolowo was personally guilty. It is within the context of the efforts of the NPC and the NCNC to obliterate their common rival that the trials demand to be understood' (Diamond, 1964: 25). In this sense, the treason case represented the fourth decisive defeat for the Action Group.

Causes of the crisis and its outcome

In seeking to understand why the conflict reached crisis proportions,

Table 4.2 Chronology of key events in Western Region crisis

Date	Events	Outcome
2–7 Feb. 1962	*Action Group Annual Congress* at Jos. Awolowo wing wins complete dominance of party offices.	Gain for Awolowo over Akintola.*
Late March	*Motion to create Mid-West Region* passes Federal Parliament and Northern and Eastern Regional legislatures but is rejected in West.	Gain for North & East over West.
20 May	*AG Federal Executive Committee strips Akintola of post as Deputy Leader* and calls unanimously on Governor to remove him as Premier.	Gain for Awolowo.
21 May	*Governor dismisses Akintola as Premier*. Adegbenro sworn in as new Premier.	Apparent victory for Awolowo.
25 May	*Western House meeting twice disrupted before Adegbenro can be sworn in*. Prime Minister refuses to recognise results of any meeting with police present.	Setback for Awolowo
29 May	*Federal Parliament declares State of Emergency in Western Region*. Regional government is suspended.	Major Blow to Awolowo, gain for NPC–NCNC coalition.
16 June	*Coker Commission of Inquiry set up* in apparent attempt to discredit Awolowo's years of AG administration in West.	Portends further blow to Awolowo.
Late Sept.	*Awolowo* (and some 30 others) *charged with treasonable felony*.	Major blow to Awolowo.
December	Prime Minister announces that AG will no longer be recognised as official opposition.	Setback for Awolowo.
1 January 1963	*Akintola reinstated as Premier, at helm of new UPP–NCNC coalition*.	*Defeat #1 for Awolowo-AG.* Victory for UPP, NPC, and NCNC.
	Coker Commission Report released. Awolowo condemned; Akintola absolved.	*Defeat #2 for Awolowo.* Victory for Akintola.
9 April	First meeting of Western House since Emergency. UPP–NCNC coalition gives Akintola huge vote of confidence.	Gain for Akintola.
28 May	Privy Council rules for Adegbenro in his appeal. Western Region overturns decision, and Federal Government ratifies this.	Gain for Akintola.
May	*Mid-West Region created.*	*Defeat #3 for Awolowo-AG.* Victory for NCNC, NPC.
14 August	Mid-West Region interim administration sworn in, with NCNC in leadership.	Further setback for AG.
11 Sept.	*Awolowo found guilty of treasonable felony* and sentenced to 10 years' imprisonment. Twenty of the other 24 defendants are also sentenced.	*Defeat #4 for Awolowo-AG.*

*'Awolowo' and 'Akintola' refer not only to the persons but to their respective party factions.

one must begin with the class structure. The increasingly stark contrast between the high living of the political class and the miserable conditions of the mass had generated a serious (albeit fractured and small) radical movement. By 1960, radical sentiment had gained sufficient momentum, especially among the nation's youth, for Awolowo to pin his political strategy around it. Thereafter, it grew significantly, fed not only by the arrogance of the political class but by the wave of radical pan-Africanism sweeping many parts of the continent. It was not a mass movement, but the division it sowed within the elite was politically explosive, given in particular the determination of the political class to preserve the system of rewards.

Chief Awolowo's effort to recast his party in a radical mould contradicted a basic feature of political parties in Nigeria – their lack of substantive definition and coherence. Being (with the exception of NEPU) broad class and ideological coalitions, united only by communal and personalistic ties, none of these parties could have survived an attempt to define a clear ideological programme. In this contradiction between social imperatives and political realities lay the origins of the Western Regional crisis. The differences of strategy and personality then deepened the ideological polarization.

Chief Awolowo's anomalous position of formal party supremacy but inferiority in his party's command of state power also contributed to the crisis. Cut off from the patronage resources he had controlled as Regional Premier, unsuccessful in his bid for Federal power, able now to promise only future rewards, Awolowo was pushed almost ineluctably to a more anti-establishment position. By the same token, with Awolowo superior in party affairs and Akintola superior in control over state resources and rewards, the two consummate politicians were bound to come into conflict. Not only did their personal ambitions cross, but the logic of their positions dictated different strategies, the one radical and anti-regionalist, the other supporting a stable distribution of rewards through the existing state and class structures. As David Abernethy has observed, 'It became pragmatic for Awolowo to "become unpragmatic" and for Akintola to remain pragmatic.'[11]

But none of this explains why an intraparty battle became a fierce *inter*party contest as well. On this plane, the deficiencies in the federal structure become crucial. The three-region system was a recipe for disaster. In the context of coinciding cleavages, it fostered an intense – and inherently unstable – tripolar competition. As long as this three-cornered contest continued, there was a strong possibility that the three competing forces would collapse down to two, as two regional power-groups joined in an attempt to eliminate the third. Probably this was one of Chief Akintola's reasons for wanting to end the competition and divide the spoils by agreement.

This dynamic was at work well before the Western Region erupted in crisis. The hints of Federal intervention in the West on the eve of Independence and afterward, Premier Okpara's attempt to get an Emergency declared there in 1961, and the Federal coalition's efforts that year to investigate the National Bank and to create the Mid-West Region all suggested an intention on the part of the NPC and NCNC to discredit and destroy their common political enemy. From the perspective of history, the Federal Government's intervention in the West gives the appearance of a well-executed plot to do just this. The bias in administration of the Emergency, the reinstatement of Akintola, and the outcomes in the Coker Inquiry and treason trials all point clearly in this direction. There is also evidence to suggest that the initiation of the crisis – the disruption in the House and subsequent declaration of Emergency – were part of a premeditated plan by the Federal Coalition partners, working in collusion with the Akintola faction.

A substantial case for such collusion is compellingly articulated by John Mackintosh (1966: 456–8). He notes Dr Okpara's declaration on 24 May (the *day before* the riot in the Western House) that 'the Federal Government would be right in declaring a state of emergency in the West'; the decision of Sir Abubakar not to recognise any votes taken with police in the Chamber (because the Prime Minister 'clearly feared that police action would allow the majority to have its way'); and the 'fine impartiality' of the police 'in using tear gas to clear the whole Chamber rather than remove the disorderly elements'. In addition, he finds it difficult to imagine why the small Akintola faction, numbering about ten in a meeting of 108, 'should have hurled themselves into such violence had it not been prearranged. . . . If there had been no expectation of outside help, the Akintola faction would simply have been courting disgrace, imprisonment, and final defeat'. Lastly, there is the fact of the calm that prevailed outside the House Chamber, the multiplicity of obvious alternatives to a declaration of Emergency, and the patent lack of any grounds for suspending the entire government, especially for six months. Few things emerge so clearly from the crisis as the eagerness of the NPC–NCNC coalition to intervene in the West.[12]

This desire to destroy the opposition outside the electoral process, even on a patently contrived constitutional pretext, reveals another contributing factor to the crisis: the shallow commitment of the key political actors to democratic values and practices. In addition to their determination to eliminate the opposition and their contrivance of the grounds for Emergency rule, the ruling coalition partners demonstrated repeated antipathy to democratic rights and procedures in their suspension of the entire Western Government, their constriction of political liberties in the West, their bias in administration of the Emergency and their failure to hold a new election at its conclusion.

But nowhere was it more clearly demonstrated than in their impatience with and often active hostility toward the judicial process, as seen not only in their manipulation of the treason trial but in their harassment and obstruction of the Action Group's court challenges. On the expulsion of the AG's British lawyer early in the Emergency, Premier Okpara commented: 'There is an emergency in a part of the country and you don't need to fumble in court in such a situation. . . . I think this democracy of ours is being misinterpreted.' This view was quickly endorsed by Northern Premier Sir Ahmadu Bello and by the NCNC in *West African Pilot*, which stated, 'Each time the Government tries to uphold the sovereignty and integrity of this country, doctrinaire constitutionalists will plead liberal democracy' (both quoted in Odumosu, 1963: 300). Writing before the Federal Government and the Akintola regime erased the Privy Council decision reinstating Adegbenro as Premier, Odumosu concluded: 'It appears the Federal Government would not tolerate a judicial decision if it is considered inconvenient' (p. 301).

The Akintola faction showed similar inclinations in disrupting the 25 May House meeting and systematically repressing the opposing faction when returned to power. But neither was the Awolowo faction impressive in its commitment to the democratic rules of the game. While less flagrant in its abuses, it, too, manipulated the system in dubious ways for short-term gain: desperately trying to avoid a dissolution of the Western House that would necessitate a new election, secretly removing Akintola through petition before a House meeting, and rejecting, at every crucial point before the Emergency when it had the upper hand, any real compromise with Akintola. In addition, there was the conclusive evidence of importation of arms and paramilitary training, with the possibility of a coup being intended by at least some radical AGers. Intolerance, distrust, unwillingness to compromise, rejection of Constitutional procedures and constraints – these were the outstanding behavioural features of the conflict.

They were hardly new to Nigerian politics. But the fact that democratic values, habits and restraints – which took decades and centuries to sink behavioural roots in Western nations – had hardly yet congealed in Nigeria cannot suffice to explain such antidemocratic behaviour. It was also heavily motivated by Nigeria's social and political structures. In a political system where the logic of success was regional dominance, Chief Awolowo's decision to pursue an aggressive antiregionalist strategy, challenging the NCNC and NPC on their home territory, was destined to draw a harsh and repressive response. And two features of the evolving class structure further pressed the contending parties toward extreme behaviour. The first was the increasingly explicit class character of Chief Awolowo's national political challenge, seeking to mobilise new lines of support and to alter the system of rewards. In this sense, the class structure and the growing polarisation around it – not yet between classes so much as within the elite, between the 'political class' and those politicians and intellectuals who saw themselves as acting for the masses – played a dual causal role in the crisis: pressing the Awolowo faction to a radical, antiregionalist challenge that split the Action Group, while motivating conservative, regionalist forces within all three parties to defeat the radical challenge at all costs.

Secondly, and perhaps most fundamentally, even if the Awolowo Action Group had not pitched its opposition on class-based themes, the mere possibility of its winning the next election was profoundly threatening to the existing power groups. For political power had become so instrumental to the accumulation of wealth and status in Nigeria that no incumbent was willing to risk its loss. This had been so throughout the 1950s, and had accounted significantly for the violent intensity of political conflict during that decade. But with independence, the state – and the scope of wealth and economic opportunity it mediated – expanded at the same time that any remaining external checks on the exercise of state power disappeared. Hence, political power was more precious than ever.

Given what was at stake in any contest for political power, and the particular stakes in a showdown between ideological and class positions, it was highly likely that one side or the other would press for a total victory. That it was the Federal Coalition, in collusion with Akintola, that did so is mainly a function of its political power at the time. Here again, the deficiencies in the federal structure are crucial. The crisis demonstrated how significant a loophole were the Emergency provisions of the Constitution, which permitted such easy and decisive intervention by the Centre. What should have been a regional conflict became a national one, fraught with danger for Nigerian democracy. The federal structure also failed in granting to the regions control over such a vast array of patronage opportunities for the acquisition of wealth that a political class was able to entrench itself in each regional government and unable to contemplate or tolerate its own departure. And both failings were related to a third deep structural flaw – the small number of regions and the coincidence of their boundaries with those of the major ethnic groups. These features contributed to the accumulation of enmity and distrust between the parties, which became another motive for destroying the Action Group.

To summarise the causes of the crisis, the growing polarisation at the level of class and ideology was most fundamental, though the regional structure helped make this possible by giving each regional political class such an enormous base of patronage. The weak commitment to democratic values was also crucial, but antidemocratic behaviour was partly generated by the polarisation around the issue of class dominance and inequality, and by the extraordinary dependence of class position on state control. The tripolar nature of the federal structure and its insufficient guarantees of regional autonomy added to the explosive mix of variables. In the context of all of these factors, the extreme ideological heterogeneity of the Action Group served as the kindling for the fire.

Ironically, it was the attempt to restructure cleavages along cross-cutting lines that made for bitter conflict. The expectations of key political actors had been built on a structure of coinciding cleavages. The political consolidation of this structure in the regional elections of 1960–61 heightened the logic of an all-party National Government or grand alliance, which Prime Minister Balewa wanted to achieve (Mackintosh, 1966: 442). But Chief Awolowo insisted on changing the rules and expectations of the game just at the moment when all other participating forces were beginning to accommmodate to them. When widely shared expectations are violated, the effort to breach traditional cleavages with a new line of contestation is unlikely to be successful and, in any case, appears profoundly destabilising.

This underscores the casual role of polarisation. Although coinciding cleavages are thought to exacerbate political conflict by making it more polarised, the Western Regional crisis reminds us that polarised conflict can also occur within a cleavage group. Within the Action Group, it is true that ideological, strategic, and personal differences coincided, but the ideological gap alone was profound enough to have made for bitter conflict. The intensity of conflict depends, in the end, on the degree of polarisation – fundamental incompatibility of goals that leaves no room for compromise – however this is brought about.

Effects of crisis on Nigerian democracy

The Western Regional Crisis had two types of effects on democracy in Nigeria. First, in decimating the Federal Opposition, thwarting the will of the Western people, and harshly curtailing political liberties it made the system distinctly less democratic. And in doing so, the Federal Coalition also undermined the legitimacy of the regime among the Opposition's committed supporters.

The latter was not simply a matter of AG partisans becoming more bitterly opposed to the Federal Coalition than ever before. The crisis generated, beginning early in the Emergency, a sense among many Westerners and Yorubas – especially the young, educated, professional, urban and more politically active Awolowo supporters – that they had been cheated and wronged, not simply defeated but routed through gross distortions of the democratic process. This generated the feeling that the parliamentary system was rigged against them, that it was a sham and a fraud. In this light, it is not difficult to imagine that when the Federal Coalition crossed the long-dreaded rubicon of Emergency rule in the West, some more militant AGers might have felt pressed to retaliate in kind and stage a *coup d'etat*. Even the sober among Awolowo's following must have seen in the Emergency a message that the Federal Coalition, and especially the NPC, would never let them come to power by democratic means, and that their political survival might now depend on extra-constitutional precautions.

While its Marxist rhetoric and polemical tone placed it on the extreme left even within the Awolowo faction, the Nigerian Youth Congress no doubt expressed the sentiments of a broader spectrum of society when it declared (in a pamphlet released in July 1962), 'Parliamentary government has been discredited in Nigeria.' Noting that 'force has been installed in Nigeria' and that political liberties had been sharply curtailed (or, in its exaggerated words 'the country is virtually a police state'), it vowed that the lower classes would fight back in kind: 'They are not likely to forget that riots in Parliament and unlimited emergency powers in addition to thugs and unconstitutional acts are all part of the rules of the game' (Nigerian Youth Congress, 1962: 16).

More generally, the crisis left a feeling among the Yoruba that they were being victimised as a people, and the feeling grew with each new escalation in the assault, from the declaration of the Emergency to the reinstatement of Akintola and the purging of Awolowo backers, to the conviction and imprisonment of Chief Awolowo and other prominent AGers (Post and Vickers, 1973: 88, 90; Worrall, 1965: 106).

While Awolowo had a committed following among radical and idealistic youth in the West, he had not yet built a truly national constituency among this social stratum. But across the country, this stratum was becoming increasingly disgusted with 'gross materialism and corruption', impatient with 'cautious pragmatism' and alienated from the country's political system (Legum, 1962; *West Africa*, 16 June 1962). It is likely that the sordid manner in which the radical challenge from the West was crushed affected young radicals everywhere (Legum, 1962; Post, 1962), as suggested by the support eventually given the AG by radical elements in the NCNC.

It also appears that the sensational findings of the Coker Commission had the effect of further discrediting politicians, and the democratic regime through which they gained power and raided the public treasury. Writing late in 1962 as a senior lecturer at University College in Ibadan, K. W. J. Post (1962: 524) observed, 'Politicians in particular are almost universally regarded as corrupt and are generally disliked; photographs in the newspapers of Western legislators fleeing in panic before the police tear-gas at the end of May were received with widespread glee.' Teaching at the same college, James O'Connell (1962: 144) found 'reason to worry about the low esteem in which politicians are held by the educated public. Too many whispers about corruption circulate.' Both men foresaw the prospect of this disaffection spreading to the civil servants.

Free's survey data, collected during the Coker hearings, supports these assessments. The proportion of the Nigerian sample listing corruption among their worries for the nation was the second highest among the twelve countries surveyed (Chapter 3), and this concern increased markedly with education (Free, 1964: 446). No doubt, this eroded the legitimacy of the democratic regime. As another astute observer wrote at the time, 'the rapid increase in corruption ... has increased the skepticism of a significant percentage of Nigerians as to the possible efficacy of democratic, parliamentary government' (Cole, 1962: 113).

There was, finally, the possible effect on Nigerian democracy of the attention the crisis focused on the basic issue of the Awolowo faction – the growing gap between the high living of the political classes and the abysmal poverty of the masses. It is difficult to determine how much of this was a direct effect, diminishing the legitimacy of the democratic regime, and how much an indirect effect, generating forces that would culminate in new, debilitating crises of the system. Probably it was some of both.

Free's survey uncovered substantial concern in the South about social injustice. This concern was not a mild unease with maldistributed wealth but a crystallising sense of indignation over the callous arrogance of 'the ruling class' and its growing moral and material distance from the poor. One respondent commented, 'My fear is that there will be a situation of inequality of wealth. The rich will become richer, while the poor become poorer. This will lead to a concentration of wealth, education and power in one class' (Free, 1964: 46). Free saw the survey data 'as an alarming indication of a widespread feeling of injustice and unfairness in the workings of the Nigerian system among the people of the Western and Eastern Regions' (p. 47). From the concern about 'victimisation and oppression' as well (Chapter 3), it would seem that the Western Regional crisis had helped to focus these feelings and thus to reduce belief in the regime's entitlement to popular allegiance.

The Western Regional crisis thus reduced the authenticity and stability of democracy in Nigeria in five respects.

Indirect effects on the prospects for Nigerian democracy

The crisis had several indirect effects on democracy in Nigeria, in the sense that they appeared likely to 'feed back' into future debilitating crises. This was probably the more serious type of effect exerted by the crystallisation of concern about inequality. Because Awolowo had staked out a clear identity in favour of the levelling of inequalities and opposed to conspicuous corruption and materialism, and because Akintola was just as clearly identified with the political class, the explosion of their conflict and the triumph of Akintola could not but sharpen the issue Awolowo was trying to draw.

The gulf between rich and poor and the public indignation over it had not reached crisis proportions by the end of 1962. But among the greatest dangers for the future was that it would. While many dirt-poor Nigerians had gotten rich overnight in the last decade, Post (1962: 524) nevertheless detected signs that 'the strata are hardening. Education, for instance, is already showing signs of division into that available for the privileged few on the one hand, and the less fortunate many on the other' (see especially Abernethy, 1969: 235–52). The crisis and its outcome seemed likely not only to focus increasing attention on this trend but to accelerate it. For with the political emasculation of Awolowo and his following, there was no base left to challenge the elitist, highly capital-intensive focus of the new National Development Plan for 1962–68 (Post, 1962: 468–70, 525–6; O'Connell, 1962: 133–4). The effect of the plan, Post and O'Connell both predicted, would be to accelerate inequalities between town and country – and, more ominously, between rich and poor within the towns – through a sharp rise in urban unemployment. By stressing so heavily capital-intensive industrialisation (financed heavily through foreign investment) and so little the raising of the productive skills and resources of the peasantry, the plan seemed certain to leave unemployed a large proportion of the estimated two million primary-school leavers in the coming years. Post (1962: 527) estimated the increase of unemployed, optimistically, at 300 000 in the West alone. O'Connell noted as well the likelihood of substantial unemployment among Southern Nigerian university graduates. Both saw this rising urban unemployment, in the context of impatient and rising popular expectations (fed, in part, by the flaunting of extraordinary wealth), as a source of radical pressure and possibly explosive discontent.

In several respects, the crisis also seemed likely to heighten political tension – which might then polarise conflict – between the coalition partners themselves. Even before the Emergency concluded, deep tensions had begun to emerge between the NCNC and the NPC, and Premier Okpara had begun to reveal doubts about what his party had done. These were expressed in his decision to keep open a line of communication to the Action Group and to call for a 'United-Front Government' in which partisan politics would be partially suspended and 'all shades of political opinion will be represented for a period of not more than fifteen years' (quoted in Post and Vickers, 1973: 79). Underlying these doubts were fundamental conflicts of interest between the two parties, especially over the competition for national resources. The negotiations between the Regional and Federal Governments over the National Development Plan had been intense and had revealed an increasingly aggressive and ambitious Northern stance (Post and Vickers, 1973: 79). In addition, tension had arisen over the results of the May 1962 census, which would be the basis for future distribution of power and resources between the regions. Two weeks before Okpara's call for a United Front, on 5 December 1962, the NCNC back-bench ministers had walked out in protest against the report of the NPC minister responsible for the census. The details of the ensuing crisis form the subject of the next chapter.

In the brief flash of conflict over the first census, a rift was opened within the NCNC and a fundamental political realignment was foreshadowed. Walking out with the NCNC back-benchers (primarily Igbos from the Eastern Region) were the remaining Action Group members. Siding tacitly with the NPC were two key NCNC Ministers, Finance Minister Chief Festus Okotie-Eboh (a Mid-Western Urhobo) and Information Minister (and NCNC First Vice-President) Chief T. O. S. Benson (a Western Yoruba). The same basic force that drove NCNC Western Regional parliamentarians into coalition with Akintola drove these Federal figures to side with the NPC: 'As non-Ibo leaders of the NCNC, unable to expect substantial rewards at a regional level, their personal and political futures had to be staked on collaboration with the NPC and assured continuing membership of the federal elite group' (Post and Vickers, 1973: 82).

With elimination of the Action Group as a serious political force, politics had been reduced in Nigeria to a bipolar struggle – ironically, divided to some extent between conservatives and progressives, as Awolowo had hoped for – and political forces were beginning to realign themselves to reflect this new reality. This reduction to a two-region struggle inevitably meant a fierce contest for control of the other two regions, most immediately the new Mid-West, and heightened tension in the coming battles over the census and the next Federal election, as the NPC and NCNC were 'left face to face without their mutual dislike of the Action Group to bind them together' (Post, 1962: 474).

As their competition drew closer and closer toward confrontation, the NCNC could only view with regret two final effects of the crisis to be noted here. First, the crisis increased dramatically the power and confidence of the dominant party in the Federal Coalition, the NPC. NCNC leaders like Premier Okpara had begun to sense this before the end of 1962 and to draw back from total extinction of the Action Group. But even early in the emergency, Stanley Diamond (1962: 8) had detected that it was the NPC that had come out the big winner:

> As a false calm settles over the country . . . it is clear that the NPC has gained immensely. 'In a very short time, the NPC will rule the whole of Nigeria,' stated Mallam [Maitama] Sule, a Federal Minister. Opportunistic Southern diversions to the NPC are beginning to occur . . .
>
> As for the NCNC, it has won too much, thus lost, for the most progressive anti-NPC elements in the West have been too drastically reduced, and not by any NCNC allies.

Related to this was the damage that had been done to the spirit and principle of federalism (Odumosu, 1963: 304–5). Parties (and hence ethnic groups) were no longer secure in their regions, even if they firmly held power. The intervention of the Federal Government in the West increased suddenly and dramatically its political power relative to the regions, a shift that had been developing simultaneously though more slowly with respect to economic powers (Post, 1962: 474). With the NPC increasingly dominant at the centre (and now controlling a slim outright majority in the Federal House) this was no welcome development for the NCNC.

5 The Census Crisis: 1963–64

'Since the mere publication of the census figures precludes a leader of a major political party from aspiring to the leadership of the nation, something must be wrong with the set-up in Nigeria when one can already know that he has won and his opponent lost a general election on the basis of census figures.'—Dr Michael Okpara, National President, NCNC, and Premier, Eastern Region, 9 March 1964 (quoted in Mackintosh, 1966: 556)

'I have no doubt whatever . . . that the Northern People's Congress has come to stay and to continue to stay and is going to rule the Federation of Nigeria for ever.'—Alhaji M. Kokori Abdul, Parliamentary Secretary, Northern House of Assembly, 4 March 1964 (quoted in Nwankwo and Ifejika, 1969: 54)

The 1962 national census was not the first in Nigeria to become embroiled in suspicion and controversy. Previous attempts to count the Nigerian population had met with popular distrust and resistance, accusations of regional bias and favouritism, and widespread suspicion of the results. These had all been sharply reflected in the most recent and professional census to date, that conducted in 1952 and 1953. Widely suspected as a plot to increase the tax burden or to spy on families and their property, the 1952–53 census was avoided by many Nigerians, and became engulfed in political controversy when the results, showing a majority of Nigerians in the Northern Region, were used to justify the assignment of half the seats in the Federal legislature to the North. Southern politicians alleged that the British administrators had inflated the Northern population figures 'to ensure that political power in the country remained with the northern politicians' (Aluko, 1965: 372–6).

As a new British census administrator prepared for the first count in a decade, under an independent Nigerian government, the implications for the balance of power in Nigeria shaped the meaning of the census. Since the 1952 census, people had come to understand the degree to which recorded human numbers determined the political weight of towns, districts, provinces, and regions – and the proportion of government amenities distributed to them.

> The more literate people became over-zealous about the value of a census and they were prepared to do anything, not only to enumerate all their people, but also, if possible, to engage in double or triple counts. The political leaders also became even more enthusiastic than others about the census returns, because they regarded them as an instrument of political power. (Aluko, 1965: 377)

It was in this spirit of feverish competition that the count commenced in May of 1962.

THE 1962 CENSUS

Even before the Western Regional crisis altered the numerical and psychological balance of power in the country, the 1962 census had become the focus of intense anticipation for Southern Nigerian politicians. They hoped, and apparently many of them sincerely expected, that it would show a population majority for the South and thus end the North's majority in the Federal House of Representatives. This had become an especially urgent priority with the NPC's sweeping victory in the 1961 Northern elections and its achievement of a unilateral majority in the Federal House. Many arguments were advanced to support these Southern expectations: British favouritism toward the North in the previous census; more widespread evasion of census enumerators in the South than the North during the previous census; and (most plausibly) further and faster spread of medical treatment in the South, leading to a more rapid decline in infant mortality (Mackintosh, 1966: 547).

Attending these expectations was a concerted campaign by Southern politicians to mobilise their constituents for the census. As the chief census officer, Mr J. J. Warren, went soberly about the task of assembling the huge administrative infrastructure, the regional governments embarked upon intensive propaganda campaigns to prepare their people for the count. Every institution and medium of communication – pamphlets, posters, radio, schools, churches, word-of-mouth – was employed (Aluko, 1965: 377–8). In the South, 'politicians were touring their constituencies urging the people "not to be left out". It was suggested that besides the distribution of seats, amenities and scholarships would be shared on a popular basis, so that there was every advantage in obtaining "a good result"' (Mackintosh, 1966: 547).

Politicians and ethnic-group leaders were 'out to win' and 'their campaign was only too successful' (Schwarz, 1968: 159). The counting took place over two weeks, commencing on 13 May 1962. By July, all the Northern and Eastern figures had been received at the Lagos headquarters. The latter were indicating an astounding increase in the Region's population of over 70 per cent in the past decade; five of its divisions reported increases ranging from 120 to 200 per cent. When the Western figures came in, they showed a comparable percentage increase. In contrast, the Northern Region's population figures indicated an increase of only about a third over the last ten years (Table 5.1). If the figures were accepted, the South would finally have achieved its historic ambition of a population majority in the nation.

Table 2.1   Official population figures, 1952–53 and 1962 censuses

	1952–53 Census (in millions)	1962 Census (in millions)	Per cent Increase
North	16.8	22.5	33.6
East	7.2	12.4	72.2
West	4.6	7.8	69.5
Mid-West	1.5	2.2	46.6
Lagos	0.3	0.7	133.3
Totals	30.4	45.6	50.0

Source: Aluko, 1965: Table I; Schwarz, 1968: 163.

As Warren and his officials examined the first wave of figures, from the North and East, they concluded that the Northern count was reasonable but that the Eastern one must have been inflated.

Allowing for a 5 per cent undercount in 1952 and for a 2 per cent increase per annum, which was what the UN demographers regarded as normal in Africa, the Northern total was just about what had been expected. In the five Eastern divisions which had shown increases of over 120 per cent in ten years, several checks could be applied .... [Most] telling, the biggest increase was in children under the age of five, and calculations showed that the women of child-bearing age could not have produced this number of births had they all been pregnant for all of the five previous years. (Mackintosh, 1966: 548)

Warren thus dismissed these figures as 'grossly inflated' and also reported, 'the figures recorded throughout the greater part of Eastern Nigeria . . . are false and have been inflated' (quoted in Aluko, 1965: 381).

Warren's Report to the Minister of Economic Development, Alhaji Waziri Ibrahim, proposed verification checks in selected areas as the only way to save the census, on which one-and-a-half-million pounds had been spent. Upon receiving the report, Ibrahim flew to Kaduna to explain matters to the NPC leaders. They agreed to a verification count in selected areas. He then proceeded to the East and obtained Dr Okpara's consent and to Ibadan, where he obtained the agreement of the Western Regional Administrator, Senator Majekodunmi. However, Dr Okpara soon backed out, possibly because he realised 'that if the West's figure had risen as much as that of the East, the North would at last be in a minority' (Mackintosh, 1966: 548). Breaking the secrecy surrounding the census results, Okpara announced that the count in the East was 12.3 million and that the Regional Government was sticking to this figure. Ibrahim decided to proceed with the verification check nevertheless, and all of the enumeration books were sent back to the Regions.

As the sixth month passed with no official report of the census results, controversy began to build. By November, the press was speculating about the political interference and appealing to the Prime Minister to reassure the nation, while Northern and Southern politicians were heatedly accusing each other of attempting to inflate the reported population figures. As the verification checks were being conducted, the issue finally erupted. On 5 December, the Federal Parliament met, and Waziri Ibrahim read out parts of Warren's Report from the previous July, emphasising its conclusion that the Northern figures appeared to be entirely reliable while those from the East were inflated.

This public accusation brought a storm of conflict. Two days later, the Action Group, the NCNC, and the UMBC joined in demanding a debate on the Census Report and walked out of Parliament when the Speaker refused their request. NCNC parliamentarians then met separately and agreed on several demands: a debate over the census motion, the dismissal of the Chief Federal Census Officer and the

Minister of Economic Development, immediate publication of the census figures, and appointment and chairmanship by the Prime Minister of a special census committee, representative of all of the Governments, to assume all further responsibility for the census. There followed 'a flood of attacks . . . by Eastern Nigerian politicians against the NPC' and the two Federal officials (Aluko, 1965: 383; Mackintosh, 1966: 549).

The prevailing political mood and the enormous stakes in the conflict were grasped by the independent, London-based weekly, *West Africa* (8 December 1962). Noting rumours that the still-secret census results gave the South a majority, it observed:

> At the same time it has been announced that 're-enumeration' has been going on in the North, which has given rise to a suspicion, prominently voiced by members of the NCNC . . . that an attempt will be made to increase the Northern figures to restore the Region's present preponderance.
>
> So far has this argument gone that whatever final figures are produced will be rejected by those whose political position they endanger. Indeed, not only the present Federal coalition, but the very survival of the Federation is at stake, since, if the census argument continues, the legitimacy of the Federal Government after the next election would be questioned. . . . It is worth remembering that, in his autobiography, the Sardauna of Sokoto noted that his Region would have to 'take measures' against a 'sudden grouping' of Southern parties to control the Federal Government. In spite of the NCNC's public rejection of the Action Group's current offer of a coalition, the rumoured census figures would make such a grouping possible.
>
> Costly though it will be, a brand new census seems the only answer – and this time, however repugnant to Nigerians, some sort of UN supervision may be the only way of avoiding chaos.

Prime Minister Tafawa Balewa did not immediately cancel the census, but his statesmanlike intervention on 10 December defused the immediate tension. While supporting the Chief Census Officer, the Prime Minister rebuked his Minister of Economic Development for accusing the Eastern Region of inflating its census figures. He then assumed personal responsibility for the census, pledging to consult immediately with the Regional Governments and to re-establish confidence.

In the absence of hard figures, however, confusion continued to rein. In December, the Ministry of Information published a pamphlet reporting the 1962 census figures as 22 million for the North, 12 million for the East, and 8 million for the West (including the Mid-West) for a total of 42 million. On 30 January 1963, the *Daily Times* quoted the final figures submitted to the Cabinet as 30 million in Northern Nigeria, 12 million in the East, and 10 million in the West and Mid-West – a total of 52 million. Neither account was denied, 'and this further convinced many southerners that northern politicians were continuing to inflate their own figures' (Aluko, 1965: 384).

By late January there were indeed two sets of figures. The latter set, the result of the 'verification checks', had found 8.5 million Northerners who had been missed entirely in the first count. The new Northern figure of 31 million represented roughly an 80 per cent increase from the 1952 census (and close to a 40 per cent increase over the original 1962 count).

The Prime Minister summoned relevant officials to a special meeting in an attempt to straighten things out, but the meeting apparently only deepened the confusion and controversy. On 19 February 1963 – nine months after the count commenced and without any definite totals ever officially being published – Sir Abubakar announced to the nation that, 'because of the loss of confidence for the figures in the various regions', the 1962 census had been cancelled and an entirely new one would be conducted later in the year. Applauding the decision, the *Daily Times* expressed the general public cynicism over the fiasco:

> The history of the 1962 census is a long process of confusion, bitterness, mistrust and the violent exchange of words during which even civil servants came in for serious reprimand. . . . We need hardly emphasize the dangers we would have been exposed to both at home and abroad were we to insist on parading the discredited figures. We fully endorse the taking over by the Prime Minister of complete control of the new census. (Quoted in Aluko, 1965: 384)

THE 1963 CENSUS

Greeted with praise and relief by much of the press and elite opinion, the Prime Minister's cancellation of the 1962 census was a statesmanlike and even-handed act that prevented an otherwise certain showdown between the North and the South, and the North and the East in particular. But cancelling the first census proved much easier than designing a second one capable of avoiding the same pitfalls, as would become all too apparent.

In September 1963, leaders of the Regional and Federal Governments met to plan the new census. Several changes were agreed upon to thwart the fraudulent practices suspected of the previous census. Enumeration would take place over a period of only four days (in November) rather than 17, to reduce the possibilities for double-counting, migration, and the like. The number of enumerators were to be quadrupled, from 45 000 to 180 000. The operation was to be in the hands of regional officials, but they were now to be observed and checked by officials from the other regions, who would conduct sample censuses. Counting by sight was to be compulsory, even for children. Finally, the results were to be subjected to demographic tests at the Lagos headquarters. To pay for all of this, the Federal Government allocated £2.5 million − almost double the amount expended in the 1962 census (Aluko, 1965: 384; Mackintosh, 1966: 551–2).

In a broadcast on 2 November preparing the nation for commencement of the new census, Sir Abubaker outlined the reasons for the new count and the elaborate procedures, checks and tests that would be employed to insure its fairness and accuracy. But his explanation − which emphasised the need for a new census to prepare for the 1964 Federal Election (Nwankwo and Ifejika, 1969: 47–8) − only served to remind Nigerians once more of the enormity of the political stakes included.

Against this political backdrop, the 1963 census proved to be an even greater fiasco. Despite the tighter Federal Control and advance agreement between the regional governments, 'the new count was held in much the same atmosphere as the old' (Schwarz, 1968: 160). Regional Governments and local politicians once again mobilised their constituencies for a 'good result'.[1] Eastern inspectors in the North met with particular frustration. Their trains were held up, even derailed, and their transport was misdirected. The mixed-sex groups of Igbo inspectors were, in themselves, a source of cultural tension in the North and 'caused intense anger' when it was announced that they would have to enter compounds and watch the counting of women in purdah (the Muslim seclusion of women from public view) (Mackintosh, 1966: 552).

By the end of 1963, the new figures were completely collected, but again, their release was subjected to a delay of nearly two months, during which the government pleaded 'the need to make detailed calculations and analyses of many thousands of figures' and then to apply 'exhaustive tests'. In the meantime, 'muted speculation and recrimination' substituted for hard figures, and the purported 'tests and checks' began to appear to a by now cynical Nigerian public as nothing more than frantic political bargaining over the figures (Mackintosh, 1966: 552; Schwarz, 1986: 158).

The original results of the second census were never officially reported or released. British journalist Walter Schwarz (1968: 158) reported the 'pre-test' total as 'the altogether incredible one of 60.5 million'. The result announced, on 24 February 1964 was 55.6 million – a total *greater* than the notoriously inflated revised count of the first census and representing an 83 per cent increase in ten years. The eastern count of 12.4 million from the first census was preserved, but the West was now reported to have more than doubled in the past ten years to 10.3 million while the Mid-West also gained over its first census figure (to 2.5 million, an increase of 67 per cent). The North reported a 77 per cent increase since 1952, just slightly less (29.8 million) than the revised first count that had suddenly discovered 8.5 million more people. This was easily a large enough increase to preserve the North's population majority in the Federation.

The figures – incredible by any rational calculation of demographic possibilities – produced an immediate storm. In a news conference on 28 February, Dr Okpara protested the Prime Minister's release of the preliminary figures without first consulting the Regional Premiers and proceeded to reject the returns unconditionally: 'I regret that the inflations disclosed are of such astronomical proportions that the figures obtained, taken as a whole, are worse than useless' (quoted in Nwankwo and Ifejika, 1969: 50). Bitterly, he condemned the Northern count as riddled with flagrant malpractices, charging in particular that areas to be sampled for the special tests 'were disclosed to the North long before the Census took place' (destroying the necessary element of surprise and violating the agreed-upon procedure). This was a lapse that even the Census Board acknowledged, and Dr Okpara contended, 'With this admission it would be seen that the main check against inflation at the census was sabotaged even before the count'. He went on to cite a host of other irregularities reported by Eastern inspectors in the North, including: counting of Eastern inspectors against the decision of the Board, double counting, counting of travellers and passers-by without staining their thumbs, counting of persons not seen, counting sample areas without the inspectors, counting after the last census day, refusal of entry into purdah, refusal to let the inspectors initial the enumeration books (Mackintosh, 1966: 552–3).

But, as Dr Okpara himself revealed, figures from all of the regions had been challenged by the demographic tests at census headquarters. The West and Mid-West had higher proportions of constituencies (57 per cent and 47 per cent) failing these tests than did the North (43 per cent), but it was mainly the Northern results he denounced. In fact, the Eastern Premier again defended his own Region's 72 per cent increase, even though 27 per cent of the constituency totals had failed demographic tests and he was declaring the not much larger increase in the North impossible. In any case, he made it clear that his government rejected the results and any attempt to use them as the basis for the next Federal Election.

THE SHOWDOWN: REGIONAL AND ETHNIC CONFRONTATION

With this rejection by the Eastern Government, the lines of conflict were drawn in sharp relief. On the same day that Okpara took his stand, the Northern Premier signalled his Government's acceptance of the census results. Chief Akintola at once positioned himself and his Government beside the Sardauna, while Chief Dennis Osadebay, the Mid-Western Premier, backed Okpara, declaring the census results to be 'the most stupendous joke of our age' (Post and Vickers, 1973: 99).

Each of the two warring Premiers, NCNC President Okpara and NPC President Ahmadu Bello, called party leadership meetings on 2 March 1964. To consider how the census might be cancelled, Dr Okpara summoned to Enugu (the Eastern capital) Premier Osadebay, Federal Finance Minister Okotie-Eboh and Chief R. A. Fani-Kayode (Deputy Premier and NCNC House leader in the West). The Sardauna, after gathering in Kaduna with top-level NPC leaders, emerged saying that he and his party were ready for a 'complete showdown' and that while the NPC did not desire to dominate anyone, 'my people, my government and my party are fully prepared at any hour of the day for any eventuality and would meet any challenge' (quoted in *West Africa*, 7 March 1964: 271). Vowing that his party would break the 'electoral truce' if the NCNC's political attacks continued, he restated his government's flat acceptance of the results and its intention to use them for economic planning and delimitation of new constituencies in the Northern legislature. He then 'proceeded to answer Dr Okpara point by point in terms of great bitterness and to accuse both the East and the Eastern inspectors in the North of deception and sabotage. The Northern Government bought full page advertisments in all the principal Nigerian papers and printed the full text of Sir Ahmadu Bello's reply' (Mackintosh, 1966: 555).

Numerous other organisations and interests took sides as the pitch of the confrontation steadily rose. Students from Nigeria's four Southern universities were the first to protest the census results. Ibadan University students 'boycotted classes and set out in lorries for Lagos, shouting "no, no"', only to be turned back ten miles outside the Capital by police firing tear gas (*West Africa*, 7 March 1964: 271). Later, more than 600 students from the University of Nigeria (at Nsukka, in the East) came to Lagos to deliver their memorandum of protest to the Prime Minister. The Action Group, the NEPU, and the Dynamic Party quickly joined the NCNC in denouncing the census figures, as did the Labour Congress, the Lagos City Council, the Zikist Movement, and the Socialist Party (Nwankwo and Ifejika, 1969: 52).

As both sides pressured their allies in the West, that Region once again became the pivot of political division and turmoil. The day after the Enugu meeting, NCNC members of the Western House heeded their party leader's call and rejected the census results. They further complained that they had not been consulted by Premier Akintola before he gave the Western Region's blessings to the figures. Chief Akintola denied this, accusing his colleagues of reversing their position on orders from Enugu, a charge inadvertently confirmed when Chief Akinyemi resigned from the Western Cabinet, declaring that he had been the only NCNC Minister in the West to vote against acceptance of the census returns (Mackintosh, 1966: 555).

The remaining NCNC ministers in the West were caught in the conflicting pull of party and personal interests, and, as had happened so often in the past in Nigerian politics, the latter won out. Complaining that their sacrifice would be pointless, and that Federal NCNC ministers had not been asked to resign, they asked, 'in what way will a further disruption of Western Nigeria change the census figures?' (quoted in Mackintosh, 1966: 556). The Region was ripe for another political realignment – indeed, it had been brewing for more than six months – and Chief Akintola showed once again his deftness of timing and manoeuvre. On 10 March 1964, he launched the Nigerian National Democratic Party, drawing in his UPP, some new members from the AG and most of the Western NCNC, including its Leader, Chief Fani-Kayode, and eight of the other ten NCNC Ministers in the West. By 14 March, the NNDP commanded the allegiance of 60 members – a solid majority – of the Western House, while NCNC strength had been reduced from 27 members to nine. The diminished NCNC contingent then joined in alliance with the Action Group (which retained its 27 members) and Alhaji Adegbenro became the new Leader of the Opposition (*Africa Report*, May 1964).

With this realignment, the last major cross-cutting cleavage in party politics was eliminated. Finally forced to choose between siding with the NPC and retaining their share of power, or siding with their own party and having to go into opposition, most of the leading NCNC politicians in the West chose to hold on to power[2] (Mackintosh, 1966: 555–6; Post and Vickers, 1973: 100).

A giant step had been taken toward the national political realignment that would make the approaching Federal Election a fiercely polarised struggle. 'From this point on', Post and Vickers (1973: 99) maintain, 'in effect the alliance between the NCNC and the NPC was dead.' The day after the Western defections were announced, statements began to flow from NCNC headquarters in Enugu stressing the need for a national union of the AG and the NCNC, a union which the NCNC had already attempted to forge (over heated intraparty conflict) for the Mid-West Regional election that February.

Growing directly out of the census confrontation, and coinciding with the defection of the NCNC's Yoruba base, was a new wave of ethnic and regional tension, especially between Northern Muslims and Igbos. On 9 March 1964, Dr Okpara answered the Sardauna's statement of the previous week in an equally combative tone.

> The only reply that the leaders ... of the NPC have given ... is a reckless attack on my person and the Ibos.... They have not stopped there but have capped this show of irresponsibility with reckless insult to the President of the Republic and threats of dispossessing Ibos, throwing them out of jobs and closure of the University of Nigeria.

Revealing to the public that the original Northern count in the abortive first census had been eight and a half million less than was finally reported after 'verification', Okpara struck at the core of the controversy:

> Since the mere publication of the census figures precludes a leader of a major political party from aspiring to the leadership of the nation, something must be wrong with the set-up in Nigeria when one can already know that he has won and his opponent lost a general election on the basis of census figures. (Both quotes from Mackintosh, 1966: 556).

Meanwhile, anti-Igbo prejudice, never far from the surface in the North, was bursting into the open again. Even before the bitter exchange between the two premiers, NPC politicians were gleefully boasting that their party would 'rule the Federation for ever' (*West Africa*, 29 February 1964: 226). As the Northern House of Assembly gathered for its annual Budget Session, in the wake of the 'successful' census results and the escalating political controversy, NPC Members were emboldened to take the offensive. Some demanded that Igbos in the service of the Regional Government or the Native Administrations should be dismissed forthwith and that Igbos should be denied land rights and expelled from mercantile houses. Others were heard to demand that all Easterners in the North 'should pack and go' back to the East. One member even pledged to 'use his position as a district head to draft all the Native Authority policemen at his command . . . to deal with the Ibos . . .' (quoted in Mackintosh, 1966: 557). A few days later (17 March), to a chorus of approval, the Northern Minister of Land and Survey informed his colleagues that he was preparing steps to prevent Igbos from owning any land in the North. Members responded with renewed demands for confiscation of all petrol stations and hotels belonging to Easterners.[3]

Expressions of ethnic antagonism were building to such intensity that even some Northern officials became alarmed, and on 24 March the Sardauna warned against victimisation of non-Northerners living in the Region. But that same day the Kano NA gave more than 2000 traders 48 hours to pack up and leave the Sabon Gari market; Igbo evictions from Katsina, Gusau, and Funtua were reported; and only the intervention of the Sardauna prevented a mass eviction in Kano (Mackintosh, 1966: 556–7; Nwankwo and Ifejika, 1969: 54).

Perhaps recalling the mass ethnic violence in Kano ten years previously, Igbo leaders became visibly concerned. A delegation of

Igbos from Kano, Kaduna, and Zaria visited President Azikiwe and asked him to intercede. Praising their restraint in the face of provocation, he urged them to be law-abiding and to seek a judicial remedy. From the Eastern Region, Dr G. C. Mbanugo, Chairman of the NCNC Working Committee there, cabled the Prime Minister asking him to act, 'and Sir Abubakar, with characteristic calm, said he had heard of no evictions and asked Dr Mbanugo to verify his facts' (Mackintosh, 1966: 557).

Meanwhile, the Eastern Government had already responded with an official statement of grievances against the North. Alleging that the North had claimed double its true population, it widened the conflict still further, suggesting that the North had used its power in the Federation to capture an unfair share of economic resources, and protesting a number of specific projects:

Take a look at what they have done with the little power we surrendered to them to preserve a unity which does not exist:

- Kainji Dam Project – about £150 million of our money when completed – all in the North.
- Bornu Railway Extension – about £75 million of our money when completed – all in the North.
- Spending over £50 million on the Northern Nigeria Army in the name of the Federal Republic.
- Military training and all ammunition factories and installations are based in the North, thereby using your money to train Northerners to fight Southerners . . . .
- Now they have refused to allow the building of an iron and steel industry in the East and paid experts to produce a distorted report. (Quoted in Mackintosh, 1966: 557–8).

Shortly thereafter, the implication of the NCNC collapse in the West came more sharply into focus as the NNDP Government joined the fray. With the former Yoruba NCNCers now able openly to champion the Yoruba cause – and, suggests Mackintosh, to 'give vent to the growing irritation [they] had felt at Eastern domination of the party'[4] – the Western Region Government published on 20 March a 'White Paper on the New Political Alignment in Western Nigeria'. The paper charged that 'a few tribalists' in positions of authority in the NCNC had gone 'all out to remove members of all other groups from key positions which are immediately filled by their relatives and tribesmen' (quoted in Mackintosh, 1966: 559). It denounced in particular the Igbo chairman of the Railway Corporation for Igbo predominance in the senior posts there and similarly objected to Igbo dominance of the Nigerian Ports Authority and of such other Igbo-led institutions as the Yaba Technical Institute, the University of Ibadan, the Ibadan Teaching Hospital and the Nigerian Airways (Mackintosh, 1966: 559).[5]

The NPC followed with the release of a pamphlet reiterating these same terms and allegations. Billed as a call for unity, it referred to a 'group' based on a tribe which was virtually a 'cult' and which it charged was bent on domination. Without naming names, it condemned the Igbos and denounced the claimed 'progressive' character of their party as a camouflage for its real, dictatorial intention (*West Africa*, 4 April 1964: 367).

There followed a spate of charges and counter-charges on the front pages of Nigerian newspapers in early April, inflamed with ethnic indignation. The Railway Corporation took full-page advertisements to rebut the White Paper's accusations. The Igbo State Union responded with similar allegations against the Yoruba Minister of Information in charge of the Nigerian Television Service, Chief T. O. S. Benson. That Chief Benson was Vice-President of the NCNC (and probably its most prominent Yoruba politician) indicates the degree to which ethnic and regional considerations were now overriding party affiliation. 'This dispute went on for a month till the tribal origins of virtually every government and corporation employee had been canvassed' (Mackintosh, 1966: 559). At one point, the independent *Daily Times* called for a conference of the Premiers to end what had 'degenerated into an alarming inter-tribal, inter-regional war of reprisals . . . . The Nigerian nation is walking on a tightrope' (quoted in *West Africa*, 4 April 1964: 367).

It was finally the Prime Minister himself who brought an end to what he called these 'disgraceful wranglings'. Sir Abubaker pleaded for political leaders to put the unity of Nigeria over tribal feeling, adding that 'it will be painful for the people to see the country break into pieces'. Bowing to his 'impressive and statesmanlike appeal', the Igbo State Union said it would make no further statement on the controversy. Other stalwarts in the conflicts similarly praised Sir Abubaker's intervention (*West Africa*, 25 April 1964: 487).

Although it receded to the background during late March and April 1964 as the ethnoregional controversy over distribution took command of the headlines, the census conflict still smouldered in a state of deadlock. The Northern and Western Premiers had accepted the results and declared their intention to use them to delimit constituencies for the new election. The Prime Minister as well – despite his accommodating stand on the first census and repeated appeal for national unity – had also accepted the results and declared them 'final'.

But the Eastern and Mid-Western Premiers had rejected the figures completely, and Okpara in particular insisted that his party and Region could not accept any reapportionment of constituencies based upon them. With the Sardauna equally firm in the opposing view, the four Premiers were called to Lagos by the Prime Minister for a meeting (11 to 14 May) of the Nigerian National Economic Council. This meeting was ostensibly to review the progress of the Six-Year Development Programme, but it was widely expected that the census would be high on the agenda. On the eve of the meeting, President Azikiwe again appealed for flexibility and moderation, calling on the Premiers 'to preserve the corporate existence of our fatherland' and to avert 'impending disaster' (*West Africa*, 16 May 1964). Two dramatic developments followed: the Sardauna reversed his position that he would not attend if the census was on the agenda and Premier Osadebay announced he was prepared to agree to the existing results in the interest of unity (Mackintosh, 1966: 559).

Osadebay's was the first major concession in the conflict and was all that was necessary to give the Prime Minister and Northern Premier some appearance of legitimacy in using the census results. While Chief Osadebay had said he would first propose an equal number of Federal seats for each Region, this was a pro forma move; he would not force the issue. Now isolated in his opposition, Premier Okpara proposed that, failing a fair census, regional representation in the House of Representatives should remain unchanged and the Senate should be strengthened in both size and powers. Ignoring his proposal, the Prime Minister announced that the Delimitation Commission would begin immediately to reallocate Federal Parliamentary constituencies on the basis of the new population figures. 'Dr Okpara returned to Enugu denouncing the meeting as a failure' (Mackintosh, 1966: 560).

But even as the redistricting proceeded, the Eastern Premier, backed by both his party and the Action Group, continued to reject the census outcome, and sought to overturn it in the Supreme Court. When (at end June) the Court dismissed the Eastern Government's suit as beyond its jurisdiction, Dr Okpara and the NCNC were left without further recourse, although they continued to insist that the issue was not settled and that the results were unacceptable (*West Africa*, 11 July 1964: 771).

The census was not the only matter of contention at the May meeting of the National Economic Council. The Northern and Eastern Regions also fought over location of the £30 million steel mill called for in the Six-Year Development Programme. The mill was of dubious economic value to Nigeria in any case, and if it were built economic experts were agreed that there was room for only one such plant and that it must be sited where costs were lowest. But politics overrode technical and economic considerations, and a 'Solomon's compromise' was instead effected, dividing the project between Idah in the North and Onitsha in the East. Premier Osadebay praised the Prime Minister for 'his sense of justice'. On one issue, at least, the Eastern Region had won a portion of its goal (*West Africa*, 23 May 1964: 579).

Also disputed at the meeting was the issue of revenue allocation, touched off by the Eastern Region's demand that revenue from oil, then coming into production in the East, be returned entirely to the region of origin rather than distributed by the Constitutional formula (50 per cent to the region, 20 per cent to the Federal Government, and 30 per cent to the Distributable Pool). It was agreed that a commission would be appointed to review the issue, but this turned out to be a single commissioner with decidedly pro-federal views. With the North dominant at the Centre and the West and Mid-West both anxious for federal financial assistance, 'the East once again found itself in a minority of one. Though the negotiations were not made public, the tone of the dispute caused serious concern among civil servants in all five governments' (Mackintosh, 1966: 561).

The May 1964 meeting of the National Economic Council marked the effective conclusion of the census crisis. Though the dominant Eastern wing of the NCNC, backed by the Action Group, refused to accept the results, the East had been defeated on the issue and the North again had won. It was in a mood of visibly heightened political polarisation that preparations proceeded for the next Federal Election, due before the close of 1964. But before the start of this battle – which would dwarf the census controversy in scale and intensity – a very different conflict along a new line of cleavage erupted in the form of a General Strike. Briefly, we turn now to other important developments that occupied political attention in 1963 and foreshadowed these subsequent two crises.

OTHER POLITICAL ISSUES IN 1963

Soon after the creation of a six-month interim administration in August, the new Mid-West Region became the site of heated political manoeuvring. The Regional election scheduled for early 1964 was regarded by all parties as a crucial prelude to the Federal election contest later that year, not simply for psychological advantage but for control of the administrative machinery and patronage that might determine how the Mid-West cast its Federal ballots. Thus, when a Federal by-election was scheduled for October 1963 in the Urhobo West constituency, it was seized upon as a 'test run' of the approaching Regional election, and the NPC made the historic decision to intervene directly in a Southern election for the fiirst time. It gave its blessing and support to a new party – the Mid-West Democratic Front (MDF) – formed to challenge the NCNC in the Region, and went so far as to send an NPC Federal Minister to head the MDF campaign. The new party narrowly snatched the House seat away from the NCNC, but more significantly, the NPC had signalled its intention to wage a larger effort in the Mid-West election, and began to talk openly of a desire to penetrate the entire South with party branches and electoral campaigns. Hence, a modest electoral initiative in an otherwise incidental election further strained the battered Federal Coalition and hastened the reorganisation of Nigerian politics around the intensifying competition between the NPC and NCNC.

On the first of October 1963, Nigeria celebrated its third year of independence by officially becoming a Republic. As the new Republic constitution took effect, Governor-General Azikiwe became President. The transition to a Republic was a moment of nationalist pride, the long-awaited shedding of the last official vestige of colonial status. But the celebration was muted by several controversies.

Intense debate had been generated in the previous two months by the Federal Government's proposals for a preventive detention measure and abolition of the independent Judicial Service Commissions, which hitherto had controlled the appointment of Nigerian judges. The preventive detention measure was proposed by the Prime Minister and the Regional Premiers as a means to 'forestall' people 'planning evil'. It brought a wave of protest at the end of July, especially in the South, where a remarkably diverse array of opinion leaders condemned it. Contending newspapers passionately editorialised against it. The Nigerian Bar Association denounced it as a 'measure to starve out liberal democracy' in Nigeria. A host of student and youth groups and most of the NCNC also protested, and the Prime Minister and the Premiers were forced to abandon it (*West Africa*, 3 August 1963: 853–4, 871). But they remained adamant in their proposal to scrap the Judicial Service Commissions and take personal control of judicial appointments. Despite vigorous protest by attorneys and by parties and organisations on the left, they prevailed, and the change was incorporated in the new constitution (Post and Vickers, 1973: 90; *West Africa*, 24 August 1963: 939).

There were other, bolder indications of growing political disaffection in the country. In February 1963, dock workers staged a strike that was marked by violent clashes with police. While this failed to escalate as planned into a general strike, the Nigerian labour movement, long bitterly divided into a welter of factions, gained strength over the course of the year and threatened to cripple and humiliate the government on Republic Day with a general strike. Negotiations defused the strike on the eve of the ceremonies, but the incident exposed the discontent of Nigerian labour and foreshadowed a much more spectacular conflict (Chapter 6).

Shortly thereafter, the Socialist Workers and Farmers Party emerged publicly, boasting among its key figures two radical labour leaders, S. U. Bassey and Wahab Goodluck, and the President of the Nigerian Youth Congress, Dr Tunji Otegbeye. While still small, the radical party, which cast its appeal on a class rather than communal basis, 'helped to swell the rising tide of discontent with the workings of the System of Rewards among segments of the participant strata' (Post and Vickers, 1973: 98). Within the NCNC, disenchantment surfaced anew in December 1963 when a radical Parliamentary Secretary, D. C. Ugwu, attacked corruption in the Federal Government at a NCNC youth rally. At about the same time, Dr Okpara condemned his own party newspaper for its leftist attacks on him. Escalating resentment of corruption was part of the fuel for the growing labour discontent, and these, interacting with the popular cynicism over the census manipulations and the protest over the preventive detention proposal, drew a portrait of a political class increasingly estranged from society.

ANALYSIS

The cleavage groups

The census crisis was a sectional conflict, and, in its perceived threat to sacred group interests, even to some extent a communal conflict. That ethnic and regional interests took precedence over political party ties was vividly demonstrated in the collapse of the NCNC's Western wing and the subsequent involvement of even some NCNC loyalists in the scathing Yoruba campaign against 'Igbo domination'. Numerous other features of the conflict attested to the predominance of regional cleavage: the intensive mobilisation by regional officials for the two censuses, the disputing of the results on a regional basis, and the common recognition that the distribution of power and resources between the regions was the primary issue at stake in the counting.

The crisis can be interpreted as a contest between the North and the East, each mobilising an allied Southern region along with the machinery of its ruling party. But the conflict was actually much more complex. First, it was originally perceived by many as a test of numbers between North and South, a struggle between two halves for control of the whole. Only after the division and destruction of the Action Group did the political leadership in the West side with the North, and even then the AG loyalists, reduced to a slim band of legislators but probably still commanding a majority of popular support, continued to stand against the North on the issue.

Second, the census conflict was not simply a competition between regions but between communities within regions. The message of mobilisation was that power and resources depended on numbers. It took little political acumen to realise that if population figures would determine which regions would get what, they would also be the basis for determining within each region the distribution of money for water, schools, paved roads, medical clinics, and the like. Local politicians framed the census issue in just such immediate, tangible terms. Indeed, *West Africa* (23 February 1963) suggested that the original inflation of figures in the East was more the product of local than regional competition, concentrated primarily in five divisions.

It is said that the areas accused in inflating their figures are actually those where population may be on the decline – which is precisely the reason why local people were tempted to misrepresent the situation. For these would be areas where the leaders fear that, unless they justify their claims by population figures, their share of Government 'amenities' will fall. If that is the case, the inflation is an effort to score against the Eastern Government, and not against the Federation.

Had the figures represented a grand design in the Eastern Region to inflate the count, its leaders would surely have been sophisticated enough to distribute the huge increase throughout the Region rather than to concentrate it in a few patently absurd figures.

The former is what appears to have happened in the North in the 1963 census. The increases it reported then over its original 1962 figures were 'very much the same in the various provinces of the North' and 'the 77 per cent increase seemed calculated just to top the increase claimed by the East in the 1962 count', suggesting 'that the operation in the North was carefully planned' (Schwarz, 1968: 160).[6] As for the East, even if the inflation was not planned and arranged from the top, Dr Okpara nevertheless doggedly defended all the Eastern figures, even the manifestly untenable ones. These facts, along with the North's 'discovery' of millions more people in the 1962 verification check and Okpara's denunciation of the 1963 Northern figures while ignoring the even more ludicrous reported increases in the West, suggest the essence of the conflict was a struggle between Northern and Eastern political leaders for control of the federation.

Leading the fight were the two Premiers and Party Presidents, Sir Ahmadu Bello and Dr Michael Okpara. Actively involved with them were the party and government officials (both federal and regional) from their Regions. With the NCNC Eastern Government stood its sister Government in the Mid-West, the Action Group, and certain radical groups which opposed all the political classes but saw the conservative NPC as the paramount enemy. With the North stood the UPP Western Government and most of the NCNC officeholders in the West who defected to it. Effectively on the fence were the two key NCNC Federal Ministers from the West and Mid-West, Chiefs Benson and Okotie-Eboh, who were concerned to maintain their warm relations with NPC colleagues in the Federal Coalition. Also uncommitted (at least officially) was President Azikiwe, whose sympathies no doubt lay with his native East, but who appealed on several occasions for accommodation between the party leaders to salvage the national unity. The Prime Minister also took an accommodating position during the first census conflict and the post-census ethnic recriminations, but on the central issue of the final census results, he had little choice but to side with his party. Still, his concern to minimise the division, and Premier Osadebay's ultimate decision to accept the results, identify both men as 'moderates' within their cleavage groups. These features of the cleavage configuration are summarised in Table 5.2.

As the Table suggests, the politicians were the driving force throughout the conflict. Although the masses were mobilised for the count, the tension and urgency of the conflict was not nearly so great at the mass level. Only in the North was there any real expression of popular feeling, and even there the tension was primarily local – a long-brewing resentment of Igbo commercial competition – and was fomented and led by Northern politicians. In the South, large numbers of students protested the 1963 census results, but this seems to have been as much an expression of disgust with the whole process and its manifestly ridiculous outcome as any defence of the Eastern or Southern position. The predominance of the politicians was especially apparent in the post-census verbal war over ethnic and regional favouritism. Indeed, in his April 1964 appeal for an end to the 'disgraceful wranglings', Sir Abubakar again placed the blame for ethnic conflict in Nigeria on the politicians, observing 'that the issue of tribal wranglings was confined to a small group of people, mostly legislators' (*West Africa*, 25 April 1964: 467).

The outcome

If the essence of the census conflict was a contest between political forces of the North and East, the outcome was clear – the North won and the East lost. Some side issues were resolved through mutual accommodation and restraint, but the zero-sum nature of the census conflict defied any kind of 'Solomon's compromise'. There were really only two possible outcomes: either the North would lose its population – and hence parliamentary – majority or it would retain it. By the time of the second census, each side had become so irrevocably committed to one or the other of these outcomes, and had so thoroughly pinned its political strategy upon it, that backing down was unthinkable. In this sense, the specific numbers and irregularities were not the real issue, and so a third census could solve nothing (*West Africa*, 7 March 1964: 253–4).

The victory of the North in the census conflict is indicated by the

Table 5.2   Cleavage alignment in 1963 census crisis

For Acceptance of 1963 Results	Effectively Uncommitted	Against Acceptance of 1963 Results
1. *Northern Regional Government–NPC:* Sir Ahmadu Bello – Premier, Northern Region; President, NPC Sir Abubakar Tafawa Balewa–Federal Prime Minister*	1. Dr Nnamdi Azikiwe–President*	1. *Eastern Regional Government + NCNC* Dr Michael Okpara–Premier, Eastern Region; President, NCNC
2. *Western Regional Government:* Chief Samuel Akintola–Premier, Western Region	2. Chief Festus Okotie-Eboh–Federal Minister of Finance (Mid-West, NCNC)	2. *Mid-West Regional Government:* Chief Dennis Osadebay–Premier, Mid-West*
3. *Most of former Western NCNC–Nine of eleven NCNC Ministers:* Chief R. A. Fani-Kayode–Deputy Premier, West Minister of Justice Olowofoyeku Minister of Works and Transport Arowojolo	3. Chief T. O. S. Benson–Federal Minister of Information** (Western Yoruba, NCNC Vice President)	3. *NCNC Western Loyalists:* Chief Olu Akinfosile–Chairman, Western Region Working Committee, NCNC** Richard Akinyemi, Minister of Chieftaincy Affairs Adeoye Adisa, Minister for Home Affairs Abiola Oshodi, Chairman of the Finance Corp. (latter three resigned their positions in the Western Regional Government).
		4. *Action Group:* Alhaji Adegbenro–Leader of the Opposition, Western House of Assembly
		5. *Other Left/Radical Parties and Groups:* NEPU, Dynamic Party, Labour Congress, Socialist Party & Southern Nigerian university students.
		6. *Lagos City Council*

*Moderates who took significant steps toward accommodation.
**Sided with Western Region (Yorubas) against East (Igbos) in post-census ethnic conflict by helping to draft Western 'White

resulting allocation of parliamentary seats. The North, while losing seven seats (about two per cent of the total), retained its majority in Parliament, with 53.5 per cent of the seats. The East lost just three seats, retaining about 23 per cent of the total. Save for the West, which increased its share of seats by about one-fifth (gaining ten seats) the allocation remained essentially the same.

While the ultimate acquiscence of Premier Osadebay gave the final figures the support of three of the four regions, Osadebay's move was incidental to the outcome. The NPC had control of the Federation, and with the additional backing of Chief Akintola's NNDP MPs, its dominance over the issue was unassailable. As in the Western Regional Crisis, the NPC was able to impose its own position. On two much less significant issues it compromised: splitting the steel mill with the East and restraining the eviction of Igbo traders in Kano, along with its own anti-Igbo rhetoric. A compromise of sorts had also been achieved in the conflict over the 1962 census with Sir Abubakar's decision to cancel it and start over. But this only postponed the inevitable showdown. On a third issue, revenue allocation, the existing federalist arrangement was preserved (with NCP support) and the East suffered another defeat.

The question of the real population size of Nigeria in 1963 remains. Impartial analyses are agreed that it was much less than the official figure of 55 million. Almost certainly, it was closer to the 45.6 million originally reported in 1962, and this itself was probably inflated, although the original Northern figure seemed about right. The final 1963 figure represented a ten-year increase of 83 per cent and an unheard of annual population growth rate of 5.7 per cent. 'This phenomenal rate of growth stands in sharp contrast with the 1.9 per cent UN-estimated annual rate of growth of the Nigerian population between 1952 and 1960' and compares incredibly even with the most rapidly growing developing nations of the period, such as Brazil (3.6 per cent), Taiwan (3.7 per cent) and Egypt (2.5 per cent) (Aluko, 1965: 386–7). Probably, Nigeria's growth rate was similar to that of its West African neighbours in this period – somewhere in the neighbourhood of two to three per cent. Assuming a 2.5 per cent annual increase (the rate accepted by the government after the 1966 coup), and adding 10 per cent to the 1952–53 Southern figures and 5 per cent to the Northern figures to allow for undercounting by the British, Schwarz (1968: 163) estimates Nigeria's population at 47.4 million in 1967. This method yields an estimated national population for 1963 of 42.6 million, or three

Table 5.3   Nigerian population figures: reported and estimated (in Millions)

Region	(1) 1952–53 Census*	(2) 1962 Census	(3) 1962 Revised	(4) 1963 Revised	(5) 1963 Estimate	(6) Upper Estimate
North	16.84	22.5	31.0	29.8	23.20	25.81
East	7.22	12.4	12.3	12.4	10.17	11.20
West	4.60	7.8	7.8	10.3	6.64	7.39
Mid-West	1.49	2.2	2.2	2.2	2.15	2.39
Lagos #	0.272	0.7	0.7	0.7	0.46	0.46
Totals	30.4	45.6	54.0	55.7	42.62	47.25

Adapted from Schwarz, 1968: 163; and Aluko, 1965: 374.
*The Northern and Western censuses were conducted in 1952 and the Eastern census in 1953. Estimates of increases (Columns 5 and 6) are calculated accordingly.
#4 per cent annual growth rate assumed in both estimates (5 and 6).

million less than the original 1962 count (Table 5.3, Column 5), and regional estimates very close to the original Northern count but way below the original Eastern and Western totals (Column 2). Allowing for a population growth rate of 3.5 per cent per annum – which the World Bank (1983) estimates to be the current population growth rate in Nigeria – and maintaining Schwarz's other assumptions, we obtain an upper estimate of 47.25 million people in 1963 (Table 5.3, Column 6). It is highly unlikely that the population was larger than this (which still shows the Eastern and Western figures to have been inflated). And unless the differential rate of undercounting between South and North in 1953 was much greater than Schwarz assumes, it is also very likely that the North did have a majority of the population.

Causes of the census crisis and outcome

The key to understanding the census crisis lies in the answers to three questions. Why did politicians at all levels mobilise their communities so intensively for the census and massively inflate the returns? Why did the conflict become so bitterly polarised around the competition between the North and the East, and why were the leaders of neither side willing or able to yield? Finally, why was the North able to triumph again, imposing returns favourable to it and unacceptable to the East?

The last answer is, by now, obvious. The NPC-governed Northern

Region had the power during this period to realise its political interests on almost any issue. The Northern majority in Parliament meant a narrow NPC majority. But the margin was too thin for comfort, and NPC leaders no doubt realised even well before the census crisis that in the long run they could not count on their coalition partner, the NCNC. Political security, and at least some appearance of political legitimacy and breadth, required a more reliable base of Southern support. This it had obtained by restoring Chief Akintola to power in the West. With the support of his Regional Government and party, the NPC had all the power resources it needed to command the census issue: the Prime Minister, two of the four regional governments, and a solid working majority in Parliament. In this respect, the census crisis was the first tangible demonstration of how much the NPC had gained from the destruction of the Action Group.

That the North had the power – i.e., the numbers in parliament – to prevail underscores once again what cannot be stressed too repeatedly: the inherent tension in the federal structure inherited from the British. The consolidation of the Northern emirates and minorities into a single region with a majority of the Federation's population was probably the most significant and unfortunate legacy of British rule. This bizarre version of federalism biased the political system toward domination by Northern conservatives and so made for a fundamental contradiction between political power, controlled by the North, and social and economic development, which found the South, quite self-consciously, at a much higher level (Sklar, 1965a: 209).

So long as the federal system retained a Northern majority, it could not have been acceptable to any political leader in the South who thought himself progressive or who aspired to political control of the Federation. Chief Awolowo did both, and so took an uncompromising stand for restructuring the Federation, which invited his political destruction. Dr Okpara did both as well, and while his ideological position was not as clearly defined as Awolowo's he aspired for his party to lead the nation, with perhaps himself as Prime Minister. Moreover, the NCNC's share of national power had always been secondary, and since the Federal intervention in the West it had been diminishing further. If the NCNC's participation in the Federal Coalition had not been, from the very start, a temporary expedient – until it could gain national power on its own or as the dominant partner – it had become so by the census crisis.

It was apparent by 1962 that if the NPC's political grip was to be loosened sufficiently to enable the NCNC to construct a national coalition of its own making, this would have to come through modification of the regional structure. In accord with their more moderate political inclination, the preference of Dr Okpara and other NCNC leaders was for a modest adjustment: elimination of the North's numerical majority. This was the most important reason why the census contest became so bitterly polarised. Achievement of a Southern majority, especially through a big Eastern population gain, meant much more than an incremental gain in power and patronage for the East. Upon this objective rested the entire political strategy of the NCNC, its hopes for ever winning national power. This is why Premier Okpara could not concede defeat on the issue, even when he was clearly defeated. It is also why, when it began to look as though the East might be defeated on the census, he came to talk increasingly of the need for fundamental overhaul of the regional structure. At the NCNC convention in Kano, just before the final 1963 returns were announced, he urged his party to consider a system of 25 small states based on the former British provinces, and quoted Professor K. C. Wheare in emphasising the failing of any federal system where one state was so powerful it could overrule all the others (*West Africa*, 29 February 1964: 231). It was a theme to which he returned repeatedly over the course of the year with increasing passion.

Two other features of the regional structure also significantly contributed to the intensity of the conflict. The small number of regions made for a system of politics that was too uncomplicated, too easily polarised. While 25 states would not have prevented North–South polarisation on the census issue – a comparable number did not prevent a civil war between North and South in the United States – they would have made polarisation less likely and enabled coalitions between some Southern and Middle Belt states. And in the context of a three- or four-region system, the coincidence of region, party, and ethnicity clearly heightened the intensity of conflict, making of it several conflicts at once. Coinciding with the NPC–NCNC political struggle – and almost perfectly so, once the Western NCNC Ministers defected – was a struggle between the Northern and Eastern Regions for national resources. Parallel with and ignited by these two cleavages was the eruption of ethnic hostility between Igbo and Hausa-Fulani and between Igbo and Yoruba. This dangerous flare-up would have been less likely in a system where ethnicity did not so much correspond to region and party on a one-to-one basis. The coincidence of these cleavages also deepened the central current of tension in the conflict. For the mere presence of a Northern population (and parliamentary) majority did not become intolerable until it became clear that the North stood politically in the Federation as an NPC monolith, and hence that a Northern majority meant an *NPC* majority.

Other factors interacted with the regional structure to produce a conflict of such polar intensity. The long record of prior ethnic and regional competition made distrust and competition between North and East, and between Hausa-Fulani and Igbo, a natural and familiar reaction. If these dispositions had been submerged in the common feeling produced by Independence and the sharing of national power, they were never far from the surface and were readily, almost reflexively, evoked in periods of interest conflict between the two groups. It was because the unity of the nation remained so fragile that President Azikiwe felt compelled to appeal publicly to the Premiers 'to preserve the corporate existence of our fatherland'.

In generating a national political crisis out of the census, class interests and class action also played a pivotal role. Despite mass mobilisation within each region, the conflict was primarily a struggle between regional political classes for power and the economic rewards it brought. In particular, it was the politicians who campaigned for 'good results', who disputed and manipulated the figures, who launched the bitter burst of ethnic recriminations, and who brought the nation to the brink of disaster. They did so on behalf of larger-scale group interests, but also out of personal ambition for status, for power, and for control of the vast resources of class formation mediated by a rapidly expanding central state. Larger shares of the national population for the areas their parties controlled meant more seats in Parliament and more control over state contracts, jobs, loans and other patronage resources. These were the stock-in-trade of the political class – the means with which not only to retain power but to translate power into personal wealth and productive assets. For the Igbo leaders of the NCNC, a census 'victory' over the NPC was crucial not only to their regional and ethnic interests but to their class interests as well. But non-Eastern NCNC politicians found they were able to cut at least as good a deal with the NPC as they had with the NCNC, in which they had played an increasingly subordinate role since Independence. Thus, most of the NCNC politicians in the Western Government defected to the

NPC side in the crisis, while at the Centre, key Yoruba NCNC Ministers refused to commit themselves in the conflict.

One other factor explains why the census conflict became so polarised and resistant to compromise – the behavioural style of Nigerian politics and politicians. This followed from the enormity of what was at stake in politics and from the paucity of experience with the give and take of larger-scale democratic politics, but it had some independent cultural and historical roots as well. Compromise was an underdeveloped art in national politics, and mutual trust across the great cultural divides was sorely lacking. The imperatives of mass mobilisation induced a preference for hyperbole over moderation. And the history of political conflict had established a pattern in which the more powerful force pressed each major contest to a clear conclusion, constrained only by the power of an outside arbiter or the complexities of a multiplayer game. With the disappearance of the former at Independence and of the latter in the Western Regional crisis, little was left to constrain the tendency of the politicians to pursue their objectives to total victory. The conciliatory instincts of the Prime Minister and the President were noteworthy but insufficient to effect lasting compromise.

Behavioural style also helps to explain why the procedural fraud and statistical manipulation occurred in the first place. Such conduct would not have been widespread in a system where commitment to democratic principles and procedures was deeply based and could be relied on to protect political and cultural minorities. In Nigeria, this commitment and this confidence were absent. Goals tended to overtake and define the means, and when one party to a conflict violated legal procedures and a basic sense of fair play its opposition was pressed to respond in like fashion. These acts fed upon each other in escalating fashion until there were no rules of the game at all – except the basic law that raw force triumphs in a normative vacuum. This dynamic of competitive escalation probably accounts for whatever it was that Action Group politicians were planning with their weapons and paramilitary training. It does much to explain the behaviour of Northern politicians after the initial discovery of inflation in the Eastern census returns. And as we will see, it powerfully illumines the accelerating slide toward chaos in the 1964 Federal Election campaign and the subsequent turbulent year.

As for the more local, autonomous census cheating, there was another important motive. The intense hunger for rapid progress in development bred high expectations for government performance and readily disposed Nigerian communities towards political mobil- isation, since the state was increasingly the source of tangible socioeconomic progress. So, when the counting of people was translated into the basis for state distribution of resources, the people rallied to their leaders' call. This popular participation was easier to wind up than to calm down. Once mobilised, it was capable of spinning out of control. In the rapid escalation of anti-Igbo animosity in the North lay a clear warning to all the nation's politicians.

Effects of the census crisis on Nigerian democracy

The census crisis converged with other developments overlapping it in time to erode further the stability of democratic government in Nigeria. As in the Western Regional Crisis, the blunt exercise of Federal power by NCP leaders left an important segment of the polity not simply defeated in a discrete contest but alienated from the system in a much more diffuse and profound way. NCNC leaders, and other progressive elements who stood behind them in the crisis, insisted that the official Northern figures were grossly inflated and therefore 'declared that they would regard as illegitimate the NPC majority which the [Federal] election seems certain to produce' (*West Africa*, 7 March 1964: 254). The census outcome, combined with the likely election results, thus promised to challenge the most basic foundation of the regime's stability – the belief that those in power were entitled to rule.

The crisis also crystallised feelings about the unfairness and hence illegitimacy of the federal system. Their defeat on the census left NCNC leaders with the same feeling as the defeated Action Group politicians before them – that there was something fundamentally wrong with a system that seemed rigged to guarantee perpetual domination by a particular region and party.

This alienation of NCNC Eastern leaders who had been part of the system was matched by a growing alienation on the part of those who had all along been outside it or on its fringe. Part of this stemmed from the general disgust among educated elites with the whole affair – the inflation, the counter-inflation, the tests and checks and verifications, the sense that politicians were cynically manipulating and bargaining with the census returns for political advantage – and part from the sense, especially strong among university students and other left groups, that reactionary Northern politicians, in alliance with a puppet ruler in the West, were seeking to perpetuate their rule by fraud. These reactions to the census crisis were reinforced by the growing disillusionment with the political class in general and the mounting evidence of its corruption. That the politicians could not execute so basic a function as counting the nation's population must have stengthened the disillusionment of those more idealistic young elites in the bureaucracy and military whose complaint against the politicians was not simply corruption but also gross incompetence.

The census thus reduced in several ways and among a number of different groups the legitimacy of a regime that had never been firmly rooted and was becoming less and less democratic.

Effects on future political developments

The census crisis also seemed likely to have several 'feedback' effects on future political developments. First by removing the single most genuine element of cleavage crosscut, the strong NCNC political presence in the West, it heightened the coincidence of cleavages in Nigerian politics, and promised further to polarise political conflict. In particular, with the reduction of the NCNC to its Eastern, Igbo base, political conflict appeared likely to invoke ethnic antagonism more readily and explicitly.

Second, the crisis appeared to augur more very serious ethnic and regional conflict in the future, for the fundamental issues in the census dispute had not been resolved. Any future political issue that tapped the census figures – elections, allocations of resources, etc. – would now be more intense and controversial, since the basis for distribution and competition was automatically tainted, and so the legitimacy of its outcome as well. In addition, the census crisis left feelings of ethnic and regional antagonism at a very high pitch. Ethnic hostility in particular, once whipped up, was not easily dissipated. In the North, an outburst of 'Igbophobia' had been checked from becoming a frenzied mass expulsion, but the underlying enmity remained dangerously alive. On the national front, the cool-headed intervention of the Prime Minister had quieted the wave of ethnic recriminations in the political arena, but here again, ethnicity had been raised to a new salience, and restraint would be required from the nation's politicians to keep it from becoming ugly in the future.

Finally, the census crisis further eroded respect for the democratic process, or what Nigerian politicians themselves repeatedly referred to as 'the rules of the game'. As in the past, violation of these rules by one party invited violation by the other. The sense that the North had used massive fraud and raw political power to preserve its population lead increased the likelihood that Southern opposition forces – including now the NCNC – would feel the need to bend the democratic process themselves if they were to have any chance of victory. Those who understood that contests without rules become bloody affairs must have watched this spiral over the subsequent two years with special fear and foreboding.

6 The 1964 General Strike

'In the present circumstances, my government will be failing in its
duty to the nation if it does not take all necessary steps in its power
to avoid a dislocation of the economic life of this country . . . The
present situation cannot be tolerated any longer.' — Prime Minister
Sir Abubakar Tafawa Balewa, in a national broadcast, 9 June 1964
(Melson, 1970: 785)

'The dismissal notices you have received are so many scraps of
paper. You can keep them as souvenirs to show your children and
remind them that today is a turning point in the history of this
country.' — Wahab Goodluck, Co-Chairman, Joint Action Committee, and President, Nigerian Trade Union Congress, to a strike
rally, 10 June 1964 (*West Africa*, 13 June 1964: 657)

As regional and ethnic competition intensified during the census
crisis, tension of a wholly different order was gathering explosive
force. Wage labourers were beginning to focus their indignation over
declining real income and gross economic inequality into militant
demands for government attention and higher pay. For a brief but
crucial year in Nigerian politics, the severely fractured trade-union
movement united in a concerted challenge to the political class. What
began as a protest over wages quickly widened into an attack on the
very basis of the regime's authority. Spanning the latter stages of the
census crisis and the preliminary manoeuvring of the Federal
Election, the conflict peaked in a thirteen-day General Strike that
brought the economic life of the nation to a virtual standstill. In the
confrontation, Nigerian workers scored a significant victory, while
the regime was discredited across a wide and crucial segment of
public opinion.

HISTORICAL DIVISIONS IN THE NIGERIAN LABOUR MOVEMENT

It is only against the historical record of chronic, rancorous conflict in
the Nigerian trade-union movement that one can appreciate what an

162

extraordinary achievement was its unification late in 1963. Since the formation of the first central organisation in 1943, the movement had been bedevilled by incessant conflict over ideology, tactics, structure, and personalities, as well as its relationship to political parties, the government, and the competing international labour federations of the Cold War. Indeed, given the intensity and variety of the antagonisms that riddled the movement prior to (and after) its 1963–64 unification, it is all the more significant that ethnicity was so peripheral a dimension of division. Urban wage labour provided the first functional bridge to cross ethnic relationships at the mass level, and trade unions became the first and most important alternative to ethnically based organisations.

Virtually as old as wage labour itself in Nigeria, trade-union organisation experienced its first burst of growth after the right of collective organisation and bargaining was conceded by colonial authorities in 1939.[1] Among its most important and charismatic early leaders was the fiery young organiser of the Railway Workers' Union, Michael Imoudu, who would play a crucial role in the General Strikes of 1963 and 1964. Imprisoned by the British after organising one of Nigeria's first labour protests in 1942, Imoudu built up a large popular following in the 1940s. In 1943, with Imoudu still in prison, 31 unions came together to form the Trade Union Congress (TUC).

This expression of solidarity was neither deep nor long-lasting, however. It cracked in its first major test, in 1945, when workers in critical public service areas (including the railways) organised a General Strike. The strike was remarkably similar in its precipitants to that which would cripple the nation twenty years later: a rapid rise in the cost of living generated demands for substantial wage increases, which met with extreme government insensitivity and arrogance. Released from prison as a government concession at the start, Imoudu played a leading role in the strike, which was backed vigorously by the nationalist press network of Nnamdi Azikiwe and by the young politician Obafemi Awolowo (who edited the TUC's bulletin and served as Secretary of the Motor Transport Owners' Union). The strike was opposed by the established union leaders (especially of the white collar unions), who attempted first to postpone and then to settle it, losing much rank-and-file support in the process. The colonial government tried to make these 'responsible' labour officials the sole legitimate leaders of the union movement. But with essential services crippled in the South, the Government was forced to concede to strike demands, enhancing the popularity both of radical labour leaders (such as Imoudu) and of the NCNC.

The NCNC's strong support for the union militants was confirmed after the strike in the election of Imoudu to the party's Executive Council. But this relationship sparked conflict between moderate and radical, or what Melson (1973) has termed 'neutralist' and 'activist' labour leaders. The former favoured a 'bread-and-butter unionism' that would eschew any explicitly political activity while the latter sought a 'political unionism' that would sponsor a socialist labour party. And while the activists favoured a unitarian constitution the neutralists supported (or were indifferent to) a federalist system (Melson, 1973: 120). These differences erupted at the TUC's 1948 Annual Conference. When the neutralists passed a motion to disaffiliate from the NCNC, the movement underwent the first in a long succession of splits, as the activist leaders – Michael Imoudu, F. O. Coker, Nduka Eze and Luke Emejulu – walked out and formed a rival federation. The following month (April 1948), all four were elected to the NCNC cabinet (Melson, 1973: 121–4).

In 1949, the rival factions of organised labour came together in the National Emergency Committee, as outrage over the killing of 25 striking coal miners at Enugu temporarily submerged class, ethnic, and political divisions in the nationalist movement. The two labour groups merged the next year into a new Nigerian Labour Congress (NLC), but tension plagued it from the very beginning, when the activist leaders took control and the moderate unions refused to transfer their assets. The NLC disintegrated at the end of 1950 under the shock of an ill-considered national mercantile strike that failed badly and ruined the career of its organiser, Nduka Eze. Coupled with this failure was a move toward moderation by the NCNC, which expelled Eze while deploring communist infiltration into the NLC. Preoccupied with their struggles to win regional power and colonial recognition, nationalist politicians had no desire to be painted as radicals and no time to support the development of central labour organisation. By the same token, the radical labour 'activists' deeply opposed the increasing regionalism of the political system and its major parties, including the NCNC. With the crystallisation of regionalist trends in the 1951 elections and subsequent developments, labour 'activists' began 'a period of isolation from Nigerian politics' that would last until 1964 (Melson, 1973: 126).

Meanwhile, within the labour movement, a new effort at unification gave birth in August 1953 to the All-Nigeria Trade Union

Federation, with a vaguely radical programme and radicals again in the elected leadership – Imoudu as President and Gogo Nzeribe as General Secretary. ANTUF enjoyed substantial success, incorporating 45 of the 57 registered trade unions and 181 000 of the 200 000 organised workers. But the activist-neutralist cleavage was again prominent from the start, with neutralist leaders such as N. A. Cole, H. P. Adebola, and L. L. Borha insinuating that ANTUF leadership was communist-infiltrated. These moderates were supported and financed, first clandestinely and then overtly, by the (US-dominated) International Confederation of Free Trade Unions (ICFTU), to which they attempted to affiliate ANTUF. Failing in this move, they withdrew and formed a rival federation in 1957. Reconciled to the regionalist system and dedicated to keeping the labour movement out of politics, the neutralist wing of labour was strongly preferred by the Federal Government, which took no comfort in the activists' increasingly pointed challenge to the status quo. When Labour Minister Okotie-Eboh granted immediate recognition to the neutralists' new federation, the radical union leaders perceived an NCNC conspiracy to undermine them and their new Nigerian Labour Party (formed the previous year by Imoudu and two new faces who would become leaders of the activist wing of labour, Samuel U. Bassey and Wahab Goodluck).

In 1959, pressure from the rank and file brought the rival labour leaders together again. At issue was the demand of public-sector workers for a government commission to review wages and salaries, as well as a vague but widespread sentiment for trade-union unity at Independence. In March 1959, the radical and moderate wings again merged in a new Trade Union Congress of Nigeria (TUCN). Compromise was effected when the radicals accepted a statement of principle denouncing communism and the moderates agreed to abandon their affiliation with the ICFTU. But the new federation began to unravel even before it got off the ground. When Samuel Bassey lost the General Secretaryship to the moderate candidate, Lawrence Borha, many radical unionists charged vote-rigging and walked out. Imoudu, who was narrowly elected President and was conscious of the rank-and-file anger that would greet another split, publicly maintained that the elections were fair. But by early 1960, renewed tension effectively destroyed the merger. Moderates retained the TUCN title, claiming 88 affiliated unions with 86 200 members, while the radicals dubbed their federation the Nigerian Trade Union Congress (NTUC), claiming 46 unions with 48 500 workers. (Some 197 unions with 142 000 members remained outside both federations in 1960.)

The split freed both wings to pursue their ideological inclinations. The moderate TUCN renewed its open affiliation with the Western-bloc ICFTU, while the NTUC joined the newly established All African Trade Union Federation (AATUF), an aggressively pan-Africanist body inspired ideologically by Kwame Nkrumah and dominated by Ghanaian unions. The NTUC, which would play a pivotal role in the events of 1963–64, then proceeded to radicalise its programme, demanding a unitary constitution and nationalisation of major industries. NTUC leaders hurled vituperative allegations at the TUCN leadership, the latter replied in kind, and there ensued an increasingly strident verbal war between the two wings of Nigerian labour. Despite repeated attempts at outside mediation and growing rank-and-file disenchantment with these leadership struggles, the conflict persisted and became more polarised, due in part to the intrusion of the international union rivalry (itself quite intense) between the ICFTU and the communist World Federation of Trade Unions, each of which was channelling material support to one of the Nigerian federations.

Late in 1961, leading politicians and academicians strenuously endeavoured to get the rival union leaders to reconcile their differences, but these efforts ended in further recriminations. Despite this setback, labour leaders from across the ideological spectrum assembled in Ibadan in May 1962 for a conference of all registered trade unions. Their purpose was to elect a common leadership and to put the question of international affiliation to a vote of the official delegates. Once again, the attempt at reconciliation collapsed amidst charges of vote-rigging, apparently blatant vote-buying, and bitter procedural wrangles.

Through 1962, the rift between the neutralist and activist wings deepened. The former, now under the name of the United Labour Congress (ULC) and enjoying Government recognition, accused the NTUC of being communist-led and inspired, whereupon the latter produced a letter (apparently a forgery) linking the new ULC President, H. P. Adebola, to American labour leader George Meaney. Factionalism ripped the two camps internally as well. Two moderate leaders – N. Anunobi and N. Chukwurra – split from the ULC to form the Nigerian Workers' Council (NWC), linking it to a Christian international labour federation that was also Western-oriented. The radical federation divided three ways. A small splinter group of Northern unionists followed Ibrahim Nock into a Northern Federation of Labour, which proceeded to forge a working relationship with the NPC. The core of the radical labour movement itself fractured on ideological grounds, with the most militantly socialist unionists following Bassey and Goodluck into a renewed NTUC, while Imoudu, Gogo Nzeribe and others established the Labour Unity Front. The move had important political implications. Bassey and Goodluck, who became NTUC General Secretary and President respectively, had forged close ties with Dr Tunji Otegbeye's hardline (and Moscow-supported) Socialist Workers' and Farmers' Party, which Imoudu and certain other left-wing labour and intellectual leaders condemned as too tied up with international politics. These leaders 'were more disposed to think of the working class struggle in national or Pan-African terms' (Cohen, 1974: 89), and in 1964 some of them would organise a rival socialist party.

Thus, the labour movement in Nigeria stood severely fragmented in 1963, torn by deep ideological differences, heated international rivalry, and bitter personal tensions and jealousies. The fourth major attempt in twenty years to overcome these centrifugal tendencies had once again failed totally. This was the organisational setting for the rapid escalation and spread of labour discontent during 1963.

THE CRYSTALLISATION OF LABOUR DISCONTENT AND UNITY IN 1963

Like the politicians, labour leaders in Nigeria grew distant from their mass constituencies in their preoccupation with struggles and strategies for power. As they fought each other, discontent spread among their members over the declining real value of their meagre wages and the increasingly stark gap between their own worsening poverty and the extravagant consumption of the political class. As it had in 1945 and 1959, this swelling discontent forced labour leaders to set aside their differences for a time and press a set of common demands.

The movement toward a united front formally began in August 1963 when the NTUC inaugurated a discussion group on wages and the other union federations decided to cooperate. This was followed on 12 September by a meeting of all registered unions in Lagos under the auspices of the moderate United Labour Congress. The meeting endorsed the ULC's call for a general revision of wages and established a Joint Action Committee (Cohen, 1974: 90–1). The JAC brought together all of Nigeria's major trade union leaders and federations: the moderate ULC, led by Adebola, and NWC, led by Chukwurra; the radical NTUC of Goodluck and Bassey, and LUF, now led by Gogo Chu Nzeribe; along with Imoudu's Railway and Port Workers' Union (an LUF member that participated independently in the JAC). In all, twenty labour leaders, drawn equally from the moderate and radical factions, sat together on the JAC (Friedland, 1965: 80; Cohen, 1974: 165). Only Ibrahim Nock's Northern Federation of Labour was missing.

While leadership of the JAC was shared between the two factions – with Bassey of the NTUC and Borha of the ULC serving jointly as Secretary-General – it was the NTUC that pressed first and most vigorously for a national strike, which Bassey proposed in August to the 'First Revolutionary Convention' of the NTUC. The convention's policy paper on the Political Struggle of the Working Class expressed the broader discontent with class domination that the strike would come to embody:

> Independence has not brought democracy to Nigerian workers and farmers. This is because the type of democracy preached and practised by the Nigerian Government is the democracy for the few rich Nigerians, the Emirs, the Obas, their families and supporters... The existing major political parties are parties of the rich and feudal aristocracy. They are dominated, controlled and financed by the agents and representatives of the rich classes. (Quoted in Cohen, 1974: 156)

The paper was especially pointed in its attack on 'Northern Feudalism', calling for abolition of the Native Authorities, popularly elected local councils and extension of the franchise to women.

While probably few Nigerian workers were able to perceive or articulate their discontent in such concrete class terms, they were aware of the widening inequalities in the society and were increasingly angered by them. Their discontent sprang from both absolute and relative deprivation. They were upset with the declining real value of their wages – which had not been increased in the government sector since 1959, despite an inflation of roughly 20 per cent in the cost of living – and with such government practices as paying workers on a monthly basis and arbitrarily maintaining most of them in a 'temporary status'. Related to this were the continuing harsh conditions of urban life, including a shortage of cheap housing. But they were even more outraged by the gap between their wages and the huge salaries of the politicians and senior administrative officials. Even for a continent in which this gap was typically extreme – 'set initially with European conditions in mind' and then eagerly preserved by the new African regimes – the imbalance in Nigeria was extraordinary. About 1964, the top salary in the Civil Service scale was 37 times the bottom salary and over a hundred times the per capita GDP (which was itself 'well above the income of the average [rural] inhabitant') (Abernethy, 1983: 11).[2] In the context of this enormous disparity, growing visibly wider as a result of corruption and visibly more obnoxious as a result of lavish and conspicuous spending by the elite, their suffering came to appear as unnecessary and unfair – not simply a burden but an injustice.

Indeed, on this basic issue of inequality in income and lifestyle, the ULC was as outspoken as its radical competitors. In its 'Programme for the Future', issued on 25 May 1962, the ULC aligned itself in sharp opposition to the political classes and framed the challenge squarely in class terms:

Independence Day ... freed us from colonial domination. It did not, unfortunately, free us automatically from colonial institutions. The edifice of privilege remains; only its proprietors are different.... This situation, in which a senior official may receive fifty times the salary of a junior official, or a daily labourer, is politically explosive and economically intolerable.... The United Labour Congress of Nigeria will fight against the continuation of this exploitation of class by class as fervently as it fought against imperialism. (Quoted in Melson, 1970: 776)

The depth of popular grievance was recognised by *West Africa* when it observed, 'Wage earners are not prepared to make sacrifices' for economic development goals 'when they see little sacrifice among the politicians.' Government Ministers and MPs, it argued, failed to

realize the resentment caused among those who can scarcely afford to feed their families by the actual and reputed scale of Government extravagance as represented by ministerial houses and overseas travel, MP's cars and their upkeep, and salaries and allowances. No longer do other Nigerians admire the man whose success is shown by ostentation. Now they ask who is paying. (5 October 1963: 1118)

Perhaps it was Samuel Bassey who expressed the theme most graphically:

> A labourer can expect to get a little more than £7 a month, or 5s 10d a day for 26 working days. He may expect to share a room 8ft. by 10ft. with two other families – and spend over two-thirds of his income on the rent. All the while, our politicians live in £30,000 air-conditioned state quarters, rent and light free. (*West Africa*, 16 November 1963: 1289–91)

This stark contrast, which workers read about in the newspapers and saw in the sleek foreign cars that whisked by them in the government capital, and of which their leaders did not fail to remind them in the most indignant terms, brought labour resentment to the boiling point by summer 1963 and forced union leaders to put aside their internecine quarrels to express it in common militant action. On 19 September the ULC, with the concurrence of the newly formed JAC, called on the Government to appoint 'a high-powered commission for the carrying out of an upward revision of salaries and wages ... the complete overhaul of the existing colonial wage structure ... the introduction of a national minimum wage and the abolition of the zonal wage-rates and the daily rated labour system' (quoted in Melson, 1970: 777). The JAC warned that if such a commission was not appointed by 25 September it would call on its member unions to strike beginning 27 September, just four days before the internationally attended Republic Day ceremonies.

Misled by the previous intense union infighting, and seriously underestimating the extent and depth of labour grievance, the Federal Government procrastinated, apparently confident that the JAC would soon collapse. It is difficult to otherwise explain its arrogant treatment of the JAC demands. On the morning when he was due to meet the union leaders, Federal Minister of Labour Chief Joseph M. Johnson went to the Lagos airport to greet the Prime Minister on his return from leave. Without consulting the JAC, the Minister then published, a day after the JAC deadline, the terms of reference for a committee to study its demands. These terms were more limited and vague than what the JAC had sought (Cohen, 1974: 91; Melson, 1970: 778). In a letter to the Minister of Labour on 27 September, Borha reiterated the JAC demands in even bolder fashion, insisting on a review of salaries and wages not only of government workers (which the Ministry was prepared to concede) but of those in the private sector as well. In addition, Borha made it clear that 'the Commission's work should result in the complete overhaul of the existing wage structure,' dating from colonial times, so as to remove 'the imbalance between the foreign-oriented upper stratum and the domestic-oriented lower stratum'. Finally, he regretted to inform the Minister that the strike 'will proceed to take effect in certain sectors and may spread unless our demands are met without delay' (quoted in Melson, 1970: 778–9).

They were not. The strike caused particularly acute dislocation and embarrassment in Lagos, where foreign dignitaries were arriving daily to unserviced hotel rooms. Within two days, it spread to most of the rest of the country, involving somewhere between 35 000 and 50 000 workers (Cohen, 1974: 91). Having already conceded to a commission and having granted workers an advance of one month's salary to mark Republic Day, the Federal Government now capitulated on the crucial point of extending the review to the private sector. On 3 October, Borha announced an end to the nationwide strike, and eleven days later, after extensive negotiations, a Commission of Inquiry was appointed with terms of reference almost identical to those demanded by the JAC (Melson, 1970: 778–80).

The six-member commission included a lawyer, an economist, and a civil servant and was chaired by the Chief Justice of the Western Region Supreme Court, Sir Adeyinka Morgan. On 24 October, the Morgan Commission began taking several months of public testimony and memoranda from labour, government, private employers and various experts.

The memorandum submitted by the Joint Action Committee (and drafted with the assistance of sympathetic leftist intellectuals, some of whom had assisted Chief Awolowo in redefining the Action Group programme) provides valuable insight into the conflict. Marshalling a wealth of statistical evidence, it implored the Commission to close the huge income gap inherited from the colonial era, which, it argued, had poisoned social relations in the nation, reproducing 'a pronounced master-servant relation expressed not only in a prestige income structure but in social snobbishness' (quoted in Melson, 1970: 781). To close the gap, the JAC proposed not only a substantial increase in the minimum annual wage (to £180) but a substantial cut in the upper income scale, from as much as £3,000 and more a year to between £500 and £960 maximum. In the prevailing sociopolitical context, the latter proposal was the more radical, entailing a basic restructuring of the social order.

The Government was still not taking the JAC seriously but rather, wishing the whole problem would simply go away. Yet to neutral observers, it was clear that the brief 1963 strike had fundamentally altered the political equation in the country. 'Organised wage-earners are now, even if still only a fraction of the population, a significant political factor in Nigeria,' observed *West Africa* (5 October 1963: 1117), 'since they can bring economic life to a standstill and are massed near the centres of political power.'

CONFRONTATION: THE 1964 STRIKE

After seven months of hearings and deliberations, the Morgan Commission presented its findings to the Government on 30 April 1964. It was then the Federal Government's turn to act. The nation awaited the release of the Report and the Government White Paper outlining the steps it was prepared to take. Again, the Government delayed. Again, workers and their leaders became angry over the Government's temporising. 'Many of the workers suspected (and this was confirmed to them by a member of the commission who leaked the general findings) that the delay was due to the report's being substantially favourable to the workers' case' (Cohen, 1974: 166). The unions alleged a plan to suppress the Morgan Report and the JAC threatened strike action if there were any delay in its publication. On 8 May, the JAC set a deadline of one week for the report's release (*West Africa*, 9 May 1964: 523; Friedland, 1965: 9).

During these tense weeks in May, the Government continued to strike a posture somewhere between casual and cavalier, still seriously underestimating the unions' power and determination.

Efforts of the union leaders to negotiate before the strike were thwarted by the absence or inaccessibility of key government officials. The Minister of Labour, Chief Joseph M. Johnson, was absent in May on a trip to the United States, from which he had to be hurriedly recalled. Nor were the Prime Minister and the President accessible to union leaders even after the strike had started. As the situation became increasingly tense, the Minister of Establishments, Jacob Obande ... dealt with the JAC in a manner that was somewhat less than deft. (Friedland, 1965: 8–9)

Tension temporarily abated on 11 May when Minister Obande met with the union leaders (after refusing to see them five days earlier) and promised publication of the Morgan Report on 25 May. When the Report failed to appear on that date, unionists stormed the Establishments Ministry looking for an absent Obande and began preparations for a General Strike. On 27 May, Obande finally handed the union leaders copies of the Morgan Report (not yet for publication) but indicated it would take another ten days to 'see eye to eye' with his colleagues before the White Paper could be released. Incensed that the Government still had not indicated its views on the Commission's findings, union leaders issued an ultimatum demanding publication of the Government White Paper within 72 hours to avert a strike. One trade union leader, Mallam Inuwah of the ULC, described the release of the Report without the White Paper as 'a wrapped parcel given by an angry father to a hungry child whose patience cannot endure for another fortnight' (quoted in Cohen, 1974: 166; Friedland, 1965: 9; *West Africa*, 30 May 1964: 607, and 6 June 1964: 619).

Union patience had run out. On 30 May, trade union leaders staged a mass rally outside Lagos declaring their intention to strike, after which they attempted to march into the Federal Capital to protest in front of the Parliament building. Enforcing a ban on public meetings, heavily armed police obstructed their path. In the dramatic clash that ensued, dozens of people were injured, including union leaders Michael Imoudu (who would wear his arm in a sling for the duration of the strike) and Alhaji Adebola. A number of union leaders were also arrested, including Imoudu, Adebola, and Wahab Goodluck (*West Africa*, 6 June 1964: 619; Schwarz, 1968: 155–6).

At midnight on 31 May, the nationwide strike officially commenced. Dockers and railwaymen were the first to come out, and by the next morning both ports and railways were effectively paralysed. In addition, several private concerns, including the United Africa Company, reported that widespread sit-down strikes had halted operations. The following day, workers in Government offices and commerce went on sit-down strikes, and postal and telecommunications joined in. Regional capitals were also hit quickly and hard. Railways, postal, electricity and textile workers in Kaduna; postal, railway, forestry, and nonacademic university workers in Ibadan; and civil service workers in almost every Ministry in Enugu all heeded the JAC call to show up for work but remain idle. Similar stoppages occurred in other large cities, such as Port Harcourt, where, by the third day of the strike, 'the work stoppage ... was virtually complete' (Wolpe, 1974: 188). On 3 June, bus crews in Lagos joined the work stoppage, leaving the Federal capital without public transport, and all of the city's main department stores shut down (*West Africa*, 6 June 1964: 619). By this time, Lagos was paralysed, and virtually the entire city of Ibadan was shut down (Melson, 1970: 785).[3]

In the absence of meaningful Government action, the strike spread day by day. Daily mass rallies in major cities kept workers informed of the previous day's events, locally and around the country, while exhorting them to continue the strike and to remain nonviolent (both of which the workers did to a remarkable degree). As more and more government workers joined the strike, troops were called in to man essential services and guard against sabotage. This did little to counter the strike's crippling effects.

On 3 June, 'the solidarity of the strikers was measurably stiffened' by the publication of the Government's White Paper, along with the Morgan Report itself (Cohen, 1974: 166). The Morgan Commission found that most Nigerian workers 'are living in penury' and, with elaborate documentation of the cost of living in various cities, recommended wage increases of 50 to 100 per cent – still not adequate to provide a living, it conceded, but enough to 'sufficiently alleviate' hardship while not completely disrupting the economy. It also recommended an end to the employment of most government workers as 'temporary' labour, a practice which it called 'unjust, unfair and immoral' in denying workers tenure, notice, sick leave and retirement benefits. In addition, the Commission recommended that economies be effected through reduction of the motorcar allowances, the children's 'separate domicile' allowances, and the substantial rent subsidies enjoyed by elected officials and senior civil servants.[4] In its White Paper, the Federal Government completely rejected the Commission's approach to the wage issue, claiming that the recommended increases exceeded inflation and were 'clearly impossible' for the Government to pay. Instead, it offered average wage increases of about twenty per cent, 'and in almost contemptuous terms rejected many of the commission's other suggestions' (Cohen, 1974: 166; *West Africa*, 13 June 1964: 649; Schwarz, 1968: 25–6).

The Government's proposals were rejected out of hand by the JAC, and the strike, which had been called to protest the White Paper's delay, continued as a demand for higher wages. Through the latter part of its first week, the strike steadily gained momentum, fed significantly by the Government's arrogant, condescending posture. Chief J. M. Johnson, Minister of Labour, had returned from his US tour for an urgent Cabinet meeting to consider the Government's response to the Morgan recommendations. But as the strike was beginning, he departed again to New York for a conference on youth problems, and thereafter, 'despite repeated telegrams from his own ministry', he 'showed a measure of reluctance to interrupt his American sojourn. The Prime Minister also failed to realise the determination of the strikers and the widely held sense of grievance' (Cohen, 1974: 166). It was not until 6 June that he broke his holiday on his Northern farm to convene a Cabinet meeting in the capital. President Azikiwe remained at his home in Nsukka through the duration of the strike. The insensitivity of the political class to union concerns 'was perhaps best illustrated when the Minister of Labour appeared at a negotiating session with strike leaders in a gold brocaded robe' (Abernethy, 1969: 227).

On 8 June, talks between JAC and Government leaders broke down when the latter proposed that the strike be called off before negotiations could begin and then issued a 48-hour ultimatum to the workers to cease the strike or face mass dismissal. The ultimatum was repeated in a national broadcast by the Prime Minister, who warned, 'The present situation cannot be tolerated any longer.' But Sir Abubakar had neither the credibility nor the power to enforce his back-to work order, which 'provoked a large measure of derision at the mass meetings' (Cohen, 1974: 167). Around the country, the union leaders responded with open defiance, exhorting their workers to stay at home and away from their jobs. The JAC's Western Regional Branch issued an ultimatum of its own for Balewa 'to resign within 48 hours' (Melson, 1970: 785). On 10 June, the Government's deadline passed without effect and Wahab Goodluck told a mass rally in Lagos:

> The dismissal notices you have received today are so many scraps of paper. You can keep them as souvenirs to show your children and remind them that today is a turning point in the history of this country. Many of you are skilled men and the Government cannot replace you all. (*West Africa*, 13 June 1964: 647)

The base of support for the strike had continued to grow over the course of the stalemate. Many domestic servants refused to work, and at rallies and meetings in the towns, workers were often joined by large numbers of unemployed. 'In a moment of farce', Alhaji Adebola even 'threatened to call out the nightsoilmen on the grounds that, as he announced it: "What is worth doing is worth doing well"' (Cohen, 1974: 166–7). By the time the union leaders rejected the Government ultimatum, leftist elements in the NCNC and the AG, along with other outspoken opponents of the NPC, were coming to the active support of the strikers. To the JAC headquarters in Lagos and Ibadan NCNC members began bringing 'not only advice and support, but the money and cars essential to the continuation of the strike' (Melson, 1970: 786).

It was only after the Prime Minister's ill-fated ultimatum, with the solidarity and popular base of the General Strike continuing to expand, that the Government finally began to negotiate seriously. With its economic advisers warning about the mounting economic consequences of the strike – the financial cost to the nation would afterwards be assessed at £2.5 million (Cohen, 1974: 167) – the Government set up a reconciliation committee chaired by Finance Minister Okotie-Eboh and the JAC decided to cooperate. By 12 June the strike reached a crucial turning point for both sides when a 48-hour ultimatum issued by the association of private employers expired. Although most firms hesitated to follow up with dismissals, this ultimatum proved more effective than the Government's. 'In sharp contrast to the still-total work stoppage in Eastern Nigeria, the strike had collapsed in the Northern Region and was continuing in name only in Lagos' (Wolpe, 1974: 192).[5] At the same time, 'it became apparent that unless some concessions were made tension would rise dangerously'. Riot police, who already had been placed on alert, were forced to move into action on 12 June to break up the crowd of thousands of applicants who answered the advertisement of a foreign firm that had dismissed more than a thousand striking employees earlier in the week (*West Africa*, 20 June 1964: 679).

That evening, negotiations resumed in earnest between the JAC and the Government's five-man Ministerial Committee. By the next day, 13 June, agreement was reached and the General Strike was ended. By the terms of the settlement, the Government agreed to withdraw the dismissal and warning notices served on striking workers, to give them leave with full pay for their absence during the strike, and not to victimise or penalise them in any way. All four Governments of the Federation, together with the JAC and the private employers, were to begin wage negotiations immediately on the basis of the Morgan Commission's recommendations. Finally, the unions agreed that the workers would return on Monday, 15 June (*West Africa*, 20 June 1964: 679).

While the Government did not concede the unions' main demand that it guarantee the Morgan wage scales before a return to work, the concessions it did make 'were of a spectacular nature' and union leaders claimed victory. Said Michael Imoudu after agreement was reached: 'Now the government has come down on its knees it is fair that we hear it first. We can always react when things go the other way. I think we have proved equal with the Government even with its soldiers and police' (*West Africa*, 20 June 1964: 679).

By 8 July, agreement was reached on a new wage scale for government workers. The increases for minimum monthly wage rates were on the order of 25–30 per cent, most of them closer to the Government's White Paper than the Morgan Commission's recommendations (for example, Lagos, for which area Morgan recommended 58 per cent and the White Paper 20 per cent, while the agreement awarded 32 per cent). But still, they were appreciably larger than the Government had originally been prepared to grant, and on the issue of when they would become effective, the unions won another important concession: the increases would be retroactive to the first of the year (the White Paper had proposed 1 April 1964 and the Morgan Commission 1 October 1963).

The aftermath of the settlement is described by Schwarz (1968: 157):

The settlement was immediately followed by a rise in prices – market women raised their food prices even before the settlement was announced – which more than offset the benefits. Many small firms with semi-redundant staff dismissed surplus workers, thus further aggravating unemployment. However, a massive protest had been made; the unions had tasted unity and power for the first time and, though they were never again to erupt during the First Republic, they could now be expected to seek to translate their power into political terms.

ANALYSIS

The cleavage

As did the other major conflicts of the First Republic, the 1964 General Strike contained within its obvious and predominant line of cleavage other, more subtle divisions. The conflict – which may be dated from the national strike of September 1963 through the

General Strike of 1964 – pitted organised labour against the Government. In an important sense, this was part of the continuing struggle for national resources, cut across a fresh line of cleavage. At the time of the strike, government was by far the largest employer in the nation. In fact, the federal, regional, and local governments together employed 54 per cent of all Nigerian wage earners – just one manifestation of the sweeping expansion of the state. Unions demanded from the government a greater share of the economic pie for their workers.

But the protest over wages was only one element of the conflict. Another powerful motivation for the strikes – without which they might never have occurred – was the extreme inequality in the official structure of wages and benefits and the glaring levels of corruption and extravagant consumption. As part of the struggle for redistribution, union leaders demanded not only pay increases for the workers but pay cuts for the senior officials. This current of discontent challenged the whole structure of domination by the political classes, including their authority to rule.

This deeper current in the conflict is evident in the composition of competing forces. In protest against the Federal Government stood virtually the entire population of organised labour in Nigeria, some 300 000 trade-union members organised into about 300 active unions, which were represented by the JAC (Melson, 1970: 774). Joining these workers in the 1964 strike at one time or another were most of the rest of the nation's wage labourers, both blue and white collar. Participation has been estimated at a total of from 750 000 to 800 000 workers in the public and private sectors (Melson, 1970: 785; Cohen, 1974: 166), against a total wage labour force of 800 000 to 1 000 000 and a total urban population of only 4 000 000. In all, the 1964 General Strike was estimated to have cost the nation from four to fourteen million man-days (Melson, 1970: 771). For a predominantly agrarian nation, the strike was of staggering magnitude.

The strike also won support from other important social and political forces. A large number of unemployed participated in protests and demonstrations, and many more were no doubt in sympathy. In Port Harcourt, 'most of the demonstrators were "applicants" – a remarkable episode in the history of strikes' (Schwarz, 1968: 24). Eventually, most left or dissident political elements came out on behalf of the strikers, including Action Group leaders and those NCNC leaders outside the Federal coalition. The Eastern Premier and NCNC President, Dr Okpara, 'was particularly outspoken in his support of the union demands' (Friedland, 1965: 9).

On the opposing side was a narrowly based coalition of the Federal Government and the nation's private employers, organised loosely into the Nigerian Employers' Consultative Association. Because most of the private employers were European (mainly British) firms – employing 38 per cent of all wage earners and 80 per cent of those in the private sector – the Government was essentially allied in the conflict with foreign enterprise. This laid it open to charges of 'neo-colonialism', a vulnerability which radical forces did not fail to exploit and which did nothing to enhance the legitimacy of the Government's position.

Three features of this cleavage alignment are of further interest. First, ethnicity was notable for its absence – for perhaps the first time in a major Nigerian political conflict. In this sense, the strike and the conflict underlying it represented a truly 'cross-cutting' cleavage. The General Strike drew both mass support and leadership from all major ethnic groups. For the labour movement, this was not a new phenomenon but a reflection of the basic irrelevance of ethnicity, even to those disputes that had deeply divided it in the past, and of the scant gains and great costs that 'communally based political strategies' promised both trade union leaders and the rank and file (Wolpe, 1974: 185). It was not surprising to find that the JAC secretary in the Western capital of Ibadan was an Igbo, while this position was held in the Eastern city of Port Harcourt by a Yoruba (Melson, 1970: 782). There is also evidence to suggest that among the workers themselves there was a good deal less ethnic antagonism and more positive feeling toward other ethnic groups than is commonly imagined.[6] Thus, despite the deeply troubling issues raised by the conflict, its transcendence of ethnicity was a hopeful sign for those who saw ethnic polarisation as the nation's greatest threat. To the extent that the workers' class-consciousness and opposition to the political class persisted, the General Strike might have represented an important step toward defusing, if not purging, the curse of 'tribalism' in politics.

On the other hand, the essential cleavage in the conflict did parallel and reflect to some extent the long-standing tension between North and South. As manifested in the strike, this was a political rather than simply ethnic or regional tension – a special hostility to the NPC, and fear of its perpetual domination of the Federation. Since well before the confrontation, this had been a concern of the more radical labour leaders, sharply reflected in their pointed attacks on 'Northern feudalism' and in their opposition to the regional system. In this sense, the General Strike touched and deepened a line of tension that had already been rubbed raw in the Western Regional crisis and especially the census crisis. 'It was lost on only a few that the Joint Action Committee was led by Southerners, most of whom supported the Action Group or the [NCNC], and that it was in confrontation with a government which was dominated by the [NPC]' (Melson, 1970: 785).

This may explain why the strike drew support from progressives in the AG and the NCNC, and finally from NCNC President Dr Okpara, who, by the time of the General Strike, had just lost the bitter showdown over the census. It may also explain why the strike was less vigorous in the North, and why it was denounced by Northern labour leader Ibrahim Nock, who had embarked upon a strategy of currying favour with the NPC (Cohen, 1974: 171).

In a second respect as well, the General Strike reinforced an existing cleavage in the country. Labour's attack on the profligacy, inefficiency, and corruption of the political class tapped a theme that had first been brought to national attention by Chief Awolowo and then dramatised during the Action Group split. Every scholarly account of the strike is more or less agreed on the importance of this wider attack on the Nigerian establishment as a motive and theme in the conflict. In this sense, the support lent to the strikers by politicians like Okpara was not reciprocal: the strike was an expression of disgust with the entire political class. One cannot read the statements and comments of labour leaders (both radical and moderate) and not be struck by this.

The outcome

Union leaders emerged from their negotiations with the Okotie-Eboh committee on 13 June claiming a decisive victory over the Federal Government. This was not some kind of rationalisation to enable them to call a halt to the strike without losing face. Most journalistic accounts and retrospective analyses have viewed the outcome of the confrontation as a victory for organised labour (*West Africa*, 20 June 1964: 670; Friedland, 1965: 9; Cohen, 1974: 168).

The final resolution of the central issue of wages was not so much a victory as a compromise: something between what the Government had been prepared to pay and what the trade unionists had sought. But the Government's original offer of wage increases – indeed, its appointment of the Morgan Commission – had themselves resulted from trade union pressure the previous autumn, and the very fact that the Government had been shaken from its arrogance and brought to the bargaining table was something of a victory for labour. In fact, perhaps the most significant outcome of the conflict was not the final wage settlement but the worker solidarity that led to it. The participation of virtually the entire wage labour force from every part of the country, the grinding to a halt of the economic life of the nation, the discipline of the strikers in eschewing violence and in persisting for thirteen days, the last few in derisive defiance of the Prime Minister's ultimatum to return to work – these remarkable features of the strike showed the trade unions to be more powerful than the Government.

This was confirmed in the Government's strike-ending concessions, which amounted to Government recognition of the strike as an expression of legitimate protest and as a legitimate *method* of protest. In particular, the withdrawal of the dismissal notices and the broad guarantee against penalisation of the strikers was a humiliating retreat from the Government's ultimatum of only a few days before, and a candid confession that it lacked the power to execute its threat.

If the conflict is viewed first and foremost as a struggle for power, the unions may be seen to have won several political victories over the ten months of confrontation (Table 6.1). In September 1963, they demanded 'a high-powered Commission' to investigate 'the existing colonial wage structure, remuneration and other conditions of service' and to examine and make recommendations on 'demands for (1) a general upward revision of salaries and wages of junior employees in both Government and Private Establishments; (2) the abolition of the daily wage rate system and the introduction of a national minimum wage'. When the Government refused to accept these terms of reference, the unions struck, and three days later the Government conceded, especially on the inclusion of private employees. The terms of reference for the Morgan Commission employed verbatim the union language save for two cosmetic changes (Melson, 1970: 778, 780). This preliminary outcome was an important victory for labour, and in 1964 it was followed by others. The General Strike paralysed the national economy and quickly brought public release of both the Morgan Report and the Government White Paper. The unions' continuation of the strike in demand for higher wages moved a frustrated Government to deliver an ultimatum that they defiantly and successfully resisted, forcing the

Table 6.1   Issues and outcomes in the labour-government conflict, 1963–1964

Issue	Union Action	Outcome
1. JAC demand (19 Sept. 1963) for commission to review wages and employment conditions in public and private sectors and Federal Government's delay.	Partially effective national strike beginning 27 Sept. 1963, and scheduled to continue through Republic Day.	*Government concedes* to appointment of the Commission under JAC's terms of reference (early October 1963).
2. a) JAC demand for release of Morgan Report and subsequently for release of the Government's White Paper (May 1964).	Launching of General Strike beginning 1 June 1964.	Immediate: National economy is paralysed Morgan Report and White Paper are released 3 June 1964.
b) JAC demand for higher pay increases than offered by Government (3 June).	Continuation and spread of strike.	Government issues back-to-work ultimatum as precondition for negotiations.
c) Government ultimatum to return to work.	Continuation of strike in defiance of Prime Minister.	*Government ultimatum fails*, and it is forced to negotiate seriously.
		FINAL OUTCOMES *Trade Union Victory* Government forced to accept Morgan Report as basis for negotiations, to withdraw dismissals, and to guarantee no penalisation of strikers.
BASIC ISSUES 1. *Trade Union power* (organised labour vs. Government authority)		
2. *Higher pay for Workers* (wage structure)		*Compromise* JAC wins pay increases higher than White Paper but lower than Morgan recommendations.
3. *Inequality* corruption, privileges, extravagance of political class		*No Resolution*

Government to back down to the negotiating table and to concede what amounted to a major political and psychological union victory. Finally, the resulting wage negotiations brought compromise, but only after the power of the unions had been firmly established and that of the Government visibly diminished.

It should be noted, however, that not all labour viewed the outcome as a clear victory. Eastern Nigerian labour leaders, overruled after strenuous argument, bitterly opposed the JAC decision to call off the strike and resume negotiations. And union leaders from Port Harcourt (and probably other labour activists as well) found the final agreement wanting in its failure to address the broader issue of inequality – the extravagant benefits and allowances of senior officials, the widespread political corruption, and so on (Wolpe, 1974: 192).

Causes of the conflict

In the immediate sense, the General Strike was provoked by 'the frustrating procrastinations of the federal and regional governments in dealing with long-standing trade union demands for wage increases, the abolition of the arbitrary system of maintaining most government workers as "temporary workers," and the establishment of an adequate machinery for union negotiations with the federal government' (Friedland, 1965: 7). But the Government's procrastination was simply the fuse for a complex resentment that had long been brewing. The specific grievances over work and wages were reinforced by more diffuse conditions that inflamed the relationship between government and labour. These other contributing factors were poverty, inequality, and corruption.

The conditions of life for the urban wage labourer in Nigeria were extremely harsh. Income was inadequate even to meet the most minimal needs of subsistence, the Morgan Commission found, and even the large raises it recommended were not sufficient to provide what it called a 'living wage'. In metropolitan Lagos, which had by far the greatest concentration of wage workers, a 1964 United Nations report found the older section of town to contain an average of twenty people per house and three people per room, with a quarter of income going for 'such very poor accommodation.' The shortage of decent, low-cost housing was accompanied by a transport shortage that necessitated a two-hour journey to work each morning for many workers. Overcrowding, dampness, and poor ventilation in housing, along with a contaminated water supply and primitive sewerage, led to extraordinary death rates from pneumonia, bronchitis, malaria, dysentery, and diarrhoea. These diseases afflicted children in particular: the UN found that more than half of all deaths in Lagos in 1960 occurred among children under five years of age (*West Africa*, 4 July 1964: 735).

Higher wages alone would not relieve these problems. Nigerians ached to see rapid socioeconomic development, and impatiently expected government to deliver it. The absence of rapid development progress since Independence was an important element in the general disenchantment with government that so heavily motivated the strikes. Young Nigerians, who were pouring out of schools by the hundreds of thousands, held especially high expectations, and for the many who could not find work the bitterness with government failure was especially severe, amounting in many cases to a sense of betrayal. After the 1963 strike, and again during the 1964, *West Africa* expressed this rising tide of frustration in some stinging questions:

> The long-term answers are obvious. But how long will it be before official bodies can make an impression on Nigerian urban housing? How long before there is everywhere enough food for the swelling millions? How long before there is adequate public transport? How long before there are sufficient sources of revenue to allow taxes on the most widely consumed imports to be reduced? In the meantime, why should Nigeria's workers be expected to make sacrifices for the sake of the development plans when they see little sacrifice among the politicians or the rich? (6 June 1964: 617)

Implicit in this last question were the causal elements that transformed deprivation into injustice and misery into militancy. The extraordinary inequality in wages between junior and senior officials was a prominent theme of union leaders, but it appears also to have been a strong motivation among the rank and file. In his survey of trade unionists in July 1964, Robert Melson found that 'when asked about the causes of the strike, more than 90 per cent indicated low salaries of workers and the salaries of senior civil servants and politicians' (Melson, 1970: 786).

Closely related to this was the corruption that supplemented these already generous salaries and allowances, the extravagant personal consumption through which this wealth was boastfully and tastelessly displayed, and the 'squandermania' that could find the money for 'prestige' edifices like multi-storey office buildings but not for low-cost urban housing. This behaviour embittered and emboldened the unions, leading them to dismiss out of hand the Government's protestations that it could not afford substantial wage increases. 'That is their job,' said Samuel Bassey when asked where the Government should find the money to pay higher wages. 'All I see is that they are spending plenty of money on themselves. It's time we got our fair share' (*West Africa*, 16 November 1963: 1291). More discreetly, the Morgan Commission suggested that the money could be found by 'rigorous pruning of expenses', especially official allowances (*West Africa*, 13 June 1964: 649). Indeed, 'the public share of [its] proposals could have been financed by abolishing the automobile allowance' (Abernethy, 1969: 251).

Diffuse disenchantment with the gross privilege, arrogance, venality, and mismanagement of the political class thus interacted with the specific working class grievances and hardships to produce increasing labour militancy. In the context of these accumulated resentments and frustrations, the haughty, dilatory response of Government officials to union demands was like a match to dry brush.

Effects on democracy

The meaning for democracy in Nigeria of the 1964 General Strike lay in its explicit challenge to the Government's authority. The unions addressed their demands to the Governments of the Federation not necessarily as employers, but, in the words of Lawrence Borha, 'as the authority of the state which not only has direct responsibility to protect workers in all sectors ... but also the obligation to bring about a more rational economic structure' (quoted in Melson, 1970: 770). Implicitly, they were arguing that the Governments had so far failed in this responsibility – calling into question their right to command state authority.

The confrontation between organised labour and the Federal Government had the effect of further eroding the legitimacy of the regime. Popular support and sympathy were behind the strikers – indeed, in the larger cities, which mattered the most politically, the strikers *were* the population. Even so crucial an extension of the state's authority as the police hesitated to back up the Government in the crisis.

In fact the strikers in Ibadan at least were able to come to an amicable deal with the police, a situation that occurred elsewhere in the country. One private informant described how, in a large British-owned motor distributor's workshop in Ibadan, the police constables played football with the strikers while the sergeant was left to score nice legal points . . . with the management. That this cooperation may have been widespread was indicated in a demand by H. P. Adebola that the police should be included in a wage settlement. (Cohen, 1974: 167)

The strike also exposed the precariousness of the Government's hold on power. The fact that it had to call upon the army and the police to suppress the strike (even though little violent confrontation resulted) was a sign of weakness. The inability of the Government to end the strike – or to prevent its near-total disruption of the economy – save through heavy concessions to the workers was an indication of outright powerlessness. The inept handling of the strike, the consistent miscalculation of the unions' determination and fortitude, and the ultimatum followed by concession further added to the impression of a weak, vacillating, ineffectual government – so vividly symbolised by the unions' scornful defiance of the Prime Minister. As a result, the Federal Government was also discredited as 'weak and incompetent' in the eyes of the employers, 'who felt completely betrayed' by its capitulation 'at the very moment when it appeared the strike might be breaking' (Wolpe, 1974: 192–3).

The legitimacy of the regime was also seriously eroded by the attention the crisis focused on rampant political corruption and waste. This had been a central theme in the challenge of the Awolowo Action Group, and it persisted in political dialogue (especially within the NCNC) even after the Action Group's destruction. It is likely that the strike – following so closely upon the Western Regional crisis, the census crisis, and the imprisonment of Chief Awolowo – heightened the growing public disillusionment with the politicians and, by extension, the political regime. This may be inferred from the findings of David Abernethy's survey of Southern Nigerian school children, administered in June and July of 1964. Perhaps more significant than the total proportion of negative perceptions about politics was the tendency for negative views to increase with greater education (and so greater exposure to and understanding of politics). Among sixth form students, negative views of the politicians were more than twice as common as positive ones. In addition, 'Greater education also seem[ed] to breed an unwillingness on the part of Nigerian students to enter politics themselves' (Abernethy, 1969: 217; 291–2). It would be consistent with other evidence to conjecture that this cynicism among the young further increased with university education and junior professional experience, as in the bureaucracy – or the army.

For the strikers, the attack on corruption was not so much a calculated move as a gradual, spontaneous release of accumulated anger, which then took on a momentum of its own. In the mass rallies in Port Harcourt, 'trade union impatience at the federal government's intransigence manifested itself in increasingly aggressive attacks on corruption and the privileges enjoyed by the political establishment' (Wolpe, 1974: 190). Robin Cohen writes:

> The 1964 strike at first represented the claims of a group who did not necessarily articulate a mass populist will against the government, but rather sought to get their own share . . . of the benefits of economic growth. As the strike progressed, however, it began to raise possibilities of a more fundamental order. Many workers during the strike were not simply begging for their share of the national cake, but were explicitly threatening the political system itself. The government had also undermined any credibility it still retained as to its preparedness to concede to democratic pressures. (Cohen, 1974: 168)

This failure to perceive in the strike a deeper threat to their whole political system was perhaps the most serious miscalculation of Federal Government leaders, who appeared little moved by the warnings of sober commentators that 'if Nigeria's political leaders do not stand together to find a just and peaceful solution to the present crisis, they might fall together' (*West Africa*, 6 June 1964: 617). Their fall was a year and a half off yet, but its roots were already visible. For the strike not only heavily damaged the moral authority of the Government but exposed what Kirk-Greene (1971: 20) has termed its 'jelly-kneed element'. 'It would not perhaps be stretching credulity too far to assert that some young majors in the Nigerian armed forces clearly perceived this fact' (Cohen, 1974: 168).

Feedback effects

If the brief 1963 strike had altered political realities in Nigeria, the thirteen-day strike of 1964 seemed, at the time, to have fundamentally transformed them. Trade unions had become a political force to be reckoned with and class had become an important political cleavage, crosscutting traditional divisions. It seemed reasonable to expect that this would carry over into the approaching Federal Election, which was less than six months away. The Socialist Workers' and Farmers' Party had been publicly launched in 1963, and among its key figures were such radical labour leaders as Bassey and Goodluck. 'Although it remained very small, the SWFP [was helping] to swell discontent with the workings of the System of Rewards among segments of the participant strata' (Post and Vickers, 1973: 98). In the fervour of the 1964 strike, Michael Imoudu had obtained a mandate to form a Nigerian Labour Party, which he launched in August of that year. The enormous popular support for the strike seemed to portend a significant electoral breakthrough by one or both of these class-based parties. If either succeeded it would mean that the strike had truly reorganised Nigerian politics. Even if one of these parties could establish an electoral foothold, and modestly loosen the pull of communal interests in elections, the complicating effect on the cleavage structure would be salutary. In the end, none of this happened (for reasons that will be explored in the next chapter), but in the early summer of 1964 it seemed a real possibility.

One outcome of the strike that seemed certain to last was the enhanced power and militancy of the unions. At the very least, they seemed likely to remain a forceful advocate of labour interests, and their power to challenge the regime on more general political grounds could no longer be disregarded. This did not augur well for the prospects of the regime so long as it continued to be dominated by the NPC, as seemed likely.

In an economic sense, labour's enhanced power had both positive and negative implications. To the extent that trade union pressure actually reduced inequality and waste, it figured to enhance the long-term stability of the regime. But strike action was costly to the nation – the lost output in 1964 ran into the millions of pounds – and the outcome of a successful strike had its dubious effects as well. For one thing, it fuelled inflation; even before the increases were announced, market women in Lagos and other cities raised their prices by margins often greater than the pay increases. And to pay for the increases, the Government announced a more than 50 per cent increase in import duties a month after the settlement (*West Africa*, 15 August 1964: 902). Strikes could also increase unemployment, as evidenced in the decision of many firms to lay off redundant workers in the face of the higher wage rates. As strikes continued throughout the summer in private industry, labour militancy threatened further to impair the already battered economic development plan.

Finally, in mobilising opposition to the NPC, the strike seemed likely to heighten the tension between North and South, especially in the political arena. NPC leaders felt betrayed by NCNC leaders from the East who 'had agreed in private to the government's proposals, only to denounce them in their own Region' (Schwarz, 1968: 164). *West Africa* would prove astute in its observation of 'signs that the strike is the last nail in the coffin of the Federal Coalition, and that the negotiations following its end may find the new NCNC-Action Group Alliance taking a different line from the NPC and the NNDP' (13 June 1964: 646).

7 The 1964 Federal Election Crisis

'I have one advice to give to our politicians: If they have decided to destroy our national unity, then they should summon a round-table conference to decide how our national assets should be divided, before they seal their doom by satisfying their lust for office. . . . Should the politicians fail to heed this warning, I will venture the prediction that the experience of the Democratic Republic of the Congo will be child's play, if it ever comes to our turn to play such a tragic role.' – President Nnamdi Azikiwe, 10 December 1964, in a 'Dawn Address' to the nation (Mackintosh, 1966: 581).

If the General Strike had deflected politics from the running ethnic and regional conflict to a fresh line of cleavage, this effect was short-lived. As the campaign for the Federal Election heated up during the second half of 1964, all of the energy of Nigerian politics was sucked into the vortex of ethnoregional conflict. Historic tensions between North and South and between the Igbos and their ethnic rivals now reasserted themselves with a vengeance. Vituperative rhetoric was joined by widespread violence and repression, as the main political parties – now polarised into two competing alliances – clashed head-on in a momentous 'struggle for supremacy' that would produce the worst political crisis in Nigerian history. Several elements of this crisis were foreshadowed in the Mid-West Regional Election of February 1964.

PRELUDE: MID-WEST REGIONAL ELECTION

A decisive shift in Nigerian politics began to unfold in October 1963 in a Federal by-election in the Mid-West, when the NPC intruded directly into Southern politics for the first time (Chapter 5). The coalition whose campaign the NPC successfully led, the Mid-West Democratic Front, was composed of Premier Akintola's UPP and 'The Apostle' John Edokpolor's Mid-West People's Congress. The

NCNC bitterly attributed its narrow defeat to 'the introduction of dirty tribal politics by the leaders of the NPC into their campaigns'. The NPC, which had not been averse to exploiting long-standing Urhobo-Igbo tension, denounced the NCNC allegations as proof that the NCNC was only paying lip-service to Nigerian unity. Earlier, Northern Premier Sir Ahmadu Bello had predicted that the NPC would win the Mid-West Regional election the following year (*West Africa*, 26 October 1963: 1211).

The stakes in that approaching election went beyond the spoils of regional power. This was the opening battle for the Federal Election, due to follow only ten months later. An NPC victory on what the NCNC considered virtually home turf would be a devastating strategic setback, given the tendency of the ruling party in each region to develop overwhelming electoral dominance. It was clear to NCNC leaders that, whatever the new allocation of seats resulting from the second census count (yet to be announced), control of the Mid-West was essential if they hoped to win Federal power. The NPC, on its part, needed a Southern political base, and it apparently lacked confidence that Premier Akintola's party could win an election in the West. An electoral base in the Mid-West would help to insure against an NCNC sweep of the South, which could give it national power if the forthcoming census revealed a Southern population majority (Abernethy, 1964: 10).

A key question in the Mid-West Election was how the Action Group (once a strong political force in the area) would align itself as it struggled to regain its political stature. On 30 November, talks between Chief Osadebay, NCNC Mid-West Leader, and Alhaji Adegbenro, Acting Leader of the Action Group, concluded in the announcement of an electoral alliance between the two parties. Both leaders emphasised the long-term national significance of the pact. Chief Osadebay said, 'It is now time for these two parties to come together. . . . It would then be a struggle between the "progressives" of the South and the "conservatives" of the North' (quoted in Post and Vickers, 1973: 93–4).

But the NCNC was bitterly divided on whether to ally (and had even been negotiating simultaneously with the UPP). In December, the NCNC Central Working Committee refused to ratify the alliance with the AG and Chief Festus Okotie-Eboh–NCNC National Treasurer, Federal Finance Minister, and perhaps the most powerful Mid-Western politician – openly denounced it as 'an act of bad faith'. With him stood the potent political machine of the Otu Edo (the communal party of Benin), led since 1950 'in bitter and successful combat against the Action Group' by Okotie-Eboh's close friend and ally, Chief Humphrey Omo-Osagie. Yoruba NCNC leaders, who had not yet defected to Akintola's new party, were also distressed by the possible association with their long-time political foe and even Chief Akinfosile and Chief Benson, who would stick with the NCNC, openly condemned it (Post and Vickers, 1973: 94–6). The pact withstood these objections, but it did not keep the Action Group from fielding its own candidates, who failed miserably.

The NCNC won a convincing victory in the election of 3 February, capturing roughly 60 per cent of the popular vote and more than 80 per cent of the seats, defeating some of the MDF's most prominent leaders (*West Africa*, 8 February 1964: 159). But while the election was generally 'free and fair' the campaign was marred by violence and rising ethnic and regional tension. NCNC campaign teams played heavily on anti-Northern sentiment: 'The MDF's alliance with the NPC was decried as the opening wedge of "Arab" interference in southern politics' (Abernethy, 1964: 10). The MDF, in turn, exploited local fears of Eastern domination, and the specific charge (accompanied by Urhobo expulsions and resignations from the NCNC) 'that Chief Okotie-Eboh was discriminating against the Urhobo people' (Abernethy, 1964: 10). Several violent disturbances also occurred, and a plot to kill an MDF candidate was alleged. In a preview of the coming Federal Election campaign, each party accused the other of thuggery, and all of them finally reached a formal agreement to abandon violence (*West Africa*, 25 January 1964: 91; 8 February 1964: 159).

The violent character and ethnic and regional polarisation of the Mid-West Regional Election – in a very small Region at a moment otherwise free of political crisis – did not augur well for the democratic prospect in Nigeria. As *West Africa* observed at the peak of the campaign, 'the "quiet period" that has prevailed over the last few months seems to be over, and we are now entering a period of "no holds barred" – a struggle for supremacy which may be decisive in determining the future history of Nigeria' (25 January 1964: 91). Although the Mid-Western election saw the involvement of two national parties outside their base region, it did not significantly counter the ethnic and regional character of national politics. Both of the direct contenders, the MDF and the mid-western NCNC, were essentially regionalist parties, and the ties of the latter to its parent party were somewhat tenuous, as evidenced in the intense opposition to the AG alliance among sections of the Mid-West NCNC. An important element of this tension was ethnic: Chief Osadebay was an Igbo, Chief Omo-Osagie and a plurality in Benin division were Binis (Post and Vickers, 1973: 96).

Osadebay himself was far from an extreme ethnic nationalist. Married to a Yoruba woman, he showed low tolerance for 'tribalism' and an increasing disenchantment (reflective of much of the younger, educated elite) with sectional politics. In an interview with *West Africa* (15 February 1964: 173) shortly after his election, the new Premier criticised the British party-system as artificial in the Nigerian context: 'The ideal thing would be for the parties to merge and then divide again into two – Progressives and Conservatives – across tribe, region, and religion.' But this would not happen, he argued, because of the opportunistic nature of Nigerian politics, and so he favoured a one-party system that would incorporate 'the essence of true democracy', which was not party competition *per se* but the right to disagree.

In the aftermath of the Regional election, tensions within the Mid-West NCNC deepened. Early in March 1964, Chief Omo-Osagie sent a circular to branches of his Otu Edo protesting the failure of the NCNC to create a promised Deputy Premiership for him after the election. Warning of the difficulty of dealing with 'Ibo organisation', the Chief suggested that the Bini people could strike a more rewarding deal with the NPC, and revealed that, because the NCNC had overriden their protest against alliance with the AG, he and Chief Okotie-Eboh were forming a new party that would be supported by the NPC (Post and Vickers, 1973: 96).

The new party never did surface, but from this time on it appeared that Chief Okotie-Eboh would swing his political machine to the NPC if ever the occasion demanded it. Coupled with the simultaneous defection of most of the major NCNC politicians in the West, this friction accentuated the declining fortunes of the NCNC. 'It was becoming more and more evident that the Northern People's Congress was the decisive force in the System. . . . Increasingly, individual politicians were coming to feel that it would be best for them and for their [cultural] sections if they aligned with the major force in the country and tried to negotiate for themselves some place in the System of Rewards' (Post and Vickers, 1973: 197).

REDUCTION TO A BIPOLAR STRUGGLE

Formation of alliances

The NCNC suffered a shattering blow when most of its Yoruba politicians defected to Chief Akintola's new NNDP, but new opportunities and imperatives quickly presented themselves. The Yoruba defections removed the most powerful opposition within the NCNC to an alliance with the Action Group and dramatically increased the importance of such an alliance to the NCNC's electoral goals. These new realities were immediately apparent to the NCNC leadership, which wasted no time in calling for a full-fledged union of the two parties. This was still stoutly opposed by the party's Mid-Western and (remaining) Western leaders, such as Chiefs Okotie-Eboh and Benson, and even by some AG elements as well. But the dominant Eastern wing of the NCNC, led by Dr Okpara, had no acceptable alternative. It had lost most of its base in the West. Its Mid-Western wing was split and even the leader of the 'loyal' faction, Chief Osadebay, was inclined toward a certain independence. Moreover, the conflict over the census had since erupted again, underscoring the impossibility of continued cooperation with the NPC. Meanwhile, the NPC was moving aggressively to forge a Southern base in the Mid-West and West. In negotiations with Chiefs Akintola and Fani-Kayode, it quietly cemented a relationship with the new NNDP in March 1964.

Recognising the urgent importance of a union with the Action Group, Dr Okpara announced a tour of the Western Region to reassure loyal NCNC elements, defying the Akintola Government's ban on public meetings and its 'clear warnings' to keep out of the Region (Mackintosh, 1966: 563). With Action Group support, the Eastern Premier commenced his tour on 31 May 1964. The following day, he announced 'to cheering crowds' in Lagos that the Federal Coalition would come to an end at the close of the present Parliament and appealed for a coalition of 'all progressive elements in the NCNC and the Action Group' (Mackintosh, 1966: 564). Press accounts of his speech were accompanied by reports from Kaduna that NPC leaders had decided to drop the NCNC from the Federal Coalition in favour of the NNDP, and to rule alone after the next elections if necessary.

On 3 June, after meeting with Alhaji Adegbenro at Chief Awolowo's home in Ibadan, Okpara announced a formal alliance between the NCNC and the Action Group. Together they vowed 'to wipe out neo-colonialism and reactionary elements from the public life of the country' and stressed the underlying similarity of their ideologies. Growing bolder in his denuciations of the NPC, Dr Okpara ended his week-long tour condemning the NNDP as 'the manoeuvre of the NPC to stifle democracy in the West' (Mackintosh, 1966: 564).

The union of the long-time bitter political enemies marked the beginning of a wave of mergers and realignments that continued throughout the summer of 1964 until the welter of parties had been reorganised into two competing grand alliances. Actually, the process had begun at the close of 1963 when the radical NEPU and the Tiv-based UMBC joined to form the Northern Progressive Front (NPF), agreeing on a common programme, symbol and list of candidates for the Federal Election. In January 1964, they were joined by two smaller opposition parties, the Kano People's Party and the Zamfara Commoners party (from eastern Sokoto).[1] Since the NEPU had long been allied with the NCNC and the UMBC with the AG, it was to be expected that the two new alliances would unite. NEPU President Aminu Kano and UMBC President Joseph S. Tarka joined Dr Okpara and Alhaji Adegbenro on the directing committee of what was rechristened on 1 September the United Progressive Grand Alliance (UPGA).

In the meantime, the NPC was drawing into its own alliance the new NNDP and various Southern opposition groups, including the Mid-West Democratic Front and a faction of the Niger Delta Congress (an ethnic minority party allied with the NPC since 1959). This grouping was formally announced on 20 August 1964, and subsequently named itself the Nigerian National Alliance (NNA).

After much discussion, the Nigerian Labour Party was also formed in August 1964 but with relatively little support, even from among radical union leaders. Michael Imoudu, its founder, would be its only candidate in the election. Moderate labour leaders opposed direct labour involvement in electoral politics while other radical leaders, such as Goodluck and Bassey, supported Dr Tunji Otegbeye's Socialist Workers' and Farmers' Party. The SWAFP negotiated for some time to join the UPGA, but these negotiations foundered on its demand for some of the choice urban seats and on Dr Otegbeye's continuing attacks on 'big men at the top of the UPGA'. Although no agreement was reached, 'it was evident . . . that the SWAFP was behind UPGA . . . and Dr Otegbeye urged sympathisers to vote accordingly where there was no SWAFP candidate' (Mackintosh, 1966: 566).

Escalating conflict

The formation of the two grand alliances was accompanied by rising political conflict between them and within the NCNC. The latter widened the continuing rift between the Eastern wing of the party and its Federal Ministers, especially those from the West and Mid-West, who had long emphatically opposed any association with the AG and who saw their privileged positions as dependent on continued cooperation with the NPC. Though neither Chief Okotie-Eboh nor Chief Benson openly attacked the new alliance once it was announced, both made their disenchantment known and sought to repair the rift in the Federal Coalition. Seizing upon the Prime Minister's endorsement of a 'national' coalition following the elections, Chief Benson called for a national Government in which each major party would play the dual role of government and opposition and all major regional interests would be represented (Post and Vickers, 1973: 116–8). Okotie-Eboh was also known to favour continuation of NCNC–NPC Coalition, and rumours, which he vigorously denied, had him trying to effect some reconciliation between the two parties in August.

More was at stake in the coming election than a possible challenge to the structure of privilege. Chief Benson may have been quite sincere, as Prime Minister Tafawa Balewa appeared to be, in his concern about the danger to national unity of an election that left one of the two alliances and hence two of the four regional governments completely shut out of Federal power. It was a concern shared by independent observers:

> Chief Benson says, as we have, that it is impossible for a Federal government to rule Nigeria effectively unless the governing parties in at least a majority of the regions, and certainly the governing party in the biggest regions, are represented at the centre. . . . As the Prime Minister said, at a later stage Nigeria will be able to 'afford' a multi-party system at the centre. Now, so serious are the problems facing the country, so fragile is its unity, so many are the threats to law and order, that a 'national' government, however constituted, seems essential. (*West Africa*, 22 August 1964: 929–30).

But the very tensions that made a 'national' government seem imperative to some also made it unlikely. With the realignment into opposing grand alliances, polarisation had proceeded too far to avoid a direct confrontation for national power. Strained by repeated conflicts of interest over the previous five years, the Federal Coalition had cracked irrevocably in the census crisis and had disintegrated further in the 1964 General Strike. NCNC reaction to Benson's proposal was extremely negative, citing not only the danger of 'populist dictatorship' but the absence of any basis of political or cultural unity for such a government.

Similar scepticism was voiced in July by the Northern Premier, who ruled out a new coalition with the NCNC under any circumstance, declaring: 'The Ibos have never been true friends of the North and never will be.' It was the responsibility of all Northerners, he added, to see that none of the Northern constituencies was won by 'the Southern politicians' (quoted in Mackintosh, 1966: 564).[2] The Prime Minister continued to express his preference for a national government including the NCNC and even possibly the AG, but conceded that the NPC was preparing its own electoral alliance (Mackintosh, 1966: 565). While urging support for the Coalition Government, the President suggested he would resign if the Coalition agreement was 'repudiated by either party'.

Early in September, the NPC–NNDP alliance was cemented with the appointment of two prominent NNDP MPs, Chief Ayo Rosiji and Chief Adisa Akinloye, to Sir Abubakar's cabinet as Ministers of State (without portfolio). The NCNC condemned the appointments as a breach of the coalition agreement, and Alhaji Adegbenro denounced them as 'a most grievous rape of democracy' (*West Africa*, 12 September 1964: 1027).

Electoral expectations

Such was the tone into which the campaign was sinking at the end of September, when Parliament concluded its last session before the general election.[3] Leaders of the NPC alliance, the NNA, were supremely confident of an election victory. Dr Okpara himself had observed that the effect of the census results was to indicate that one party had won and another lost before the election ever took place. By any dispassionate analysis, the NNA was the overwhelming favourite. Throughout the Federation, each ruling party was continuing to tighten its grip on the politics of its region, and this trend had been especially dramatic in the North, where the opposition, falling from 33 victories to ten between 1959 and 1961, had since disappeared due to carpet-crossing, internal dissension, and lack of support. The NEPU was weakened by internal conflict, and the Bornu Youth Movement and Ilorin Talaka Parapo had both collapsed. 'Only in Tiv division was any serious will to resist evident' (Mackintosh, 1966: 582). By 1964, it seemed impossible for the NPC to be defeated in the North in more than a few constituencies. And even if its alliance partners were completely shut out in the East and Mid-West, the NPC could count on the NNDP to win some seats in the West. Indeed, given Akintola's control of the regional government for the preceding two years, there was reason to believe his party could win the bulk of the 57 Western seats. Considering as well the poor state of Action Group finances and organisation, it was difficult to imagine how the NNA could be denied a majority of the 312 Federal seats (Post and Vickers, 1973: 138–9; Mackintosh, 1966: 581).

And yet 'in the early days of the campaign Dr Okpara and Alhaji Adegbenro talked and behaved as if they really thought victory was possible' (Mackintosh, 1966: 581). Not unrealistically, the NCNC assumed it could sweep the 70 Eastern and 14 Mid-Western seats, and in the West NCNC and AG organisers conceded just a few seats to the NNDP, figuring that an appeal to Yoruba unity, focused around the principles of Chief Awolowo and the memory of prosperity under his rule in the West, could rally popular support and show Akintola's regime to rest on the thin foundations of coercion and NPC support (Post and Vickers, 1973: 140). These assumptions and a sweep of the four Lagos seats would give UPGA roughly 140 seats, just 17 short of a majority. Given the 1959 victories of 25 and 8 seats by the UMBC and NEPU respectively, UPGA leaders believed the necessary margin could be won in the North with a vigorous campaign. 'Indeed UPGA hopes went beyond this, since it was firmly believed that the Kano People's Party would bring it a number of seats', as a result of Kano resistance to the forced resignation of Emir Sanusi (Post and Vickers, 1973: 139).

In the end, these assumptions proved extremely naïve, shaped by what Mackintosh has called 'an element of irrationalism' – imagining 'that sending money, lawyers, thugs and speakers a few months before an election could undo the damage and decline of the past five years'. Perhaps this was self-delusion induced by the grim imperatives of the situation. More likely it stemmed from the same ignorance as the Action Group's stunning miscalculation in 1959. Mackintosh (1966: 582) concludes:

> The only explanation that carries any conviction is the simple failure of Southern leaders to study or understand the North. Long before, when Chief Awolowo had heard that elections in the North were to be direct and secret, he declared that the AG was sure to win as the Northern *Talakawa* were bound to cast aside their feudal rulers. He was completely wrong in his assessment of Northern voters and their outlook and yet such delusions persisted. In 1964, each Eastern Cabinet Minister was given some money and told to take his official car and campaign in an allotted area of the North. How it was thought that Ibo ministers, unable to speak Hausa, with no local knowledge, were to win over Northern peasants whose chief feeling for Ibos was one of dislike, is hard to imagine.

CAMPAIGN ISSUES

As with past elections, the 1964 campaign featured a 'high road' and a 'low road'. The former articulated lofty, if rather vague statements of principles and policy goals. The latter, the plane on which the election was actually fought, saw the politicians once again mobilise popular support through rank appeals to ethnic and regional prejudice.

Issues of policy and ideology

The high road of the campaign was officially launched on 10 October with the release of the UPGA election manifesto. As would the NNA manifesto two weeks later, the UPGA programme contained a number of proposals (which 'tended to be vaguely worded and full of generalities') to bring rapid social and economic development. Often their proposals were similar. Their differences in development strategy mainly concerned the role of government, with the UPGA emphasising comprehensive government planning (Post and Vickers, 1973: 108–9).

What most sharply distinguished the two alliances was the issue of political structure, with the UPGA advancing a number of proposals for 'Political Reconstruction', in particular the creation of more states. But UPGA itself could not agree on a specific formula, and the AG, which had long favoured strong regional powers, blocked an endorsement of Dr Okpara's proposals for a new system of some 25 states and a much stronger Centre. Thus, UPGA remained vague in its pledge to create new states, mentioning specifically only the Middle Belt and Calabar states the AG had long championed, along with the Kano state sought by the Kano People's Party. It also promised a Constituent Assembly to 'remove all defects' in the Constitution.

NCNC themes that had been muted in the alliance manifesto were given full play the day after its release, when Dr Okpara launched the UPGA 'Crusade for Total Freedom' in Lagos. Beyond the NCNC plans for new states and increased Federal powers, Dr Okpara also reiterated his proposal from the previous February to give the President authority over the Public Service Commission, the Electoral Commission, the Census and the Audit – four of the most sensitive areas of administrative responsiblity. He further called for a Privy Council – comprised of the President, a new Vice-president, President of the Senate, Prime Minister, Chief Justice, Speaker of Parliament, and Regional Governors and Premiers – 'to decide on all major operations of the Army and Police as in times of war or emergency' and for an amendment to give the Senate concurrent powers with the House (Okpara, 1964: 26). Both of these changes would have reduced Northern control of the state.

The UPGA manifesto went further than Okpara in its attack on the structure of privilege in the country. Renewing themes from the Action Group crisis and the General Strike, it declared the country 'divided between the forces of reaction, feudalism and neocolonialism on the one hand, and those of progress, democracy and socialism on the other'. The power of the 'reactionary elements' perpetuated 'a colonial system of wages' and brought a 'systematic attempt to silence opposition parties and to curtail freedom of expression'. The manifesto denounced the 'general craving for money', which had 'led to moral degeneracy..., a diminishing sense of social justice, ... corruption, selfishness', and deceit and violence by the nation's politicians and political parties (quoted in Post and Vickers, 1973: 111).

Such rhetoric, and the manifesto's emphasis on good relations with the trade unions, appeared designed to appeal to the growing numbers of people who felt alienated from the political system and the political class (Post and Vickers, 1973: 112). But there was reason to doubt the enthusiasm of the NCNC for serious social and economic reforms, and the UPGA statement stopped well short of the radical analysis and proposals advanced by the SWAFP, which called (in orthodox Marxist-Leninist terms) for the building of genuine socialism (Post and Vickers, 1973: 114).

Not surprisingly, the NNA manifesto was conservative in tone and substance. 'Peace and stability' were its watchwords. It pledged 'a fair and equitable distribution of the wealth', 'equal opportunity for all' and efforts 'to see that all ethnic groups are adequately represented in the civil service' and the various government boards and corporations. The NNA manifesto saw no conflict between competing interests – viewing the governments, the workers, and the private employers as 'members of a family' – and no need for any changes in economic or political structure, especially creation of new states. Condemning the opposition alliance for offering 'nothing except a vague ill-understood Utopia' and for wanting to destroy 'African institutions', it promised a measured pace of change that would preserve continuity with the past, working through 'our traditional institution(s)' while modifying and improving them (quoted in Post and Vickers, 1973: 112–113).

Other issues divided the two alliances as well. Although the NCNC's own Jaja Wachuku was Foreign Minister, the UPGA criticised Nigerian foreign policy for being too partial to the West and, in particular, for condoning the Western intervention in the Congo (Harris, 1965: 27). Committing the alliance 'inflexibly' to non-alignment, Dr Okpara pledged strong support for the UN and the OAU and denounced 'the dangerous attempt being made by the NPC leaders to drag Nigeria into the Arab-Israeli conflict' (Okpara, 1964: 27). Dramatising the new political alignment, the Eastern Premier now condemned Chief Awolowo's continued imprisonment, pledging that the first act of an UPGA Government would be to release him within 24 hours.

While the latter pledge carried emotional and symbolic significance in the Western Region, the alliance manifestos were mostly a sideshow for intellectuals. 'There is no real evidence that the issues of policy raised in these programmes played any part in shaping the voting decision of the average elector in 1964' (Post and Vickers, 1973: 108). Even the broad question of corruption and inequality receded from its peak salience in June as politicians drew the campaign around their most reliable, familiar and explosive issue – ethnicity.

The ethnic issue

At the peak of the census controversy in early 1964, political leaders had waged a fierce verbal war over issues of ethnic favouritism and prejudice. While the exchange of charges and epithets abated in April, the underlying animosity remained. From the start of the Federal Election campaign, it played a major role and grew in importance and intensity until it had become the dominant theme. Chief Akintola and his NNDP campaiged relentlessly against alleged ethnic favouritism and discrimination by the Igbos, resuming issues from his Government's 'White Paper' of March. The controversy over that document revealed an increasingly zero-sum view of the competition for positions and material resources: what another group achieved could only have come at the expense of one's own. Such perceptions predestined conflict.

A fitting symbol of the campaign was provided in October when the Alafin of Oyo 'was induced to bestow upon Chief Akintola the title of *Are Ona Kakanfo*, or Commander-in-Chief' (Post and Vickers, 1973: 122). The campaign was one of cultural warfare. Part of this involved the NNDP's own attempt to rally Yoruba unity, but the leading element was a crude and systematic effort to incite ethnic hatred against the Igbos, not only among the Yoruba but among Southern minority peoples as well. Broadsheets and cartoons warned that the 'mushroom army of shopkeepers and shop-owners from across the Eastern Bank of the Niger' threatened 'the total elimination of Yorubas from business and commercial fields and, of late, from market stalls and shops'. This propaganda depicted the Igbos as attempting to swallow up the government, the corporations, everything. Typical was the exhortation, 'Wake up and live. Drive UPGA Ibos from your capital city' (Post and Vickers, 1973: 124). The Region's newspaper was also employed, warning that 'the philosophy of Iboism' meant that Ibo 'unity, progress and hegemony ... must be maintained and built on the disunity, retrogression and slavery of non-Ibo' peoples (Post and Vickers, 1973: 124).

Appeals to sectional pride and prejudice were the stock-in-trade of the other parties as well, though none seemed to match the raw, pervasive bigotry of the NNDP. In the Mid-West, the main themes of the MDF were its objection to Igbo or Eastern domination and its promise of a windfall of benefits with an NNA victory.[4] The Niger Delta Congress 'also indulged in anti-Igbo propaganda' and told the minority peoples of the river delta that only the NNA would create their cherished goal of a Rivers State. As it had previously, the NPC campaigned in the North on its accomplishments for the Region, on pride in being a Northerner, and on the charge that 'its opponents were aliens in the North or, in the case of Hausa-Fulani in NEPU, irresponsible wastrels' (Mackintosh, 1966: 572–3).

The UPGA employed anti-Northern propaganda everywhere except the North, where it pledged freedom from oppression by the Native Authorities and soft-pedalled its call for new states. In the South, UPGA campaigned against Hausa–Fulani domination, alleged that the North had used its Federal power to obtain an unfair share of development resources, and vowed to create new states in the North so as to break its domination of the Federation. In its native Eastern Region, the NCNC 'capitalised on the deep resentment at the way Ibos in the North had been treated' (Mackintosh, 1966: 573).

As they had during the census crisis earlier in the year, the President and Prime Minister both became alarmed by the rising tide of 'tribalism'. Sir Abubakar closed the final meeting of Parliament warning that tribalism was the greatest danger and that it had to be fought if Nigeria was to survive as a nation (*West Africa*, 3 October 1964). Shortly thereafter, in his Independence Day broadcast, President Azikiwe bluntly denounced the atmosphere of 'mutual antagonisms, bitter recriminations and tribal discrimination'. Referring directly to the election struggle, he asked how politicians could take such delight 'in beating the tom-tom of tribal hatred' in a nation whose many religions taught love, kindness and charity, and how some leaders could carry hate to the point where 'private armies are said to be organised in order to liquidate political opponents'. Pleading for 'our interest to our motherland', Azikiwe beseeched the politicians to pursue moderation (*West Africa*, 10 October 1964).

It was the first of several Presidential appeals, which would become increasingly urgent and even apocalyptic in tone over the course of the election campaign. Among the most distressing threats to Nigerian unity and democracy, Dr Azikiwe warned, was the denial of the right to campaign to 'some opposing political parties' and the general attitude by which 'the citizens of one nation always regard their compatriots as interlopers'. This was apparently in reference to the harassment and obstruction Premier Okpara encountered as he attempted to lead an NCNC campaign tour of the Northern Region. By November, widespread official frustration of opposition campaigns, along with police repression and party thuggery, had become a major issue and a grave threat to the integrity and legitimacy of the election.

THE CONDUCT OF THE CAMPAIGN

Though the campaigns were not officially launched until October, partisans of each alliance were heatedly engaged by midsummer. As the party machineries and electoral administration were being readied, a climate of violence and extremism was developing, and reports from around the country were giving a picture of growing chaos:

> Party leaders in the Western Region have asked for police protection, the Tiv Division in Northern Nigeria (scene of much bloodshed in 1960) has experienced dozens of deaths and hundreds of arrests. Criminal gangsters become bolder and bolder in Eastern Nigeria. Trade unions, determined not to be cheated after their general strike victory, are threatening to strike again to secure all the concessions to which they feel entitled. The President is dragged into political controversy, and there is bitter recrimination between two government-controlled regional newspapers.
>
> The general election, in these circumstances, it might be thought, would appear to offer Nigeria an opportunity of choosing a Federal Government which would be sufficiently broad-based to ensure stability and produce calm. Instead, too many politicians seem to look at it as an opportunity for excluding from all power parties or leaders whom they dislike, even if these have substantial followings. (*West Africa*, 8 August 1964: 881)

As the campaign progressed, restraint further disintegrated, and anti-democratic behaviour systematically obliterated the freedom and fairness of the 1964 Federal Election. The campaign misconduct was of three types: *thuggery*, the use of hired and organised ruffians to harass, intimidate, brutalise and eliminate political opposition; *obstruction*, using the legal powers of local and regional administration to prevent the opposition from conducting speeches, rallies and campaign tours; and *repression*, legal coercion and punishment, through arrest, imprisonment, tax levies, revocation of licences and so forth, to discourage opposition and prevent it from campaigning. These practices were especially pervasive in the Northern and

Western Regions, not simply because the two NCNC governments were less inclined toward repression (having in the East no local government police), but because the UPGA strategy called for carrying the election campaign into the very heart of opposition territory. Because the UPGA was able to draw upon Chief Awolowo's still considerable popular following, and the widespread resentment engendered by Premier Akintola's heavy-handed methods of rule, the contest in the Western Region was the only one in which the victory of the ruling party was not assured. For this reason, it was also the most violent.

For the most part, violence in the 1964 campaign was not the spontaneous eruption of partisan passion but the organised, tactical deployment of hired thugs.

> Violence was not intentionally indiscriminate but had a definite place in the campaign. First, there was little if any violence used by members of one cultural section against another, despite all the appeals to primordial loyalties and invocation of hostile stereotypes. . . . Second, thuggery was not employed against the persons of leaders of opposing parties conducting campaign tours outside their own regions, partly, perhaps, because their importance gave them some immunity. The technique used in their case . . . was obstruction. (Post and Vickers, 1973: 141–2)

Organised violence appeared earliest and widest in the Western Region, where NNDP thuggery, along with the 'nervous atmosphere' generated by a Regional ban on public meetings and rumoured political purges of civil servants and teachers, led the AG to recruit its own strong-arm men. Opposition grievances by June included attacks on the NCNC's Ibadan headquarters, burning of AG cars, and damage to the houses of two AG officials. On 18 June, Alhaji Adegbenro charged there was a 'breakdown of law and order' in the Region and urged that the local government police be merged with the less blatantly partisan Nigeria Police (Mackintosh, 1966: 576–7).

No action was taken, and tension mounted steadily through the summer. In July, one of the AG's few remaining MPs was attacked and severely wounded by thugs. In August, two NNDP ministers were injured in attacks by thugs, and two other NNDP men were killed (one was dragged out of his home and beaten to death by a crowd). That same month the Region's Obas appealed to the Prime Minister for emergency legislation against thuggery and hooliganism. Such was the political climate in the West, said a coroner in his report on the death of an NNDP thug, 'that no leading politician can go out without being armed for self-defense, and that his carrying a few dangerous weapons would not be out of place' (Mackintosh, 1966: 577; *West Africa*, 29 August 1964: 923).

Probably the largest scale of violence was in Tiv Division, which seethed with mass resentment over NPC attempts to repress Tiv political organisation and with rivalry between pro- and anti-NPC factions. Rioting in February 1964 was so severe the Army had to be called in, and by September it had left hundreds dead (including many policemen), almost a thousand arrested, and a steadily deepening reservoir of hatred (*West Africa*, 5 September 1964: 999, 1007; Dent, 1966: 506–7). But the unrest continued unabated throughout the year. In October, rioters interrupted rail services. With the campaign now in full swing and the Tiv Division a major target of the UPGA, 'the NPC claimed that the disturbances were instigated and the rioters subsidised by the NCNC government of the Eastern Region. UMBC supporters put the blame on arbitrary taxation and victimisation by clan heads who were trying to force them to support the NPC' (Miners, 1971: 91). In mid-November a new wave of violence moved the Prime Minister to again call in the Army.

Obstruction and repression by government authorities were significant impediments to the UPGA campaigns in the West and North. When Okpara's campaign in the West was launched on 24 October, he was refused permission to speak at the University of Ife, and university authorities 'were lucky to avoid a riot when they attempted to restrain the students from attending it at its alternative venue at the nearby University of Ibadan' (Post and Vickers, 1973: 143, 147). On 26 October, Dr Okpara and Alhaji Adegbenro were prevented by a police roadblock from entering Premier Akintola's home town of Ogbomosho. Throughout the Western Region, NNDP 'management committees' (which replaced local government councils dissolved for their loyalty to the AG) used their control of local administration, police and courts to frustrate the UPGA campaign and punish its supporters. As the campaign wore on, they banned such activities as campaigning at night, the shouting of party slogans by children under sixteen, and in one instance, 'unnecessary alarms, provocative shouting..., offensive songs, unwholesome parades and aimless wandering' (Post and Vickers, 1973: 142, 147).

On a joint campaign tour of the North in November, Dr Okpara, Alhaji Adegbenro and NEPU President Aminu Kano were similarly confronted with bans on meetings and were barred from entering Katsina and Bauchi, home of the Prime Minister. 'They passed through village after village in which the inhabitants had been told to close their businesses and stay indoors. In the end they abandoned their tour three days early' (Post and Vickers, 1973: 148; Mackintosh, 1966: 578).

Harsher measures were employed against lesser UPGA figures in the North. The Native Authority Police and the local alkali courts came down severely upon Igbo residents who attempted to organise for the NCNC. Many were forced to flee their towns. Thousands of UPGA supporters were arrested and locked up in 'awful stinking police cells'. Many were beaten and sentenced to prison for six months or more. 'At the NEPU headquarters in Kano, confused and disoriented political refugees appeared, homeless after their farms had been burned to the ground' (Feinstein, 1973: 208). UPGA candidates and their highly resented Southern lawyers also became targets of repression. In October, NPF co-leader Joseph Tarka was arrested for incitement, and by 30 November some 45 UPGA candidates were in jail. Some of the lawyers (who were not allowed to practice in the Native Courts) were themselves arrested (Post and Vickers, 1973: 148–9; Mackintosh, 1966: 579).

Failed attempts at peace and freedom

The escalating violence, obstruction, and ethnic tension in the campaign became a source of deep concern to many Nigerians. Newspapers and traditional leaders in the West appealed for an end to the thuggery, as did the President and Prime Minister repeatedly. Many of the administrative elite '– probably a majority – remained bound by the values of impartiality and efficiency. Even some of the politicians at times drew back in alarm when they saw the forces they might be unleashing' (Post and Vickers, 1973: 152).

Periodically over the course of the election campaign, several attempts were made to contain the abuses of parties and governments. The first effort came early in September, when the Prime Minister and Regional Premiers agreed to place local police forces under the operational control of the Nigeria Police. While the latter were independent of local and regional politics, and many of their local commanders were quite dedicated, this effort brought only limited success.

In October the Premiers called a two-day conference of political party leaders, presided over by the Prime Minister. While Okpara, Adegbenro, and Akintola all were present to head their party delegations, NPC President Sir Ahmadu Bello saw no need to attend. And, in the wake of a mass-arrest of some 300 UPGA supporters in the North, Dr Okpara arrived in a bitter mood, deepened the next day when local-government police in Ibadan raided UPGA head-quarters and detained thirteen party stalwarts. The delegations differed sharply in their perceptions of the urgency of the problem; UPGA delegates demanded a strong, written guarantee of campaign freedom while NNA representatives dragged their feet. Finally they agreed upon a 'Nine-Point Plan', providing for integration of the local police into the federal police for the election; freedom of movement and assembly for all parties; equal time and space for all parties in government media; cessation of thuggery, hooliganism and abusive verbal attacks; and a lifting of all existing bans on public meetings (Post and Vickers, 1973: 152; Mackintosh, 1966: 578).

But no written agreement could dissipate the years of accumulated bitterness and distrust nor diminish the huge electoral stakes. The very day it was signed, Dr Okpara condemned the NPC as 'lazy and indolent'. Two days later NNDP authorities barred Okpara's campaign entourage from entering Ogbomosho. By then, it was apparent that the peace plan was a total failure. Harassment and obstruction of opposition campaign teams continued, as did physical attacks and destruction of property. Each new peace agreement or pronouncement only underscored the futility of the preceding one.

Frustration with these repeated failures was vented in President Azikiwe's dramatic broadcast to the nation at dawn on 10 December, two days after Parliament had been formally dissolved and the date of the election set for 30 December. Fearing for the fate of 'our embryo republic', the President told of receiving 'hundreds of letters and telegrams pleading that I should use my good offices to ensure a free and fair election'. After recounting the grievances at length, he cited ten 'intimidatory instances' of 'calculated deprivation' of constitutional rights, drawn rather obviously from UPGA's allega-tions of violations by the NNA, especially in the North. Once again, he denounced the deliberate efforts to 'incite tribe against tribe'. While praising the Nigerian Police and Army for their efforts to maintain order, he charged that official power was being used 'not only to stifle opposition but also to prevent the forthcoming elections from being free and fair'. He then concluded with a stunning warning:

And I have one advice to give to our politicians: If they have decided to destroy our national unity, then they should summon a round-table conference to decide how our national assets should be divided, before they seal their doom by satisfying their lust for office.

I make this suggestion because it is better for us and for our many admirers abroad that we should disintegrate in peace and not in pieces.

Should the politicians fail to heed this warning, then I will venture the prediction that the experience of the Democratic Republic of the Congo will be child's play, if it ever comes to our turn to play such a tragic role. (Mackintosh, 1966: 581)

The President's suggestion that national disintegration was at hand brought an immediate, sharp rebuke from the Northern Premier, who stressed that the 'constitution has no provision for secession or disintegration', and dismissed as 'arrogant utterances' alleged statements to the effect that NCNC leaders would seek secession. Backing up President Azikiwe, the UPGA conditioned its effort to keep 'our federation one country' on the absolute cooperation of the NNA, and Dr Okpara warned that the NNDP and NPC 'denigration campaign' against the Igbos could easily lead to civil war (*West Africa*, 19 December 1964: 1419; Post and Vickers, 1973: 155).

The day after the President's address, a local UPGA leader was killed in an interparty 'free for all' outside Lagos, and two lorries were burned by UPGA 'party stalwarts'. In the North, 'the violence rose to a crescendo. Pitched battles continued. Opposition supporters were stoned, homes and cars burned to the ground' (Feinstein, 1973: 209). What little chance Azikiwe's speech might have had of quieting the violence was probably dashed by its partisan appearance, which 'suggested a one-sided attack on the NNA'. In fact, the President's neutrality had long since been tarnished by partisan remarks, such as his statements in October accusing Akintola of using the NNDP to 'stir anti-Ibo tribal hatred' (Post and Vickers, 1973: 144–5, 155).

A final attempt to restrain the escalating turmoil of the campaign was made in a national radio broadcast on 18 December by Inspector-General Louis Edet, Commander of the Nigeria Police. His list of 'Eight Don'ts' to minimise interparty thuggery underscored the violent character of the campaign,[5] as did the extraordinary provisions he recommended to guard against sabotage on election day: armed police at every counting station, searching of candidates or their agents before entry into vote-counting places, armed guards at power stations and electric counting centres. By the time of Edet's broadcast, however, the issue of thuggery and obstruction had been overtaken by a more pressing conflict which threw the troubled campaign into crisis.

CONFRONTATION: NOMINATIONS AND THE BOYCOTT

As violent as the campaign was, it was the disastrous administration of the election that produced the actual crisis. Controversy engulfed the process early on with the long delay in the preparation of the voters' list, then shifted to internal conflict within UPGA over candidate selection, and finally exploded over severe malpractices in the filing of nomination papers.

Preparation of the electoral machinery

The administration of the election was in the hands of a six-member Federal Electoral Commission, chaired by E. E. Esua (a member of an Eastern ethnic minority) and including official representatives from the four regions and Lagos. Esua had been an educator and General Secretary of the Nigerian Union of Teachers. Only one Commissioner was a professional administrator. Subordinate to them, and responsible for implementation of the electoral laws and procedures, were the professional administrative personnel at all levels of government. Local government officials were drafted to provide the bulk of the electoral officers, especially at the polls. Like the higher administrative officials, they were caught between the competing demands of impartial administration and loyalty to their ethnic group and party.

The first task of the FEC, delimitation of the new Federal constituencies, was accomplished in the months following final announcement (in July 1964) of the new census figures, and approved by the Federal House of Representatives on 25 September. But the second task provoked considerable protest. Lists of eligible voters were to be compiled by extracting from the census the names of all persons over 21 (men only, in the North), who were to have been given voter registration cards during the census. But these cards were widely manipulated for political advantage. In the North and the Delta Province of the Mid-West, and perhaps elsewhere, numerous residents entered on the census roll had not received voter registration cards, without which they could not legally object if their names did not appear on the Preliminary List of Voters. Other tactics were employed as well to confuse opposition voters and keep them off the lists. People were placed in the wrong wards, names were misspelled and addresses were jumbled or omitted. During the period of revisions and claims in September and October, thugs discouraged the filing of grievances, registration officials with the requisite forms became mysteriously absent, and other 'ingenious schemes' were employed, particularly by the NPC and NNDP (Post and Vickers, 1973: 130).

As the hearing of claims and objections dragged into November, the printing of the final voters' lists was delayed, stalling the dissolution of Parliament and selection of an election date, and the UPGA became restive, charging the Government with incompetence and deliberate procrastination (Post and Vickers, 1973: 131; Mackintosh, 1966: 576). It was not until 8 December that Parliament was dissolved and a date for the election – 30 December (virtually the latest possible) – was announced.[6] The final voters' list was urgently needed because the formal nomination of a candidate required the support of two validly registered voters, and nominations were scheduled to close on 18 December. As this deadline approached, UPGA protested that it could not reasonably be maintained since the final register of voters was not yet available.

Selection of party candidates

Before a party could contest the election, it had to select its candidate in each constituency. For the Progressive Alliance, whose two Southern parties overlapped in regional strength, the task became delicate and complex. To the traditional rivalry within the NCNC was now added the prospect of serious intra-alliance disputes.

In the East, the NCNC again faced the problem of disappointed NCNC aspirants standing as Independents, but more serious was the problem in the Mid-West, where the simmering tension between the Otu-Edo and the younger members of the 'pure NCNC' faction led to conflict in a number of constituencies, with Chief Omo-Osagie and his Otu-Edo machine decisively prevailing. The AG, denied any of the 14 Mid-West nominations, was forced to settle for only four of the 70 nominations in the East, despite its hollow claim of continued strong support among Eastern minority groups (Post and Vickers, 1973: 162; Mackintosh, 1966: 568).

In Lagos, there emerged a bitter dispute involving Chief T. O. S. Benson, over whose fierce objection the local NCNC decided to choose its four nominees by election in constituency caucuses. When an Igbo candidate soundly defeated him and the party rejected his appeal, he resigned from the NCNC to stand as an Independent candidate. While the NCNC greeted Benson's departure 'with great relief', it was a major blow, depriving the party of its most important remaining link to the Yoruba people.

> The resultant increasing domination of Dr Okpara and other Eastern Ibo leaders reinforced the tendency to interpret the political scene in simple sectional terms. Immediately upon his resignation Benson raised such a theme by chiding Okpara for refusing to state categorically that Chief Awolowo would become Prime Minister in the event of a UPGA victory. Inevitably, also, the NNDP made much of Benson's selection defeat at the hands of an Ibo. (Post and Vickers, 1973: 165).

In the Western Region, rivalry between AG and NCNC aspirants plagued the selection process in many areas. Eventually, the leaders of the two parties were able to agree (after several AG concessions) to a division giving the AG 37 of the 57 nominations, but local party organisations were less inclined to cooperate. Conflict between the two party branches in Ibadan Division became so bitter that it threatened to consume the whole alliance, and led to dual candidacies in three of the seven constituencies (Post and Vickers, 1973: 168–9). By contrast, UPGA nominations in the North fell naturally along demarcated lines of strength. Thus, the UMBC took the Middle belt, the AG the heavily Yoruba Provinces of Kabba and Ilorin, and the NEPU all remaining seats save the seven in Kano Province, where the KPP was to nominate candidates.

The NNA suffered little internal conflict, since all its constituent parties were regionally concentrated and the main two, the NNDP and NPC, were able to use their regional power to discourage dissident candidacies and compensate disappointed aspirants. In the West, however, the NNDP was forced to select its candidates centrally, since its organisation was weak or nonexistent at the divisional level (Mackintosh, 1966: 567–72).

The 'drama of the unopposed'

The rivalry within the UPGA and the NCNC was overshadowed in mid-December by a grave challenge to the integrity of the election. As the 10–18 December nominations period drew to a close, it became apparent that a number of UPGA candidates in the West and especially the North were being prevented from being officially nominated by the same thuggery, obstruction and coercion that had plagued the campaign. UPGA candidates 'were arrested or kidnapped' – and on occasion murdered – 'letters of withdrawal were extracted by beatings, and nominators were attacked' (Mackintosh, 1966: 585). These malpractices were documented by the UPGA in a submission to the Federal Electoral Commission.

> Examples of the evidence it contained are the account of the attempts to nominate a candidate in the Prime Minister's own constituency of Bauchi South West. At the first attempt the nominators were arrested. The second time the nominators were carried off by thugs. On the third occasion they were kidnapped and held until the lists closed. In Gwadabawa North 'NA police refused candidate entry into the town. Candidate subsequently killed.' For Binji-Tangaza-Silame it was the same story. 'Sarkin of Tangaza prohibited candidate from entering town. Candidate was eventually killed.' (Both these cases were in Sokoto.) (Mackintosh, 1966: 585).

Other abuses were stirring UPGA alarm as well, such as the absence of the final lists of voters and complaints that the flimsy construction of polling booths would not ensure the secrecy of the balloting. Charging that electoral officers in the North were deliberately 'dodging the receipt of nomination papers from UPGA candidates', the NCNC warned, 'Unless the Electoral Commission steps in at once and takes action to enable UPGA candidates to file their nomination papers we shall regard all the seats where our candidates' nominations are dodged as won by the UPGA'. On behalf of the UPGA, Eastern Attorney-General C.C. Mojekwu cabled the FEC Chairman demanding a five-day extension of nominations (Post and Vickers, 1973: 173).

As telegrams alleging arrest and intimidation poured into Lagos, the Electoral Commission granted a one-day extension and flew to Kano to investigate complaints. The Commission found that the NPF candidates had been able to lodge their nominations in Kano. But in the NPF Kano headquarters, 'all 25 candidates for Sokoto, 12 of the 14 for Katsina, and one for Biu [Bauchi] were sheltering as they were unable to proceed to their constituencies'. Ignoring Alhaji Aminu Kano's complaint that opposition in these Provinces was in physical danger, the Commission chose not to investigate further, allowing its one-day extension to expire on 19 December (Mackintosh, 1966: 583).

In the following days, the extent of the damage became known as the numbers of unopposed candidates filtered in. By 21 December, there were 61 unopposed NPC candidates (including the Prime Minister and many other NPC notables).[7] It should not have been surprising that the UPGA would refuse to accept this outcome. Dr Okpara had indicated as much on 9 December when he warned that if the election was not fairly conducted 'the UPGA won't allow anybody to assume power' (Post and Vickers, 1973: 171); and since the UPGA had found the men and money to contest every seat, such returns could only have been produced by massive coercion and fraud.

The NCNC immediately protested upon learning of the number of unopposed in the North, but even before this the alliance may have determined that the election was unacceptable as it was shaping up. Mackintosh (1966: 582–3) suggests that during or immediately after Dr Okpara's tour of the North in early November, UPGA leaders began to realise that they had seriously overestimated their election prospects there. He speculates that Dr Okpara and Dr Azikiwe then very likely 'began to be seriously alarmed about the probable outcome of the election' and to look for a face-saving way to avoid a humiliating defeat, which might trigger the defection of the Okotie-Eboh wing and leave the NCNC largely an Eastern party. The massive irregularities, so glaringly reflected in the unopposed returns, seemed to offer a way out.

No doubt, moral indignation coincided with political imperatives, for by then UPGA, perceiving the inevitability of defeat in a rigged election, saw the unopposed returns as the crowning outrage in an escalating pattern of electoral maladministration. Even midway through the nominations period, the mounting irregularities moved UPGA to call for immediate dismissal of Prime Minister Tafawa Balewa's 'Caretaker Government', and on 16 December Alhaji Adegbenro wired the President urging appointment of an all-party interim Government. The following day, the student AG branch at the University of Ibadan endorsed the call for dismissal of the Tafawa

Balewa Government but proposed a more ominous alternative – suspension of the elections while the Nigerian Army managed the nation's affairs for a period of three months. Sir Abubakar rejected the calls for a new government with considerable irritation, insisting that he could not be dismissed until a new government was formed after the election. Noting the provisions of the Constitution that confirmed the Prime Minister's position, the Northern Premier expressed confidence that the President would not act contrary to the Constitution. Alhaji Adegbenro disputed this interpretation of the Constitution, while UPGA militants insisted there were 'other ways' in which Sir Abubakar's Government might be dismissed (Post and Vickers, 1973: 171–3).

As nominations closed on 19 December, the Western Region grew more tense as the twelfth and thirteenth towns declared curfews, followed by six more the next day. As news of the number of unopposed returns surfaced, the NCNC Central Working Committee went into emergency session in Enugu for the second time in a week, amidst new reports of deadly political violence (*West Africa*, 2 January 1965: 3).

On the evening of 19 December the crisis deepened when Dr Okpara described the election as a 'colossal farce' and declared, 'There will be no election at all'. This was the first clear indication that UPGA would demand postponement or cancellation of the election. In the enraged and apocalyptic tone that would colour so many public statements in the following two weeks, the Eastern Premier declared, 'Nigerians [are] today facing the worst excesses of a Hitlerite regime in Northern Nigeria', and he squarely blamed the Northern Premier for 'the impending disintegration of the country'. At the same time, in one of many such threats and rumours, Mokwugo Okoye, General Secretary of the Zikist Movement, reportedly threatened secession by the East and Mid-West if the election was not cancelled (Post and Vickers, 1973: 174). Two days later the NNDP claimed that NNA candidates had been nominated for nine of the fifteen unopposed seats in the East, and the Prime Minister attacked the NCNC as a 'great liability to UPGA' who would blame their AG partners if they lost the election (*West Africa*, 2 January 1965: 3; Post and Vickers, 1973: 174).

Caught in the crossfire was FEC Chairman Esua, who had been criticised both for allowing only a one-day extension of nominations and for permitting any extension at all. In a national broadcast on 22 December, Esua conceded that there were cases where more than one candidate had been validly nominated but one candidate had 'been announced as returned unopposed'. Striking a cautious balance, he announced that elections would be held in two such constituencies in the North and one in the East (*West Africa*, 2 January 1965: 3). Neither side was satisfied. The NPC National Legal Adviser, Alhaji Abdul Razaq, characterised Esua's statements as 'unfortunate and preposterous' and vowed to challenge in court any FEC reversal of unopposed returns. Dr Okpara warned that 'this country is finished' if the NPC continued to act in divisive ways and that the UPGA parties had reached 'the limit of our endurance' (Post and Vickers, 1973: 175–6).

Indeed, they had. At this point, the Progressive Alliance dramatically raised the stakes in the confrontation.

Postponement or boycott

On 23 December, Alhaji Adegbenro set out the UPGA position: installation of a provisional government and postponement of the election. If this was not acceptable, then, at a minimum, nominations in all constituencies with unopposed returns would have to be cancelled. In a separate statement, Dr Okpara suggested that the Army should supervise the elections in the North. The next day, against the warning of the NPC not to drag the President into politics, a delegation led by Dr Okpara, Alhaji Adegbenro, and Chief Osadebay told Dr Azikiwe and then the public that they would boycott the election unless it was postponed (*West Africa*, 2 January 1965: 3).

Motivating this request, claims Mackintosh (1966: 586–7), was 'the lingering only half-abandoned view that if the election was fairly conducted, if this could be arranged given more time, UPGA could win', coupled with the belief that the Constitution would permit the President to appoint a temporary government if no valid election were held. 'Under such (presumably UPGA) leadership, the Census figures could be revised and a fresh election held with the full Federal machinery of government in UPGA's hands and under these circumstances victory would be assured'. That UPGA leaders could believe the NPC would stand for such a move indicated the increasing desperation of the struggle. A constitutional crisis was now clearly foreshadowed.

In his Christmas message, President Azikiwe appealed for calm and requested Nigerians to go to the polls with all sense of honesty and purpose. The following day, this sign that the election would go forward appeared to be confirmed when, after the President met with all four Regional Governors, a statement was released appealing for national unity 'whatever the outcome of the election' (*West Africa*, 2 January 1965: 3). But UPGA leaders intensified their pressure on the President, and on Sunday, 27 December, Dr Okpara apparently managed to convince him that the election should be postponed. Later that day, the Eastern Premier promised a Lagos rally of some 20 000 UPGA supporters 'an important announcement' the following day. The rally, backed by the SWAFP and the JAC, was held under the shadow of troop manoeuvres in the streets of Lagos. Clashes occurred with riot police as the demonstrators proceeded to the State House to give President Azikiwe their resolutions, emphatically reiterating the grievances, demands and warnings of the previous days, including a call for the Army to referee the elections. Smaller rallies were held in other major cities as well (Post and Vickers, 1973: 178).

A new stage of confrontation began on 28 December – just two days before the scheduled election – with a two-hour meeting between the President and the Prime Minister. President Azikiwe urged that the election be postponed for six months and that UN experts and advisers be asked to supervise it. Curtly rejecting this request, 'Sir Abubakar said he saw no reason for postponement and argued that it would be humiliating to admit any need for outside assistance' (Mackintosh, 1966: 587). In an attempt to break the deadlock, a meeting of Regional Governors and Premiers was summoned for the following day. Unrest mounted through the day as police broke up another UPGA demonstration in the capital while a motorised column paraded in the streets with fixed bayonets (*West Africa*, 2 January 1965: 3).

The election boycott

On 29 December the last attempt to avert a boycott failed when the Northern and Western Premiers and Governors failed to show up for the noon meeting at the State House. Even before the meeting, it became apparent that there would be no compromise when Sir Abubakar met with the heads of the Army, Navy and Nigeria Police to review last-minute instructions to ensure 'a peaceful and orderly poll'.

It was a day of intense manouevring. President Azikiwe, who had been advised by the Federal Attorney-General that he lacked power to form an interim government or to assume executive powers, nevertheless agreed to a boycott of the election in a lengthy meeting with UPGA leaders that afternoon, but warned that he could only refuse to recognise the election results and assume 'executive powers' if the boycott was effective in three of the four regions (i.e., throughout the South). Support had already been given the previous day in a meeting between UPGA and radical labour leaders. Now JAC co-President Wahab Goodluck (without the support of his more moderate co-Presidents, Adebola and Chukwurra) called a sit-down strike to support the boycott. News of the election boycott was broadcast throughout the latter part of the day by radio and by UPGA vans touring Southern cities and towns exhorting people not to vote. The six-man Federal Electoral Commission announced it was deadlocked on the question of holding the election, and its Eastern and Mid-Western members resigned, soon to be followed by a third (Mackintosh, 1966: 587–9; Post and Vickers, 1973: 180; *West Africa*, 2 January 1965: 3).

In a broadcast that same day, the Sardauna said he failed to attend the summit meeting because it had been called to consider the possibility of boycott and secession by the East. While not dismissing the possibility that 'other Nigerians' might concede the right of the East to secede if it insisted, he warned that such 'a complex matter ought not to be decided at this tense and critical point of time' (Post and Vickers, 1973: 181). Since the discovery of oil in the East, he added, the NCNC had been getting steadily colder in its relations with other parts of Nigeria, trying to 'make themselves so intolerable that other Nigerians will take the initiative of getting Eastern Nigeria outside the Federation and thereby winning sympathy for the NCNC in the world at large' (*West Africa*, 2 January 1965: 3).

The boycott of the polls on 30 December was only partially successful. Official voter turnout declined sharply from nine million in 1959 to roughly four million, perhaps a quarter of the electorate at most (Sklar, 1966: 154). In failing to prevail in three regions, the boycott was, by the President's yardstick, a failure. Only in the Eastern Region was it a complete success. There, polling stations were reported 'silent as graveyards' as the electoral officers (mostly Eastern Regional officials) failed to appear with the ballot papers and booths. In Lagos, polling booths were destroyed by UPGA supporters, and the boycott foreclosed voting entirely in three of the four constituencies. Only in Lagos did the sit-down strike enjoy even mixed success. Bus, port and railway workers all struck, but moderate union leaders kept their men at work, and elsewhere in the country the strike was hardly evident (Post and Vickers, 1973: 181–4; Mackintosh, 1966: 589).

In the Western Region, the boycott met with very mixed results, due largely to deeply conflicting attitudes toward it within the Action Group. Although the AG fell into line behind its Acting Leader the day before the election and announced it would 'stand by our decision to boycott the poll', a large segment of the party protested, feeling the most urgent priority was for the party 'to prove that it still commanded the allegiance of the mass of voters in the West', which would then give it the confidence and momentum to recapture power from the NNDP in the next regional election. As a result of this division, the boycott call came too late to reach the hinterlands and many UPGA candidates remained reluctant 'to throw away their chance of election'. Despite the destruction of several polling stations, interparty violence in Ibadan, and a delay in balloting, voting was heavy in a number of constituencies and moderate in many others (Post and Vickers, 1973: 181–3).

Perhaps the most grievous setback came in the Mid-West, where Premier Osadebay reversed the boycott in a dramatic noon broadcast announcing the opening of polling stations and urging all his followers to go and vote. In the North, the boycott was little felt, as a day of 'brisk voting' began promptly in an atmosphere of relative calm. Only in the largely Igbo Sabon Garis, particularly in Kano and Jos, was there any evidence of a boycott.

On the evening of the election, the UPGA vowed not to accept the authority of any government formed on the basis of the elections, saying this would be 'compromising with evil', and called on the President to summon a conference of all political leaders to 'break up the Federation peacefully' (*West Africa*, 2 January 1965: 1–3). This uncompromising tone reflected the now totally polarised character of the confrontation between the two alliances.

As the results came in over the next two days, it became apparent that the UPGA had suffered a crushing defeat. While constituency returns were never published (and would have been meaningless anyway), the NNA won 198 of the 253 seats awarded in the election, giving it virtually a two-thirds majority in the House regardless of the outcome in the remaining 59 constituencies.[8] Defeat was especially crushing in the North, where the UPGA won only four of 167 seats (all of them in Tiv division, and even here the NPF lost ground).

Eighty-four of the 98 UPGA candidates in the North lost their deposits. Few if any of these defeats could be attributed to the boycott, since the great distances and poor communication in the rural North made it difficult to circulate the last-minute order.[9] The boycott was most damaging in the West, where it cost the UPGA some eighteen seats 'which it would otherwise almost certainly have won' (Post and Vickers, 1973: 1851). What would have been a clear UPGA victory became instead a solid triumph for the NNDP, although several prominent Akintola backers were defeated. Only in the Mid-West was UPGA successful (precisely because Premier Osadebay had defied the boycott). It scored landslide votes in most of the Region, winning every constituency but one (which was left undetermined when the vehicle carrying the ballot papers to a recount was burned) (Mackintosh, 1966: 596–601).

Once again, the Eastern leaders of the NCNC had badly miscalculated. In the ruins of their strategy they stood more isolated than ever before, unable even to rely on their own party leaders in the West and Mid-West. More than ever, the confrontation was polarised around the conflict between the political leaders of the North and East. The electoral obstruction by the former and rejection by the latter had created an unprecedented constitutional crisis. In the feverish manoeuvring of the following five days, the future not only of the civil regime but of the nation hung in the balance.

CRISIS AND COMPROMISE

The new year began with each side hardening its position and assessing its strength. The essence of the stalemate hung on whether or not President Azikiwe would call on Sir Abubakar to form a new government, as the Constitution appeared to require, given the Prime Minister's renewed position as Federal Leader of the majority in Parliament. At issue was the scope of Presidential authority under the Constitution, and underlying it, the long-gathering tension between Dr Azikiwe's formal position as President – which, as the symbol of Federal authority and national unity, required a nonpartisan stance – and his *de facto* role as leader of a particular people and party – which had led him to increasingly partisan involvements in the previous year and now drove him to abandon any pretence of impartiality.

On the afternoon of 1 January 1965, it was announced that the President would broadcast a speech on the crisis that evening, to which the Prime Minister would reply. Abruptly at the last minute it was cancelled, but the text (already released to the press) became public. In his prepared remarks, President Azikiwe vowed to prevent the Prime Minister from forming a new Government on the basis of the election results. Reviewing the repeated frustration of attempts to ensure a free and fair election, and Sir Abubakar's rebuff of his request for postponement and UN supervision, he said they had finally agreed to allow the Federal Electoral Commission to take 'appropriate action'. But when the FEC failed to postpone the election and three of its members resigned, he felt morally compelled to reject the election result (and by extension, Sir Abubakar's entitlement to form a new government) (Post and Vickers, 1973: 191).

Although never formally released, the Prime Minister's reply was published on 4 January. Sir Abubakar insisted that postponement of the election had never been discussed between them; that only the FEC could call off the election and only the courts could remedy irregularities; that his supporters had won a clear majority in the elections and that the President therefore had no choice but to reappoint him. He concluded with a pointed attack on the Eastern NCNC, suggesting that unscrupulous individuals were using the supposed election issue to ventilate other grievances, as had happened during the census. 'Do you think these people will ever accept the result of another election if it is still not in their favour?' he asked (Post and Vickers, 1973: 192; Mackintosh, 1966: 590).

In the deadlock over constitutional authority, the contest became a trial of strength. The President could rely on the support of UPGA leaders and their Governments in the East and Mid-West, along with 'the vocal backing of the few left wing groups, the sympathy of all Ibos, and, much more important, the Lagos mob organised by the JAC'. The Prime Minister was backed by the NPC, which controlled the Northern Government and most of the key Federal ministries (including Defence), and by the NNDP Government in the West. His constitutional position was also supported by an impressive cross-section of legal authorities, including not only the Federal Attorney-General, T. O. Elias, and the Chief Justice of the Federal Supreme Court, Sir Adetokunbo Ademola, but the Solicitor-General and Chief Justice of the Eastern Region, Dan Ibekwe and Sir Louis Mbanefo (Mackintosh, 1966: 590). Their collective judgment was crucial, because in any naked showdown the armed forces and the Federal Police would decide the issue, and their commanders appeared determined to abide by a strict interpretation of the Constitution. The Prime Minister had already demonstrated his control over the military and readiness to deploy it in the tense final days before the elections.

As the confrontation hardened following the election debacle, President Azikiwe made his own play for control of the armed forces. Summoning Army Commander Major-General Welby-Everard, Navy Commodore Wey and Police Inspector-General Edet to the State House, Azikiwe 'is alleged to have pointed out that they owed allegiance first to him as President of the Republic' and Commander-in-Chief. Anticipating such a claim, the service chiefs had sought constitutional advice, which confirmed that operational command of the three services was clearly vested in the Prime Minister or his designate. Commodore Wey told the President he could take orders only from the Prime Minister. As an expatriate, General Welby-Everard did not wish to get enmeshed in a political dispute and politely withdrew, but then circulated to all his officers an explanation of the constitutional position, in particular 'to remove the doubts felt by some Ibo officers. Thus the President found that he did not have the armed forces or the police on his side' (Mackintosh, 1966: 592).

It was very likely this realisation that convinced President Azikiwe to begin the process of retreat reflected in the cancellation of his New Year's Day broadcast. By 2 January he was clearly no longer sure of his ground. The next three days saw him torn agonisingly between the competing pressure of his supporters – the leaders of the Eastern NCNC and of the unions' JAC, who urged him to stand firm – and the Prime Minister and chief legal authorities of the nation, who told him his position was without constitutional foundation.

On Sunday, 3 January, the basis for a compromise emerged when a delegation led by the Federal and Eastern Chief Justices presented Dr Azikiwe with a six-point formula for resolving the deadlock. Its key provisions were: that 'a broad-based national government . . . be formed on the results of the last election'; that the legality of the election be determined in the courts and the results upheld, except where the number of voters was so small as to require another election; that arrangements be made within six months for a Commission (and then a constituent assembly) to review the Constitution and the electoral machinery; and that the Western

Regional Government be dissolved 'to enable the people of that Region to express their will as to who should govern them' (Mackintosh, 1966: 592–3).

Later that day, the President consulted with the national leaders of the four UPGA parties along with other UPGA and JAC figures. Appearing greatly strained, he presented the compromise proposals and related his fears that the NPC would try to remove him from office. The UPGA leaders 'each in turn urged the President to stand firm' in refusing to reappoint Sir Abubakar, assuring him that 'any threats of force would be met by the overwhelming support of the Lagos populace' (Mackintosh, 1966: 594–5). Subsequently, Dr Azikiwe met with Premier Osadebay and NCNC Federal Ministers Okotie-Eboh and Mbadiwe who almost certainly urged acceptance of the compromise.

The two Chief Justices believed Dr Azikiwe had agreed to a modified version of the compromise, but tension rose that Sunday afternoon when his expected broadcast announcement was not forthcoming. It was suspected that the President had been pressured to back out by the JAC leaders, who were 'virtually encamped on the ground floor of the State House'. The Army and the Police stood ready to arrest the radical union leaders, but were dissuaded by NPC leaders, who chose to escalate the pressure on President Azikiwe by threatening to invoke a Constitutional provision for his temporary removal from office during illness. With rumours of such an impending move rapidly spreading, the State House issued a statement in the middle of the night affirming the health of the President (who had indeed been ill recently) (Mackintosh, 1966: 595).

The following morning (4 January) the two Chief Justices informed the President that Sir Abubakar had accepted the compromise formula save for the dissolution of the Western House, which he felt was unnecessary since the law required a new election within eight months anyway. Dr Okpara then pressed a nine-point UPGA counterproposal calling for the release of Chief Awolowo; fresh elections for all seats with unopposed returns or less than a 50 per cent turnout (or perhaps 30 per cent, as an extreme concession); an immediate election in the Western Region; a broadly based national government, with two-thirds of the Cabinet going to UPGA; and a rapid and thorough Constitutional review, with the creation of new states as a precondition.[10]

By this time, President Azikiwe appears to have decided to accept the modified compromise. As the day wore on, he granted the police permission to remove the labour militants from the State House, following which a heavy guard was deployed on the premises. In a surprise broadcast that evening, he announced the compromise settlement of his conflict with the Prime Minister, whom he had decided to reappoint for the sake of national unity.

The crisis was over. But what the international press assumed was a genuine compromise UPGA soon determined was a profound defeat. The vision of a 'broad-based national government' turned sour on 7 January when Sir Abubakar named the first 17 members of his Cabinet. Fifteen were NPC men, all former Ministers; only Chief Okotie-Eboh and Dr Mbadiwe were drawn from the NCNC. Two seats were allocated to the NNDP and later filled by its existing members. A bill was introduced in Parliament arranging for elections in the East, after which the NCNC would be given two more Cabinet seats. 'There was no word of any constitutional revision' (Mackintosh, 1966: 596).

AFTERMATH

Just as besieged groups pull together in the heat of combat, so they often fracture in the wake of shattering defeat. Such was the case with the UPGA and its constituent elements in the weeks following the triumph of the NNA.

Familiar divisions emerged anew within the AG and especially the NCNC, whose Western and radical elements indicated that they felt betrayed by the 'compromise agreement'. A prominent long-time NCNC leader in the West, Chief Adeniran Ogunsanya, launched the protest on the very day the agreement was announced, condemning the absence of any commitment to release Chief Awolowo and the vagueness of the pledge for a 'broad-based' government. The latter concern was intensified with the first round of ministerial appointments. At a stormy NCNC National Executive Committee later in January, the bitterness poured out in a torrent of criticism against Dr Okpara – who had been very grudgingly persuaded by intermediaries to accept the compromise – and Chief Osadebay and Dr Mbadiwe (Post and Vickers , 1973: 195–6).

NCNC and other radicals denounced the agreement as an utter capitulation that entrenched 'reactionary' and 'feudal' domination 'through a rigged election and the betrayal of the masses'. Members of the Zikist Movement condemned the pact as a 'gross betrayal of those nationalists whose sacrifices had made independence possible', and many Zikists resigned (Post and Vickers, 1973: 197–8; see also *West Africa*, 23 January 1965: 99, and 6 February 1965: 156). The radicals' disillusionment with their one-time source of inspiration, Dr Azikiwe, was especially sharp, and was shared by much of the UPGA and NCNC mainstream. In agreeing to defeat in the name of compromise, the President had, in their belief, shown himself to be a weak leader. For most NCNC members of the political class, this disaffection was based more in their exclusion from the Federal system of rewards than in any ideological revulsion.[11]

The NPC crudely played on these divisions, attempting to split off NCNC Federal officials like Okotie-Eboh, Mbadiwe, and Azikiwe from the party's more militant Eastern wing. In its press organ, the *Nigerian Citizen*, the NPC repeatedly praised President Azikiwe and condemned Premier Okpara, distinguishing true Zikism from 'Okparaism, . . . this vague, baseless doctrine built on pragmatic tribalism and sectionalism' (Post and Vickers, 1973: 198). The effect of this transparent strategy was to deepen resentment and further polarise the conflict between Northern and Eastern party leaders.

Fissures in the opposition continued to proliferate. The Action Group bitterly debated (and its leadership moved with alarm to kill) a proposal to form an alliance with the NNDP in the West to win Chief Awolowo's release. A UMBC leader (who had testified against Chief Awolowo), Alhaji Ibrahim Imam, was expelled after allegedly trying to seek readmission into the NPC. In mid-February the UMBC President, J. S. Tarka, was sentenced to four months jail for 'abetting' the rioting in Tiv Division the previous year (Post and Vickers, 1973: 199–200). And ten days after the ill-fated election-day general strike, Co-Chairman Adebola pulled out of the JAC, which he alleged Wahab Goodluck was trying 'to transform . . . into an arm of the SWAFP', and formed a new trade union council, thus renewing the fragmentation of Nigerian labour into activist and neutralist federations (*West Africa*, 6 February 1965: 137–8).

As the Progressive Alliance struggled through its multiple divisions, the national conflict subsided. In early February, Dr Okpara emerged from a meeting with the Prime Minister to declare that everything in Nigeria would now be 'plain sailing', which *West Africa* took to be 'the official end of the "crisis"' (13 February 1965: 166). The following week, legislation was passed enabling elections in March for the seats left unfilled by the December boycott, and an

Igbo, Brigadier J. T. U. Aguiyi Ironsi, was promoted to Major-General and Commander of the Nigerian Army to replace the departing Welby-Everard. In appointing Ironsi from competition with a Northern and two Yoruba generals, the Prime Minister appeared to be making a significant 'politial gesture of conciliation', which the NCNC press welcomed 'with exultant gratitude ... in practically the first cheerful editorials these papers carried since the election' (Miners, 1971: 148–9).

But, as a writer for the Eastern Government's *Nigerian Outlook* observed, the surface calm of February was but 'a very thin plaster over a deep crack' (*West Africa*, 6 March 1965: 251). In the North, a militant NPC faction was voicing disenchantment with the Prime Minister's moderation, asserting that the party should have maximised its advantage after the election by awarding all the top Federal positions to the NNA. This uncompromising mood reopened the festering wounds of ethnoregional conflict. A 3 March editorial in the *Nigerian Citizen* declared:

> Today I am weeping because the North has foregone all its advantages brought to it by its natural position – majority in population, expanse of land and majority in parliament.... The head of the Police Force goes to Eastern Nigeria, the Navy also goes East. Where is the Army now? Eastern Nigeria has captured it too.... What has the Northern Alliance gained from winning the election? Two UPGA men who should not be ministers are there. Why? Dr. Mbadiwe and Chief Festus Okotie-Eboh are Sir Abubakar's personal friends. The opinion of all elites in the country is that Sir Abubakar should be recalled home to Bauchi if he cannot carry out the great tasks devolving upon him. (Miners, 1971: 149).

The 'little election'

The campaign in February and March for the remaining 59 seats in the Federal House was a relatively mild affair. Most of these seats were in the Eastern Region, where the ruling NCNC mounted an intensive campaign in the hope of a clean sweep. The AG lent support in those Eastern minority areas where it retained some strength, but the NPC and NNDP did little to support their minor party allies in the East, other than to echo their charges of thuggery, obstruction, and harassment. These were given continuous play in the *Nigerian Citizen*, which mimicked UPGA's December election stand when it demanded that the Army be called in to maintain law and order in the East during the campaign. While the charges appear to have had some substance, they were probably greatly exaggerated (Post and Vickers, 1973: 211–12).

The returns from the little election on 18 March gave the UPGA a resounding victory. It swept the four remaining seats in Lagos and the Mid-West and carried 53 of the 55 in the East (Table 7.1). While rather bitter fruit, given the preceding humiliation, UPGA leaders were nevertheless cheered and their parties rejuvenated by the results, which denied the NNA the two-thirds majority necessary for such legislative actions, as creation of new states or amendment of the Constitution (*West Africa*, 27 March 1965: 339).

Table 7.1   Distribution of federal parliamentary seats after elections of December 1964 and March 1965

	NPC	NNDP	NCNC	AG	NPF	Inds.	Totals
North	162	–	–	–	4	1	167
West	–	36	5	15	–	1	57
Mid-West	–	–	13 + 1*	–	–	–	14
East	–	–	15 + 49*	4*	–	2*	70
Lagos	–	–	1*	2*	–	1	4
Final Party Totals	162	36	84	21	4	5	312

*Result from the March little election. The fifteen Eastern seats won by the NCNC in the December election were in unopposed constituencies.
From Post and Vickers, 1973: 213, Table 7.

In what was seen by the disaffected as a fittingly farcical conclusion to the drawn-out contest, the Prime Minister announced his final Cabinet appointments on 1 April. Attempting to accommodate both the victorious and the defeated parties, Sir Abubakar doubled the number of Ministers to 54 and named 26 parliamentary secretaries as well. In this bloated Executive body were 22 NPC ministers, 14 NNDP, 15 NCNC and three pro-NPC Independents along with twelve NPC parliamentary secretaries and seven each from the NNDP and NCNC.

But if sheer numbers gave the appearance of a broadly based government, the assignment of ministries revealed the NPC's tightening grip on Federal power. Of the 21 Cabinet-ranked ministers with executive authority (the remaining were Ministers of State), the

NPC controlled all the strategic centres of economic and coercive power–External Affairs, Defence, Internal Affairs, Economic Development, Mines and Power, Establishments, Lagos Affairs, Works, and Transport.[12] At the head of two other pivotal ministries, Finance and Justice, remained trusted friends of the NPC elite – the NCNC's Okotie-Eboh and the independent T. O. Elias. The NCNC was otherwise consigned to the periphery of power, taking the Ministries of Communication, Housing, Trade, and Aviation (whose new Minister was replaced at External Affairs by the Prime Minister himself). The NNDP was given the portfolios for Information, Labour, Education, and Natural Resources.

The newly filled Parliament convened at the end of March. From the Government came not a word of the promised constitutional review, on which UPGA had pinned its hopes for political change.

ANALYSIS

The cleavage alignments

A superficial analysis of party alignments in 1964 might suggest that historic regional cleavages had finally been bridged with the formation of the two grand alliances. In fact, the opposite was true. The year-long Federal Election struggle was essentially a confrontation between the nuclei of the two alliances, the NPC of the North and the NCNC of the East. As the conflict progressed, it increasingly polarised around these two dominant poles. While political or ideological themes were raised in the campaign, they did not cut across traditional regional, ethnic, and party cleavages as they had during the General Strike. When proponents of class-conscious, ideological themes finally aligned with one side, ideology melted into sectionalism. The regional and ethnic character of the conflict was evident throughout, from the preliminary skirmish in the Mid-West through the violence and ethnic vituperation of the campaign to the tense final weeks of crisis, rife with threats and rumours of Eastern secession.

An important feature of the conflict, foreshadowing the subsequent tragedy of secession and civil war, was the recurrent political isolation of the Igbos, who were left at critical moments to face their ethnic antagonists in the North and West without appreciable support from their party brethren and political allies in the Mid-West and

West. This was demonstrated in the ethnic controversy of March 1964, when even NCNC loyalists joined the Western Region's tirade against Igbo domination of the country. It was evidenced again in the electoral showdown, when the bulk of the Action Group leadership balked at the boycott proposal. But it was most visible in the continued ambivalence of the Mid-West NCNC, dominated by minority ethnic groups. It was this wing of the party that had most stoutly opposed alliance with the AG and whose abandonment of the election boycott most damaged its credibility. Though some Eastern leaders talked of taking the Mid-West with them if they seceded, Mid-West political leaders (including Premier Osadebay) repeatedly indicated that they would not follow the East in secession (e.g., *West Africa*, 2 January 1965: 3). Chief Osadebay had never had much stomach for the extreme sectionalism of his Igbo brethren who led the Eastern NCNC, and he believed the financial precariousness of his Region precluded an irretrievable break with the dominant party in the Federation. As Chief Okotie-Eboh asked (in a question equally applicable to his personal situation), 'Is it right that we should kill the goose that lays the golden egg?' (*West Africa*, 12 December 1964: 1393, 6).

If NCNC and UPGA solidarity crumbled when it came to defence of the Igbo cause, the attack on the Igbo was the only theme that held the Nigerian National Alliance together. Both NPC politicians in the North and, with special fury and crudity, NNDP politicians in the West attacked the Igbo leaders of the NCNC for alleged ethnic imperialism and cited Igbo domination of the UPGA as the main reason to vote against it. Allied minority parties in the East and Mid-West also played heavily on the threat of Igbo domination.

The primacy of ethnicity in the election struggle was underscored by the dramatic decline in salience of class identification as the campaign accelerated. In no way did such a decisive resurgence of ethnic and regional identification appear inevitable in the triumphant aftermath of the General Strike. Certainly there were vehicles, in the Socialist Workers' and Farmers' Party and the Nigerian Labour Party, for a class-based vote across ethnic lines. But these parties failed to mount a serious challenge; SWAFP contested only twenty seats (all in the South) and the Labour Party only one. Neither party garnered more than a fraction of the vote anywhere, and the SWAFP repeatedly sought to gain entrance into the UPGA, giving it vigorous backing in the election boycott and crisis.

Interview data gathered between July and December 1964 indicate that the potentially strong appeal of a labour party to Nigerian workers declined precipitously between the end of the General Strike and the time of the election.[13] The percentage of workers who appeared significantly cross-pressured between their class and ethnic identifications declined from well over half in July to something like one out of five in December, and a post-election survey showed a strong tendency for workers to endorse in principle a labour party but to support in fact an ethnically based party (Melson, 1973: 586–92).

It is important to try to understand why this happened. One significant factor was the factionalism within organised labour, which found moderate union leaders supporting the established parties (Lawrence Borha, for example, ran on the NCNC ticket in the Mid-West) while radical leaders divided between the SWAFP and Imoudu's NLP. A more fundamental cause, however, was the weakness of organised labour in Nigeria. Nigerian trade unions had never been able to stake a primary claim on the attention and loyalty of their members. The social benefits and activities that trade unions in more developed countries provided or won for members – such things as old age and sickness benefits, scholarships, leisure association – were supplied in Nigeria by communal associations. Hence, Nigerian workers probably had limited expectations of their trade unions, turning to them for assistance only at special and irregular moments (Cohen, 1974: 129, 132–3; Sklar, 1963: 496). Politically, labour militants were also up against the vigorous and pervasive ethnic mobilisation of the electorate by the political class. For years, the voters had been regularly encouraged to see the competition for power and resources in sectional and zero-sum terms. In the atmosphere of ethnic and regional polarisation that gathered through the election campaign, this appeal assumed exceptional urgency. Melson (1970: 787) concludes, 'Workers may have been opposed to the politicians as corrupt individuals, but they were not opposed to the institutions and interests that the politicians represented. In his capacity as a member of this or that ethnic group or region, the same worker who denounced all politicians in one breath supported *his* man in the next'.

But if ethnicity was the dominant cleavage in the election, it was not the only one. Coinciding with the broad polarity of ethnicity and region was a significant, if rather vague, ideological division. For Southern progressives, this involved the conviction that the NPC was a party of a reactionary ruling class intent upon preserving a grossly unjust social system, which was protected by the anomalous and unfair regional structure. Indeed, it was opposition to the political dominance of the Northern aristocracy that drew together the constituent parties of the UPGA. This had been an important current in every major conflict since Independence, and the related equalitarian and anti-regionalist themes had been primary in both the Action Group crisis and the General Strike.

The configuration of group actors in the conflict is depicted in Figure 7.1, which places the parties and other key actors horizontally on the spectrum of polar conflict between the NPC and the Eastern NCNC and vertically in terms of their standing within each alliance's system of rewards (e.g., nominations and prospective Cabinet seats). Three conflicts are depicted: the election struggle between the two alliances; the controversy over the boycott and election results, in which the Mid-Western NCNC, though ranking higher than the AG in the UPGA reward hierarchy, deserted the dominant Eastern branch, while the AG belatedly supported it and the radical union leaders strongly did so; and the implicit cleavage over the threat of secession by the East, in which the Igbos and the Eastern NCNC were utterly isolated.

As the top of the figure shows, the President, the Electoral Commission, and the various levels of administration below them – what Post and Vickers term the 'Structural Frame' – were supposed to be above the conflict. In fact, the President became increasingly identified with the UPGA cause, and whether or not he favoured secession (placement on the figure is deliberately ambiguous here), he wound up negotiating an end to the crisis as the *de facto* UPGA leader. Members of the FEC and the lower layers of electoral administration also wound up crossing the boundaries of neutrality and favouring one side or the other based on ethnic and regional ties. While some members of the bureaucracy retained their professionalism, in the end it was only the judiciary that remained relatively uncontaminated and hence able to act as arbiter and intermediary.

Two other features of the character and configuration of the cleavage are significant. First, the conflict was mainly among the political classes. Ultimately, large numbers were mobilised to demonstrate on UPGA's behalf in major Southern cities, especially Lagos, and people were everywhere mobilised to vote or to boycott. But, for the most part, it was a struggle for power within a thin stratum of society, which was then projected into a grave ethnic and regional crisis that gripped the entire nation. Until then, the people did not appear to be deeply involved. Even in the heat of the election

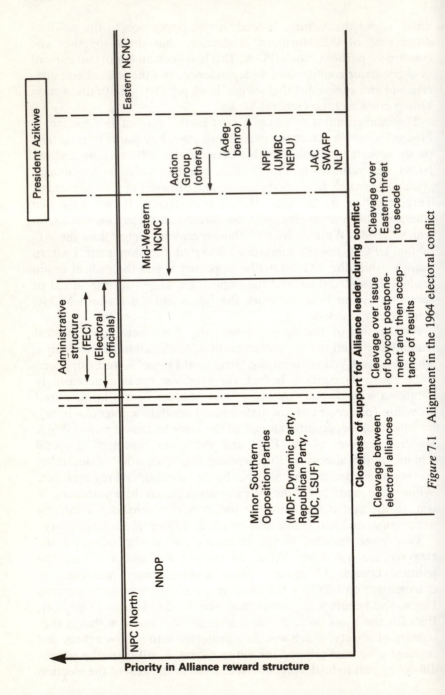

Figure 7.1 Alignment in the 1964 electoral conflict

campaign, a correspondent observed that 'people at large are remarkably phlegmatic, in face of the barrage of propaganda, much of it vitriolic, to which they are subjected' (*West Africa*, 12 December 1964: 1396). And although the militant union leaders became actively involved, their rank-and-file this time did not. *West Africa* observed: 'It is perhaps revealing that some workers on 30 December are reported to have said that they weren't quite sure why they had been called out on strike. Last June it had been perfectly clear' (6 February 1965: 138). If President Azikiwe had acted as militant politicians and union leaders had urged him to do and rallied the Lagos masses, the conflict could well have engulfed very large numbers of people, but it might also have spiralled into civil war. In the end, this spectre must have weighed heavily in the President's decision to back down.

The possibility of secession and mass violence and the widespread brutality, repression, obstruction and bigotry of the campaign indicated the extraordinary bitterness and polarisation of the cleavage. This was the worst conflict the nation had yet suffered: the most intense in its prosecution and the gravest in its implications. A catastrophe was perhaps only narrowly averted. 'Maintenance of the attitudes expressed immediately after the election could have led to secession even if nobody really wanted it. One false step by those responsible for law and order could have led to bloodshed in many areas' (*West Africa*, 9 January 1965: 29).

Outcome of the conflict

The outcome of the 1964 Federal Election crisis involved little in the way of real compromise or reconciliation. Although *The Times* of London and the *New York Times* praised the President and Prime Minister for reaching a compromise that had preserved national unity, Western observers closer to the scene saw the outcome more accurately as a resounding defeat for the UPGA (Mackintosh, 1966: 596; Schwarz, 1968: 177). UPGA leaders had little illusion about this, notwithstanding the hopeful poses many tried to strike. Even the semiofficial Eastern newspaper, the *Nigerian Outlook*, condemned the settlement, implying obliquely what the radicals were saying openly about the President's 'betrayal' (Nwankwo and Ifejika, 1969: 83).

An examination of the points of contention in the election crisis reveals the extent of the UPGA's capitulation and defeat. These are

Table 7.2 Key issues and outcomes in the 1964 federal election conflict

Issue	UPGA Position: Okpara 9-point Plan	NNA Position: Balewa's Stand	Example of Compromise (Six-Point Compromise)*	Ultimate Outcome	Winner
1. Unopposed returns	New elections for all such seats, with chance to file nominations free from harassment.	Acceptance of all unopposed returns as final.	FEC investigation of all unopposed returns. Guarantees of safety and freedom to file opposing nominations.	Acceptance of all unopposed returns as final.	NNA
2. Boycotted constituencies	New elections for all constituencies with less than 50% (30%) turnout.	New elections only for vacant seats.	(New elections where turnout was so small 'as to make a mockery of democracy') – less than 25%?	New elections only for vacant seats.	NNA
3. Authority in the West	Immediate election in West to determine which party had majority support.	Election only later in the year, as scheduled.	(Dissolution of Western Government & election of a new Regional Government).	Election only later in the year, as scheduled.	NNA

Table 7.2 cont. Key issues and outcomes in the 1964 federal election conflict

Issue	UPGA Position: Okpara 9-point Plan	NNA Position: Balewa's Stand	Example of Compromise (Six-Point Compromise)*	Ultimate Outcome	Winner
4. Makeup of Federal Government	Broadly based government drawn from main parties of East and North, & from winner in Western Regional election (2/3 of Cabinet for UPGA).	Vague commitment to broad-based government (militant sentiment for pure NNA government).	Broad coalition government, continuation of previous party balance. (Broad-based national government on basis of election results.)	Superficial coalition. NPC takes all strategic ministries. NCNC downgraded.	NNA
5. Regional & political structure	Rapid & thorough constitutional revision by a commission drawn equally from all 4 Regions (creation of new States).	Private opposition to any fundamental constitutional changes.	(Appointment within six months of a Constitutional Review Commission, to be followed one year later by Constituent Assembly).	Long delay; eventually a commission, but it never got off the ground.	NNA
6. Chief Awolowo	Immediate release of Chief Awolowo.	No release.	Release or sharp reduction of sentence.	No release.	NNA

*Entries in this column taken from the six-point compromise are in parentheses.

traced in Table 7.2, which reviews each side's negotiating positions. It must be recalled, however, that through most of the crisis UPGA leaders, especially those from the Eastern NCNC, opposed any point-by-point compromise or negotiation. Regarding the election as hopelessly fraudulent, they demanded to start from scratch, beginning with the fraudulent census that had put them in the bind of probable defeat. Thus, they urged upon President Azikiwe a constitutional coup to effect this political reorganisation. The President's decision to negotiate instead was seen by many in UPGA as an acceptance of defeat. But after negotiations began, the UPGA militants came up with a negotiating plan of their own, as a counter to the six-point 'compromise' drafted by the Chief Justices. Their nine-point plan was extreme in a few specifics but accorded with much of the six-point plan and could have served as the basis for serious negotiations. Whether out of physical exhaustion or, as some NCNCers intimated, concern for retaining his office and financial assets, or the belief that only the six-point plan could end the crisis, Dr Azikiwe agreed to its provisions (minus the sixth on Western elections) and promptly reappointed Sir Abubakar. Unfortunately for UPGA, he not only failed to bargain for their counterproposals but also neglected to obtain firm assurances on the five agreed points.

Outraged by the unopposed returns in the North, the UPGA nine-point plan demanded new elections and a fair nominations process for all of these seats. The six-point plan was silent on this subject and so was the final agreement. A reasonable compromise might have ensured investigation of all complaints and guarantees for the integrity of the nominations process and physical safety of aspiring nominees. Instead, all of the unopposed returns stood – a major victory for the NNA (Table 7.2, Row 1).

A second UPGA demand was that it should not be made to suffer for its boycott – which was meant to protest the very abuses the nine points addressed. Its demand for new elections in constituencies that failed to obtain (as an absolute minimum) a turnout of 30 per cent would seem to have been reconcilable with the six-point plan's provision for new elections 'where the number of voters was rather small as to make a mockery of democracy'. Though the latter was among the accepted five points, it was never acted upon. New elections were held only for vacant seats – another clear NNA victory (Row 2).

As for the dissolution of the Western House, the UPGA and six-point plans were more or less agreed that the people of the Region should be allowed to decide soon who would govern them. Sir Abubakar objected to this point, however, and it was removed; another victory for the NNA (Row 3).

A fourth issue – the object of the electoral struggle – concerned the makeup of the Federal Government. The UPGA demanded a broad-based government drawn from the major parties in the East and North and whichever party was chosen by voters in the West. Its demand for two-thirds of the Cabinet was ridiculous but presumably could have been negotiated. In fact, a truly broad-based coalition government could have been a crucial step toward resolving the crisis, and even perhaps the pattern of recurrent crises. For more than a year, Premier Osadebay called for such a government as the only hope for long-term stability in Nigeria, and Premier Okpara had similarly proposed (first in 1962 and again in 1964) a 15-year United Front Government. Sir Abubakar accepted the compromise provision for a broad-based government (which he himself had long favoured), but militant sentiment within his alliance would not permit him to honour the spirit of it. Torn by contradictory political pressures, he swelled the Cabinet to absurd proportions while consolidating NPC control of the critical power centres. The NNA clearly won this ultimate objective of the competition (Row 4).

An even more fundamental issue for UPGA involved the structure of government in Nigeria. A paramount grievance in all four post-Independence crises had been the ability of the emirate North to dominate the Federation because of the imbalanced regional structure. Now UPGA determined that if the census could not be overturned and power won at this election, a thorough and prompt constitutional review must at least reorder political possibilities for the future. While the North would hardly have agreed to the creation of new states as a pre-condition of the review, this might have been conceded in the negotiations and won in the review process, which UPGA also hoped would transfer to the Presidency the executive powers it had proposed. While this process of constitutional review was one of the most explicit provisions of the compromise agreement, it was anathema to the NPC, and little ever came of it (Row 5). The persistence of a Federal structure widely viewed as unstable and unfair would continue to undermine the legitimacy of the First Republic in its remaining 12 months.

The final key demand in the UPGA plan was the immediate release of Chief Awolowo, a subject on which the compromise agreement and the Prime Minister were silent. A genuine compromise might have set an early date for his release as a gesture to national unity. Instead, Chief Awolowo remained in prison through the fall of the First Republic (Row 6).

On all of these six issues, the NNA clearly won and the UPGA clearly lost. While the final parliamentary lineup was not as skewed as it might have been, given the UPGA sweep in the 'little election', it was still a grim occasion when an alliance that had hoped to gain power was forced to console itself with having barely kept its opposition from a two-thirds majority.

Causes of the crisis

The most proximate cause of the election crisis was the polarisation of conflict between the two alliances, and especially between the ruling parties of the North and East. No general rule of social action is more graphically demonstrated in this period of Nigerian history than the close connection between the degree of polarisation of conflict and the difficulty of its peaceful, constitutional resolution. The components of conflict polarisation – the gathering of forces around opposite extremes, the disappearance of moderate or mediating forces and of salient cross-cutting cleavages, the erosion of the rules of competition and of belief in the possibility of mutual benefit – had been steadily developing through the successive political conflicts since Independence. While the deterioration was not yet so complete as to obliterate any possibility of compromise, it had made political conflict extremely intense, explosive and crisis-prone.

Therefore, to explain why the election conflict degenerated into crisis, we must explain why it became so polarised. As we have seen, the process was rooted in the tensions and contradictions of the colonial period, and the recurrent ethnic and regional conflict they generated. The legacy of this recurrent conflict was apparent in several lines of sectional cleavage underlying the 1964 UPGA–NNA competition: North versus South (and especially East), Hausa-Fulani versus Igbo, Yoruba *vs.* Igbo, and minorities *vs.* majorities. The historical accumulation of enmity and distrust through these conflicts presented an increasing challenge to the forces of accommodation and an increasing strain upon conflict-regulating institutions.

Against this background, two features of the post-Independence pattern of conflict advanced the process of polarisation. First, a key factor contributing to the fluidity, complication and so containment of political conflict had disappeared – the existence of a three-player game. With the decimation of the Action Group and incorporation of the Western Regional Government into the orbit of the NPC, politics was reduced to a bipolar struggle and most of the potential for shifting coalitions was removed. Second, this and the subsequent census crisis had engendered acute bitterness and resentment. For both the NCNC and the AG, UPGA's humiliation in the election crisis represented a second successive defeat in confrontation with the NPC, and made the creation of more states an increasingly urgent condition for the defence of their basic group interests.

The federal structure was thus another contributing factor to the polarisation of competition. By 1964 it was clear that so long as the North remained one Region, the NPC would dominate it and the federation (though faith and desperate hope for a time seemed to overcome the clarity of this reality for UPGA strategists). The AG and NCNC simply could not accept this. The NPC could not accept otherwise. With each new crisis their positions hardened and became more irreconcilable.

As in previous conflicts, the more brutal and unrestrained the methods of competition became, the more intractable conflict became. In this sense, the style of political behaviour contributed to the polarisation, but the relationship was complex and reciprocal. Polarisation also fed extremist behaviour – violence, repression and invective. And to a great extent, antidemocratic behaviour fed on itself. Thus, the use of thugs by one party inspired retaliation in kind by its opponents. Violence begat violence, and in the West massive obstruction and oppression often also begat violence by angry and frustrated opposition partisans. By the same logic of injury and retaliation, threat and response, one violation of the rules of the game begat another, and often a larger one. Thus, the repressive obstruction of its nominations and campaigning led the UPGA to boycott the election and explore a constitutional coup to remove the Prime Minister. This produced sentiment for a 'pre-emptive' coup by the NNA to remove President Azikiwe from office first. Neither coup was effected but both came close, and either could have plunged the nation into a much deeper spiral of truly massive bloodshed.

Several factors further explain the antidemocratic methods of competition. We have seen (Chapter 3) that Nigerian politicians, as a group, had a weak commitment to democratic values and behavioural styles and only a vague understanding of what democratic politics required in the way of reciprocal obligations and restraints. Structural factors did tend to impel elites toward extremist methods, but the values restraining elites against such behaviour were weak. So shallow was the appreciation for democracy in the North that often the simple presence of opposition was enough to invoke a repressive response. This 'utter contempt for the principle of permitted opposition' (Post and Vickers, 1973: 179) motivated the obstruction of UPGA nominations in the North and so was an important cause of the election crisis. It stemmed not from the fear of defeat ('the pressure came almost entirely in NPC strongholds') but from the assumption by NPC Provincial Commissioners 'that open opposition was insulting and should be prevented' and that their party leaders would reward such actions (Mackintosh, 1966: 584).

In the context of regional conflict and the obsessive concern for regional security, it may be too much to attribute this intolerance simply to what Post and Vickers term 'the arrogance and desire for domination of the northern leaders'. But certainly this factor, at the intersection of class and culture, played a role. The Muslim aristocracy at the helm of the NPC believed that domination was its right and destiny by birth, and boasted that it would rule Nigeria 'forever'. To be sure, there were moderates within the party (mostly men of much more modest social rank, such as Tafawa Balewa) who were inclined toward a more generous and conciliatory approach. But it was aristocrats like the Sardauna of Sokoto – committed to economic and political modernisation but equally to preserving the traditional class structure of the emirates – who controlled the party and state machinery. To these noble born, as to their fathers, opposition to their authority was cultural and religious blasphemy, and anything that might unravel their authority – such as a breakup of the Northern Region – could not be countenanced. In that it compelled the NPC to retain control over the Federation at all costs, the structure of class domination in the Muslim North and its attendant values and beliefs must be seen as an important cause of the election crisis and of the entire pattern of crisis and conflict in post-Independence politics.

However, none of this adequately explains the eager, often malicious manipulation of ethnic competition and distrust that deepened the polarisation and fed the other elements of antidemocratic behaviour. This demogoguery was partly motivated by the previous animosity and conflict, but more so by the same factors that gave rise to that previous tension. Primary among these factors was the competition within the 'new and rising class' for scarce resources and rewards, and for a position of class dominance that could only be formed and consolidated upon the foundation of state power. This competition had prominently motivated the major previous political conflicts and was perhaps the most revealing clue to their intensity. In the election crisis, it was a significant cause of conflict polarisation and the collapse of the 'rules of the game'. Militant forces on both sides aspired to secure total control over the system of rewards.

The election struggle was viewed by many observers, both Nigerian and expatriate, as essentially an affair between politicians. This view assigns to the politicians and their class action the chief blame for the crisis that was generated. Such was the implication of the *Daily Express* editorial of 28 December, which suggested that the crisis was the result of inordinate ambition on the part of some politicians (Post and Vickers, 1973: 177). Many Nigerian college students appeared to share this sentiment. Observing a formal debate between Nigerian university students in London on the motion 'that the present constitution of the Republic of Nigeria is a failure', a columnist for *West Africa* concluded, 'although the motion was carried by four votes there seemed to be a general feeling that it was the politicians rather than the constitution that had failed' (30 January 1965: 117). The Prime Minister and the President themselves repeatedly identified the politicians as the worst peddlers of ethnic antagonism.

That the ethnic current in the election crisis was the construction of politicians and not the eruption of popular sentiments is suggested by two additional pieces of evidence: the absence of interethnic violence not directly related to the campaign (indeed, the tendency for most of the violence to be *intra*ethnic), and the results from a survey of 509 Nigerian workers (conducted between September 1963 and April 1964 in Lagos and Ibadan). Expecting strong ethnic feelings, the study found surprising levels of interethnic tolerance and acceptance among the ethnically heterogeneous work forces sampled. Comparing cooperation in politics with that in daily life, it concluded that 'inter-ethnic relations are much better where the population works together – e.g. in a factory – than where politicians collaborate. Political tensions between ethnic groups cannot be taken as an adequate measure of the relations between all the members of these groups, who usually work quite harmoniously together' (Seibel, 1967: 228).

Paradoxically, however, the same ambitions for which politicians made the election into a crisis may also have contained the crisis from escalating into civil war. In the end, claims Mackintosh, politicians took great care 'not to break legally punishable rules or to violate the Constitution', the NNA leaders because they scarcely needed to do so to win, and the UPGA leaders because they had seen in the treason trials what fate awaited those who gambled everything and lost. Even in defeat at the federal level, they still controlled two regional governments and even some federal posts. Their personal stake in the system was too great to take such a risk. 'Most of these men were relatively wealthy, had interests in business, land or the professions... they had much to lose. To be worsted politically and remain as junior, even barely tolerated, partners in the Nigerian governing elite, still meant large houses, car allowances and very considerable personal prosperity' (Mackintosh 1966: 606–7).

Independent of their class interests, UPGA leaders were surely not eager to risk destroying the political system and possibly the lives of their people. Once the Police and Army affirmed their loyalty to the Prime Minister, the conflict could not have been pressed further without substantial bloodshed and almost certain defeat. Like the President, the Prime Minister appears to have agonised over the danger of mass bloodshed. In an interview with Walter Schwarz in March 1965, he confided that he had restrained a militant impulse within his own alliance:

> I think I can say with trust that I was the only Nigerian leader not in favour of force and bloodshed at that moment. I ... heard day after day people urging me to call out the police, the army, the navy: to arrest the President and so on. I said to them I had been Prime Minister for seven years and they might feel the time had come for me to go because I couldn't see things the way they did. ... I told them I would not mind seeing millions of Nigerian lives lost if I felt it was for a good reason. But what was that reason? Just because some people wanted to get power for their own selfish reasons, we were plunged into this crisis. I was not willing to see lives lost for this. There are numerous Northerners, men, women, and children, living in the South and millions of Southerners living in the North. Who could say how many of them would die once fighting broke out? It could not be controlled. (Quoted in Schwarz, 1968: 175)[14]

Such a catastrophic outcome might not have been averted without the intervention of two rare members of the administrative elite –

the Chief Justices – who had remained sufficiently above politics to be able to mediate the conflict. But such scarce resources of arbitration could not be relied on to rescue the system a second time.

Direct effects on democracy in Nigeria

Through succeeding crises and mounting signs of corruption and profligacy, the legitimacy of the regime had been steadily eroding in the three years preceding the 1964 Federal election. In addition, the regime had manifestly been failing the Constitution's standards and expectations of democratic performance. The effect of the 1964 Federal Election was to advance significantly both of these trends.

The touchstone of liberal democracy is free and fair competition for power, especially through elections. For many years, regional governments had been violating the spirit and increasingly the letter of this basic principle, until each region had become a virtual one-party state. It could be argued that this manipulation of state power for electoral advantage differed perhaps only in degree from what ruling parties in every democracy (including those in Britain and the United States) do to try to retain power. But the degree of overt repression, especially in the North, and the subjugation of the Action Group through a manifestly fraudulent and partisan use of Federal emergency power, were of a wholly different character, fundamentally inconsistent with liberal democracy. And yet, in the wake of the Western Regional crisis, there remained elected legislatures with effective power in the Federation and the regions. The Action Group, though gravely and unjustly weakened, would have a chance to reclaim the government of the West in an election within three years, and opposition elements in the Federation would have their turn to compete for power even sooner. As the Federal election campaign approached, Nigeria retained some significant properties of liberal democracy.

The 1964 Federal Election erased most of what remained of the democratic character of the system. That the election had not been 'free and fair' could not be doubted. NPC leaders demonstrated that political opposition would not be tolerated in the North, and so long as they were able to control virtually all of its parliamentary seats, they could control the Federation and so block the structural changes that were needed to make it possible for anyone else to win Federal power. The elimination of opposition in the North thus effectively foreclosed competition for Federal power as well. Because of this, the abuses of the 1964 Federal Election represented much more than a new increment of democratic decay. In an important sense, they marked the end of democracy in Nigeria.

Certainly, it was perceived this way by a great many Nigerians – especially the young and educated elite – who were coming to regard the entire system, and the politicians who operated it, as a failure. Such disenchantment was evidenced in the debate among Nigerian university students in London that declared the Constitution a failure and blamed the politicians. The call by Southern university students for suspension of the election and a three-month Army takeover was further evidence of this, as were the rumours and expectations in some circles of an Army coup (Post and Vickers, 1973: 187, n. 29).

But it was not simply educated and idealistic young Nigerians whose disillusionment was deepened by the crisis. The 'colossal farce' of the election seriously eroded the legitimacy of the regime among the population at large, in the view of many scholars and journalists who observed it at the time:

Perhaps most disturbing of all, the public's faith in the electoral process, if not the existing system of government in Nigeria, has been shaken. (Harris, 1965: 31)

Reactions to the solution were varied. Those with a prime interest in stability were relieved that chaos had been averted. Others were indignant that democracy had been violated. Perhaps the most characteristically Nigerian reaction was one of cynicism: what can you expect of politicians, after all? (Schwarz, 1968: 177)

What effect will this episode have on Nigeria's political future? It has naturally aroused cynicism about politics and politicians, even if there is increased respect for the Prime Minister and the advisers who carried most of the burden. The particular settlement, constitutional and necessary though it was, might even increase the resentments that were at the back of the crisis. (*West Africa*, 9 January 1965: 29)

As the crisis fever subsided, it was apparent that fundamental issues remain unresolved. Nor could either side derive much satisfaction from the state of affairs. While the NNA had nominal control of the federal government, that government's authority and legitimacy were gravely impaired. (Sklar, 1966: 155)

This broad-based erosion was accompanied by the specific alienation of much of the political class in the Western and especially Eastern Regions, who had not simply been defeated again but, they believed, cheated and defrauded (again) so grossly as to diminish the prospect that their interests would ever be seriously accommodated in any future conflict with the North (much less that the system would be altered to allow for fairer competition).

This explains why some UPGA leaders began talking of secession; why the alliance vowed, in the aftermath of the election, not to accept the authority of any government based upon its outcome; and why so much of UPGA felt betrayed when President Azikiwe finally conceded to Sir Abubakar's authority. From now on, political leaders throughout the Eastern Region, and probably the bulk of their followers, would no longer recognise any NPC federal government as legitimate in its authority, though they would, for utterly pragmatic reasons, grudgingly accept it. Such alienation and cynicism were also growing in the Western Region, where 'the NNDP by a mixture of persuasion, force and fraud, secured a larger number of seats but in doing so intensified popular support for the AG' (Mackintosh, 1966: 602).

Indirect effects on Nigerian democracy

Another damaging effect of the election crisis, which would become fully apparent only in the following months but which observers could clearly discern even in its immediate wake, was the extremely unbalanced outcome. The hollow compromise failed to resolve any of the basic issues in the conflict and so ensured that they would re-emerge, perhaps with even greater force. The acute need was for change in the political structure to enable genuine competition for national power. But NPC leaders would never agree to this, and it probably came as little surprise that the promise of swift and comprehensive constitutional review was never honoured.

Here, *West Africa* seems to have missed the essential point in suggesting (9 January 1965) that moderation by the politicians could save the situation over the long term:

> The remedy, easy to define but very difficult to apply, is in the politicians' own hands. It is simply that the victors should show magnanimity and the vanquished responsibility, and that neither side should behave as though any particular election was their last chance. For if they do behave like that they will destroy even the electoral freedom Nigeria now enjoys.

The latter prediction was on the mark, and certainly the scarcity of magnanimous and responsible behaviour had helped to produce the crisis. But behaviour was heavily shaped by structural imperatives. If magnanimity did not extend beyond sharing out the rewards of power that one party could count on controlling indefinitely, if responsibility meant accepting the structural impossibility of free and fair competition for national power, these could be no more than 'a thin plaster over a very deep crack'.

It is possible that by the end of the 1964 campaign, these fissures were too deep to be closed – that no amount of moderation and statesmanship and even political resourcefulness could have defused the explosive accumulation of grievance and suspicion, or found a way to resolve the crippling contradiction between the North's control of the Federal Government and the South's huge advantage in educational and economic development (Sklar, 1965a). Post and Vickers (1973: 215) maintain that the long-gathering regional and ethnic antagonism 'between the North and East particularly . . . had been afforded no opportunity for a cathartic expression but instead, suppressed by the "deal" between East and North party leaders, had been internalised. An explosive potential, therefore, was being confined within regional bounds'. Yet still, there were conciliatory forces on each side, and the very brinkmanship of the politicians suggested their capacity to work a better 'deal' if an explosion seemed imminent.

As Post and Vickers suggest, another negative effect of the election crisis was the further polarisation it produced. Existing tensions and contradictions had not simply been left unresolved, they had been deepened and further inflamed. In the process, militant viewpoints on both sides had gained and moderate ones had lost ground; witness the increasing sentiment for Eastern secession within the NCNC, the increasing pressure within the NPC to exclude the UPGA parties completely from the new government, and President Azikiwe's loss of esteem within the NCNC, which figured to weaken his ability to forge compromise in the future.

Perhaps most ominously, the election crisis drew the Army into political conflict more fully than ever before. Though it sided with the Constitution and attempted to remain as far above the conflict as possible, it had been forced to take sides. And increasingly, the Army was being called upon to quell and contain the unrest that the politicians had generated, which meant using its coercive power and authority in support of the NPC Federal Government. More and more, the Army was coming to be seen as the only force capable of refereeing political conflict. If many politicians and opinion leaders were maintaining that only the Army could fairly and efficiently administer the elections, what were the officers themselves to think? In fact, it appears that a number of middle-ranking officers, including perhaps three Lieutenant-Colonels, 'seriously discussed whether the military should intervene to resolve the crisis' (Luckham, 1971: 238).

Finally, the ultimate outcome of the election left the Action Group, once again, alone and isolated in opposition at the Centre, as the NCNC rejoined the Federal Cabinet with reduced power but increased emoluments. The AG gained nothing from the conflict, not a Cabinet seat, nor the release of Chief Awolowo, nor immediate dissolution of the Western House – not even new elections in the Western constituencies it had boycotted. For the AG (and others) this smacked of a sellout and seemed likely to generate new friction between the UPGA partners, without in any way reducing the tension between the NCNC and NPC. The Federal Election crisis thus deepened the alienation of the Action Group and its substantial following in the West, just eight months before its chance to regain power there would finally come.

8 The Western Election Crisis and the National Crisis of Confidence, 1965

'I had an uneasy and perhaps unwarranted feeling that here, among all Chief Awolowo's legal books, by flickering candlelight, was being enacted the funeral rites of the Westminster model as a practical proposition in African politics.' — A journalist (in reference to post-election press conference of Action Group Leader Dauda Adegbenro, 12 October 1965) (*West Africa,* 16 October 1965: 1151)

'I have told people all along that we are not ripe for a system of government in which there is a fully fledged Opposition.' — Prime Minister Abubakar Tafawa Balewa, 14 January 1966 (*West Africa*, 29 January 1966: 113)

Throughout 1965, the Nigerian political system was ravaged by the tensions and strains that had been developing through years of political conflict and decay. In March, a bitter struggle over the Vice-Chancellorship of the University of Lagos reignited the issue of 'tribalism', paralysing the University for months. A scandal over a Federal Minister's private land deal also briefly took command of the headlines, crystallising the escalating disgust with rampant political corruption and waste. In particular, younger intellectual, professional and administrative elites were becoming bolder in their criticism, openly questioning whether Nigeria could afford a competitive party system in which the urgent need for economic development was overwhelmed by struggles for power and wealth within a narrow dominant class.

In the midst of this mounting disillusionment, a new election was conducted in October for control of the Western Region. In an atmosphere of 'do or die' for both parties, the campaign was once again dominated by crude appeals to ethnic prejudice, opposed by indignant condemnations of repression and reaction. The election itself was consumed by massive official obstruction and fraud, hopelessly blurring the real outcome. When the dust had settled, the

NNDP remained in power with an even greater parliamentary majority, and popular protest exploded into open rebellion and chaos in the Western Region.

THE UNIVERSITY OF LAGOS CRISIS

The ebb of ethnic controversy following the compromise of 4 January was brief. Two weeks before the March little election, a new wave of ethnic conflict arrived, battering this time the university system. On 26 February 1965, the Provisional Council of the University of Lagos, now controlled by the NNDP, announced its decision to replace Vice-Chancellor Eni Njoku (whose first three-year term was expiring) with Dr Saburi O. Biobaku. For several reasons, this decision outraged most of the University's faculty and students and became the subject of heated political controversy. A crucial element was the fact that Njoku was an Igbo and Biobaku a Yoruba. But three other factors also weighed heavily.

First, Dr Njoku had been widely praised as the architect of the University's phenomenal growth in its first three years. One of the country's most renowned academicians, Dr Njoku had attracted distinguished academic staff from Africa and the West and generous foreign grant support. When his replacement was announced, only a few months remained until the University produced its first crop of graduates and moved to the permanent campus he had been instrumental in planning (Nwankwo and Ifejika, 1969: 57–9; Idem, 1965: 32; *West Africa*, 2 January 1965: 1).

Second, Dr Biobaku – though himself an eminent historian – was seen as partial to the NNDP. During his tenure as Pro-Vice-Chancellor of the University of Ife, he produced a storm of controversy when he mandated, in December of 1963, that academic staff support the Government of Western Nigeria or resign or be dismissed. A number of outstanding academicians did resign, leaving the University of Ife in a slump from which it had not yet recovered (Nwankwo and Ifejika, 1969: 63–4).[1]

A third element in the protest was procedural. Dr Njoku, whose reappointment would have been routine under normal circumstances, had been unanimously recommended for reappointment by the University (Faculty) Senate. The decision of the (federally appointed) Provisional Council to replace Njoku was supported by all seven Yoruba members (many known NNDP partisans) and opposed by the remaining three members (Nwankwo and Ifejika, 1969: 60–2). Moreover, the reversal of the Senate recommendation came virtually without warning, and with no justification other than the approaching completion of Njoku's contract, fanning suspicion among students, and many newspapers and politicians (especially Igbo and NCNC), that the replacement was purely 'tribally' motivated. In fact, the move had been openly predicted by Dr Samuel Aluko, a Yoruba economist who resigned from the Ife faculty rather than pledge an oath of loyalty to the Regional Government. Late in 1964 he wrote:

> If the NNA wins the Federal election, it is going to interfere more and more with the academic rights of the universities. The NNDP has not hidden its determination to appoint Vice-Chancellors of universities on the basis of tribe; it made a public statement challenging the rights of the Ibos to the Vice-Chancellorships of the Ibadan and Lagos universities. It has lined up puppets to replace one or both of these illustrious Nigerians, should the NNDP win. (quoted in Nwankwo and Ifejika, 1969: 55).

Protest against Njoku's dismissal was swift and intense. Groups of students barricaded the University and boycotted lectures. Fighting among students at the barricades resulted in a number of arrests and hospitalisations. Forty-one senior academic staff signed a letter of protest, as did five Deans, including L. C. B. Gower, formerly Head of the Department of Law at the London School of Economics and Political Science, who resigned in protest as the Senate's lone representative on the Provisional Council (*West Africa*, 13 March 1965: 283).

With the University in turmoil, the Provisional Council voted on 4 March to suspend all undergraduate students and to close the campus temporarily. The students vowed to challenge the mass suspension in court and continued to defy the Administration, which had to summon the police to disperse them from the campus. On 29 March the University Senate voted no confidence in the Council, instructed the students to disregard its order that they sign declarations of good behaviour, and directed staff to cease lecturing until the Senate determined that conditions were suitable for instruction (Idem, 1965: 32; Nwankwo and Ifejika, 1969: 65–7).

The University reopened on 7 June to further protest and violence. As the new Vice-Chancellor attempted to deliver his inaugural address the next day, he was shouted down by students and later physically attacked and injured by a Yoruba law student. In the ensuing rioting, police again had to be summoned to restore order, and the entire student body was again temporarily suspended (Idem, 1965: 32; *West Africa*, 12 June 1965: 659).

As unrest mounted, both University and Government authorities attempted to link the protest to 'neo-colonialism' – namely, the expatriate Deans. Pressure became especially severe on Professor Gower, who was indirectly accused by the new Federal Minister of Education (and NNDP General-Secretary), Richard Akinjide, of inspiring the crisis (*West Africa*, 17 April 1965: 435). On 15 June, the University dismissed the five expatriate Deans, and 50 of the 75 members of the academic staff resigned in protest, denouncing the change in Vice-Chancellors as an act of 'sudden chicanery' that 'violated ... law, ... ethical principles and universally recognised academic conventions' and 'subjects the University to political and tribal domination' (*West Africa*, 19 June 1965: 687).

The Deans did take a leading role in the faculty protest, but hardly for personal or 'neo-colonialist' motives. Their objection was to the intrusion of politics and ethnicity into academic affairs. Osuntokun's (1982: 186–7) well informed biography of Akintola maintains that the replacement of Njoku with Biobaku was wholly a political move planned by the two top NNDP leaders, Akintola and Akinjide, 'to sow seed of discord between the Action Group and the NCNC'. Knowing that Biobaku and the AG Acting Leader, Alhaji Adegbenro, came from the same home town (and that they were fellow Muslims and distantly related to boot), Chief Akintola correctly calculated that Adegbenro would welcome Biobaku's appointment, to the distress of the NCNC.

The political and ethnic character of the conflict became increasingly blatant. On 4 March the NNDP identified itself openly with Dr Biobaku, and NNDP politicians visited the campus, denouncing the protests as tribally motivated and impugning the integrity of expatriate faculty protestors. While Adegbenro applauded the appointment, many younger Action Group activists were offended by it, and pro-AG Yoruba students joined the widespread student protests. The issue became even more a political and 'tribal' one when Igbo and NCNC organisations openly condemned it as such.

Given that 'few appointments in Nigeria carry the prestige of that of a Vice-Chancellor', it was not surprising that the replacement of an Igbo by a Yoruba in one of the two Federal universities would be interpreted in terms of long-standing ethnic and regional competition (*West Africa*, 24 July 1964: 815). In the East, the NCNC newspapers headlined the story as 'another shock for Ibos' and termed it a planned anti-Igbo move by Igbo-phobists (Idem, 1965: 33). Although NCNC leaders did not become involved, the crisis was a serious setback to the brief inter-ethnic peace brought about by the Zik-Balewa agreement. The mood was reflected in a 4 March editorial of the Eastern Government's *Nigerian Outlook*:

> We have always been prepared to give the Abubakar 'broadly based' government a fair trial, but are the present happenings in the country in the true spirit of President Azikiwe's broadcast of last January 4? . . . It is to be hoped that no one gets the stupid idea that the Ibos are going to stay like a punching bag for any group of mischievous but cowardly clots. (Miners, 1971: 150)

CONTINUING DECAY OF THE FIRST REPUBLIC

Between and concurrent with the University of Lagos crisis and the Western Regional Election were a number of other developments in 1965 which marked the continuing rapid decay of the First Republic. Prominent among these was further scandal and discontent over the corruption and profligacy of the political class. A central figure in this regard was the NCNC Federal Minister of Aviation, Dr Kingsley O. Mbadiwe. Several Nigerian newspapers demanded Mbadiwe's removal early in March after a newspaper columnist alleged that a company of his had leased a piece of Government land and then subleased it to a government corporation for more than twice the original rent. Mbadiwe denied any wrongdoing, claiming that he subleased the land for a 'chicken-feed rental' and that the press (which was feeling increasingly constrained as a result of the 1964 Newspapers Act) was being flagrantly abused 'to distort, lie and assassinate character' (*West Africa*, 6 March 1965: 253).

Shortly thereafter, Prime Minister Tafawa Balewa announced that Dr Mbadiwe, in the overall interest of the country, had decided to return the plot of land to the Nigerian Government, but that no further action would be necessary. This hardly relieved the growing public concern over political corruption. Neither did it abate when Sir Abubakar soon reappointed Mbadiwe to his new Cabinet as Minister of Trade, nor when the NCNC passed a unanimous vote of confidence in him, nor when that party's national legal adviser, Chief Kolawole Balogun, offered this controversial defence of his colleague's behaviour:

To say that financial transactions in land and landed property by many leading citizens of Nigeria have not become a gainful pastime is to start deceiving ourselves. All top Nigerians, Ministers, parliamentarians, top civil servants, journalists, ... indulge in these transactions. When it suits our purpose we quote conventions surrounding the British parliamentary system. When it again suits our purpose, we close our eyes to certain practices.... Our journalists must make up their minds which system they are going to uphold in Nigeria. The British parliamentary conventions or the Nigerian way of life as it exists today, where everybody regards it as fair to make money. (*West Africa*, 6 March 1965: 255).

Another continuing theme of protest and alienation concerned official salaries and emoluments. This resentment was sharply intensified when Sir Abubakar more than doubled the size of his Government to 80 members. Adding up the basic salaries and allowances (house rents, utilities, car, upkeep of house and grounds, and so on), *West Africa* (10 April 1965: 390–1) calculated that each minister or Parliamentary Secretary earned roughly £8230, suggesting a total cost of £650 000 – close to one percent of the 1965–66 Federal Budget. This did not include substantial associated expenses in travel, housing and support staff, and an estimated £1 300 000 in basic salaries and allowances for Regional Ministers and Parliamentary Secretaries. Added to the salaries and allowances of the remaining Federal and Regional MP's, all this amounted to an increasingly significant drain on the nation's resources. Protest was lodged not only in the press but on the floor of Parliament, where a number of demands were made (to no avail) for reduction of Ministerial salaries (*West Africa*, 1 May 1965: 475), and more circumspectly, in the civil service, where a staff report on the progress of the National Development Plan complained that all five governments of the Federation were spending too much on administration and not enough on production (*West Africa*, 31 July 1965: 841). Disaffection was further heightened by the widespread recognition that it was not primarily the wealthy stratum of society that would bear the increased tax burden. Tax evasion among this group was so extensive – and so damaging to Regional revenues – that all four Regional Finance Ministers were forced to take account of it in their annual budget speeches (*West Africa*, 10 April 1965: 406).

Disenchantment with corruption, inefficiency, injustice and stagnation also became more cogent and articulate in 1965. Significant
was the introduction of a monthly magazine of trenchant commentary and analysis, *Nigerian Opinion*, published by the 'Nigerian
Current Affairs Society', based in the Faculty of Economics and
Social Studies at the University of Ibadan. Edited by Nigerian
political scientist B. J. Dudley, in collaboration with O. Aboyade
and J. O'Connell, its chief aims were 'to put to the public the critical
and constructive thinking of the intelligentsia' and to propose specific
'political and economic alternatives' (*Nigerian Opinion*, January
1965: 1). The magazine was outspoken in condemning the budgetary
drains caused by the nation's political excesses: the Federal Election
crisis (which it estimated to compare with the two million pounds
swallowed by the second census), the creation of new ministries,
extravagant ministerial salaries and official corruption (*Nigerian
Opinion*, February 1965: 2, April 1965: 2). The latter concern was
evidenced in its commentary on the Mbadiwe land scandal.
Observing that abuse of office 'has now reached such proportions
that short of discrediting the country and the political leadership as a
whole, Ministers of State will have to be protected against
themselves', the magazine proposed several reforms, such as
requiring Ministers to declare publicly all their assets and to give up
all direct connections with their business interests (March 1965: 1).

Accompanying these specific complaints was a thinly veiled disgust
with the politicians as a group, who these intellectuals believed were
obstructing the nation's economic development in their political
struggles and frantic accumulation of personal wealth. There was still
time, said a *Nigerian Opinion* commentary following the Federal
Election, 'for our politicians ... to convince people that they are
serious about economic growth and are willing to make sacrifices
themselves to promote it' (January 1965: 2). But it held out little
hope that the reconstituted government would bring any improvement: 'There is no new breed of leadership on the horizon. Also,
looking back at the electioneering campaign over the last three
months ... the battle cry has been who gets what and at whose
expense. There has been little thought for how to solve the more
fundamental question of continuously increasing the size of the
national cake' (January 1965: 3). A few months later, the magazine
put the challenge even more directly. Charging that the government
was over-estimating the economic growth rate and failing to meet the
four per cent target in the National Plan it warned: 'No government

can hope to stay in power unless it promotes relatively rapid economic growth and makes employment opportunities available' (June, 1965: 4).

Erosion of respect and support for the regime continued among Nigerian labour as well, which aggressively renewed its protest themes from the 1963 and 1964 General Strikes. At its annual congress in July 1965, the moderate United Labour Congress proposed abolition of the salaries of parliamentarians. Paying them only living allowances, it reasoned, would reduce the intensity of the desire for office and discourage 'bitter rivalry and thuggery in election campaigns'. In a separate resolution, the Congress called for a ceiling on the amount of property that politicians and top civil servants could acquire (*West Africa*, 17 July 1965: 795).

In August, threatened nationwide strikes by the ULC (in sympathy with strikes at three foreign-owned enterprises) and by Nigerian teachers were averted when certain concessions were made (*West Africa*, 21 August 1965: 930). Then the Joint Action Committee threatened to strike in protest against 'repeated arbitrary increases in prices', which it blamed on recent increases in import duties. This strike also was averted when the Minister of Labour agreed to forward to the Government the JAC's demand for review of the progress made since the 1964 renegotiations, but by then the issue had already erupted in three days of mass demonstrations in Lagos and a boycott that closed most of the Nigerian-owned shops in the city. Twice demonstrators had to be dispersed by tear gas, and when it was over the Federal Government imposed a two-month ban on public meetings in the Capital (*West Africa*, 4 and 11 September 1965: 991, 1026).

Growing disillusionment with competitive party democracy

Along with the deepening cynicism over politics and politicans, acute doubts were surfacing in public discussions about the system of multi-party competition. A growing proportion of the educated elite was coming to question the appropriateness of the Westminster model. This concern was frequently evident in *Nigerian Opinion*. It was illustrated in a series of letters appearing in *West Africa* during the spring of 1965, in which the relative merits of 'no-party' and 'one-party' states were debated, in particular the capacity of these alternative systems to restrain the abuses of politicians. But even the defenders of the existing system could not defend the politicians, and what was to be concluded when only one type of individual ever got elected?

The issue took an intriguing turn in April when the Mid-Western Region became the first in Nigeria officially to become 'one-party', as eight of the nine MDF members in the Mid-Western House of Assembly crossed over to the ruling NCNC. In welcoming the former opposition members, Premier Dennis Osadebay said they had chosen unity over disorder, and declared himself a believer in the one-party system of government: 'It is natural, it is African, it is efficient' (*West Africa*, 17 April 1965: 417).[2]

The Northern and Eastern Regions were effectively one-party as well, but neither had achieved such a fusion of government and opposition. The conviction underlying the move – Chief Osadebay's belief that the ethnic and regional character of Nigerian politics were not conducive to formal party competition and opposition – was akin to the thinking behind the various proposals for a National or United Front Government. Generally favoured by moderate political elements, the idea also captured the interest for a time of NCNC President Dr Okpara and of many radical intellectuals (whose concept of the composition of such a government, however, was very different).[3]

CONSTITUTIONAL REVIEW

A key provision of the January compromise agreement had been a timely review of the Constitution. For the NCNC, it was perhaps *the essential* provision, as Dr Okpara underscored on 8 April, when he warned that the continued existence of Nigeria as a nation would be threatened if the constitution were not reviewed (*West Africa*, 17 April 1965: 435).

Late in March, President Azikiwe laid out his vision of constitutional change in an article in the American quarterly, *Foreign Affairs*. His proposals to transfer certain strategic executive responsibilities to the Presidency and control over the armed forces to a new Nigerian Privy Council conformed precisely with the changes Premier Okpara had called for the previous year, as did his call to give the Senate significant concurrent powers (see Chapter 7). Pointing to the North directly, Dr Azikiwe called for granting women the right to vote or reducing Northern representation in Parliament by half, and proposed reducing the authority of Islamic *Alkali* courts and *Sharia* courts of appeal in favour of greater federal uniformity and control. Most importantly, he pleaded for division of the country into more Regions so that 'no one region would be in a position to dominate the rest' (Azikiwe, 1965). Closely reflecting NCNC/UPGA positions, the article once again cast the President in a partisan role.

Opposition to such sweeping constitutional changes was not confined to the NPC. It was also voiced by one of the country's most esteemed constitutional experts, former Western Region Attorney-General and long-time Legal Adviser to the Action Group, Chief Rotimi Williams. While arguing for certain changes in the judicial structure – in particular, restoration of the Judicial Service Commission to remove judicial appointments from political manipulation and control (a move also strongly urged by the Federal Chief Justice) – Chief Williams criticised the proposed increase in Presidential powers as a 'dangerous experiment' that would put 'two captains in one boat' (*West Africa*, 27 March 1965: 333–4). Indeed, it was difficult to see how this would have enhanced the position of the East or the UPGA, since the Sardauna had repeatedly stated that if a directly elected Executive President were established he would give the vote to women in order to ensure that the President was a Northerner. In June, he reiterated that if an Executive Presidency were approved, the post would have to be declared vacant, and he had his candidate for the job (*West Africa*, 19 June 1965: 687).

Against this dubious background, the machinery for constitutional review was set in motion by the Prime Minister on 25 May 1965 with the announcement of a summit of the Regional Premiers in early August. There they agreed to a committee to arrange a conference to review the Constitution. But with the stalemates over the regional structure and the Executive Presidency, with the NPC also unwilling to consider changes in the Northern legal system, with the Premiers ruling out restoration of the Judicial Service Commission, and with the regions having recently and amicably agreed to modest changes in revenue allocation,[4] it appeared 'most unlikely that anything will be proposed, far less approved, that will alter significantly the present pattern of the Nigerian Republic' (*West Africa*, 11 September 1965: 1009).

The planned constitutional conference not only failed to take form at the urgent pace ('within six months') envisioned by UPGA in January, it never got off the ground. Overwhelmed by the Western Regional Election crisis, it was rendered irrelevant a few months later by military coup.

THE WESTERN REGIONAL ELECTION CAMPAIGN

With dissolution of the Western House of Assembly constitutionally required before 28 September 1965, the campaign of the two rival alliances began heating up in September. The previous eight months since the Zik-Balewa agreement had been a period of relative calm. No firm arrangements (and no focused conflict) had yet emerged with regard to the constitutional review, and even during the University of Lagos uproar, the NCNC's most prominent leaders remained conspicuously silent, quietly consolidating their weakened position in the Federal Government. The smooth acceptance of the new recommendations for revenue allocation was interpreted as a sign of 'an underlying readiness to co-operate'. Despite the tensions of the approaching election campaign, despite the persistence of 'corruption, nepotism and greed for power' which were eroding respect for government, it was still possible to believe that the regime would endure. In a lead commentary on 'Nigeria's Prospects', *West Africa* observed: 'It is her capacity for overcoming successive political crisis, and not the absence of strife which suggests that this is basically a stable country' (25 September 1965: 1065).

What prevailed was only an illusion of stability, however, for none of the major crises had yet been overcome in the sense of any mutually acceptable resolution. As the wounds from previous conflicts festered, each new one became more bitter, more violent, and more resistant to compromise. The Western Regional Election would bring the final and most violent crisis in this destructive cycle of polarisation.

Both sides viewed the election as a 'do or die' struggle. For the UPGA, the campaign was 'a last desperate attempt to challenge the hegemony of the NPC' (Schwarz, 1968: 178). A solid victory in the West would not change the grim balance in the Federal House, but it would give it control of three Regions (as well as Lagos), and hence a commanding majority in the Senate, where it could block much critical legislation. A defeat would likely mean further heavy defections from the AG and the NCNC in the West, where the costs of continued loyalty to the UPGA parties had been eased by the expectation that the unpopular Akintola Government would be booted from office in the next election. For Premier Akintola and the NNDP, it was also 'do or die'. Despite almost three years in office (first as the UPP) and a powerful political machine, the new party had been unable to establish a strong grassroots base. In the absence of active popular support, it had come to rely increasingly on blunt manipulation of the rewards and sanctions of Regional power. If it lost this advantage, it was unlikely ever to rebound politically.

The election was also of great consequence for the NPC. Completely shut out in the East and Mid-West, the NPC badly needed to retain its government ally in the West in order to preserve some legitimacy for its domination of the Centre. An UPGA victory in the West would give the opposition complete control of the South and make of national politics a naked struggle between North and South that might be impossible to control, even with a firm NNA majority in the Federal House.

Despite the advantage of incumbency, the NNDP faced formidable difficulties. Extensive official victimisation might have done much to cow open opposition but it also embittered old enemies and created new ones, engendering hatred of the ruling party in many areas. The NNDP knew its victory the previous December was a hollow one, owing heavily to UPGA's disastrous election boycott. And it had the misfortune of having to face the electorate at a time of sharp decline in world cocoa prices (and, after years of political abuse, exhaustion of the Region's financial reserves), which severely depressed the regional economy and fanned persistent rumours of an imminent slash in the Government's guaranteed price to cocoa farmers. Finally, there was the continued bitterness over the imprisonment of Chief Awolowo.

The content of the campaign differed little from that of the previous year. Once again the NNDP portrayed itself as the champion of the Yoruba cause and warned against the threat of 'Ibo domination' as represented by the UPGA. On 1 September, a chief NNDP propagandist declared, 'More and more Ibo business interests are pouring into Lagos and Ibadan and the Ibos are striving might and main to penetrate the Western economy, thereby exploiting our wealth and riches for the benefit of themselves'. That this would be the chief election issue was clearly signalled on 25 September when Chief Akinjide officially launched the NNDP campaign with the warning that 'the members of the UPGA are now shamelessly seeking for the votes of the people of Western Nigeria to enable them [to] carry out their plan to establish "Ibo empire" in Nigeria' (both quoted in Post and Vickers, 1973: 221).

The other face of the NNDP campaign was familiar as well – the rewards of state control. These were more tangible now that the NNDP was firmly positioned in the Federal Government, controlling such patronage-rich Ministries as Education and Industry. The party's 'Fair Share Manifesto' promised that with an NNDP government in the West, 'The Yorubas will no longer stand as spectators watching other tribes enjoying milk and honey' (Anifowose, 1982: 213). Indeed, it had already 'delivered' a Vice-Chancellorship and the lion's share of Federal Scholarships in 1965.[5] Control of the Regional Government enabled some timely announcements, such as loans for farmers in hard-pressed areas, and the withholding of others, namely the government price for cocoa in the coming buying season (which was slashed nearly in half shortly after the election) (Post and Vickers, 1973: 221–2).

The UPGA centred its campaign on the political abuses and economic hardship it charged the Akintola Government with inflicting upon the people of the Region:

> People are victimised for no just cause; thugs are let loose on innocent women and children; schools are closed down as a political vendetta on individuals and even professors and lecturers are sacked on the flimsiest excuse. Produce buyers, liquor sellers, goldsmiths, have their licenses withdrawn and market women have been deprived of their stalls for failing to team up with the NNDP. (quoted in Schwarz, 1968: 180)

The UPGA manifesto promised 'as its first and most immediate duty' to seek the release of Chief Awolowo. It pledged drastic reductions in the size of Premier Akintola's bloated Cabinet (in which 49 of the 54 NNDP Members of the Western House served as Ministers or Parliamentary Secretaries) and in the number of directors of public corporations. And it sharply contrasted the prosperity under Chief Awolowo (when cocoa prices were high and revenues seemed boundless) with the severe recession under Akintola (Schwarz, 1968: 180).

On 18 September, the Western Regional House was dissolved and the election date set for 11 October. The shape of the coming campaign was indicated on the last day's sitting of the old House, when the governing party passed over fierce objections a series of blatantly partisan changes in the electoral regulations. If any candidate declared elected 'unopposed' were murdered, nominators were empowered to return a new one to office. Electoral officers (who were controlled by the Regional Government) were empowered to postpone elections in any constituency where there had been rioting or violence during the campaign. And on election day the polls were to close at 4:00 p.m. instead of 6:00 p.m. – enabling employers (in particular, the Government) to prevent workers from voting at all. The day the House was dissolved, the Government banned public meetings and processions for the entire duration of the campaign and five weeks thereafter (*West Africa*, 25 September 1965: 1082; Schwarz, 1968: 180–1; Anifowose, 1982: 216–17).

The ban on public meetings could not but grossly distort the campaign and handicap the UPGA forces, which heavily depended upon rallying their grassroots support. While Chief Adegbenro did not publicly protest the ban, Dr Okpara condemned it as a 'panic measure' and proceeded to Lagos to launch a personal campaign in the West. But there he remained, not wanting to provoke disturbances that might justify postponement of the election. Campaigning had to be conducted in the form of house-to-house canvassing. Still, a number of other Eastern and Mid-Western NCNC leaders joined in the UPGA campaign. The active support of Mid-Western Premier Osadebay and his NCNC branch, who had stood their distance from the UPGA in the Federal election, was a sign of the critical importance the NCNC attached to an UPGA victory in the West. Ironically, the ban forced the last-minute cancellation of a scheduled NNA campaign tour of the Region by the Northern Premier, a tour which UPGA leaders had welcomed as a progressive turn in Nigerian politics (*West Africa*, 25 September and 2 October 1965: 1082, 1102).

There were much graver problems for the UPGA, however, than the ban on public campaigning. As in the North the previous year, the nominations process was grossly abused by the ruling party. This time the UPGA anticipated the attempt to return many candidates of the ruling party 'unopposed' and took extraordinary precautions. As soon as the House was dissolved, it published the names of its candidates in each of the 94 constituencies. 'Not content with this, it paid all their deposits and, to make doubly sure, made all of them swear affidavits before magistrates that they intended to stand and that no letter of withdrawal purporting to come from them should be considered valid without oral reference to them' (Schwarz, 1968: 181). Still, the UPGA faced the inherent difficulty of all electoral oppositions in the First Republic: electoral administration was in the hands of officials (primarily local and regional civil servants) responsive to direction and pressure from the region's ruling party. The Chairman of the Federal Electoral Commission would later lament the FEC's inability to exercise control over the Western

Nigeria Electoral commission and its partisan staff (*West Africa*, 27 November 1965: 1354).

As a result of pervasive malpractices by the NNDP, the administration of the election broke down completely, beginning with the nominations process. As in the North in 1964, electoral officers mysteriously disappeared from their constituencies once the NNDP nominations were filed, and the filing of UPGA nominations was intimidated by thuggery. On 26 September, the day before nominations were due to close, the Progressive Alliance again released the names of all its 94 candidates and, protesting that only 80 had been able to file nominations, requested an extension of the deadline. The request was ignored, and two days later twelve NNDP candidates were declared elected unopposed. By 30 September, the number had risen to 15, despite the UPGA's claim to have received certificates of validity for 86 of its candidates.[6] Four days later it was announced that Premier Akintola's opponent had withdrawn (*West Africa*, 9 October 1965: 1121; Post and Vickers, 1973: 225–6).

Angrily, the UPGA protested that it had legitimate candidates in all 16 'unopposed' constituencies and that the Premier's opponent had 'not willingly withdrawn'. Two court challenges were filed seeking injunctions against the unopposed return of NNDP candidates, but both were quickly dismissed. By 6 October, the Progressive Alliance decided to let the issue rest for the time being, boosting its supporters with the observation that 78 seats still remained to be contested (Post and Vickers, 1973: 226).

Caught in the crossfire of fraud and protest once again was the Chairman of the Federal Electoral Commission, E. E. Esua. When evidence of malpractice began surfacing soon after nominations opened, Esua met with UPGA officials to consider their complaints. For this he earned scorn from both sides. An Action Group official predicted, 'The man is going to bungle the whole thing again', while the NNDP called for his resignation, denying his authority to 'sack or appoint electoral officers'. Against vigorous NNDP resistance to any FEC interference, Esua travelled around the Region with other Commission members and did, in fact, sack and replace some of the offending officers. But his limited efforts were largely frustrated by the Regional Government, which refused to recognise some certificates issued to UPGA candidates by the new officers and managed to restore some of the dismissed officers. In a radio broadcast on 28 September, Esua candidly conceded that some electoral officers had been kidnapped and others had had their lives threatened to prevent them from discharging their duties. But, to continued condemnation from both alliances, he could only protest helplessly that the scope of the FEC's powers did not enable it to 'perform the miracles expected by some people who themselves were privy to the making of these laws and regulations' (quoted in Post and Vickers, 1973: 225; Schwarz, 1968: 182).

The Progressive Alliance was also seriously weakened again by internal conflict over nominations. In a number of constituencies, local Action Group branches, desperate to reassert their positions in the Region's structure of rewards, refused to accept central party decisions allocating seats to the NCNC. In the end, the NCNC nominated 35 candidates (3 more than agreed to by the AG) but in 20 of these contests the AG also nominated a candidate (Post and Vickers, 1973: 226). This vote-splitting appears to have cost the UPGA at least five or six seats (*West Africa*, 23 October 1965: 1194).

THE ELECTION

Despite the many debilitating obstacles to a free and fair campaign, the UPGA may very well have won the election – if by winning is meant receiving the largest number of legitimate votes in a majority of the seats. The truth will never be known, so extensively were the balloting, counting and announcement of returns riddled with fraud. By a series of wilful, ingenious, and, it would appear, carefully premeditated actions, the election was hopelessly rigged.

Through the ban on public gatherings and the deployment of 7000 Nigerian police – nearly half the total Federal force – the brief campaign had been kept unusually peaceful and orderly. But as the 11 October polling date approached, rumours of election rigging proliferated. During the final days before the election, word spread in UPGA circles that the results would not be announced locally but only through the government's Western Nigeria Broadcasting Service. This was denied by authorities, but the apprehension of foul play was heightened by the rejection of several UPGA proposals to guard against the wholesale falsification of the results that was widely feared. Once again, the opposition called for the Nigerian Army and Police to take charge of the most sensitive elements of electoral administration (Post and Vickers, 1973: 227).

On election eve, the mounting anxiety and months of pent-up anger finally snapped. An 18-year-old Electoral Officer was shot dead in his office in Ibadan, and a curfew was declared there that night. The next day worried parents kept their children home from school as voters went to the polls, and the violence that would reign in the Region until the fall of the regime began to pour forth. Two more electoral officers were shot and killed, along with two party polling agents. In Ibadan, an NNDP jeep was burned by UPGA supporters. In a Mushin constituency (outside Lagos), UPGA supporters set fire to ten houses, including two said to belong to the Electoral Officer whose postponement of the polling there precipitated the arson. Army troops and Nigeria Police opened fire on the crowd, killing two people. Other reports of violence and disorder around the Region staggered into Ibadan throughout the day (*West Africa*, 16 October 1965: 1151, 1155).

The motivation for the violence – the belief that the voting was being rigged – was well founded. An authoritative account of the day's events reported:

> The main idea at this stage was to try to prevent the official polling agents of the opposition from being present in the booths, while enabling the government party agents to stay on. All accredited agents had to be issued with special identity discs. At the last moment, however, it was decreed that these discs had to be counter-signed on the reverse side by an electoral officer. When polling day dawned, the government party agents had their duly countersigned, while those of the opposition found theirs were not. Needless to say the electoral officers were nowhere to be found. These were only the more obvious devices. Behind the scenes, large numbers of ballot papers mysteriously disappeared from police custody, presumably to find their way into the government party boxes. A number of supporters of both sides were arrested in possession of illegally obtained ballot papers, but prosecutions were squashed. (Schwarz, 1968: 182–3)

Rigging was apparent in the counting as well. In many constituencies, UPGA polling agents and candidates were kept away from the ballot counting by various means, including dusk-to-dawn curfews in the major cities and, in at least one constituency, at gunpoint by the local government police. And despite the assurance to the contrary, the UPGA's worst fear was realised: instructions were issued not to announce the results in the constituencies, as the electoral regulations required, but to report them to the Premier's office for broadcast over the regional government network. This enabled the government, when all else failed, to simply reverse the results. 'In several well-attested cases, the UPGA candidate was declared elected by the returning officer and even given a certificate to the effect, only to hear his opponent declared elected over the radio' (Schwarz, 1968: 183; Miners, 1971: 151).[7]

The results did not begin to trickle in until the early hours of the following day, but as they were broadcast throughout the morning from Ibadan, it was clear that the NNDP was taking a commanding lead. By noon it had won a majority of the seats. Or so its Broadcasting Service claimed. Incredibly, the Eastern Nigeria Broadcasting Service was reporting an entirely different set of figures, which the UPGA was releasing from Chief Awolowo's house in Ibadan, where it was receiving its own information from the constituencies. These were showing an electoral landslide for the UPGA. On 13 October, as most newspapers were leading with the news of Akintola's new Government, UPGA newspapers were headlining Alhaji Adegbenro's dramatic claim of an UPGA victory the previous evening (*West Africa*, 16 October 1965: 1149).

Adegbenro's press conference that evening of 12 October was perhaps the climactic moment in the life of the First Republic. Throughout the day, the Action Group acting leader had sought an audience with the Governor, Sir Odeleye Fadahunsi, to complain of the massive irregularities and seek redress, warning that he would form an interim government of his own if Chief Akintola were appointed to form a new government. Declining to see him, the Governor had instead acted on the official reports of an NNDP landslide and reappointed Chief Akintola Premier. Now, in the library of Chief Awolowo's home, an exhausted Adegbenro released returns showing the UPGA winning 68 of the 94 seats (compared to 17 seats in the official returns). Declaring himself 'convinced that the UPGA has won the election' he announced formation of an 'interim government' with himself as Premier. A correspondent conveyed the mood of desperation and foreboding that gripped the room the occasion:

It may, indeed, be partly exasperation at his own constituency result that has driven Alhaji Adegbenro to extreme action. His claims about his votes seemed mythical, and his statement that he was nominated by nobody ('I nominated myself') was that of a man who had thrown caution to the winds. The pressures on this unlikely rebel must have been enormous. Though widely respected as a God-fearing and moderate man, . . . he seemed at the end of his tether.

It was a strange and improbable scene; there was a power cut as soon as he started to speak, so candles were brought out. I had an uneasy and perhaps entirely unwarranted premonition that here, among all Chief Awolowo's books, by flickering candlelight, was being enacted the funeral rites of the Westminster model as a practical proposition in African politics. (*West Africa*, 16 October 1965: 1150)

The following day, Chief Adegbenro and some of his 'Ministers' were arrested for unlawfully forming 'an interim executive council'. By then, the people of the Western Region were already rising up in rebellion against the government they believed had returned itself by fraud.

AFTERMATH: DESCENT INTO CHAOS

The final returns gave the NNDP a massive victory (roughly three quarters of the seats). But they were utterly without credibility: 'Everybody knew that the election had been rigged and that there was no shred of truth in the official results' (Osuntokun, 1982: 192). Although the NNDP remained in office, it no longer could be said to govern. With its authority completely shattered, the Akintola Government proved powerless to halt the waves of protest and violence that swelled in the aftermath of the election rigging.

The descent into chaos began with the election itself. A week of relative calm followed, the result of a four-day curfew imposed on election night and of uncertainty over the election outcome. As the curfew was ending on 15 October, Premier Akintola's first post-election speech was displaced from the airwaves by a masked gunman who forced engineers at the Ibadan station to broadcast a substitute tape demanding, 'Akintola get out, get out and take with you your band of renegades who have lost all sense of shame' (Schwarz, 1968: 188). There were disturbances in Adegbenro's home town of Abeokuta following his arrest.[8] In Ilesha (the home town of the Governor) the Governor's private residence and other houses were attacked. Students demonstrated against the election returns and clashed with the police at the University of Ibadan. Market women were dispersed by police with tear gas in Lagos and Ibadan after attempting to march on the official residences of the Prime Minister and Governor. Along with the riot police, soldiers patrolled the streets of Ibadan in armoured cars (*West Africa*, 23 October 1965: 1194). As his authority was collapsing, Chief Akintola was shattered by the death (apparently by suicide) of his eldest daughter, who had been his most cherished aide and confidante (Osuntokun, 1982: 195).

The protest was not confined to the West. There were also demonstrations in the East and Mid-West, whose Premiers denounced the election results and backed up Alhaji Adegbenro. Some militants among the hundreds of demonstrators in Enugu chanted, 'Give us guns' – presumably to do battle against a government in the West that Dr Okpara had called 'illegal and undemocratic' (Schwarz, 1968: 185). Debate in the Federal House over the conduct of the election became so enraged that the House had to be adjourned. Meanwhile, the Prime Minister gave no sign of appreciation of what was taking place. The present 'confusion' in the West, he suggested, 'had been deliberately planned'. In a gloomy tone he declared to Parliament, 'If politics will turn into this way for innocent people, I think it is time we think of the future of this country. Democracy does not mean that one can do what one likes' (*West Africa*, 23 October 1965: 1195). With that, the Prime Minister departed for an OAU conference in Ghana, leaving behind an opposition indignant at his inaction.

Early in November, the long-festering anger in the West erupted in 'spontaneous armed rebellion' (Post and Vickers, 1973: 229). Realisation that Akintola would not be dislodged combined with his Government's announcement of a drastic cut in the guaranteed price for cocoa to spark a new wave of violence, unprecedented in its scale and ferocity. Within a month of the election, some eighty persons were reported killed in Ondo Province alone, and heavy casualties were reported in many other areas as well (Anifowose, 1982: 244).

Many deaths and injuries resulted from large-scale clashes between demonstrators and police, who, in several instances, opened fire at point-blank range. But there were also numerous incidents of selected violence against the symbols of NNDP authority. In Chief Awolowo's home province of Ijebu, a customary court judge was driven from his home by armed men and beheaded, and fighting broke out between the Yoruba and the Hausa settlers, who were associated with the NNDP in the popular mind. Elsewhere, another customary court judge was killed and several court buildings burned. In Ilesha, demonstrators attempted to burn down the residence of the Governor. Arson was increasingly employed against the NNDP Government and its prominent supporters, many of whose homes were also attacked and looted. (Post and Vickers, 1973: 229–30; *West Africa*, 13 November 1965: 1283; Schwarz, 1968: 187). As in previous episodes of political violence, party thugs – heavily armed, extensively financed and centrally directed – figured prominently in the wave of attacks and clashes (Anifowose, 1982: 232–4).

The NNDP responded with official and unofficial repression. Its thugs struck back by burning the Ibadan printing workshop of the *Nigerian Tribune*, the Action Group newspaper. When this failed to eliminate the newspaper, the Government arrested its staff several times, but somehow the paper staggered on (Schwarz, 1968: 187). Even before this, the (NNDP-controlled) Ibadan City Council had banned the *Tribune* and six other UPGA newspapers and fixed a penalty of £100 or six months in jail for reading them. The Council also forbade listening to the Eastern Nigeria Broadcasting Service. A dusk-to-dawn curfew was reimposed in Ibadan and several other areas of rebellion, including Ikeja and Mushin. Reinforcements of Nigerian Police, already heavily deployed in the West, were summoned. The Fourth Battalion of the Nigerian Army, stationed at Ibadan, was also employed (Post and Vickers, 1973: 230; *West Africa*, 13 November 1965: 1283).

Repression worked for a time, and the violence subsided to sporadic incidents by mid-November. By then, however, most of the remaining fabric of Nigerian democracy was unravelling. Local councils in the Eastern Region banned three newspapers from the West and a University lecturer who condemned the ban as undemocratic became the target of intense political attack. Editors of two pro-UPGA newspapers were arrested on federal charges of sedition and false publication stemming from their reporting of the alternative Western election returns. As the atmosphere of repression thickened, the increasingly intimidated press stepped up its own self-censorship (Schwarz, 1968: 187).

On November 20, the Federal Electoral Commission Chairman came forward with his sensational letter to the Governor confirming charges of election fraud and calling for sweeping changes in the electoral law, without which, he warned, 'we may as well say farewell to parliamentary democracy and the rule of law in Nigeria' (quoted in Nwankwo and Ifejika, 1969: 94–5). Declaring that Esua's letter showed that elections in the West had been rigged, Premier

Osadebay observed, 'You cannot rule the people with soldiers and police all the time. You can only rule if the people want you' (*West Africa*, 27 November 1965: 1354).

Pressure was building upon the Federal Government to act to save the situation. Alhaji Adegbenro cited Esua's letter in demanding a 'high powered public commission inquiry' into the election and proposed a provisional government with equal representation from both parties, headed by a Federal administrator. Other UPGA leaders went further. Noting the decay of law and order in the West, they called for the Federal Government to declare a State of Emergency and remove the Akintola Government altogether, paving the way for fresh elections under impartial administration. If an Emergency could have been declared over a scuffle in the Western House three years ago, why not now, when large numbers of people were in open rebellion against the Government? To such an appeal from a delegation of University of Ibadan students on 16 November, the Prime Minister replied that he had no intention of declaring an Emergency, and that UPGA should seek to redress its grievances in the courts. As rebellion spread, public pressure on the Prime Minister intensified, but he steadfastly refused to ask Parliament to declare an Emergency. Throughout these final weeks of the First Republic, 'Balewa was either unwilling or unable to convince his party leadership in Kaduna that the political disadvantages that would arise from the fall of Akintola were far less serious than the general calamity which now promised to overtake the whole regime' (Schwarz, 1968: 189).

The UPGA made its own position on the deadlock clear again in early December, declaring that recourse to the courts (which had so far proved fruitless for individual candidates) was a waste of time and money. Public opinion should decide, said the UPGA. In the absence of Federal action, it was deciding – in the streets and fields.

A new and larger wave of riots and arson – sparked in part by the murder of two popular Action Group organisers in Ijebu – began at the end of November. Again, the property of Government supporters was attacked and destroyed. Flit guns, normally used to spray cocoa trees with pesticides, were now employed to drench property – and sometimes people – with gasoline before setting them afire. This was known as 'wetting'. Farmers burned the houses, crops and cocoa plantations of NNDP 'Big Men' and drove them from the countryside into Lagos or Ibadan, where police and army troops maintained tight control. On his return from a visit to Ibadan, a local Oba in

Ijebu was 'wetted' and burned to death by his subjects. Police posts and barracks were attacked and burned; police on patrol were ambushed and killed (Post and Vickers, 1973: 230–1; Miners, 1971: 151).

As a result of the massive violence and destruction, the Akintola regime began to haemorrhage at the local level. By the end of November, the *West African Pilot* was daily reporting the recantations of former NNDP customary court judges and local councillors. Two NNDP House members also changed allegiance, each 'at the request of my constituents' (Miners, 1971: 152).

But Premier Akintola refused to yield.[9] A mediation effort by a 'Peace Committee' of Yoruba elders, headed by Federal Chief Justice Ademola, proved fruitless. The *Daily Times'* call for an all-party government in the West until a new election could be peacefully conducted had no effect. Repression escalated with the violence. Deaths from police action rose (Post and Vickers, 1973: 231–2).

The final weeks in December and January were a time of accelerating political, social and economic disintegration in the West. Armed with guns, cutlasses, bows and arrows, and petrol, angry mobs challenged police and searched for targets of retribution among the NNDP elite. More government buildings were attacked and burned. Telephone wires were disconnected. Payment of taxes virtually ceased. Demonstrators in Ilesha finally succeeded in burning down the Governor's residence. In other towns, UPGA demonstrators set up roadblocks to prevent NNDP politicians from returning with force to quell their protests. NNDP ministers and party leaders travelled with armed police escorts, and were themselves armed with revolvers. Lawlessness reigned on the highways as bands of thieves, thugs and angry unemployed youths stopped motorists and demanded money. The Nigeria Police, reinforced with detachments from the North but now identified with a hated government, were powerless to stop it. The chaos in Mushin became 'so intolerable that large numbers of ordinary people began to move out of the area' (Post and Vickers, 1973: 232). Economic activity withered as harvesting was disrupted by the violence and markets and motor-parks were boycotted or shut down (Miners, 1971: 153–4; Schwarz, 1968: 187–8; First, 1970: 157; Osuntokun, 1982: 196).

To the rise of common banditry and mayhem in these final weeks was added another sinister development – the growth of ethnic violence between the Yoruba and the Hausa, who were settled in small merchant communities in most Yoruba towns and who migrated to Western fields on a seasonal basis to help with the cocoa harvest.

These Northerners naturally supported the party of the Sardauna's ally, Chief Akintola, and their property suffered from the indiscriminate attacks on all followers of the NNDP. Drivers of large trucks which brought produce down from the North to Lagos found it necessary to assemble in convoy before crossing the Western Region border in order to avoid being individually waylaid and murdered on the road. Cars with Northern Region number-plates were liable to be stopped and burnt. (Miners, 1971: 153)

This new turn in the disintegration of the West began to generate doubts within some Northern circles about the NPC policy (to which the Sardauna had committed the full weight of his power and prestige) of backing the NNDP at all costs. Through late December and early January, any reappraisal awaited the return of the Sardauna from his annual pilgrimage to Mecca. On 10 January 1966, the *New Nigerian* (owned by the Northern Government) editorialised:

Facts must be faced ... and the facts are that thousands of people in the West are convinced that the last elections there were not fairly conducted. They remain convinced that Chief Akintola has no right to be in power ... Force is having to be used to prevent the violence in the West from spreading ... In the North we cannot sit back doing nothing while our kinsmen are being killed in other parts of the Federation. (Miners, 1971: 153)

The Sardauna did not return until 13 January. By then, Sir Abubakar was apparently seeking some kind of compromise settlement, working with Chief Justice Ademola and others. In an interview on the evening of 14 January, he indicated that while the Action Group had accepted his mediation the NNDP so far had not. Resolution of the conflict, he conceded, would have to take the form of some kind of coalition government. 'I have the solution at my fingertips – I could solve it in five minutes,' said Balewa, 'if only everybody could come together, could forget the past' (*West Africa*, 29 January 1966: 113). The powers in the ruling coalition, the Sardauna and Chief Akintola, had no such intention. Earlier in the day, Chief Akintola had flown to Kaduna to see the Sardauna. It is believed that they discussed a plan for drastic Army and police action to crush popular resistance and protest in the West, involving the removal on leave of General Ironsi (suspected of UPGA sympathies), the disbandment of some (presumably Igbo-led) army units considered unsafe, and 'the massive arrest of dissident politicians, officials, writers, and journalists in the West' (Schwarz, 1968: 190; Ademoyega, 66–8).

In fact, Muffett (1982: 12–13, 19–21) maintains that the Army crackdown, 'Operation No Mercy', had been authorised by the Council of Ministers in December and set to begin on 17 January (having been postponed from 1 January for the Commonwealth Conference in Lagos), but that its purpose was simply to restore order. Moreover, he claims (pp. 17–19) that Chief Akintola was aware that the Prime Minister and the Sardauna were prepared to withdraw their support and 'to go for a vote on a State of Emergency' in the Western Region 'if Akintola showed the slightest sign of a continuing inability to reach a political settlement after order was restored and relative peace reigned'. This does appear to have been Sir Abubakar's sentiment; whether it was also the Sardauna's may forever remain in dispute.[10]

In any case, there can be little doubt that Akintola was then demanding strong Army action in support of his government. As he flew to Kaduna on 14 January, the beseiged Premier was driven by a sense of urgency, having been warned that a military coup was imminent and that he and the Sardauna would be among its principal targets (Muffett: 20–1). Perhaps from fatalism perhaps from arrogant confidence, the Sardauna apparently rejected these warnings. Although the Prime Minister had discounted these same warnings after reassurances from the Special Branch of the police, the tone of his interview that evening suggests the mood of a man who nevertheless knew that time was running out.

Time *had* run out – for both compromise and repression. By the morning of 15 January 1966, all three men were dead and the First Republic was finished.

ANALYSIS

The cleavage

It was one of the many paradoxes of politics in Nigeria's First Republic that an election struggle within one region, among one people, should have served as the stage for the final showdown between the bitterly opposed parties of two other regions and ethnic groups. As they had in 1962, the Yoruba people became the victims of political designs to exploit their internal conflict in the struggle for control of the Federation. Even more than in 1962, the West was the pivotal region in national politics. In each of the other regions, a single party was dominant. Only in the West did the government lack a clear popular mandate. Only in the West was the outcome of a free and fair contest for power in doubt.

Once the 1962 crisis removed the third force in Nigerian politics, the West became the primary battleground for the remaining two sides. For the NPC, a firm grip on federal power required an ally in power somewhere in the South, and the West was the only possibility. Without this, the NPC could probably cling to a majority in the most powerful chamber of Parliament, but would face deadlock by the Senate and, more importantly, would be forced to govern over a North–South fault line that might split the Federation permanently in two. For the NCNC, control of the West – even if through a reluctant alliance with its old nemesis, the Action Group – was its only hope for survival as a serious contender for national power. A defeat in the West, leaving the wily and determined ally of the Sardauna to consolidate his power there for five more years, would almost certainly have foreclosed the possibility of the NCNC ever rising above its decidely junior position in the Federal Government.

The election was a 'do or die' struggle for both of the Western parties as well, since a victory by either one would likely have implied the expiration of the other as a viable political force. There is no doubting the depth and bitterness of the continuing cleavage within the Yoruba West along personal, ideological, sub-ethnic, and emotional/symbolic lines. This cleavage cannot be seen as a mere reflection and appendage of North–East political conflict; since early 1962, and to some extent long before that, it had been developing a momentum of its own. But it became engulfed by the larger national cleavage, so that the 1965 Western election was at once a continuation of the 1962 conflict in the West and the 1964 conflict in the Federation.

A third cleavage exploded into prominence after the election. This involved a peripheral collective actor in most of the previous political conflicts, what may loosely be termed 'the masses'. Most observers believed that Chief Awolowo's party commanded a much greater popular following than did Chief Akintola's. Certainly Awolowo's popularity became both wider and more emotionally intense as his trial and imprisonment cast him in the role of martyr of the Yoruba people. While Akintola and his party had certain clear areas of popular strength – such as his ethnic homeland of Oshun, and Oyo, the historical rival of Ijebu – their chances of electoral success in 1965 rested mainly on the support they had induced or coerced through manipulation of the rewards and sanctions of regional power.

Even for a people who had come to expect a certain amount of corruption and coercion from their political leaders, the performance of the NNDP in its three years of power had been an outrage. Coercion had become ruthless, corruption obscene. In the orgy of greed, favouritism and victimisation, development needs were denied attention, imagination and funding in the West, as in the Federation overall. Of course, the corruption and decay had begun before Akintola became Premier. And 'few of his methods – coercing people into supporting the party by the threat of petty prosecution, the withdrawal of trading licences, the denial of privileges, the harassment of opponents at elections – were new to the West. They had been practised in the days of Action Group power – when the same Akintola was their chief planner' (Schwarz, 1968: 188). But, faced with a horrendous economic slump and pervasive and intense opposition, the Akintola regime transformed the familiar coercion into an unfamiliar ruthlessness. For when an unwanted regime is determined to remain in power, force and intimidation must substitute for legitimate authority, casting the ruling politicians as oppressors in the eyes of the people. Popular opposition then turns to hatred, which may ignite in spontaneous rebellion. The acts of rebellion were most prevalent in areas, such as Ijebu and Ekiti, where popular support for the Action Group had remained particularly steadfast, and hence where coercion and victimisation (including the denial of development resources) had been particularly harsh. But violent disturbances occurred in virtually all of the Region's sixteen administrative Divisions and appear to have elicited support and participation from a wide range of social and economic groups: farmers, market women, other self-employed people both in the countryside and the cities, intellectuals, and university and secondary school students (Anifowose, 1982: 230–1, 238–40).

Thus, the chaos following the election reflected something much broader and more profound than partisan alienation extended to the mass level, or historic sub-ethnic rivalries. It expressed a generalised disgust with the greed and arrogance of politicians, a protest, like the General Strike, 'against the whole way the polity worked' (Post and Vickers, 1973: 232). Looters and highway robbers were aware that their behaviour differed only in its openness from that of the politicians. Said one young man as he threatened to ignite a car he had stopped on the highway, 'Akintola has had his share. Now we want ours' (Schwarz, 1968: 188).

Most rioters were engaged not in indiscriminate violence but in a kind of traditional retribution 'against the wealthy and arrogant', who, in using their political leverage to enrich themselves at a time of widespread hardship and oppression, had offended against the community. Post and Vickers write (p. 233):

at least in the areas where defections to the NNDP had been most blatant and unpopular, the newly rich and arrogant had to be punished. Sometimes they were killed, but more often they were chased away and their property destroyed. Frequently they were warned first, to give them time to leave, and the bullroarer would be sounded from the bush to announce the approach of retribution when it came with its petrol. Thus, with a nice sense of discrimination, the palace of an Oba who had supported Akintola against the majority of his people was left untouched, but all his houses in the town, his personal property, were burned. Other dimensions of traditional community values were hinted at in stories concerning various incidents. When the chief was burned alive in Ijebu, it was said that the women ritually beat him first to degrade him publicly. . . . By the time of the military coup, the West, at least, was being shaken by tensions and antagonisms which went much deeper than just inter-party rivalry.

Antipathy for the political class was growing throughout the country in 1965, especially among educated Nigerians in the intelligentsia, the civil service and the military, who constituted an alternative elite to the political class. While this cleavage was not the primary one in the Western crisis, it was deepened by it (as we shall see) and by numerous other developments throughout the year: the crisis at the University of Lagos, the exposés of scandal and corruption, bloated government, wasteful spending, and economically dislocating political crises.

The rift between the people and the political class widened further during the final months of the regime. Popular and progressive indignation was aroused anew in mid-October, when Members of Parliament voted themselves a two-thirds increase in salaries and allowances, along with new pensions and gratuities. In condemning the move, Lawrence Borha, Secretary-General of the United Labour Congress (and by now an NCNC MP from the Mid-West), protested that millions of Nigerian workers found it hard to make ends meet. An AG MP was shouted down in debate when he said the government was being asked to condone 'daylight robbery' (*West Africa*, 23 October 1965: 1178).

Perhaps the crowning symbol of the pretentiousness and arrogance of the political class was presented in December, when K. O. Mbadiwe (the same NCNC Minister whose corrupt land dealings had been exposed in March) celebrated the completion of his opulent mansion in his home village of Arondizuogu in the East. A columnist wrote, 'Its three storeys, its blue terazzo walls, its gilt furniture, its red carpets, its fountain and its swimming pool – as well as Dr Mbadiwe's generous hospitality – came as a great surprise after the laterite road by which you approach it, and the mud and thatch houses which border the road' (*West Africa*, 1 January 1966: 13). The widely reported event (which brought some 2000 invited guests, including leading federal and regional politicians) reinforced the deepening popular resentment of the political class. Particular attention was given to Dr Okpara's opening remarks, which noted what a great achievement it was for 'one of the priests of pragmatic socialism' to have been so clever 'as to be able to accommodate this building within the context of pragmatic African socialism' (quoted in *West Africa*, 1 January 1966: 13). When the coup came, some three weeks after his gala reception, the inimitable Mbadiwe would be lucky to escape assassination.

His fellow Minister-tycoon, Chief Festus Okotie-Eboh, would not be so fortunate. As Finance Minister, he was the chief architect of the nation's failed trade and development policies, and disenchantment with him intensified in the latter part of the year. During the summer of 1965, sharp popular protest greeted his announcement of higher import tariffs, which fell heavily on basic commodities. In August 1965, his speech on the Budget recognised for the first time 'a serious balance of payments situation' – after ten years of persistent deficits. A commentary in *Nigerian Opinion* blamed the government's 'open-door policy in the uses of foreign exchange and its lack of internal financial discipline', and condemned Okotie-Eboh's new measures as 'no more relevant to the nation's economic ills than curing lung cancer with aspirin' (September 1965: 2). The following month the magazine pointed similar criticism at the government of the Western Region.

By January 1966, then, several cleavages were coming together to ravage the First Republic. The continuing political conflict within the West flowed together with the struggle between the ruling parties of the North and East to produce the fraudulent and violent election battle in the West. The resistance of the Western people to the return of a corrupt and patently undemocratic government then exploded in open rebellion. At the same time, a national crisis of confidence was gathering over the political class and its entire regime, swelling in particular among strategically placed young elites in the universities, the press, the civil service and the military, and also among the unions and radical parties that had successfully confronted the regime the previous year. The first three cleavages underlay the crisis in the West. The fourth drew its final burst of momentum from that crisis to bring down the Republic.

These cleavages are depicted in Figure 8.1 (which employs the model of Tilly (1978)). Inside the box representing the polity are shown the elite cleavages and alliances within the Western Region and the Federation. Outside is the opposition to the regime of a growing disaffected elite and of the people at large. Popular alienation was most intense in the West, where it was dramatically and violently expressed, but it was increasingly felt throughout the South and in at least some portions of the North, especially the Tiv Division.

The outcome

The proximate outcome of the Western election crisis was a massive NNDP victory, which was widely viewed as patently fraudulent. Victory was forcibly imposed by the ruling NNDP, the ally of the NPC, against a Progressive Alliance that now appeared to command the support of all three Southern regions. This was the fourth time in four years that the NPC (with its Western allies) had imposed its position as the outcome of a major political conflict (the others being the 1962 Western Regional crisis, the census crisis, and the Federal Election crisis), and the third time in three years that it had defeated the Eastern Region and the NCNC. Each of these four victories came at the expense of any serious compromise. Each was interpreted by the opposition as having been achieved by illegitimate means. Each

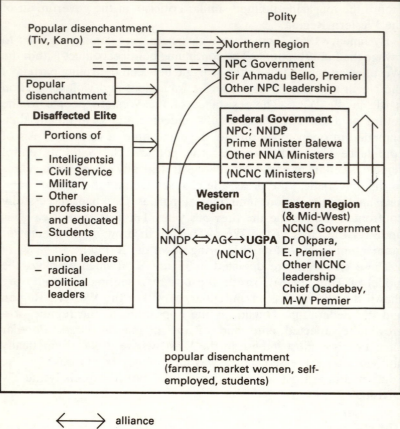

Political System

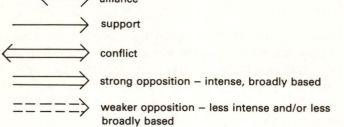

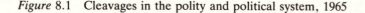

Figure 8.1   Cleavages in the polity and political system, 1965

further consolidated the national dominance of the NPC.

As with the Federal Election crisis, a compromise agreement might have been possible – even after the intense electoral conflict and widespread fraud – to avoid the total alienation of the defeated alliance and its supporters. The outlines of such a possible compromise were suggested by *West Africa* and were no doubt similar to what Chief Justice Ademola and other Yoruba elders (and, it appears, the Prime Minister as well) were trying to bring about. These involved a coalition government in the West between the NNDP and the UPGA, the early release of Chief Awolowo and consideration of electoral reforms as a high priority in the constitutional review. But Chief Akintola was determined to hold on to total power by any means, and he was vigorously backed in his intransigence by the dominant figure in the NPC, the Sardauna.

Causes

As the 1965 Western crisis was the product of past crises and conflicts in the Federation, its causes are to be found among the social and political tensions that generated previous crises. The cumulative pattern of previous conflict was, in itself, a contributing factor. The polarisation of political conflict between the UPGA and the NNA, which almost broke the Federation apart in the Federal Election crisis and was hardly relieved by the superficial compromise, was an important reason why the Regional election was so intensely fought and why neither alliance was prepared to accept defeat. Paralleling this was the polarisation that had been developing in the West since 1962 between Chief Akintola's ruling clique and what remained of the Action Group and the Western NCNC. By 1965, this also involved the deepseated alienation of much of the population from their own Regional Government. As this took violent form in the wake of the election, each new escalation of official repression produced a more ferocious burst of anger and violence, which induced steadily more ruthless repression.

As with the Federal election crisis, a number of structural and cultural factors underlay the polarisation. Prominent again was the peculiar Federal structure. First, because there were so few regions, control of any one of them was crucial in determining the balance of power in the Federation. Neither alliance would have had quite the same stake in the election had it been taking place in one of ten or twelve regions. Second, the coincidence of region and ethnicity (and then party as well) not only helped to polarise Nigerian politics but also invested the Western election with particular significance. In facilitating the pattern of single-party dominance in each of the few regions, this cleavage coincidence also made of any region where the pattern was broken an extraordinary opportunity that the other regional parties could not fail to exploit. Thus, even if the split in the Action Group had had nothing to do with national politics, there would have been powerful pressure on the NCNC and the NPC each to take a side in the conflict. But the new alignment of Yoruba against Yoruba in national politics was not real cross-cutting cleavage. Rather, it divided between two culturally homogeneous political competitors a third force that was no longer capable of autonomous, coherent action. This only intensified both the Western conflict and the national one. Finally, the Federal structure concentrated in the regional governments enormous power to reward support and punish opposition. Premier Akintola's heavy-handed use of this power was an important cause of the intensity, anxiety and polarisation of the electoral struggle. Action Group leaders knew their party could not survive another five years of relentless victimisation. And NNDP leaders knew their devices would be turned against them if they lost (and that their popular base was too limited to rebound to power even if the AG governed with greater restraint). As indicated by Anifowose's interview data (1982: 263–9), the corrupt exercise of this immense regional power also heavily motivated the violent rebellion that followed the election.

Flaws in the system of electoral administration also contributed to the crisis. Perhaps the greatest problem was that regional elections were administered by regional civil servants, 'who in the last analysis will obey the regional governments – which can also mean parties' (*West Africa*, 23 October 1965: 1177). Thus, as the Chairman of the Federal Electoral Commission protested in his impassioned letter to the Governor, 'while the effective organisation and control of the details of the election were left directly in the hands of the Government of the day, the Commission was left utterly helpless . . . to remedy the abuses which came to light' (Nwankwo and Ifejika, 1967: 94). Chairman Esua proposed a number of reforms to insulate the electoral system from partisan manipulation, including greater independence for the electoral commissions in the appointment of senior staff (Schwarz, 1968: 186–7). But in a country so short of administrative talent, 'It is impossible to imagine a Federal Electoral Commission employing enough staff to make itself independent of the Regional Governments. Only the politicians themselves can create the atmosphere in which this body can function as the constitution meant it to' (*West Africa* 23 October 1965).

Indeed, the fundamental problem was the politicians and their overpowering desire for power. No system of electoral administration could have been secure against a ruling party that was determined to win at all costs and was prepared to carry rigging to the point of broadcasting mythical election returns when all else failed. By the same token, 'No regulations can ultimately satisfy a dissident party which can see no explanation except rigging for its defeat' (*West Africa*, 20 November 1965: 1294).

A major cause of the Western election crisis, and of virtually every major political crisis in the First Republic, was that the politicians never really understood the role or appreciated the importance of opposition in a democracy. Especially in a system where so much depended on the control of the state, they were prepared neither to assume this function nor to tolerate it. Nowhere was the tragedy of the First Republic more vividly expressed than in the weary lament of Prime Minister Tafawa Balewa in his last interview, only hours before his death:

I have told people all along that we are not ripe for a system of government in which there is a fully fledged Opposition. In Nigeria, no party can agree to be in opposition for long. A political Opposition in the Western-accepted sense is a luxury that we cannot afford ... The trouble is that the Nigerian Member of Parliament wants to criticise the government and to be in it at the same time. (*West Africa*, 29 January 1966: 113)

Several factors were involved in this failure as it was manifested in the 1965 Western Election. There were, to begin with, the symptoms: the pervasive repression and intimidation of political opposition by the NNDP, the flagrant corruption and self-enrichment by NNDP officials at every level, the brazen rigging of the election, the refusal of Akintola to compromise and of the Federal Government to intervene. As we have seen, these abuses polarised political conflict in the West and irretrievably alienated much of the populace, destroying the legitimacy of the regime.

Beneath these were the basic motivating factors. The weak commitment to democratic values of Nigerian politicians has repeatedly been cited. Intolerance of opposition meant that ruling parties were willing to go to any lengths, to violate any laws and procedures, to stamp it out. For the NNDP in 1965 (in contrast to the NPC in 1964), this became a tactical necessity for retaining power, and so that party carried familiar abuses to extremes that were uncharacteristic and unacceptable among the Yoruba. A natural companion of intolerance is unwillingness to compromise. Thus, Premier Akintola adamantly rejected any settlement of the crisis that might diminish his power. And possible resolution of the crisis through Federal intervention was vetoed by the Sardauna and other militant NPC leaders, against whose wishes the more moderate Prime Minister was powerless to act. Also, motivating the NPC leadership was, again, its determination to dominate the Federation and its belief, deeply rooted in the history and culture of the emirates, that its sacredly ordained destiny was to complete its 'conquest to the sea'.

Yet these elements of political culture alone do not explain why politicians were so desperate for victory and fearful of defeat. Another reason has already been noted here: that, given the way the political system was structured and operated, electoral defeat was likely to mean permanent exclusion from power. But this is simply to say that power was too dear to those who held it to allow any chance that it might be lost, and for most politicians, even five years of exclusion from the rewards and perquisites of power was too painful to contemplate.

It may be that some UPGA politicians were motivated mainly by political principles, or by the simple conviction that the ruthlessness of NNDP rule, the scale of its corruption and the stagnation of its economic management could not be endured by the Region for another five years. But corruption, stagnation and abuse of power were commonplace in UPGA governments and ministries as well. It may be that the UPGA abhorred continued NNA domination of the West and of the Federation because it viewed the NNA as reactionary. But commitment to their official philosophies of 'pragmatic' and 'democratic' socialism did not keep politicians of the two UPGA parties from opposing each other in twenty of the 94 constituencies.

Whatever role was played by political principles and ideology appears in both alliances to have been secondary to the desire for the material rewards of power. The NCNC, for example, was not so disgusted with the 'reactionary' character of the NNA that it was unwilling to accept a share of the spoils that made eight of its MPs Cabinet Ministers, another seven Ministers of State and eight more Parliamentary Secretaries. And what could be said of an NNDP regime in which every one of its 53 MPs (many of whom had only recently left the NCNC) held an office in the Western Government or Parliament? Faced with the problem of now having to satisfy 73 NNDP MPs, it was not surprising that Premier Akintola was unwilling to bring any UPGA politicians into his new Government.

At the root of the fraud and repression and corruption that brought chaos to the West was the process of class formation – the ambition for wealth, for privilege, for prestige, for control that could only be satisfied in the political arena. The stakes were enormous: for a minister, not only a princely salary but a rent-free, air-conditioned residence, replete with stewards and gardeners, a driver and generous car allowance, an entertainment budget, free telephone and free electricity (which alone might exceed the total salary of the average teacher or civil servant). Unofficially, illicitly, top positions in the ruling party, the government, and the civil service meant the opportunity to translate control over state resources into enormous personal wealth and wealth-producing assets (especially land).

Because state office or patronage was virtually the only means to attain a position in the emergent dominant class, and yet state resources were too limited to satisfy all comers, competition for state control was inevitable – and inevitably tense. No candidate or party could afford to lose an election, for that would mean exclusion from the resources of class formation. Having triumphed initially, none could afford to risk defeat, for that would mean losing the means with which to consolidate the structure of class dominance, and one's own position in it. And for most politicians, it would mean as well a traumatic decline in income and status, a return not to some respectable level of comfort and security but to a marginal social position. This point is vividly conveyed in Chinua Achebe's *A Man of the People*:

We ignore man's basic nature if we say, as some critics do, that because a man like Nanga had risen overnight from poverty and insignificance to his present opulence he could be persuaded without much trouble to give it up again and return to his original state.

A man who has just come in from the rain and dried his body and put on dry clothes is more reluctant to go out again than another who has been indoors all the time. The trouble with our new nation ... was that none of us had been indoors long enough to be able to say 'To hell with it.' We had all been in the rain together until yesterday. Then a handful of us – the smart and the lucky and hardly ever the best – had scrambled for the one shelter our former rulers left, and had taken it over and barricaded themselves in. (Achebe, 1966: 34)

This interaction of state and emergent class structures powerfully motivated the electoral anxiety, fraud and violence that generated the final crisis of the First Republic.

Effects on Nigerian democracy

If the Federal Election cast serious doubt on the democratic character of the regime, the Western Election of 1965 removed any trace of ambiguity. So naked and fundamental were the Government's violations of the principles of free and fair elections that the episode rendered the democratic constitution, in the West at least, a total sham. Because the West was pivotal to control of the Federation, the same could be said for the entire regime. The Federal Electoral Commission Chairman said as much in his letter substantiating charges of rigging and warning that, in the absence of sweeping structural reforms, 'we might as well say farewell to parliamentary democracy and the rule of law in Nigeria' (Nwankwo and Ifejika, 1967: 94–5).

But by October 1965, it was not only election rigging that was effacing democracy in Nigeria. Political leaders had long been chipping away at fundamental freedoms and checks and balances. The elimination of the Judicial Service Commission in 1963 and the Amendment of the Newspaper Act in 1964 were significant steps in this erosion. Political pressure was building upon the judiciary again, especially in the West. One who steadfastly resisted was Justice Oyemade, who angrily rejected an attempt at political pressure with the declaration:

I will not allow myself to be intimidated into sending innocent persons to jail. Even if this means losing my job, I am still sure of leading a decent life. The only thing we have now in this country is the judiciary. We have seen politicians changing from one policy to another and one party to another. But the only protection the ordinary people have against these inconsistencies is a fearless and upright judiciary. (Schwarz, 1965: 246)

Not all judges were so fearless (though many political prosecutions of UPGA politicians and supporters failed to bring conviction). But in any case, the judiciary was becoming increasingly irrelevant in the aftermath of the Western election, as both sides took justice into their own hands. The banning of opposition newspapers in both the Western and Eastern Regions was a clear sign of the openly authoritarian direction in which the system seemed to be moving. The reported plan of the Sardauna and Chief Akintola for mass arrests was another.

The election crisis was also the final blow to the stability of the regime. Within the Western Region, the massive rigging shattered all remaining vestiges of the legitimacy of the regime. A hated government was now compelled to turn to sheer force to maintain itself in power. As rebellion spread, the application of this force was having to become increasingly ruthless and promising to become still more so. Even if the coup had not intervened, it is doubtful that the plans for wider repression would have restored stability.

The final destruction of the regime's legitimacy in the West was only one of several deathblows to the stability of the First Republic. The delegitimation of the political system that followed from the Western election was not limited to the West. Walter Schwarz (1968: 187) has written, 'Popular disillusionment about democracy, already far advanced after the federal elections, was now almost total'. This may be somewhat exaggerated. We do not know the reaction to the crisis of the average Nigerian in other parts of the country. In many parts of the North, where the NPC enjoyed stable popular support, it is doubtful that the abuses and unrest in a distant part of the country much affected the average villager, if he were even aware of them. But in areas of popular resistance to the NPC – the Tiv Division, urban pockets of radical sentiment and of stranger (especially Igbo) settlement, perhaps Kano emirate – news of the events in the West was likely viewed as an ominous development. Furthermore, if the editors of the Government newspaper were calling for a rethinking of the NPC's unyielding support of Akintola, it is likely that there were other educated elements in the North whose disaffection, though not openly expressed, was much more thorough.

Even if disaffection with the system was not widespread in the North, it was throughout the South. Newspapers in the East and Mid-West stridently reported the theft of the election by the NNDP and the subsequent open rebellion. These were given especially sensational play in the widely read *West African Pilot*. And politicians as well, including Premier Okpara and Premier Osadebay, were telling their people that the election had been rigged and that the NNDP was attempting to prevail with guns and bayonets over the popular will. After the humiliating defeats for the Eastern Region in the census and Federal Election crises, this news was further confirmation that the political system of the Federation was profoundly flawed and unfair.

Probably the most devastating effect of the crisis was on the attitudes of sophisticated elements in the country, whose education and occupation set them apart from the mass but whose beliefs and self-perception set them apart from the regime as well. The 1965 Western election crisis, and the unwillingness or inability of the Federal Government to resolve it, clearly deepened their disaffection. In the midst of the furore over Chairman Esau's letter to the Governor, *West Africa's* columnist observed:

> There is now deep cynicism in the Republic not only about the Western Region election but about all future elections. For the first time I find people openly saying – and this includes many very important people indeed – that nobody any longer pays any attention to the constitution. (27 November 1965: 1327)

Indirect effects on Nigerian democracy

The First Republic came to an end as the Western Region was still burning in a state of rebellion. Since the immediate effect of the crisis – the total delegitimation of the regime – brought down the regime in short order, consideration of its potential indirect effects seem superfluous. But we can note two other effects of the crisis which may have hastened the end of the Republic. First, like the outcomes of other major crises, the 1965 Western election failed to resolve the conflict and its multiple grievances but, instead, left the competing social forces more bitterly polarised than ever. This was mainly because the defeated party refused to recognise the outcome – and the system which produced it – as legitimate, and thus continued to contest it with the only means left to it: petrol and cutlasses and stones. But there was more than the question of legitimacy involved. The inclination of more powerful parties in Nigeria to press their opponents to the wall repeatedly had the unanticipated effect of hardening rather than dissolving opposition. Because of this winner-take-all posture, no major crisis could ever be resolved; each one festered, further polarising the political terrain and straining the political system. This ensured that the underlying conflict would resurface with even greater intensity and then prove even more difficult to manage and contain. Inevitably, this meant greater violence and disorder, both as a result of the confrontation between opposing forces and as a means of protest against the system. The 1965 Western election did more than any previous crisis to advance this polarisation and decay – to the point where the political system was collapsing in rebellion and repression.

This then produced a related effect. When law and order began to unravel from either source of conflict – group against group, or group against the state – the regime had to call upon the military. Each time the military was summoned to quell violent political conflict or protest, it was dragged more deeply into politics. Eventually, military leaders were bound to question why they were continually being called upon to restore order out of the chaos generated by politicians. Eventually, they were bound to begin asking themselves whether, if they were always suppressing chaos and the politicians always making it, *they* shouldn't be in power and the politicians out of it. That politicians themselves were repeatedly looking to the military as the only impartial referee and that military coups were then sweeping across the continent like a prairie fire could only have sharpened these questions and doubts.

9 Conclusion: Why the First Republic Failed[1]

'In short, the rulers used power that they held constitutionally to do unconstitutional things. In the process they destroyed themselves. Nigeria had censuses that were not censuses, elections that were not elections, and finally governments that were not governments.' — *Nigerian Opinion*, February 1966: 16

There are always many levels at which a complex social phenomenon can be explained and understood. To begin at the surface, the First Republic was overthrown because the people lost faith in it – not because some disaffected colonels were worried about their careers, not even because a disaffected ethnic group was worried about its position in the Federation. The former worry may have existed, and certainly the latter did. But they explain neither the success of the coup attempt nor the outpouring of joy and relief that greeted it across the country. The First Republic's loss of popular legitimacy was a remarkably deep and broadly based – and, by the end of 1965, thorough – phenomenon.

Why the loss of faith? In the declarations of the coup-makers and opinionmakers, the proximate causes are clearly exposed. The people – and particularly the stratum of educated and politically-aware Nigerians outside the political class – had become disgusted on the one hand with the 'ten wasted years' of corruption, incompetence, and gross abuse of office, and on the other, with the incessant political crisis and internal strife, the political violence and repression, and finally the descent into political chaos. Although these were widely seen to be the failings of a rotten class of politicians and associated recipients of state patronage, the newness of the system caused it to be swallowed up in opprobrium as well. With no past record of regime performance on which to judge, the failings of the politicians became the systemic failings of the First Republic, of which there were also plenty.

The disillusionment with corruption and waste spread like a cancer through the body politic – steadily but gradually for many years, and then with a vengeance when the 1964 General Strike thrust the

288

gathering resentment to the centre of national politics, where it boiled over into rage at the government's arrogance and intransigence. Although the cleavage between the people and the political class receded from the front lines of political conflict with the end of the strike, it did not subside in public feeling. Rather, it became more widespread and intense as corruption and extravagance increased.

The other process of deligitimation was more episodic in nature, and more focused around the cultural and political groups that were defeated in the successive conflicts. This process began with the educated, progressive young elites who identified with Chief Awolowo's Action Group, and then spread to encompass the Yoruba people generally. Similarly the census crisis alienated the political leadership of the East, but also increasingly its entire population as it dragged on into ethnic recriminations and as the Igbo East was left isolated and decisively defeated in its stance. The blunt outcomes of the first two crises also fanned the growing alienation of young, progressive and more idealistic political observers around the country. These latter elements, along with organised labour and other urban dwellers, became further disillusioned by the government's grossly inept and insensitive handling of the 1964 General Strike, which also exposed the shallowness of the government's authority. The Federal Election crisis six months later deepened the alienation within the Igbo East, and in all those areas that identified with the defeated alliance – which included most of the South and significant elements of ethnic and political resistance in the North as well. But the repression, fraud and nearly catastrophic confrontation of that experience also deepened the alienation from the system of educated professionals who had no particular political stake but the efficient administration and rapid development of the country. If these various social elements had any faith left in the institutions of the First Republic, it was irrevocably shattered by the 1965 'election' in the West, which seemed to obliterate any remaining vestige of the Republic's democratic character.

The surface manifestations of democratic decay were apparent, then, in these two lines of historical development – the secular deterioration through corruption, profligacy and waste, and the episodic deterioration through the sequence of exhausting and unresolved crises. The explanation of the failure of Nigeria's First Republic is to be found in the causes of these two processes. We turn first to the latter, which has been the primary focus of this study.

CAUSES OF THE MAJOR CRISES

In the analyses of each of the post-Independence crises, we have identified, case by case, the factors that were most significant in generating the conflict and in producing its unfavourable outcome. Now the causal pattern across crises must be discerned. By identifying those factors that most consistently and significantly shaped these explosive turns in Nigerian politics, we will move toward a more general explanation of the failure of the First Republic. We begin by dealing, and dispensing, with popular but superficial explanations.

Ethnic division and conflict

It can hardly be denied that bitter and increasingly polarised ethnic conflict heavily contributed to the fall of the First Republic. It was the dominant feature of the census crisis and the 1964 Federal Election, and was more or less dangerously present in every other election contest. It also festered in a number of smaller but still significant incidents, such as the 'ethnic wrangling' following the census, and the University of Lagos crisis. It motivated, at least partially, the 1962 assault on the Action Group, and the subsequent Yoruba feeling of victimisation. Of all the major instances of political conflict, only the General Strike was relatively free of ethnic jealousy, resentment, competition and recriminations.

But little is learned by pointing to ethnic antagonism as the cause of political instability. Ethnic conflict was not deeply rooted in Nigerian history; different tribes exchanged goods amicably more often than they warred and, in any case, were less centralised in scale and much less regular in their external contacts. Nor was ethnic antagonism a natural mass phenomenon; most peasants were simply unaware of the vast array of peoples beyond their limited horizons.

If 'tribalism' was not a primordial phenomenon, then it must have been generated in the course of modernisation. Indeed, the evidence in the Nigerian case powerfully supports Melson and Wolpe's (1971: 5) generalisation that, 'in a culturally plural society, the competition engendered by social mobilisation will tend to be defined in communal terms'. Where ethnic antagonism developed spontaneously among ordinary people, it was in the cities, where people of different cultural backgrounds competed for economic opportunities and rewards. But mass ethnic socioeconomic competition does not explain the centrality of ethnic conflict in politics. More helpful here is the proposition that political party competition tends 'to further politicise and intensify communal conflict' by encouraging 'aspirant politicians to make appeals to the most easily mobilised communal loyalties' (especially in the absence of crosscutting cleavage) (Melson and Wolpe, 1971: 19). However, this ethnic manipulation must itself be explained in terms of the country's political and social structures.

Similarly, it is of little help to attribute democratic failure to primordial ethnic divisions by another name, i.e., the lack of national unity or failure of national integration. One can blame the British for failing to provide integrating national symbols and institutions during colonial rule and for encouraging regional and ethnic, as opposed to national, loyalty. But Britain decided only very late in colonial rule that Nigeria would pass to independence as a single nation, and when this was decided, the far more debilitating colonial legacy concerned the political structure it constructed and the social order it preserved.

Political culture

Most Nigerian political leaders manifested a weak commitment to democratic values and behavioural styles. From the very start of electoral competition, this was apparent in the vituperative and inflammatory rhetoric of political competition and conflict, the lack of respect and tolerance for opposition, and the unwillingness to compromise with it. Through the late 1950s, antidemocratic behaviour grew more pronounced, as incumbent governments abused their powers in increasingly bold attempts to eliminate opposition and rhetorical fervour spilled over into physical violence. With the departure of the British, repression, obstruction, fraud and other violations of the 'rules of the game' escalated sharply.

These violations not only raised the temperature of political conflict and eroded public faith in democracy, they also unleashed a dynamic of competitive escalation that assumed a momentum of its own. This was evident in the manoeuvring for power between the competing Action Group factions in 1962, culminating in the suspension of democratic government in the West and then the alleged intended coup; in the competitive bidding up of census figures until numbers seemed to be drawn from mid-air; and of course, in the successive election struggles. Moreover, this competitive escalation of abuse occurred not only within each crisis but across them. Thus, each ended with a more serious breakdown in constitutional safeguards and democratic norms than the last, as each one became more bitter and more polarised than the last.

The increasing bitterness and polarisation were partly the product of these escalating violations. But deeper factors lay beneath this chain of reciprocal causation, and 'political culture' does not suffice as an explanation. Democratic commitments may have been weak, but they were not absent. Many Nigerian political leaders manifested a considerable pride in their democratic system and a sincere desire to make it work. A number of them had studied in Britain or the United States and acquired an intellectual and moral commitment to democracy. And the political traditions and values of many Nigerian peoples had significant democratic features. Even if Nigerians had not before experienced the phenomenon of *institutionalised* political opposition, it was not inevitable that they would demolish it.

A democratic political culture was not strongly rooted in Nigeria. But, save for the case of the Northern emirates, neither were Nigerian political values steadfastly authoritarian. Hence, it is not analytically profitable to maintain that democracy failed because Nigerian politicians didn't value it. This does not explain why political competition became a kind of warfare. We must, instead, look for the social and political structures that generated antidemocratic behaviour.

The federal structure

There can be no doubting the contribution of Nigeria's deeply flawed federal structure to the failure of the First Republic. In both crises in the Western Region, in the census controversy, and in the Federal election crisis, the tensions and contradictions in the regional structure played a pivotal role.

The most basic flaw in the federal structure – certainly the one most often stressed by aggrieved Southern leaders – was the fact that one region was more populous, and hence (after the 1958 decision to alter federal representation to a per capita basis) more politically powerful, than all of the others combined. In a system where political power was expanding to encompass an ever larger share of social resources and popular aspirations, and where economic imperatives were continuously concentrating power (especially over finance) in the centre, this meant that the most important guarantees of federalism were endangered – that one region had the potential to dominate the others and to appropriate to itself the bulk of national resources. Although NCNC leaders appeared confident in 1959 that their greater political experience and sophistication could enable them to prevail in the federal coalition government despite their much weaker parliamentary standing, it was becoming clear by 1962, and was made abundantly so in the census crisis, that Northern political leaders were fully capable of effecting their determination to tilt the balance of Federal resources to their region. This was a crucial reason why the census and the 1964 Federal Election became such desperate struggles.

The tension flowing from the anomalous weight of the Northern Region was aggravated by the disparity in development levels between North and South, which widened still further during the early 1960s. Hence, Northern leaders sought to use their power in the Federal Government to 'catch up', concentrating the bulk of federal development spending (under the 1962–68 Development Plan) in the North. Almost all of the scheduled spending on defence, and much of that allocated for roads, health and education, was directed to the North (Dudley, 1966: 21–2). Paradoxically, however, the much higher development level of the South constituted a burden as well as an advantage: the pace of social and economic progress had to be sustained and even accelerated if upheaval was to be avoided. With some 300 000 unskilled Nigerians, mostly from the South, leaving primary school each year to enter the labour market (Arikpo, 1967: 105), and with urban unemployment running more than twice as high in the South as in the North in 1962 (29 per cent versus 13 per cent) (Dudley, 1966: 24), the need for developing spending simply to keep pace with social mobilisation was much higher in the South than in the North.

But the contradiction between political power and socioeconomic development was not the only explosive element in the North's federal predominance. Culture, history, class, and ideology also deeply divided Northern and Southern political leaders and sharply accentuated Southern anxieties over Northern domination. The prominent role of Islamic religion and law in Northern society, the conservative, authoritarian social structure and values of the emirates, the historic expansionist tendencies of the Fulani empire – symbolised in Tafawa Balewa's 1948 vow to complete its 'conquest to the sea' – and the history of political and ethnic conflict during colonial rule all intensified the refusal of AG and NCNC politicians to accept Northern domination.

Another flaw in the federal system was the small number of regions, which heavily contributed to the extraordinary degree of political polarisation. The only way to break the offensive dominance of the Northern Region was to divide it into two or more regions, as Southern progressives insisted. And the only way to diminish the polarising coincidence between region and ethnicity was to divide the three major ethnic groups into multiple states. Moreover, the three- (four-) region system afforded little possibility for the flexibility of position, the shifting coalitions, and the bargaining, negotiation and compromise found in federal systems with a larger number of states. What scope for fluidity in conflict patterns there was derived from the calculus of a three-player game. But tripolar structures tend to collapse into bipolar struggles, as happened in Nigeria.

The small number of regions contributed to political instability in three other senses as well. First, by leaving several large and politically active ethnic minority groups without states of their own, it generated a persistent source of tension and insecurity within each region that was mobilised in national political struggle. Second, it meant that regional political parties could not fail to take an interest in and exploit the internal political conflicts of any other region (such as the West), because control of any one of them was crucial to control of the centre. Hence, federalism could not decentralise conflict and reciprocally insulate the centre and the regions. Finally, in the context of a swelling state and immense regional autonomy, the small number of regions meant an enormous scope of patronage resources in the control of the regional governments, and hence a huge premium on winning control of them.

Had the ten or more regions envisaged by Chief Awolowo been created, it is reasonable to conjecture that political competition and conflict would have been much less likely to degenerate into a polarised struggle between the nation's three largest ethnic groups. The greater dispersion of government power would have more effectively decentralised political conflict and might, for example, have enabled the Western Region to resolve its conflicts free of federal intervention.

Coincidence of regional, ethnic and party cleavages

What was seen by many colonial officials as a positive feature of the federal structure – that each of the three major ethnic groups enjoyed the cultural, economic, and political autonomy of their own regions – became instead one of the most persistent sources of political conflict and instability. This structural reification of the major ethnic boundaries made it almost inevitable that political competition would be waged through ethnoregional parties, thereby polarising conflict along the cumulative cleavage of region, ethnicity and party.

This cleavage coincidence fed upon itself during the 1950s, as ethnic parties quickly took power in each region and hardened their bases there, effectively making of each region a one-party state. This gave rise to a host of conflicts during the 1950s, which became incessant and inflamed in large measure because they were repeatedly tapping the same coinciding lines of cleavage. British mediation helped preserve some fluidity and moderation in the pattern of conflict (see below), but after Independence, the conflict pattern rigidified along the major cumulative divide.

The cooperation of the NPC and the NCNC in their mutual design to destroy the Action Group was to be the last significant bridging of this divide. Even before it was over, the NCNC recognised that in destroying its erstwhile Southern antagonist it had also removed an indispensable brake upon the North's march to total political dominance. From then on, conflict reduced to a bipolar struggle between North and South, Hausa-Fulani and Igbo, and their respective political alliances. Even the one conflict along a truly distinctive cleavage line, the 1964 General Strike, tapped an undercurrent of this polarisation. That both the census and the 1964 Federal Election were approached as struggles for control of the Federation between North and South, and ended as fierce showdowns between North and East, owed much to the regional structure and the coincidence of cleavages it produced. The final chapter in this bipolar struggle, the 1965 Western Regional crisis, was the culmination of fifteen years of conflict between these regional/ethnic/political formations.

The political party structure might have been very different had the regional and ethnic cleavages not coincided as they did. The creation of several ethnic minority states would have complicated the cleavage pattern, affording multiple possibilities of shifting coalitions across different issues. In breaking the monolithic unity of the North, it would have made much less likely the devastating polarisation of half the South (the East) against the entire North. And a multi-state system like that envisioned by the NCNC would also have entailed splitting the Yoruba, Igbo, and Hausa-Fulani heartlands into multiple states;

thus activating intraethnic political cleavages, such as the historic tensions between the Ijebu and Ibadan Yoruba (Sklar, 1963: 284–320), between the Onitsha and non-Onitsha Igbo (Sklar, 1963: 146–8, 151–7), and between Sokoto and subsidiary emirates, such as Kano. In such a federal system, these autonomous minority and sub-ethnic political interests would have compelled a much more nationally-oriented strategy by the major political parties, like that which the NCNC originally followed before the formation of regionalist parties in the West and North forced it to fall back upon its Eastern, Igbo base, or that which the Action Group later pursued with such spectacular futility.

In the context of the peculiar federal structure, the coincidence of region, ethnicity and party was most damaging in its effect on the North, where it enabled the NPC so thoroughly to entrench itself in power that, through its control of the North alone, it was able to gain unilateral control over the Federation. This is why the Middle Belt was the key to the politics of the Federation. It was doubtful that the NPC could retain control of the Middle Belt as a separate region. And even if it could have maintained its monolithic hold on the constituencies of the Upper North – which would have been unlikely if they were fractured into the separate Sokoto, Kaduna, Kano, Bauchi and Borno states that now exist – it would still have needed to score substantial gains or forge a major alliance in the South to achieve national power. Without the same formidable parliamentary strength from the North, such an alliance would have been more difficult for the NPC to forge and substantially more difficult for it to dominate.

In all likelihood, a multistate structure would have forced political parties to compete directly in all regions of the country, would have yielded a less predictable pattern of party control of the states, and would have generated much more fluid alignments from issue to issue, splitting not inevitably according to ethnic or regional reflex, but now and then according to cross-cutting interests, such as the formula for revenue allocation (pitting oil against non-oil states in the South), the location of universities (pitting 'have' against 'have-not' states) and the allocation of development resources.

Nevertheless, it would be a serious mistake to infer that a complex, multistate federal structure would have enabled the First Republic to mature into a stable democracy. There were other factors inflaming conflict and other problems gnawing at the First Republic. Even if ethnic and regional conflict had been less polarised and predictable under a multi-state federal structure, it would probably still have been fomented and manipulated by the politicians. More importantly, even if there had been no ethnic differences to manipulate, it is likely that political competition in the First Republic would still have been consumed by fraud, repression and violence, and underlying these, the determination to win at all costs. At bottom, these were the product not of flawed political institutions, nor of historic ethnic antagonisms, nor of 'uncivilised' political cultures, but of the dynamic interaction between class and state structures.

Class and state

Perhaps the core problem of democracy in Nigeria during the 1950s and 1960s was that, in the midst of desperate poverty and intense ambitions for a better life, government at all levels was coming to absorb and distribute 'a larger and larger share of the public wealth' (Mosca, 1939, 143). When the essential means to 'a life more abundant' (as the Action Group put it) are increasingly controlled by the state, when control of the state becomes the essential foundation for class formation (Sklar, 1979), when 'all moral and material advantages depend on those who hold power, ... there is no act of chicanery or violence that will not be resorted to in order to attain power', to belong to the class that controls the resources, the political class (Mosca, 1939: 144).

Those who aspire to position in the dominant class must aspire to position in or intimate access to the expanding state. This puts an extraordinary premium on political power, which in turn motivates what Claude Ake (1973) has termed a preference for 'efficiency norms to legitimacy norms' – a willingness to violate the legitimate methods of contestation to whatever degree necessary to capture and retain power. The breakdown of constitutional norms, in the context of the high premium of power, generates a high level of political anxiety – 'the fear of the consequences of not being in control of the government, associated with a profound distrust of political opponents' (Ake, 1973: 359). On the surface of politics, these forces manifest themselves in antidemocratic attitudes and behaviour – intolerance, distrust, fanaticism, unwillingness to compromise. But these features of political culture do not in themselves constitute an explanation of democratic failure. Similarly, the extraordinary premium on power and anxiety with which its loss is contemplated motivates the pervasive mobilisation of ethnic jealousy, fear and prejudice as a strategy for winning, retaining and expanding power. But the fact 'that conflicts and violence in Africa are commonly channelled along tribal divisions ... tells us little about the actual causes of intergroup conflict and violence' (Sklar, 1971: 44). In their competition for the resources of class formation, the politicians of the First Republic channelled their conflict into Nigeria's major line of social division, ethnicity. Had it not existed, they would have seized upon some other cleavage at the mass level, or invented one. In fact, to a considerable extent, the modern ethnic identifications that clashed in mortal political combat were not primordial, but the constructions of cultural entrepreneurs who sought to ride them to political and class dominance.

At the root of democratic failure – and of the accelerating ethnic polarisation that culminated in civil war – were the processes of class formation and class action. But if class, rather than region or ethnicity, was the most destructive cleavage, how could it not have been more apparent? In part, of course, class cleavage was becoming increasingly apparent in popular resentment over the widening gulf between the political class and the people, as the 1964 General Strike made apparent. But why, then, did the intersection of class and ethnic cleavage not moderate rather than inflame the latter? Why were the politicians able to use 'tribalism as a mask for class privilege' (Sklar, 1967: 6)?

In part, we have seen that the absence of sustained crosspressures followed from the capacity to compartmentalise the two cleavages over time, and from the way in which the flawed federal structure focused attention on sectional cleavages and facilitated their mobilisation by the politicians. Both these factors were evidenced in the rapid 'retribalisation' of the political climate in the months between the General Strike and Federal Election in 1964. But two features of the class structure also prevented effective psychological crosspressures and sustained political mobilisation of class cleavage: the inability of the dominant class, and for different reasons, the inability of the lower classes, to develop any national coherence or solidarity.

In the case of the emerging dominant class, this owed significantly to the limitations of its resource base. Given the poverty of the country – which permitted only a relatively impoverished state, despite the increasing proportion of social resources controlled by the state – and given the rapid expansion of the educated elite, especially in the South, the number of aspirants for entrance into the political class vastly exceeded the available state offices and rewards.

This scarcity made intense competition inevitable. The competition became organised along communal lines for several reasons: the absence of other crosscutting or functional solidarities, the presence of real cultural differences, the extreme aggravation of these differences by the federal structure, and the natural tendency for people in competition to seek assistance from those with whom they share the most in common culturally.

For the bulk of the lower class, the peasantry, who did not compete on an ethnic basis in a direct way, the chief obstacle to solidarity was isolation. Although the urban lower and working classes were able to overcome divisive political manipulation and unite impressively in the General Strike, this action bypassed the peasantry. Extreme underdevelopment meant that few Nigerians were employed in the urban wage economy, the sector most conducive to development of class identity. Most Nigerians farmed for a living in the villages where they were born – where cleavage was understood in terms of being in or outside the cultural community, and where education and independent sources of information were extremely limited. As a result, allegiance to traditional authority remained strong, and political participation was mobilised from above on the basis of ethnicity and clientage. The process of socioeconomic modernisation – the spread of literacy, education and the mass media, the migration to cities, the commercialisation of agriculture – could be expected to weaken these traditional authority relations and generate a more autonomous form of mass political participation based on functional interests (Huntington and Nelson, 1976: 54–6; Almond and Verba, 1963; Inkeles, 1969). But in the Nigeria of the 1950s and 60s, such a transformation of politics and society – a condition for lower class political mobilisation – was only beginning. Indeed, in the North, it had not yet begun.

The political impenetrability of the upper North was a crucial obstacle to the forging of a national political challenge along class or ideological lines. Many outsiders (Southern Nigerians as much as non-Nigerians) judged that the authoritarianism and social injustice of the emirates made them a ripe target for popular rebellion, and progressive and radical forces sought to mobilise an uprising at the ballot box. Their failure cannot be explained by the substantial electoral repression and obstruction in the North, although these probably reduced the opposition vote significantly, especially in the cities. In most parts of the North, the *talakawa* simply did not rise to the call to overthrow their rulers. The literature on peasant revolution helps us to understand why. Where multiple, strong institutional links – through production, commerce, protection, arbitration, welfare, religion and so on – bind the peasantry in hierarchical fashion to the upper classes, peasants do not rebel against the social order. For this to happen, the vertical ties between patron and client, lord and peasant must be broken and replaced by autonomous binding linkages among the peasantry (Moore, 1966: 469–70; Popkin, 1979: 27, 184–267; Skocpol, 1979: 112–57). In Northern Nigeria during this period, there was nothing like the political organisation or penetration of modernisation necessary to accomplish this.

Thus, as Nigeria lacked the conditions for a trans-ethnic dominant class, so did it also lack the conditions for effective lower class mobilisation. Consequently, the competitive agonies of the process of class formation found their primary expression in ethnic political conflict. Four of the five major crises were generated to at least a significant degree by competition within the emergent dominant class for control of the locus of class formation, the state. This was true of both crises within the Western Region. It was true as well of what seemed the most purely sectional conflicts, the census crisis and the 1964 Federal Election. In both these conflicts, and indeed in every election, ethnic mobilisation was the calculated strategy of dominant-class elements locked in bitter competition for control of state power and resources. If not consciously a mask for class action, such tribalism was certainly a manifestation and tragic consequence of it.

Northern social structure

Most of the major causes of democratic failure in Nigeria – the federal structure, the coincidence of cleavages, the structures of class and state and the ethnic polarisation and antidemocratic behaviour that followed from these – tap general theoretical dimensions applicable across countries. But to these causal factors must be added a more historically specific one, the social structure of the Hausa-Fulani emirates in the North, and the consequent determination of the NPC to dominate the Federation. The structure of class dominance in the North interacted in complex fashion with the other causal agents. The federal structure preserved it intact and served its domineering ambitions. The coincidence of party, region and ethnicity, in turn, flowed partly from the monolithic dominance it insisted upon throughout the North. The national structures of class and state made control of the regional and central state essential to its preservation. And it, too, was a significant source of the political intolerance and ethnic polarisation that were the proximate causes of incessant crisis.

Nothing was so fundamental to the peculiar political balance of the First Republic as the NPC's determination to control the Federation and to continue to control it indefinitely. Part of this was the pride of a dominant class that was more established and culturally quite different from its emergent counterpart in the South, oriented to the Islamic Middle-East rather than to the West. Part was the resentment and insecurity of a class and a people who were far behind the South on every dimension of modernisation and determined to catch up. Part involved the familier hunger for the modern instruments of power, wealth and status. And part was the need to control the Federation in order to preserve the structure of class dominance.

That the structure of Northern class dominance was still fundamentally intact at Independence owed heavily to the British strategy of colonial rule, coupled with the skill and 'savvy' of a new generation of Northern leaders in using the new political institutions to modernise the traditional social structure without altering its hierarchical and religious character. But if these new leaders were to continue to preserve the essence of the traditional structure – the power of the Native Authorities (if not of the Emirs themselves), the *alkali* courts, the general social dominance of the titled classes – they had to retain complete control over the pace and content of modernisation in the North. Southern domination of the Federal Government – and with it, the possible break-up of the Northern Region – would mean loss of such control. It would mean that men from profoundly different cultures could use federal power to level traditional social gradations and alter or eliminate traditional institutions. This possibility could not be allowed. Hence, the NPC had to control the Federation, and to do this, it had to preserve the Northern Region as one.

A final motive for Northern domination may be linked to the historic expansionist urge of the Fulani empire, and the desire of the younger aristocratic elite, most notably the Sardauna, to complete the mission of the jihad and extend the empire's dominance to the sea. The cultural pride of the more traditional and religious Northern leaders became increasingly aggressive as NPC control at the centre was consolidated. In his later years, the Sardauna 'became obsessed with religion, conducting crusades at which vast numbers of "converts" were claimed among the pagans,' and spoke of North-South confrontation in terms of 'a holy war to protect our religion' (Schwarz, 1968: 238, 239). Lesser figures in the NPC began to boast confidently that their party would rule the Federation forever. This arrogance particularly grated against Southern sensitivities and further inflamed and polarised the conflict of interests.

The Northern determination to dominate the Federation, heavily rooted in the social structure and the cultural and historical traditions of the North, played a role in every major crisis. It was an important motivation behind the Federal Government's intervention in the West in 1962 and its multifaceted assault on the Action Group. It was the basic reason why the NPC was determined to preserve a Northern majority in the census. Indirectly, it was an element in the disaffection of Southern labour that exploded in the General Strikes in 1963 and 1964. As Northern power was wielded more aggressively, it weighed more and more heavily upon the battered Republic. In 1964, it motivated the NPC's sweeping repression of political opposition and absolute unwillingness to compromise that turned the Federal Election into a grave crisis. In 1965, it motivated the NPC's decision to back the Akintola Government unconditionally in the face of overwhelming popular resistance and outrageous electoral fraud.

THE CUMULATIVE PATTERN OF CONFLICT

One of the central findings of this study is the importance of the cleavage structure across conflicts, over time. The theory of crosscutting cleavages suggests that when individuals are crosspressured by the simultaneous pull of competing and more or less equally salient loyalties, the resulting conflict is less intense, hence less politically destablising. Coinciding cleavages, by contrast, tend to polarise and inflame conflict. Analysis of Nigeria's political conflicts before Independence and during the First Republic lends support to this hypothesis. But the pattern of these conflicts also suggests that crosscutting and variation in the cleavage structure *over time* can as well dampen the intensity of conflict. Three elements of the longitudinal cleavage pattern are important:

1. *The lines of cleavage.* In a longitudinal sense, the most ideal arrangement is for the lines of cleavage to crosscut over time, so that

any given conflict is succeeded by one along a wholly different line of cleavage, recombining political actors in very different ways. Even if particular conflicts tap deep cleavages and generate intense feeling, polarisation will be minimised if the bases of conflict are constantly changing and the alignments continually shifting, uniting previous antagonists and dividing previous allies.

2. *The alignment of cleavage groups.* Even if conflicts keep tapping the same line or reinforcing lines of cleavage over time, they will be less intense if the configuration of antagonists is constantly changing. This requires more than two cleavage groups, however. If multiple groups align in different combinations across conflicts, this can have a somewhat salutary effect. On the other hand, when successive conflicts not only fall repeatedly along the same broad line of cleavage, but also pit the very same alignments of social forces against each other time and again, the consequent polarisation can produce conflicts of disastrous intensity.

3. *The outcomes of the conflicts.* If there is recurring conflict along the same cleavage and between the same competing forces, polarisation may still be attenuated and stability preserved if group leaders are regularly able to reach some kind of compromise or accommodation, or (as a less promising condition) if the distribution of victories and defeats is not one-sided and predictable over time. Since the effect of cleavage polarisation is to reduce the inclination to compromise, and to erode the very basis for compromise, accommodation requires, in these circumstances, a peculiar structural arrangement: either an external referee more powerful than any of the actors or some type of consociational arrangement. The success of a consociational system depends on several pre-conditions, such as strong command by group leaders over their members and a powerful elite commitment to compromise and restraint. Where cleavages and alignments recur over time, a balanced distribution of victories and defeats would seem particularly elusive, and even if there were a fine balance of power between competing forces, this might only produce a succession of savage stalemates.

These propositions are supported by the pattern of political conflict in Nigeria between 1951 and 1966. During the first decade of political competition, conflict fell incessantly along the same broad, coinciding cleavage of party, region, and ethnicity. Some relief was provided by the faint rotation between these three cleavages during the 1950s, but the key factors maintaining fluidity in the conflict pattern and limiting its intensity were two others: the role of the British and the presence of a constantly shifting, tripolar pattern. The British colonial authorities effectively arbitrated between the three often bitterly opposed groups, working out compromise formulae for such explosive questions as the allocation of revenue and the timing of self-government. Where compromise was not possible, the victory of one side did not signal any long-term pattern, as colonial adminstration prevented raw political power from simply crushing the weaker competitors. Moreover, in administering the elections, the colonial authorities also kept the competing parties in bounds with regard to means as well. Colonial administration thus served, not always consistently or evenly but nevertheless forcefully, a classic referee role.

The intensity of conflict was also restrained by the constant shifting of alignments in the pre-Independence period. If certain issues found the North and South bitterly opposed, there were others that pitted West against East (or Yoruba against Igbo, or AG against NCNC), others still which embodied genuinely three-cornered competition, and a final outcome to the decade of conflict which spanned across the North-South fault line in making the Federal Coalition.

Both of these moderating forces evaporated after Independence. The first did so immediately, but its effect was not really felt until the crisis in the Western Region in 1962–63. This was the first test of whether there had developed, since the departure of the British, indigenous institutional or cultural forces that could bring about compromise, or whether sheer political force would settle differences. The instrusion of the Federal Coalition and the systematic assault upon the Action Group indicated that competing cleavage groups would, to the full extent of their capacities, press their opponents to the wall.

Still, there remained a large element of fluidity in the pattern of conflict during the first few years of the new government. Crises did not fall in any kind of neat succession but overlapped with each other and with lesser conflicts. Thus, as the Federal Coalition partners began their assault on the Action Group in 1961 by attempting to investigate its National Bank and to sever the Mid-West from its control, they also came to quarrel with each other over the division of powers between President and Prime Minister. As the assault proceeded in 1962, the census was conducted and tabulated, and then it exploded into bitter controversy between NPC and NCNC MPs that December. Even before the Prime Minister ordered a new census, conflict along a wholly different line of cleavage emerged with the strike by Lagos dock workers, foreshadowing much more serious troubles. Continued Action Group woes were interrupted in the summer of 1963 by the heated flash of debate over conservative attempts to retrench on democratic safeguards in the constitution, tapping a line of cleavage that cut across party, region, and ethnicity. In September 1963, class conflict occupied the political arena again as the trade unions launched a General Strike that nearly ruined Republic Day. Through the end of 1963 and early 1964, party competition in anticipation of the coming Federal Election was interspersed with intense regional conflict over the census.

This was the beginning of an important change in the longitudinal pattern of conflict, because the essential cleavage was the same in the census and Federal Election – the party of the Northern aristocracy struggling with the Eastern-based and Igbo-dominated NCNC for control of the Federation. But as this cleavage sharpened through the first half of 1964, it was suddenly interrupted by the devastating General Strike, which again cut across the predominant cleavage.

Through the 1964 General Strike, the character and configuration of conflict was constantly shifting, even more than it had been during the 1950s. Although conflict was incessant and intense, there was uncertainty about which issue would erupt next and what kind of political alliances would form around it. Even in the three major conflicts, we see an intra-party, intraregional conflict of personal, class and ideological interests succeeded in 1963–64 by a regional conflict between North and East, succeeded by a showdown between the unions and the NPC/NCNC Federal Government.

This conflict pattern contained two very dangerous features, however. First, the main internal factor keeping conflict fluid was eliminated with the destruction of the Action Group, which reduced politics to a two-player game and left one player substantially stronger than the other. This led to the second ominous element – the NPC's consecutive massive victories over the Action Group in 1962–63 and the NCNC in early 1964. These successive uncompromising triumphs began to establish a pattern, which even the eruption of a totally different line of cleavage could not erase.

The failure of the First Republic was sealed in the subsequent final two crises, for these manifested the classic polarising formula. First the basic *cleavage* was the same in both: political and regional conflict, now congealed into North-South struggle. Indeed, the fundamental issue in each was the same as that in the census crisis:

whether the Federation was to be controlled by a Northern-based conservative alliance, led by the NPC, or a Southern-based progressive alliance, led by the NCNC. Second, the *alignment* of parties was the same: the NPC and its client party in the West, opposed by the NCNC and the Action Group opposition in the West. This had not changed since the census crisis either. Finally, the *outcome* was the same in all three conflicts. In fact, including the 1962–63 Western crisis as well, one observes an unbroken string of four decisive triumphs for the NPC and the North, in each case leaving one or both Southern antagonists not simply defeated but feeling cheated and gravely wronged.

Even though each of these four conflicts was waged primarily at the level of the political class, the recurrent nature of the cleavage, alignment and outcome polarised and embittered them to the point of exhausting all potential for conciliation. Post and Vickers (1973: 234) have written:

> Already by mid-1965 the Nigerian political system was suffering from a severe case of metal fatigue. Its structures had lost their flexibility and become more and more rigid; a little more strain and they collapsed. They became more rigid because they failed to diffuse and control conflict, serving rather to exacerbate it and focus it along one particular line. Thus, the System of Rewards was essentially a system of competition, and one which never succeeded in establishing generally-accepted ground rules to control its participants' behaviour. While it involved the mass of the people at its lower levels, it was essentially an elite affair, and its only real possibilities of conflict control were dependent upon the wheeling and dealing of elite strata, and more especially elite group members. The Zik-Balewa Pact as the last of these deals, and the inequality of its terms portended the failure of this method. Five years of cumulative competition pushed some members of the political elite strata, especially in the West, so far towards the margin of the system that they were increasingly inclined to replace wheeling and dealing with more direct methods.

Our analysis of the five major crises of post-Independence politics is summarised in Table 9.1. The reinforcing succession of outcomes and cleavage configurations, broken only briefly by the General Strike, can be observed, along with the previously summarised causes and effects of the crises. The final column indicates the cumulative effects of the longitudinal pattern of outcomes. Each of the four political/regional conflicts had significant negative feedback effects on future crises. The failure in each case to resolve the basic conflict in a way even minimally acceptable to the weaker party ensured that it would recur with even greater intensity than before. Hence, every time the more powerful party unilaterally imposed its preferred solution on its aggrieved competitors, the regime lost a precious portion of its diminishing legitimacy. With each new instance of momentous showdown and uncompromising triumph, a layer of the behavioural restraint vital to democratic stability crumbled. With each new version of the previous crisis and each new replay of the previous outcome, another piece of the First Republic's foundation disintegrated. When the majors finally struck, there was nothing left.

CLASS CONFLICT AND INSIDIOUS DECAY

A weakness in the crisis-case approach of this study is that it tends to miss the gradual, insidious evolution of destabilising factors that do not fully erupt into crisis until they bring the system down altogether. The key factor here was the widening class cleavage, and the pressures and frustrations that accompanied or followed from it. Where it crystallised in discrete political conflicts, in 1962 and especially 1964, the destablising effect of this class cleavage has been noted. At points in the analysis, we have also noted the insidious decay of the First Republic induced by mounting corruption and profligacy, the increasing economic and psychological distance between the political class and the people, and the accumulating frustrations of sluggish development. These factors progressively eroded the popular legitimacy of the regime – especially among the crucial sectors of the intelligentsia – as surely as did the succession of major crises. In the end, they were probably equally responsible for the military coup. They require more explicit attention in conclusion.

Corruption, extravagance, inequality and waste

Corruption in and of itself did not destroy democracy in Nigeria. The use and abuse of political office for personal pecuniary gain is a common, perhaps inevitable, feature of the political development process (Wraith and Simpkins, 1963), and, in any case, it was in

Table 9.1 Analyses of major crises and conflicts in Nigeria 1960–65

Crisis	Cleavage Groups	Outcome	Causes	Effects on Democracy	Feedback Effects
1. Western Regional Crisis 1962–63	*Class/Ideology:* 'populist' anti-regionalist *vs* 'conservative' regionalist *Political:* NPC & NCNC *vs* AG *Regional* N & E *vs* W	Victory for regionalists imposed by (N-dominated) Federal Government Defeat & humiliation for Awolowo/AG Defeat for W Region–separation of M-W	Growing inequality between political class & mass, Extreme dependence of class position on state power Flawed federal structure – too few regions – wide scope of patronage resources at stake – constitutional provisions for Emergency Coincidence of party, region, and ethnicity Weak commitment to democratic values Ideological and structural incoherence of parties	Erosion of democracy – obstruction of majority will Erosion of regime legitimacy among: – Progressive elites in W (AG) – Yoruba people – Southerners in general (concerns about corruption, inequality)	Increased prospect of NPC–NCNC polarisation due to: – elimination of third force (AG) – increased NPC power – destruction of federalism Growing urban unemployment & disenchantment
2. Census Crisis 1962–64	*Regional:* N & W *vs* E & MW (N *vs* E) (Political: NPC & UPP *vs* NCNC & AG)	Victory for N (NPC) & its W-Government ally Defeat for E (NCNC)	Flawed federal structure – one region dominant – two few regions Coincidence of party, region, & ethnicity Low level of national unity (pattern of previous conflict) Class ambitions of politicians Antidemocratic behavioural	Erosion of regime legitimacy among: – NCNC – Easterners at large – portions of bureaucracy & intelligentsia – students & Left	Polarisation of future conflict due to: – Defection of most of West NCNC – Continuing E refusal to accept census figures

			style of politicians Popular desire for rapid socioeconomic development		– Continuing high salience of ethnic regional conflict
3. General Strike 1964 (& 1963)	*Class:* Urban workers (& sympathisers) *vs* the state & the political class	Victory for unions over government on symbolic issue of union power & right to strike Compromise on issue of pay	Specific labour grievances Poverty; development stagnation Extreme income inequality Corruption; profligacy of political class Arrogant, dilatory response by Government to union demands	Erosion of regime legitimacy among: – urban workers – unemployed sympathisers – portions of bureaucracy & intelligentsia – radical & progressive elements	Increased political salience of labour (possible cleavage crosscut) Greater possibility of future strikes & class tensions Greater N-S political tension
4. 1964 Federal Election	*Party:* NNA *vs* UPGA NPC *vs* NCNC (Region: N *vs* E) (Ideology: Regionalist *vs* antiregionalist)	Massive electoral victory for NPC (N) & its ally (NNDP) Humiliating defeat for NCNC & its UPGA allies Complete rejection of all NCNC demands in post-election crisis	Polarisation as a result of recent conflicts & historical pattern of conflict Federal structure – one region dominant – too few regions Antidemocratic methods & values Northern social structure; NPC desire for domination Elite campaigns of ethnic vilification	Heavy erosion of regime democraticness Further bitter alienation & heavy erosion of regime legitimacy among: – NCNC leaders & supporters in E Region	Conflict polarisation due to: – intensity of this conflict – failure to resolve basic issues Increasing political/civil involvement of army–increased likelihood of military coup

Table 9.1 cont. Analyses of major crises and conflicts in Nigeria

Crisis	Cleavage Groups	Outcome	Causes	Effects on Democracy	Feedback Effects
			Class position and ambitions of politicians, resulting from interaction of class dominance and state power	– AG leaders & supporters in W Region – Young, educated, & people at large (cynicism over elections & entire political class)	Further conflict polarisation– failure to resolve underlying conflict
5. 1965 Western Regional Election Crisis	*Party:* NNDP *vs* AG (NCNC) (NNA *vs* UPGA) (Region: N *vs* E; N *vs* S) *Ideology:* Disaffected progressive & anti-regionalist elites (& West masses) *vs* political regime	Victory (by gross fraud) for NNDP, & so for NPC Complete defeat for UPGA; no element of compromise or conciliation	Polarisation resulting from past conflicts Federal structure – too few regions – wide scope of patronage resources at stake Coincidence of cleavages Flawed electoral regulations Massive violation of democratic 'rules of the game' NPC desire to dominate federation Structure of class dominance and state power	Gross violation of essential features of democracy Complete shattering of regime legitimacy among W region people Further serious erosion of legitimacy in E & MW too Complete disillusionment and alienation among educated strata	Increasing involvement of military in political conflict, hence greater disposition to intervene & overthrow regime

keeping with prevailing expectations and norms in Nigeria (Mackintosh, 1966: 617; Achebe, 1966: 136, 140). Had Nigerian politicians observed greater discretion and restraint in their misappropriation of public resources, and had they delivered on expectations for government performance and contained their political conflicts, it is doubtful that political corruption alone would have brought the downfall of the regime. Self-enrichment by the politicians did not threaten their survival until it became apparent that this was draining the energy and resources needed to deliver the rapid socioeconomic progress so anxiously awaited by the people. It was only after several years of stagnation and dashed expectations that dominant class action began to provoke popular reaction in the General Strike and the Western rebellion.

The scale of avarice was enormous in some cases; the size of the personal fortunes built up by men like the Finance Minister, Chief Okotie-Eboh, will probably never be known, but some ran into the hundreds of thousands and millions of pounds. These were extraordinary sums in such a poor nation. The total misappropriation by the political class must have amounted to a significant portion of the capital available for development spending. Federal Ministers' official salaries and allowances alone amounted to one per cent of the Federal Budget. When one considers that this was only a fraction of their total take: that others were helping themselves up and down the political and bureaucratic ladders; that contracts were let at hugely overpriced sums, often to wholly incompetent firms; and that the portion of the budget spent on official salaries and benefits was particularly large in relation to that for productive investment; the accumulated drag on the development process looms large indeed. And this does not include the other elements of waste, the unproductive expenditures on prestige projects and buildings, which did little to improve peoples' lives or to stimulate economic growth.

If the mass of the people did not have the knowledge or sophistication to make the necessary links, there were intellectuals, journalists, students, union leaders, bureaucrats and military officers who did, and whose disgust spread to wider and wider circles till it engulfed, by 1964, large numbers of town dwellers especially. Pride in successful sons of the soil increasingly gave way to resentment at the growing inequality. By flaunting their wealth, the members of the political class played into this escalating resentment. Dr Mbadiwe's extravagant and widely publicised coming-out party for his 'Palace of the People' symbolised a regime of men who had sunk with their ill-gotten wealth into fatal insensitivity. O'Connell (1967: 151) has observed: 'Strangely enough, the politicians continued right up to the time of their overthrow to ignore the whispers of corruption – charges that were loudening into shouts and that were gradually undermining their standing among the leaders of opinion of the towns and the countryside'.

The failure of development

It is interesting to contemplate whether any of this could have been otherwise – whether the abject poverty of the nation, the virtual absence of a middle class and of private, non-state routes to wealth, and the importation through the colonial system of Western standards of consumption did not predestine corruption, inequality and stagnation under the new political leadership. Certainly the pervasiveness of this pattern in so many new nations of this period suggests a general dynamic beyond the specifics of the Nigerian case and the avarice of selfish individuals.

Nigeria's poverty was a kind of vicious circle. The above syndrome cannot be understood apart from the pervasive poverty of the nation, and yet its effect was to obstruct escape from poverty. In the context of the extraordinary popular expectations for personal and national progress, this failure insured the demise of the regime.

The odds against sufficiently rapid progress to satisfy expectations would have been long in any case. The 1950s had been a time of economic growth and prosperity: increasing external reserves, large-scale spending on infrastructure and education, rapid induction and promotion of Nigerians in the bureaucracy, and high prices for agricultural producers (O'Connell, 1970: 1023–4). These were auspicious circumstances in which to begin nationhood, but, ironically, they may have set unrealistically high standards for measuring the first few years of independence. This was especially so, given that the prosperity of late colonial rule owed heavily to an unstable factor – the consistently high world prices of Nigeria's principal export commodities, especially cocoa. By the end of the 1950s these had begun to fall sharply.

Falling commodity prices were not the only serious economic difficulty at Independence.

Universal primary education schemes were filling schools with millions of hopeful pupils. The secondary schools were also multiplying. But the top ranks of the senior civil service were nearly filled, and in a service that was no longer expanding rapidly there came to be less room in the lower and intermediate ranks than there had been.... With the arrival of independence, foreign capital grew cautious and there was less foreign private investment than had been hoped for by economic planners. The export of oil had not yet begun to make an impact on the economy. The cities were being crowded and their social facilities strained by ill-educated young job-seekers who remained unemployed indefinitely or for long periods and who depressed the standard of living of the working brothers and cousins with whom they lived. (O'Connell, 1970: 1024–5)

To be sure, there were enormous agricultural, mineral and human resources on which to build a foundation of stable growth (Schwarz, 1968: 284–5). But to get the economy moving quickly enough, and effectively enough directed at the most pressing bottlenecks, in order to prevent the aggravation of ethnic socioeconomic competition and the swelling of popular discontent was an enormous challenge. The 'Independence' generation of politicians was simply not up to it.

The hopes for rapid and widely diffused development were dashed not only by corruption and waste but by unfortunate priorities in planning, inefficient administration and widespread political interference. With respect to planning (or at least broad goal-setting, for of planning in the rigorous sense there was little), the chief failure was in stressing industrial over agricultural development and in banking so heavily on foreign investment. In the process, manufacturing did achieve remarkable annual rates of growth (e.g., 25 per cent in 1963–64) (Schwarz, 1968: 290), but this growth did relatively little to relieve the nation's most pressing economic problems. Because it was such a poor country, and because rampant corruption and inefficiency discouraged foreign investors (Schwarz, 1968: 295), Nigeria had to give away much of the yield of foreign investment in order to attract it. Generous incentives attracted by 1963 almost £40 million in foreign investment, 68 per cent of total investment (Cohen, 1974: 40–1; Schwarz, 1968: 286).

No quantitative, cost-benefit analysis is available, but two factors suggest that this investment bias may have done more harm than good – or at least less good than would have come from a different development strategy. First, it did relatively little to solve the most urgent (certainly the most politically explosive) problem – urban unemployment. Although employment in large-scale manufacturing tripled in roughly five years, the modern wage sector never employed more than a few per cent of what was throughout a predominantly agararian labour force. Even in the cities, industry made little dent on unemployment, which was estimated at 14.6 per cent nationwide in 1963, and up to 45 per cent by 1965 in such cities as Lagos, Ibadan, and Onitsha (Cohen, 1974: 54; Green, 1965: 6). This was because foreign investment was overwhelmingly oriented, as was Nigerian public investment, to capital-intensive industrialisation (Cohen, 1974: 53). Second, the stress on building factories at any cost, and the bias in favour of foreign expertise and high technology, led to many foolish government investments in foreign 'turn-key projects', under which 'the foreign "investor" made his profit by selling the machinery, irrespective of the viability of the industry' (Schwarz, 1963: 290). By this arrangement, the Nigerian government assumed virtually the entire risk while the foreign investor could not fail to make a large profit. By 1966, Nigerian debts from such projects totalled £55.3 million (Schwarz, 1963: 290–1). The inherently dubious value of such arrangements was further diminished by the outright charlatanism of some investors and the corruption and imcompetence of the Nigerian officials who joined hands with them.

In retrospect, what was needed was a strategy emphasising small, indigenous manufacturing enterprises and especially agricultural development.[2] While some analysts have challenged the wisdom of emphasising small enterprises (Cohen, 1974: 45–6), in the one area of the country where it was attempted, the Eastern Region, the strategy appears to have yielded promising success. Small enterprises employed three times as many workers as large industries with roughly one-thirtieth the investment, while training people in technical and business skills (Schwarz, 1968: 267).

However, the heart of any development strategy for Nigeria had to be in agriculture, where the overwhelming bulk of the people were. Here Nigerian policy makers were caught on the horns of a familiar dilemma. If they did not steer development resources to the towns and increase employment there, instability would likely result. But if they neglected the countryside at the expense of the towns, they risked, if not widespread peasant unrest, at least a continued flow of young migrants into the cities, overwhelming the benefits of development spending there. Moreover, the neglect of agriculture would mean neglect of the economy (both domestic and export), since agriculture accounted for the largest share of gross product.

But development strategy focused rather little on the countryside. The one-time Eastern Minister Okoi Arikpo observed (1967: 121–2): 'The modern social services, the industrial projects and all those government policies which enable Nigerians to increase their earning power have so far been concentrated in the towns. ... the practical outcome of public policy has been a relative lowering of peasant-living standards compared with those of the wage-earners'. In the Western Region, development planning called for expansion of food production and diversification beyond cocoa, but production fell miserably short of targets across the board. This was officially blamed on 'shortage of materials, inadequate funds and equipment and administrative and technical problems', but the consumption of Western Market Board Reserves in political graft was probably a major factor (Schwarz, 1968: 276).

The deterioration of rural conditions and agricultural prices in the Western Region contributed directly to the collapse of the regime through the eruption of peasant rebellion there late in 1965. Massive electoral fraud and repression was the fuse for this explosion, but it had been building through years of severe neglect. Government information services failed to keep farmers abreast of improvements. Medical facilities, water supplies, roads, and electricity were inadequate or absent altogether. Children were being sent to primary schools, and many to secondary schools, only to fail in the search for a job. At the same time, this process was drawing them off the Region's farms, contributing to a scarcity of labour that caused a fall in food production there in 1964 and 1965. And atop it all were the persistent rumours of fantastic corruption (O'Connell, 1970: 1028–9).

Corruption, waste, inefficiency and misguided development strategies were compounded by politics. Regionalism worked against effective planning and often led to counterproductive competition, as in the fruitless tug-of-war over the steel mill in 1965 (Schwarz, 1968: 298). Politicians interfered with civil servants in the execution of development policy, and often failed to seek their advice on key policy decisions (*Nigerian Opinion*, December 1965: 8–9).

As a result of these factors, the Six-Year Development Plan had fallen severely, perhaps irretrievably, short of its targets by the time it had half expired. Costs were running out of control, due to what one progress report referred to as a 'gross imbalance' in the Plan between 'Development' and 'Administrative and Social' expenditures (*West Africa*, 1 May 1965: 473). The latter (especially government flats and offices) were proceeding much faster than envisioned in the Plan while directly productive investment was only 30 per cent of the halfway target (Green, 1965: 7).

'WHAT IF'S'

Throughout the five-year First Republic, and especially in its later years, a number of structural changes were proposed in the political system. Proponents believed these changes would relieve the deep tensions in national politics and rescue a regime that was, in the final two years, clearly reeling toward collapse. What might have been the prospects for stable democracy if these structural changes had been effected?

With respect to the calls for a truly federal system, breaking up the regional structure and, in particular, the North's domination of the Federation would have at least reduced a major source of political tension and conflict. If federalist guarantees of group security had been preserved (by retaining states' autonomy over their internal affairs), a multistate structure could have complicated the cleavage pattern and worked against the polarisation of sectional conflict. It is doubtful, however, that this alone would have been enough to save the system. There would still have been a fierce contest for the material rewards of political power. The basis of this struggle would have been different in a multistate system, but none of the underlying socioeconomic and class pressures would have been altered. It is difficult to see how any change in political structure could have made stable democracy a likely outcome in the absence of wide opportunities for status attainment outside the political arena.

Aside from the creation of many more states, the most promising structural alternative was the United Front government proposed in one form or another by many Nigerian political leaders, and floated in *Nigerian Opinion* after the Federal Election crisis by Richard L. Sklar (1965b), then teaching at the University of Ibadan. The basic idea was that since the parties were essentially regionalised anyway, party competition would be suspended for a time – Dr Okpara had suggested a period of ten years – in order to end the fierce succession of sectional conficts, settle long-term structural questions, and get on with the business of development. The parties would have continued to exist as distinct entities (Sklar opposed any legal infringement on the right to form parties for electoral competition), but they would have divided up the parliamentary seats in advance, and then divided up power and resources at the centre in some fashion. If a stable formula for allocation of seats and ministries could have been agreed upon – perhaps parallelling the formula for revenue allocation that the parties managed to arrive at, then renegotiate – this alternative would have resembled Lijphart's consociational system.

But it is doubtful that such a system could have worked. A true consociational system involves not only the sharing of central power in grand coalition but decisional autonomy for each subgroup over its own affairs, and veto power over major national policies. It involves not only the proportional division of public funds and political offices but of civil service positions as well.

Only some of this was plausible. While political leaders often talked of coming together and dividing up all of this on some kind of rational, amicable basis, the intensity of competition lengthened the odds against a stable allocation. Even within the electoral alliances – in which the politicians faced more intense pressures for internal accommodation than they would have in a grand coalition – such agreements broke down in the hunger for office. Thus, even in the face of an extraordinary common threat in 1965, the Action Group/ NCNC alliance collapsed in some 20 Western constituencies where both parties contested. Given the more sharply conflicting interests between the NNDP and the AG, and between the NPC and NEPU/ UMBC, it is difficult to see how any elite allocation of parliamentary seats would not have degenerated in practice into intense party competition in the constituencies – which could have unravelled all other agreements. This is one reason why a consociational system, if it had been imposed, would probably not have been democratic. In order to work, it would have had, in effect, to suspend or repress electoral competition. And in the absence of such competition, the most important lever of accountability would have disappeared.

Beyond this, there are a number of conditions which Lijphart (1977: 53–103) identifies as important to the success of consociational democracy, few of which held in the Nigerian case. In particular, Lijphart's model predicts that the following features of the Nigerian system would have worked against consociational success: the centralised balance of power between the major ethnic groups, in which one stood in hegemonic position over the others; the inferior socioeconomic position of one group; the absence of overarching loyalties; the large size of the nation; and, most important, the absence of a tradition of elite accommodation or of some historical factor – such as the degeneration of previous conflict into civil war – which leaves a collective memory of horror that drives elites away from the precipice of polarisation in what Lijphart calls 'a self-negating prophecy'.

In addition, there were other reasons why a consociational system – if it could have been constructed and maintained – was unlikely to have been democratic in practice. The main impetus for a consociational-like system came from the conservatives and instrumentalists in the political class, like Chief Akintola and Chief Okotie-Eboh, who had little interest in democracy. These men saw a grand coalition as a way to further entrench the system of regional security and divide the spoils of rule on a stable basis. It is possible, as Sklar envisioned, that progressives might have adapted to this system and eventually engineered some constitutional and territorial changes. The greater likelihood, however, is that elections would have become a total facade, feebly masking authoritarian rule by the political class. This was the direction in which the political system had been steadily moving for a number of years. Had the Action Group and the progressives in the NCNC conceded to join such a long-term United Front, it would have removed the primary resistance to this trend. Class polarisation would have continued in the form of growing popular resentment of the political class, and the outcome would likely still have been, as it was in Ghana for similar reasons, a military coup.

Constitutional changes proposed by UPGA to limit Northern power in the Federation – raising the Senate to a coordinate legislative chamber and transferring from the Prime Minister to the President such substantive areas of responsibility as the census, the elections, and the federal public service – similarly failed to address the fundamental problems. Apart from the fact that the NPC was no more likely to approve these changes than to concede to the division of the Northern Region, it is difficult to see how they would have defused the cumulative pattern of conflict. At most, they would have evened somewhat the power resources of the competitors, which might only have produced more paralysing deadlock.

And so it would have been with proposed changes in the electoral system. The election of candidates through proportional representation in each Region rather than by districts (*West Africa*, 11 October 1965: 1177) might have prevented manipulation of the nominations process (since there would have been a single list for each party), but the underlying motivation to obstruct the democratic rules would simply have been manifested in some other way. The same difficulty plagued the reforms proposed by Chairman Esua of the Electoral Commission in 1965: welcome as greater civil service control may have been, it could not have prevented electoral fraud on the part of a ruling party that was determined to retain power at any price. And so, as well, with proposals for stricter constitutional protection of fundamental rights and enhanced judicial independence (Sklar, 1966: 161–2; Dudley, 1968: 287). These changes might well have been helpful – and point in the direction of institutional innovations Nigeria should consider in the future to insulate the democratic process from partisan abuse (Diamond, 1984a, 1985) – but they did not get at the underlying threat to democracy. As Billy Dudley noted (1968: 288), 'No constitution, however consistent and laudable a document it is, can be made operable if there does not exist that willingness and cooperation, the determination to play according to the "rule of the game", on which the political system itself rests'.

If there was to have been a real possibility for stable democratic government in Nigeria, the ethnic and class imperatives that led politicians to overrun democracy had somehow to be altered. A multistate federal system might have modified the former, but it would not have changed the latter. The only structural alternative addressed to these class imperatives was the proposal of the United Labour Congress to abolish parliamentary salaries (paying only living allowances), and to limit the amount of property that politicians and top civil servants could acquire. Had these limits been respected – and rigorously policed through some Code of Conduct mechanism to monitor, try and punish corruption in office[3] – they would have reduced the fixation of class ambitions on politics. But this also required a reduction in the size of the state and the scope of its intervention in the economy, as well as the invigoration of private enterprise. And the class imperatives for Northern control of the political system would have remained so long as the Federation was structured as it was.

THE FLOW OF CAUSATION: A SUMMARY

The major causes of the failure of the First Republic can now be summarised and linked together, as depicted in Figure 9.1. There is first the most elementary fact – the poverty of the nation. The low level of national development and the narrow base of modern

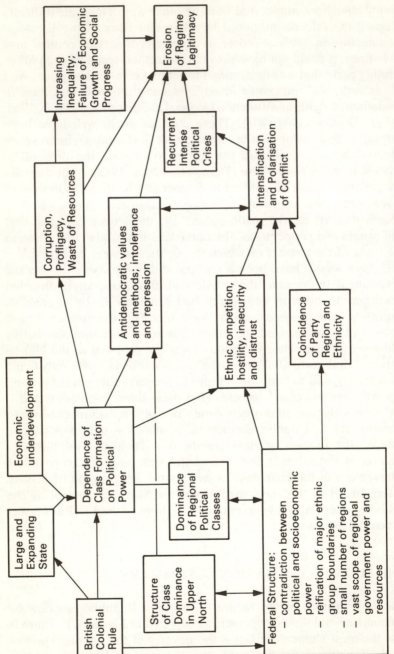

Figure 9.1   The flow of causation in the failure of the First Republic

economic institutions, opportunities and talents presented obstacles to rapid economic growth and provided fertile soil for mushrooming corruption and waste, which only compounded the difficulty of generating economic growth. But poverty in itself did not generate corruption and stagnation, or polarisation and violence. These resulted from the interaction of an underdeveloped economy and an oversized state. The extreme weakness of indigenous entrepreneurship and scarcity of social mobility opportunities in the private economy, coupled with the relatively large and expanding stock of resources and rewards controlled by the state, generated an extreme dependence of class formation on political power. This gave rise to a class of politicians, administrators and politically-connected businessmen whose most important motivation was the advancement and entrenchment of their class interests. By manipulating power, they could reap vast rewards with little investment and even less risk. The incentive to innovate, invest and produce withered, not only in the urban economy, but also in agriculture, where wealth was extracted by the omnivorous state. Hence, the tight connection between the process of class formation and the control of the state generated the corruption, mismanagement, distorted incentives and waste of resources that sapped the potential for economic development; the increasing intolerance and antidemocratic behaviour that intensified conflict and eroded the people's faith in the Republic; and the large-scale ethnic conflict that inflamed and polarised political crises.

While the weight of what was at stake in politics was clearly the primary reason for the antidemocratic character of political behaviour, British colonial rule also bears some responsibility. The postponement of indigenous political competition until the twilight of colonial rule did not allow sufficient time for commitment to democratic values to develop through experience with the process. The more significant colonial legacies, however, were the concentration of resources in the state; the establishment of a pattern in which the dominant class was the group in control of the state, and the profoundly flawed federal structure.

In several respects, the federal structure was a basic source of democratic crisis and decay. It heavily contributed to the polarisation of political conflict by generating the coincidence of ethnic, regional and party cleavage, by placing such a premium on political control of each region, and by reifying the ethnic boundaries of the three major groups while heightening the insecurity of minority groups. These causal linkages are depicted in Figure 9.1, which also shows the contribution of the federal structure to the formation or preservation of regional political classes, particularly that of the North. In reciprocal fashion, these regional classes then acted to preserve the most critical feature of the federal system, its three regions.

From these fundamental factors of class, state, ethnicity and regionalism followed the tribalism, repression, intolerance, corruption and recurrent political crises that consumed the popular legitimacy of the First Republic and so brought it down.

CLASS, ETHNICITY AND THE DEMOCRATIC PROSPECT

What of general significance does all of this imply about the conditions and prospects for democratic government in the Third World? There are, of course, the obvious truisms that democracy requires a popular belief in its legitimacy and democratic behaviour and commitment on the part of political leaders. There is the clear lesson, as well, that democratic leaders must perform effectively if people are to value democratic government, especially where the democratic system is not infused with deep historical or traditional legitimacy. This means at least some measure of visible and broadly diffused improvement in the material conditions of people's lives, and effective limits on political corruption and social inequality. It was in part Prime Minister Balewa's unwillingness (or inability) to jettison manifestly corrupt ministers that led to his downfall, despite his personal reputation for honesty and moderation.

Effective performance also means the reasonably effective management of political and social conflict, at least so that it does not paralyse government or destroy civil order. This demands responsible partisanship from elites, but it also requires a favourable set of structural conditions. In this regard, the experience of the First Republic, and the decade of competition preceding it, support the theory of crosscutting cleavages and the modifications subsequently proposed by Nordlinger (1972). Conflict is more intense when cleavages coincide. There is no way around this social law save for a consociational arrangement, which is difficult to sustain amidst the deep divisions and pressing economic imperatives of Third World countries. Moreover, the success of consociational systems in such developed nations as Austria and the Netherlands does not demonstrate their viability in the more pressured circumstances of the contemporary Third World (witness Lebanon). On the other hand, judicious adoption of some consociational mechanisms, such as the political pacts that ended 'La Violencia' in Colombia, or the more elaborate federal system and requirements for ethnic distribution that reduced ethnic polarisation in Nigeria's Second Republic, can make a difference.

The history of Nigerian politics calls attention to the pattern of cleavage in political conflict over time. It suggests that the polarising effect of coinciding cleavages may be at least partially mitigated by fluidity of alignments and/or alternation in outcomes. The latter in particular will be more likely to obtain if there is a powerful arbitrating mechanism that can insure the fairness of the process and veto or overturn domineering, oppressive and unfair outcomes. There will likely never again be an external presence like colonial rule to perform this task – and such a presence would contradict the meaning of democracy. How then can free political competition and the need to avoid a consistent, cumulative and alienating pattern of outcomes be reconciled?

One method is through various kinds of consociational mechanisms: constitutional safeguards and power-sharing arrangements. Some surrogate for the colonial referee might be another. Here the most obvious candidate in the Third World is the military, and the parallel between the 1959 Federal Election, when the steel frame of British rule contained abuses, and the 1979 elections inaugurating Nigeria's Second Republic, when the military performed a like role, is instructive. (Equally so is the sad parallel between the subsequent Nigerian elections of 1964 and 1983.) To the extent that the military remains the ultimate political authority in the nation, democracy is diminished. However, it may be possible to assign to military supervision certain specific functions critical to the regulation of democratic politics, such as the administration of elections and of the laws and institutions restricting corrupt practices in office. Such specific, supervisory functions for the military can, in principle, coexist with civilian, democratic government, even with civilian control over the funding and deployment of the armed forces (Diamond, 1984a).

There is a more democratic candidate for the arbitrative role, though one less capable of administering. That is the judiciary. Indeed, it would appear that a vigorous, powerful and fearlessly independent judiciary is an indispensable condition for stable democracy, particularly in nations where the tendency to perversion of democratic institutions is high. During the Second Republic, vigorous assertions of judicial independence played an important role in maintaining some democratic balance between government and opposition (Sklar, 1982: 6; Diamond, 1983b: 51). Unfortunately, this fragile balance was overwhelmed in the elections by the sheer scale of the abuses and malpractices.

The First Republic also had significant constitutional provisions for judicial independence, and at least some democratically committed judges. Indeed, it was the judiciary that played the key mediating role in breaking the deadlock over the 1964 Federal Election and averting potential mass violence. But this did not avert democratic collapse, or even effectively resolve the underlying conflict. It is unlikely that any judiciary can contain the enmity of cumulative cleavages and grievances. In the long run, stable democracy is much more likely where crosscutting cleavages develop.

In this regard, a federal system is a crucial resource, in that it represents one of the few cleavage structures that is relatively open to rapid and deliberate rearrangement. The Nigerian case powerfully demonstrates the importance of using the federal system to break up large-scale, sub-national solidarities and to complicate the cleavage structure. This was acutely perceived by many Nigerian progressives even before the start of formal political competition. Indeed, the fact that both subsequent military regimes – Ironsi's and then Gowon's – moved early and decisively against the old regional system reflects the degree to which it had become identified with the traumas of the First Republic. Ironsi's declaration of a unitary system moved in the wrong direction, however, for in a deeply divided society, federalist protections of decentralised power and local autonomy are a crucial condition for the development of mutual trust and security between cultural groups. On this point it is difficult to dispute Lijphart. And one may also agree with Sklar (1982: 5) that 'truly federal governments are necessarily liberal governments'. But if governments are to be 'truly federal', there must be enough units to ensure mutual security. This is what General Gowon recognised in creating twelve states in 1967 – and so finally breaking the structural guarantee of Northern political domination. The subsequent military regime of Generals Muhammed and Obasanjo explicitly recognised the importance of crosscutting cleavages in creating a total of 19 states, and in writing into the 1979 constitution provisions requiring that political parties demonstrate a broad national presence, that the winning presidential candidate show trans-ethnic support (by scoring a quarter of the vote in two-thirds of the states), and that major

Presidential appointments 'reflect the Federal character' of the country. Such institutional innovations began to produce a more complex pattern of political alignments and increased the prospects for stable democracy in the Second Republic (Whitaker, 1981). Although the Second Republic failed as well, polarised ethnic conflict was not a cause (Diamond, 1984a).

The failure of the Second Republic underscores a central conclusion of this study: that constitutional innovations cannot succeed without the necessary social foundations. Even the most shrewdly crafted constitutions may be relentlessly abused. Democratic constitutions matter if politicians respect them – or at least if enough politicians do to permit democratic checks and balances to work. But where parties and politicians are determined to win and retain power at all costs, no written constitution can safeguard liberal democracy. Here the relationship between the process of class formation and the structure of the state assumes decisive importance. Where the underdevelopment of the economy and the overdevelopment of the state require state control or access as a condition for the accumulation of wealth and achievement of status, new and aspiring entrants into the dominant class can be expected to use any means to compete for political power, and dominant classes can be expected to use power in every way possible to hold on to what they have and to accumulate more. It is of little use to attribute such chicanery to antidemocratic values or excessive greed. Dominant classes always manifest a certain measure of greed, and complex societies have always had more or less dominant classes. The question is whether members of the dominant class and aspiring entrants – and others as well who seek merely a comfortable middle-class existence, or perhaps only an escape from grinding poverty – must control political power in order to satisfy their ambitions for 'a life more abundant'.

This raises the relationship between the close structural linkage of the state and class formation, on the one hand, and democracy on the other. Where the accumulation of wealth and status depends almost totally on political power, both those who aspire to high class standing and those who wish to consolidate it need assured access to the state, if not position within it. Under an authoritarian state sympathetic to the dominant class, such access and support can be confidently secured. In a democratic state, and particularly one lacking a social consensus legitimating the capitalist accumulation of wealth, it cannot be. It is at risk in every election and must continually be renewed through elections. Hence, elections become brutal and bloody affairs. Moreover, in ethnically divided societies, these elections, and the ongoing legislative and political conflict that is the stuff of democratic politics, become the vehicle not only for protecting the general process of capitalist accumulation but also for promoting accumulation by one cultural section of the dominant class in competition with others. Thus they become a major expression of ethnic conflict. And because manipulation of mass ethnic feelings is often the surest instrument of electoral success, democratic competition serves to fan ethnic conflict at the mass level as well.

Thus, ethnic division and competition, an emerging dominant-class structure heavily dependent on state control, and electoral democracy interact to produce an intense polarisation of politics around ethnicity. Given the first two alone, elite ethnic competition would lack such regular political outlets and weapons, and, if elite access to state resources could be assured, might instead be eliminated by some stable division of state resources like that sought by regionalist forces in the First Republic. Given the emergent class structure and democratic competition in a more ethnically homogeneous society, conflict might become intense and even polarised, but not along ethnic lines. Given ethnic divisions and democracy but a pluralist economic structure, where the position of the dominant class had either a secure base or at least ample opportunity for formation and consolidation outside the state, elites would not depend so heavily for their class position on political victory, and so would be under less pressure to manipulate ethnic tension and to trounce the democratic 'rules of the game' in pursuit of victory.

The Nigerian case thus suggests several general propositions. First, in ethnically divided societies with low levels of socioeconomic development but relatively large state sectors, ethnicity is mobilised by elites as a resource in their competition for the scarce but expanding resources of class formation controlled by the state. Since these conditions are typical of contemporary Asian and especially African countries, this suggests that the ethnic conflict that has commonly plagued and polarised their politics has been, to a significant degree, the product of the process of class formation, and cannot be explained simply by the stimulus to competition for new resources and rewards introduced by modernisation. Second, in such a context, electoral competition may make mass ethnic conflict – and its polarisation into bitterness, violence and even secession – more likely, by inducing politicians to mobilise mass constituencies along ethnic lines in their struggle for state control (Melson and Wolpe, 1971: 19). Third, because such ethnic polarisation is more a phenomenon of class than political structure, attempts to generate crosscutting cleavage through constitutional innovations, in the absence of changes in socioeconomic structure and in the nature of class formation, are likely to prove disappointing.

These propositions are consistent with the experience of Nigeria's Second Republic. The new federal system and constitution visibly reduced ethnic polarisation; ethnicity remained the primary current of political alignment and conflict, but at a much more decentralised level. At the national level, new ethnic coalitions and alliances emerged, and new fissures developed as old ones widened within the major groups. At the same time, the sweeping pace of social and economic change and the heightening inequalities and contradictions generated by the oil boom thrust class-based cleavages into politics more resolutely than ever before (Diamond, 1983b). Indeed the familiar cleavage between a remote and self-aggrandising political class and the mass of the people was, even more decisively than for the First Republic, the crucial precipitant of democratic collapse.

In this sense, the root problem of the First Republic continues to haunt Nigeria's quest for democratic government. State power – control over government contracts, jobs, development projects, import licences and so forth, and the coercive machinery to preserve that control – remains the primary locus of national wealth and the primary arena of class formation. As a result, the premium on political power remains as high as ever, and 'a desperate struggle to win control of state power ensues since this control means for all practical purposes being all powerful and owning everything. Politics becomes warfare, a matter of life and death' (Ake, 1982: 1162–3). Unless this relationship between state and society is altered, it is likely that the politics of a future Third Nigerian Republic will be similarly plagued by the violence, intolerance and venality that destroyed the first two attempts.

There has been a rising and virtually irresistible pressure in the contemporary world to expand the revenues consumed by the state, the structures administered by the state, and the services rendered by the state. Apart from the need of nations for strong states to compete in an increasingly interdependent world, and from the autonomous interest of state elites themselves in an ever larger and more powerful state, this inexorable expansion has had the worthy goal of improving the welfare of the people. In developing nations, there has further been the understandable pressure to expand the state much more rapidly than was historically the case in older nations in order to speed up the process of development. But separate and apart from the serious questions about the effectiveness of such a centrally directed march toward progress, there is the increasingly inescapable fact of its incompatibility with liberal democracy.

If liberal democracy is to survive and mature in the Third World, the growth of the state in proportion to the rest of society must be halted, and in many cases, reversed. This would seem to require the development of an authentic, indigenous capitalism: a class of entrepreneurs and producers, both *grand* and *petit*, who are able to profit from productive, risk-taking investment without controlling the state – in other words, a real bourgeoisie. More generally, opportunities must be opened for promising and ambitious young men and women to succeed independent of political power and connections, and for incumbents of state power to exit and still enjoy a comfortable and rewarding life, both materially and psychologically. Where society is deeply divided along ethnic lines, a reduction in the size of the state and the scope of public resources would similarly reduce the group stakes in politics, and so 'tone down the invidious quality of ethnic politics' (Rabushka and Shepsle, 1972: 216). Stable democracy requires not only that people care about politics, but that they be able not to care as well, and that they do not care too much. This is an essential condition for the tolerance and mutual restraint that are the lifeblood of democracy.

This does not mean that a nation must be wealthy, or economically 'developed' in the sense the word is commonly understood. What it does require is a broad diffusion of at least moderate socioeconomic progress, and a sizeable and growing middle class 'whose economic position is virtually independent of those who hold supreme power and who have sufficient means to be able ... to serve their country with no other satisfaction than those that come from individual pride and self-respect' (Mosca, 1939: 144).

In many contemporary developing nations, two important conditions for such a social arrangement exist: a reasonable base of wealth and a sizeable educated population. More frequently, however, the conditions of state and class structure do not obtain. Many changes will be necessary if the new attempts at democratic government in the Third World are to succeed. Some of these changes are historically specific to particular nations; others are more general. Among the most important general conditions is that the historic process of state expansion begins now to be arrested, and a foundation of economic pluralism and private initiative developed that can produce and distribute growth. For the remainder of this century, this will likely be the most crucial and difficult challenge for liberal democracy in the Third World.

Notes and References

2 The Origins of Crisis

1. In addition to the ruling class (*sarakuna*) and lower class (*talakawa*), Paden (1973: 25–26) distinguishes three other social classes in Kano (and presumably by extension, other Muslim emirates of Northern Nigeria): the wealthy Hausa merchants (*attajirai*); the educated senior personnel of the Civil Service (most of whom were Fulani, many of lesser noble birth); and the middle class Hausa traders. The *talakawa* encompasses five subcategories: peasants, petty traders, craft and skilled workers, labourers and beggars.

2. A former colonial Lieutenant Governor of the Northern Region, Sir Bryan Sharwood-Smith, explained in his memoirs (1969: 222): 'It would have been a travesty of democracy to have required this uninformed and uninterested peasantry to elect an unknown candidate with an unknown policy', hence the decision to conduct the election in stages 'through the medium of electoral colleges', which even many critics in Britain attacked as 'undemocratic'.

3. This profoundly important historical process, which challenges the earlier conceptions of modernisation, is articulated in absorbing detail in the landmark study of C. S. Whitaker, Jr (1970). In many other African nations as well, traditional ruling classes used the opportunities of modernisation to consolidate their dominance (Markovitz, 1977: 152–72).

4. Corruption was rife in local government as well, as was extensively documented by a number of colonial commissions of inquiry (Storey, 1953; Floyer, *et al.*, 1955; Grant, 1955; Gunning, 1955; Nicholson, 1955). For a summary of local and regional corruption and a provocative comparative analysis, see Wraith and Simpkins (1963).

5. In this they were assisted by colonial administration, which, seeing the chieftaincy system as 'the one sure bulwark against the future domination of the region by a ruthlessly despotic party machine', sought to 'purge' it of its 'worst abuses' (Sharwood-Smith, 1969: 290; 243; 279; 289).

6. The label one attaches to this social formation has important theoretical implications. In his original pathbreaking study of Nigerian politics, Sklar (1963: 474–505) used the term 'new and rising class' to describe the emergent dominant class distinguished by high levels of income, education, and occupational status, and business ownership or control. His subsequent adoption of the term 'political class' followed Mosca in denoting that class which controls 'the dominant institutions of society' (Sklar, 1965a: 203–4). This term was frequently misinterpreted as encompassing only politicians. To overcome this confusion and to emphasise the role of the private and public business elite, Sklar (1976:

81, 91 n.51) adopted the term 'managerial bourgeoisie', which encompasses as well other upper-level bureaucrats, members of the learned professions, and high government officials. This term, like Markovitz's (1977) 'organisational bourgeoisie', is more broadly conceived than 'bureaucratic' or 'state' bourgeoisie in that it seeks 'to comprehend the dominant class as a whole' (Sklar, 1979: 544–7), and is more precise than Ekeh's (1975: 93) simple designation of these groups as 'bourgeois', which 'connotes the newness of a privileged class which may yield much power, but have little political acceptance'. Precisely because this class forms and consolidates its social dominance through political power, I favour the term 'political class'.

7. Melson and Wolpe (1971: 19–21) persuasively advance the general proposition that 'democratic political institutions which encourage mass political participation and competitive political parties' 'tend to further politicise and intensify communal conflict', by inducing political elites to make communal appeals to the mass, which 'exacerbate communal tensions', which in turn encourage the recruitment of leaders who will make communal appeals and demands', and so on in a vicious cycle.

8. This important conceptual distinction introduced by Sklar is at odds with Melson and Wolpe (and many others), who use the term 'communal' in reference to any type of cultural identity and assertiveness – racial, religious, linguistic or ethnic – at any level of social aggregation. These four types often overlap, with ethnicity typically involving 'some notion of common kinship or origin' (Melson and Wolpe, 1971: 1–2; Paden, 1971: 114).

Throughout this study, I will use ethnicity to mean, as Barth (1969) has conceptualised it, an exclusive category of ascription and identification attributed to an actor by both self and others on the basis of social origin and current behaviour, emphasising in particular the cultural content – values, beliefs, symbols, lifestyles – of this identification and behaviour. A virtue of this formulation is that it fits well the reality of shifting ethnic boundaries and multiple levels of ethnic identity. Paden (1973: 36–8), distinguishes eight levels of 'communal' identity among the Kano Hausa, including religion, clan, birthplace, language, nation and race. Wolpe (1974: 68–77) similarly distinguishes four levels of 'communal' identity in Port Harcourt (including race, nationality and 'geo-ethnicity'). I will use the term 'sectional' in the way Melson and Wolpe and Paden use 'communal' to refer to any kind of cultural or community identity or cleavage. This will include ethnicity, sub-ethnic (clan) divisions, language, religion and region, i.e. the formal components of the federal system. Although each region contained numerous ethnic groups, its political identity and position was typically defined by the dominant group. 'Ethnoregional' will thus refer to the simultaneous overlapping involvement of both ethnic and regional cleavage.

9. My use here (and elsewhere) of the singular form is a matter of style and should not be read as implying the existence of a unified, national political class. Again, consolidation never reached beyond the region during the life of the First Republic.

3   Conspiracy of Optimism: Nigeria at Independence

1.   This survey, part of an extensive, twelve-nation study of people's hopes and fears, was conducted between September and November 1962, when the Federal Government was ruling directly in the Western Region after having dissolved the government there and declared a 'state of emergency' (Chapter 4). This atmosphere of political crisis no doubt coloured the survey responses, particularly in the Western Region itself.

2.   A key component of the survey was to ask each respondent to rate the past, present and future standing of his nation and of his own personal life on a ten-step ladder, with the top step representing the best possible life (or national condition) he could imagine and wish for and the bottom step the worst he could imagine and fear (Cantril, 1965: 21).

3.   This was reflected in his appointments in 1961 to a 'National Reconstruction Group' formed to develop new economic and social policies. The twelve men, ranging in age from 28 to 38, were all to the left of centre politically. Some of them were not actually members of his party. Fully half came from the university; only two were full-time politicians (Post and Vickers, 1973: 75; Sklar, 1966: 130).

4.   This flatly contradicts the thesis of Wallerstein (1963: 668) that the involvement of ethnic groups in providing for social security and economic progress functions to 'divert expectations from the state to other social groups' and so serves 'as an outlet for political tensions'. In fact, the formation of ethnic unions, and their involvement with the socioeconomic needs of their members, not only failed to relieve but very probably stimulated popular expectations and demands upon the national state.

5.   Part of this difference was likely due to the spectacular revelations of corruption in the West surfacing in the Coker Commission hearings at the time of the survey, but the persistence of this regional difference when controlling for education led Free to suggest that 'the Northerners appear either to have more confidence in their officials or to not care as much about graft and corruption' (Free, 1964: 45).

6.   This vulnerability was demonstrated a few months after Independence when Dr Chike Obi was arrested for distributing a pamphlet stridently critical of the nation's politicians and their 'squandermania'. The Supreme Court upheld his conviction for sedition as consistent with constitutional guarantees of freedom of expression, interpreting the Constitution as forbidding anyone 'to criticise the government in a malignant manner . . . for such acts by their nature tend to affect the public peace'. Reportedly, Prime Minister Balewa and the Regional Premiers were planning even stronger measures against radical dissent when they met in December 1961, including a possible Preventive Detention Bill, which never materialised (Schwarz, 1965: 184–5).

7.   Chief Awolowo's testimony to the role of opposition in a democracy bears recalling here and in subsequent chapters: 'It is universally agreed that the quintessence of a democratic way of life is the freedom

of all citizens . . . to hold and express divergent and opposing views on any issue of the day without let or hindrance. From this . . . I deduce that the soul of democracy is the open, unfettered and uninhibited existence of a strong and organized Opposition in and outside Parliament. It is political heresy of the worst kind to think of a democracy without an organized opposition which also serves as the alternative choice open to the electorate in any succeeding elections' (Awolowo, 1960b: 7).

4 Crisis and Conflict in the Western Region, 1962–63

1. Some have interpreted the personal rivalry between Awolowo and Akintola as the overriding element in the widening party rift. Despite his embrace of democratic socialism, Awolowo, Mackintosh writes (1966: 443), 'had established forms of government-aided party and private enterprise which fell into no clear ideological category,' while also attracting some of the party's big businessmen to his side in the dispute. In this interpretation, the businessmen and Obas around Akintola resented more Awolowo's 'intellectual arrogance' than his socialist platform *per se*. Even in the dispute over strategy, Mackintosh stresses the personal component. Chief Akintola had served with Sir Abubakar in the first Federal Cabinet in 1957 and had remained on good terms with him after he became Prime Minister in 1959, while Awolowo had always been on bad terms with Sir Abubakar and refused to consider joining him in coalition (Mackintosh, 1966: 442–3). While not ignoring the obvious personal component, other analyses (Post, 1962; Sklar, 1966; Sklar, 1971; Post and Vickers, 1973) have seen the ideological conflict and the threat perceived by vested class interests in the West as quite real, and have treated Awolowo's turn toward socialist programmes as something more than mere political rhetoric or opportunism.

2. Specifically, Dr Okpara, speaking at the September 1960 Annual Convention of the NCNC, issued a 'final warning' that if the 'coercion and persecution' of opposition by the Action Group government in the West did not cease, AG supporters in the East could expect 'precisely the same treatment' (Okpara, 1960: 10). More ominously, National Secretary F. S. McEwen observed in his speech to the same Convention: 'one wonders whether with a party like the Action Group, other means of combating their fascist methods should not be employed' (McEwen, 1960: 11).

3. Stanley Diamond (1964) makes much – probably too much – of this possible 'united front of the disaffected'. The Action Group actually lost ground in the Middle Belt in 1961, and the NPC victory in the Muslim North was crushing. But still, some base of opposition remained among a core 30 per cent of the voters in the North, and the NPC leadership was disposed to view with alarm even the faintest prospect of a coalition between its chief sources of opposition.

4. This account is confirmed in its essential details by Richard Sklar (1966: 134), F. A. O. Schwarz (1965: 135), and A. Osuntokun (1982:

144). Mackintosh interprets the 'fire on the mountain' exclamation as 'a signal to start the disorders'.

5. Why offending members could not have been impartially identified and then evicted, in place of a full-scale State of Emergency in an otherwise peaceful Region, the Prime Minister did not explain. Chief Awolowo condemned the motion as 'a violent assault on democratic institutions in Nigeria'.

6. As Sklar (1966: 138) notes, the Commission concluded that Akintola did not know that the National Investment and Properties Company had been formed to finance the Action Group, nor that it had borrowed heavily from the Regional government for that purpose (on one occasion with his alleged approval). The image of Akintola as 'a veritable deputy who all along the line had relied upon his leader' simply does not square with the reality of the shrewd, proud politician who resisted Awolowo's interference in Regional affairs and sought to build an independent base within the party.

7. Writing after several months of Commission testimony, Colin Legum (1962) observed, 'There is little doubt that another election in the West would confirm him as still the strongest party leader there'. Osuntokun (1982: 151) maintains 'the NPC and NCNC knew Awolowo's Action Group would win' an election.

8. Indeed, it appears that the AG and UPP had actually agreed on a merger in mid-1963, but that heavy pressure on Akintola from the NCNC sabotaged the reconciliation (Mackintosh, 1966: 550; Post and Vickers, 1973: 89).

9. Sir Abubakar himself apparently found the charges against Awolowo incredible. In a 1965 interview he recalled: 'I just couldn't believe it. I thought it would make us a laughing-stock and told them to release him. But they assured me it was true. I just couldn't believe Awolowo would be so foolish' (Schwarz, 1968: 138).

10. Miners (1971: 134) argued that a popular uprising was planned by the conspirators rather than a military coup precisely because 'there were very few Yoruba officers ... and only six of these held senior rank' (five of whom were not in command of any troops in Nigeria).

11. Private communication, 22 July, 1980.

12. An observer of the drama reported at the time that neither Dr Azikiwe, then Governor-General, nor Prime Minister Tafawa Balewa 'has shown a particular liking for the job of discrediting Chief Awolowo. But behind them stand the determined political bosses of both the NCNC and the NPC. . . . Many of these leaders have bitter old scores to settle with Chief Awolowo' (Legum, 1962: 23).

5 The Census Crisis: 1963–64

1. Chief Akintola personally headed the intensive effort in the West, stressing that the last census (in which the West reported a 70 per cent increase) still left the Region grossly undercounted. Observed *West Africa* (5 November 1963: 1231) on the eve of the count: 'And more

ominous was the threat . . . by Mr Okafor, Parliamentary Secretary to the Minister of Justice, that all three regions of Southern Nigeria would secede . . . if the census collapses as a result of "intrigue" by Northern Nigerians. This is what is at stake next week.'

2. The move was the final resolution of the pressures that had long been building on the Western NCNC. Since November 1962, it had been wrestling with the dilemma of whether to join with the UPP and enjoy immediate (though thinly based) power, or to join with the AG, the more likely victor in the next election. Younger and more militant NCNCers favoured alliance with the AG and opposed any dealings with the NPC, even indirectly through Akintola's new party. But a UPP–NCNC alliance in the West was a logical sequel to the NPC–NCNC coalition at the Centre, and alliance with the AG in the West could not but further strain the NCNC's already tense relations with its Federal partner. Thus, the mid-1963 reconciliation negotiations between the AG and the UPP were scuttled by vigorous NCNC protest to Akintola, and especially intense opposition from the more nationally oriented leaders of the NCNC, including Dr Okpara and two Yoruba Federal Ministers, Chief T. O. S. Benson (Information) and Chief Olu Akinfosile (Communications). 'It became evident that with the UPP and the AG each trying to present themselves as the only hope for the Yoruba, there was no place for the Western Wing of the NCNC.' Ultimately, the issue came down to 'how the Western electorate could best be handled and whether "Yoruba unity" was best preached with anti-Hausa or anti-Ibo overtones' (Mackintosh, 1966: 549–51).

3. The terrible ugliness of ethnic prejudice was underscored in the Eastern House on 19 March when attention was called to two cartoons published in the *Nigerian Citizen* (a daily newspaper supported financially by the Northern Government) crudely depicting Igbos as cannibals (Mackintosh, 1966: 558).

4. This was not the only source of resentment over the ethnic character of the NCNC. In the minority areas of the Eastern Region, non-Igbos saw both the NCNC and the Regional Government as 'communal institutions to which they had little access' (Wolpe, 1974: 184).

5. Significantly the White Paper was originally produced not by the Western Government but by former Yoruba leaders of the NCNC in the West – including Chiefs Fani-Kayode and R. O. A. Akinjide – and by the two Yoruba federal ministers, who remained loyal to the NCNC – Chiefs Benson and Akinfosile (Dudley, 1966: 294, n. 57).

6. Mackintosh (1966: 554) as well concludes that the inflation of the Northern figures in the 1963 census was 'produced by careful organisation with overlapping areas and systematic double counts arranged so that most of the Eastern inspectors were quite unaware of what was going on'.

6 The 1964 General Strike

1. This brief history of the Nigerian labour movement is drawn from the

outstanding account of Robin Cohen (1974: 70–109, 159–64), except where otherwise noted.

2. Of the eight African nations for which Abernethy presents data, Nigeria was the second most extreme on each of these two measures. In Ghana, for example, the top salary was 29 times the bottom and 40 times the per capita GDP.

    While the 'few and fragmentary' studies have shown the degree of overall income inequality in Nigeria during this period to have been 'moderate' relative to other developing nations (Diejomaoh and Anusionwu, 1981: 97–8), the data have 'serious limitations' and in any case show a concentration of income (38 per cent in one study) in the top 5 per cent of the population that would be considered extreme anywhere.

3. A reporter described the scene in Lagos thus: 'Lagos has had the appearance of a beleaguered city; refuse has been lying in the streets since sanitation workers joined the strike. Hundreds of people were reported to be searching the city for food shops as food has been running short, and rotting because of a breakdown in refrigeration services. Queues of lorries . . ., heavily laden with produce, were said to be stretching for three miles outside the city. . . . Forty-one ships were counted idle in and around Apapa. Water failed on Thursday of last week. . . . On Sunday, there was a total blackout due to a faulty boiler' (*West Africa*, 13 June 1964: 647).

4. Two minority reports addressed this issue in even more emphatic terms, one recommending a cut in the salaries of high officials, both to provide money and to give the workers 'a sense of satisfaction' (*West Africa*, 13 June 1965: 749). Criticising the Labour Ministry severely, the Commission also proposed a series of measures to provide a permanent machinery for continuing review and negotiation of wages. These measures included a network of Joint Industrial Councils for industry-wide collective bargaining, a National Wages Advisory Council, regional Industrial Courts to adjudicate labour disputes, and new legislation to control strikes and lockouts. These proposals were accepted in principle by the Government White Paper (*West Africa*, 20 June 1964: 684).

5. This raises the question of why the Government yielded when labour solidarity was finally breaking – an about-face that particularly troubled the employers, whose ultimatum the Government had privately supported. Wolpe (1974: 281, n. 16) advances three possible motives: the (rumoured) threat of a local police uprising in Lagos, the reported discovery of an anti-government plot by a British lecturer and two Lagos trade unionists, and 'the NCNC's reported withdrawal of support from the government's White Paper'.

6. The evidence comes from a 1963–64 survey of 509 workers drawn randomly from ten industrial firms in Lagos and Ibadan. The survey found that 'attitudes and actual behaviour are more in favour of ethnic heterogeneity than ethnic homogeneity – not only at the working place but to an increasing extent during leisure' (Seibel, 1967: 227). (See also Chapter 7, Analysis).

7   The 1964 Federal Election Crisis

1. The Kano People's Party was the much more significant of the two.
    The KPP had been formed in protest against the Northern Gov-
    ernment's deposition of the Emir of Kano, Muhammad Sanusi, who
    had rivalled the Northern Premier, Ahmadu Bello for power and
    authority. As the Premier was also Sardauna of Sokoto, this was
    widely interpreted by Kano people as an attack on their kingdom by
    Sokoto, 'its ancient suzerain'. The effect of this complex political,
    religious and communal conflict was not only the formation of the KPP
    but an outpouring of Kano nationalism that would congeal in 1965 into
    a broad movement for a separate Kano State (Paden, 1973: 266–72,
    330–1; Post and Vickers, 1973: 102; Feinstein, 1973: 199–202).
2. Shortly before the Sardauna's statement, animosity between the Igbos
    and the Muslim North surfaced again in a brief but fierce exchange
    between the NPC and the NCNC. This began when the Eastern
    Government's *Nigerian Outlook* printed an article declaring that
    'there is something radically wrong with the NPC and some of its
    cattle-rearing legislators.... These ignoramuses must realise that it
    was Allah himself who installed Dr Azikiwe in the State House and
    made him the overlord of all citizens of Nigeria, including Emirs,
    District Heads and all'. As Mackintosh (1966: 562) observed, 'This
    was too much for the *Nigerian Citizen* (the NPC organ) which
    countered that Zik was President by the grace of Sardauna and that
    many others could have done the job. But once installed by agreement
    with the NPC, the "half-naked fellows in the East" should respect the
    President.' Dr Azikiwe then delivered a 'voluminous reply' protesting
    the 'tirade' against him and emphasising the 'persecution' the Igbos
    had 'been obliged to endure in Nigeria'.
3. As the session drew to a close, controversy briefly arose over a
    government-sponsored amendment to the Nigerian Newspaper Act,
    stiffening the guidelines and penalties for reporting of rumours,
    confidential information, defamatory statements, or anything 'likely to
    be prejudicial to the defence of Nigeria, or to the public safety, public
    order, public morality, or public health thereof' (*West Africa*, 19
    September 1964: 1063). The proposed amendment inspired intense
    opposition from the press and from progressive politicians. Newspap-
    ers alleged that the aim was 'to make it impossible for the press to
    expose the activities of certain political parties'. After the amendment
    was modified to remove some of its most objectionable passages and to
    reduce the sentences for offenders, it passed by a vote of 189 to 22, but
    many continued to condemn it as the first step to a totalitarian regime.
    This issue again found the leading NCNC Federal Ministers – Benson,
    Okotie-Eboh, and Mbadiwe – in sharp disagreement with the
    progressive wing of their party (*West Africa*, 3 October 1964: 1119).
4. Because of the enormous revenues at stake, the recent inception of oil
    production in the Niger Delta area was to become enmeshed in the
    gathering sectional conflict. During the 1964 campaign, the MDF cited

the fact that Mid-Western oil pipelines had their outlet in the East as evidence of Eastern domination (Post and Vickers, 1973: 150).

5. For example, 'Don't set fire to the motor vehicle of your political opponents. . . . Don't over-indulge yourself in alcohol . . . or Indian hemp for the purpose of whipping up "Dutch courage" to tackle your thuggery duties efficiently. . . . Don't arm yourself with broken bottles, matchets, sticks and and so on when accompanying your political leaders' (Post and Vickers, 1973: 156).

6. Under the circumstances, even the 30 December date was something of a gamble; it was not until the 17th that the final registers were printed, and then only through round-the-clock crash employment of every available computer in the country.

7. The total number of NNA unopposed candidates rose to 66 shortly thereafter with the announcement of several 'withdrawals' of NPF candidates in the North and two unopposed NNDP candidates in Ife constituencies, where the Action Group was strong and expected to win. Fifteen NCNC candidates had been returned unopposed in the East, but most of these seem truly to have lacked opposition from the scattered coalition of small parties that comprised the NNA in the East (*West Africa*, 2 January 1965: 3).

8. Three of these were in Lagos, one in the Mid-West and 55 in the East, where only the NCNC's 15 unopposed candidates were 'elected'.

9. Nor could the NPC sweep be ascribed to the unopposed returns, since most of these came in areas where the NPC was strongest and where highly political Provincial Commissioners were simply determined to stamp out any opposition whatsoever (Mackintosh, 1966: 584).

10. It is doubtful that UPGA leaders seriously imagined that the NNA, still so clearly in the superior position, might accept such patently unfavourable terms. More likely, they intended them to be the basis for negotiation. The failure of President Azikiwe ever to put these points to Sir Abubakar and to attempt to bargain from them was a major element in the bitter disillusionment that followed his agreement to the Chief Justices' compromise.

11. The controversy surrounding Dr Azikiwe heightened considerably with the release of his 'State House Diary', tracing the secession threat and the election boycott to Dr Okpara, while depicting the President's paramount concerns as the preservation of the Constitution and the unity of the nation (*West Africa*, 16 January 1965: 53–4). The effort to evade responsibility offended many UPGA leaders. UMBC Leader J. S. Tarka denounced its publication as 'in very bad taste. . . . The main attempt to visit the sins of the constitutional crisis on the UPGA has simply misfired. The masses know too well who betrayed them. . . . It is not Okpara, Adegbenro, not Aminu Kano and just not I' (Miners, 1971: 259, n. 18).

12. The Ministry of Mines and Power controlled not only coal-mining and electricity, but the oil production that was finally beginning to produce substantial revenue by 1965, with the prospect of untold export earnings to come (*West Africa*, 27 February 1965: 233).

13. The five samples were small and nonprobabilistic, overrepresenting

educated workers and active trade unionists. But they appeared to have been roughly comparable to one another, and hence permit us to draw inferences about changes in workers' preferences (Melson, 1973: 602–5).

14. A different informant from these deliberations contradicts this account, however, claiming that the Prime Minister had agreed with NPC Ministers and the service chiefs to proceed with the plan to remove Dr Azikiwe from office and that it was the expatriate commander of the Army, General Welby-Everard, 'who persuaded Balewa to allow one final effort to persuade Azikiwe' (Schwarz, 1968: 176).

8 The Western Election Crisis and the Crisis of Confidence, 1965

1. The uniquely detailed account of this crisis by Nwankwo and Ifejika is not disinterested. Samuel Ifejika was one of the students who protested Njoku's dismissal, and he was convicted of assaulting a lecturer during the June disturbances on campus (*West Africa*, 14 August 1965: 915). However, many of their key assertions and interpretations are confirmed by other accounts.

2. The NPC immediately condemned as 'shameless' the carpet-cross, which wiped out its political partnership in the Region in a single stroke. Later in the year, Northern Premier Ahmadu Bello attacked the idea of a one-party system as amounting to dictatorship. Chief Osadebay, in turn, called opponents of such a system 'mere hypocrites,' explaining that 'Nigeria is already headed for a one-party system of Government' because Federal and Regional opposition had 'sunk to insignificant' (*West Africa*, 14 August 1965: 914).

3. Dr Okpara continued to oppose a one-party system because of what he saw as inherently undemocratic features. But in August 1965, he restated his public disenchantment with the Westminster system of institutionalised opposition, calling for parliamentary representation of parties on a proportional basis and a cabinet outside parliament (Post and Vickers, 1973: 219–20).

4. The final agreement, unanimously adopted by Parliament in October, allocated a larger share of recurrent revenue to the regions and compromised on the distribution formula. The East accepted a reduction of its share in the distributable pool (from 32.6 to 30 per cent) in exchange for maintenance of the 50 per cent share of mining rents and royalties for the region of origin, promising a windfall of oil revenue for the East in coming years (*West Africa*, 14 and 21 August, 23 October 1965: 897–8, 929, 1183).

5. The latter development became known in September with the publication of the results, which showed 'that the Igbo were discriminated against and that most Yoruba who applied got federal scholarships'. This coup by the Federal Minister of Education, Chief Akinjide, was 'immensely popular in the West and was equally hated in the East' (Osuntokun 1982: 185–6). The grandest promises of

future rewards were made by Federal Minister of Industry A. M. A. Akinloye, who pledged a £5 million investment in Ibadan Division and a £10 million iron and steel industry for Ondo Division 'very soon' (Post and Vickers, 1973: 221).

6. Five of these were in Ife division, the home base of Deputy Premier Fani-Kayode. As Minister of Local Government, he had dissolved all the Region's local government councils and replaced them with NNDP management committees, which played a key role in the fraudulent administration of the election. Osuntokun (1982: 191–2) traces the character of the election significantly to the role of Chief Fani-Kayode, who 'blatantly told the electorate that if they did not vote for the NNDP "Angels" would vote for the party, implying that the NNDP would win one way or the other'.

7. See Anifowose (1982: 220–1) for specific instances of such brazen fraud. Many charges of rigging were confirmed by FEC Chairman E. E. Esua in a bitter letter to the Governor of the Western Region on 15 November, which he later released to the press. Esua protested not only the abuses in the nomination process (reiterating his earlier statements) but also that ballot papers were widely found in the hands of unauthorised persons on election day, that 'some persons in Local Government Police uniform had proved themselves to be nothing but thugs in their operation', and that the refusal of returning officers to declare the election results locally after the count clearly violated electoral regulations and 'gives good cause for misgiving about the authenticity of the results' (*West Africa*, 27 November 1965: 1327, 1354; Schwarz, 1968: 185.–6).

Nwankwo and Ifejika (1969: 91) report other allegations of fraud:

> On the election day over 500 000 ballot papers were recovered from both the NNDP leaders and the NNDP electoral officers when they tried to dump them into the ballot boxes. Some 'pregnant' NNDP women were caught with ballot papers bulbously wrapped over their stomachs, while NNDP men were arrested with bundles of ballot papers conveniently hidden in the spacious depths of their *agbadas*, the Yoruba native dress. Ballot boxes already filled with ballot papers were recovered before polling began. The police also recovered lists of election results which the NNDP had prepared long before polling day.

8. Adegbenro and his fellow UPGA leaders were denied bail until the declaration of an interim government was retracted. He was discharged after he told a press conference at the police station that his earlier declaration did not mean that he had actually attempted to form a government and that his party would pursue its aims by constitutional means (*West Africa*, 23 October 1965: 1194).

9. After the coup, a reporter reflected upon an interview with the Premier in December: 'It was clear to me that he would never voluntarily relinquish power, however much violence there was in the region; nor would he consider a coalition with his opponents, which was the only hope of peace' (*West Africa*, 22 January 1966: 93).

10. According to the back cover of his book, 'David Muffett served as an administrative officer in Nigeria from 1947 to 1963', and 'had a particularly close working relationship and friendship with the late... Sardauna..., whom he greatly admired'. His account is therefore probably better informed of the Sardauna's real sentiments and intentions than virtually any other, but also more inclined to present the late Sardauna in the most generous possible light. Some elements of his account are implausible at least. For example, Muffett maintains that Akintola flew up to Kaduna on the 14th unscheduled and unannounced, and that the Sardauna only promised to convey his plea for open Army backing to the Prime Minister. This is difficult to reconcile with the presence at their meeting of Brigadier Ademulegun, commander of the 1st Brigade, and Lt. Col. Largema, commander of the 4th Battalion in Ibadan (Miners, 1971: 160).

9 Conclusion: Why the First Republic Failed

1. Portions of this chapter are adapted from Diamond (1983a).
2. The former was urged by Nobel Prize-winning economist W. Arthur Lewis in his review of the Nigerian economy for the OECD in 1967.

> Given the private enterprise system, the only way to industrialize Nigeria adequately is to produce a large class of Nigerian entrepreneurs with industrial experience. Small enterprise is the university where this class receives its training. Thus ... it is more important to lay the foundations of an industrial class by helping small entrepreneurs than it is to build a few large factories – all the more so when 70 per cent of value added by large factories accrues to foreigners. (Quoted in Cohen, 1974: 45).

3. For an analysis of how the Code of Conduct Bureau and Tribunal failed to function in the Second Republic and needs to be restructured in the future, see Diamond (1984a: 912–19).

Bibliography

I. Theoretical sources

AKE, CLAUDE (1973) 'Explaining Political Instability in New States', *Journal of Modern African Studies*, 11 (3): 347–59.
— (1976) 'Explanatory Notes on the Political Economy of Africa,' *Journal of Modern African Studies* 14 (1): 1–23.
— (1981) Presidential Address to the 1981 Conference of the Nigerian Political Science Association, in *West Africa*, 25 May 1981: 1162–3.
ALMOND, GABRIEL A., and POWELL, G. BINGHAM, Jr. (1966) *Comparative Politics: A Developmental Approach* (Boston: Little, Brown & Company).
— (1978) *Comparative Politics: System, Process and Policy* (Boston: Little, Brown and Company).
ALMOND, GABRIEL A., and VERBA, SIDNEY (1963) *The Civic Culture* (Boston: Little, Brown & Company).
BARTH, Frederick (1969) *Ethnic Groups and Boundaries* (London: George Allen and Unwin).
BATES, ROBERT M. (1974) 'Ethnic Competition and Modernization in Contemporary Africa', *Comparative Political Studies* 6(4): 457–84.
BINDER, LEONARD (1971) 'Crises of Political Development', in Leonard Binder, James S. Coleman, Joseph La Palombara, Lucian W. Pye, Sidney Verba, and Myron Weiner, *Crises and Sequences in Political Development* (Princeton: Princeton University Press).
BOLLEN, KENNETH (1979) 'Political Democracy and the Timing of Development', *American Sociological Review* 44 (4): 572–87.
— (1983) 'World System Position, Dependency and Democracy: The Cross-National Evidence', *American Sociological Review* 48(4): 468–79.
COHEN, ABNER (1969) *Custom and Politics in Urban Africa* (Berkeley: University of California Press).
COLLIER, DAVID (1979) 'Overview of the Bureaucratic-Authoritarian Model', in David Collier, ed., *The New Authoritarianism in Latin America*: 19–32 (Princeton: Princeton University Press).
CUTRIGHT, PHILLIPS (1963) 'National Political Development: Measurement and Analysis', *American Sociological Review* 28(2): 253–64.
DAHL, ROBERT A. (1971) *Polyarchy: Participation and Opposition* (New Haven, CT: Yale University Press).
DIAMOND, LARRY (1980) 'The Social Foundations of Democracy: The Case of Nigeria'. Unpublished Ph.D. thesis, Stanford University.
DOMHOFF, G. WILLIAM (1983) *Who Rules America Now?* (Englewood Cliffs, NJ: Prentice-Hall).
EMERSON, RUPERT (1971) 'The Prospects for Democracy', in Michael F. Lofchie, ed., *The State of the Nations* (Berkeley: University of California).
GEORGE, ALEXANDER (1979a) 'Case Studies and Theory Develop-

ment: The Method of Structured, Focused Comparison', in Paul Gordon Lauren, ed., *Diplomatic History: New Approaches* (New York: Free Press).

— (1979b) 'The Causal Nexus Between Cognitive Beliefs and Decision-Making Behavior: The 'Operational Code' Belief System', in Lawrence Falkowski, ed., *Psychological Models and International Politics* (Boulder, CO: Westview Press).

HANNAN, MICHAEL T. (1979) 'The Dynamics of Ethnic Boundaries', in John W. Meyer and Michael T. Hannan, ed., *National Development and the World System: Educational, Economic and Political Change, 1950–70* (Chicago: University of Chicago Press).

HANNAN, MICHAEL T., and CARROL, GLENN P. (1981) 'Dynamics of Formal Political Structure: An Event-History Analysis', *American Sociological Review* 46(1): 19–35.

HOROWITZ, DONALD L. (1971) 'Three Dimensions of Ethnic Politics', *World Politics* 23(2).

— (1975) "Ethnic Identity," in Nathan M. Glazer and Daniel F. Moynihan (eds.), *Ethnicity: Theory and Experience* (Cambridge, MA: Harvard University Press).

HUNTINGTON, SAMUEL P. (1968) *Political Order in Changing Societies* (New Haven, CT: Yale University Press).

— (1984) 'Will More Countries Become Democratic?' *Political Science Quarterly* 99(2): 193–218.

HUNTINGTON, SAMUEL P. and NELSON, JOAN M. (1976) *No Easy Choice: Political Participation in Developing Countries.* (Cambridge, MA: Harvard University Press).

INKELES, ALEX (1969) 'Participant Citizenship in Six Developing Countries', *American Political Science Review* 63: 1120–41.

INKELES, ALEX, and DIAMOND, LARRY (1980) 'Personal Qualities as a Reflection of Level of National Development', in Frank Andrews and Alexander Szale (eds), *Comparative Studies on the Quality of Life* (London: SAGE).

JACKSON, ROBERT H. and ROSBERG, CARL G. (1982) *Personal Rule in Black Africa: Prince, Autocrat, Prophet, Tyrant* (Berkeley: University of California Press).

KORNHAUSER, WILLIAM (1959) *The Politics of Mass Society* (Glencoe, IL: The Free Press).

LIJPHART, AREND (1968) 'Typologies of Democratic Systems', *Comparative Political Studies* 1(1): 3–44.

— (1969) 'Consociational Democracy', *World Politics* 21(2): 207–25.

— (1977) *Democracy in Plural Societies: A Comparative Exploration* (New Haven, CT: Yale University Press).

LINDBLOM, CHARLES (1977) *Politics and Markets: The World's Political-Economic Systems* (New York: Basic Books).

LINZ, JUAN (1978) *The Breakdown of Democratic Regimes: Crisis, Breakdown and Reequilibration* (Baltimore, MD: Johns Hopkins University Press).

LIPSET, SEYMOUR MARTIN (1960) *Political Man* (Garden City, N.Y.: Doubleday & Company, republished in expanded form by Johns Hopkins University Press, 1981).

- 1963 *The First New Nation* (Garden City, N.Y: Doubleday and Company).
LIPSET, SEYMOUR MARTIN and ROKKAN, STEIN (1967) *Party Systems and Voter Alignments* (New York: Free Press).
MAFEJE, ARCHIE (1971) 'The Ideology of "Tribalism" ', *Journal of Modern African Studies* 9(2): 253–61.
McCRONE, DONALD J., and CNUDDE, CHARLES F. (1967) 'Toward a Communications Theory of Democratic Political Development: A Causal Model', *American Political Science Review* 61(1): 72–9.
MELSON, ROBERT AND WOLPE, HOWARD (1971) 'Modernization and the Politics of Communalism: A Theoretical Perspective', in Robert Melson and Howard Wolpe (eds), *Nigeria: Modernization and the Politics of Communalism* (East Lansing: Michigan State University).
MILIBAND, RALPH (1969) *The State in Capitalist Society* (New York: Basic Books).
MOORE, BARRINGTON, JR., (1966) *The Social Origins of Dictatorship and Democracy* (Boston: Beacon Press).
MOSCA, GAETANO (1939) *The Ruling Class: Elementi Di Scienza Politica.* (New York: McGraw Hill).
NAGEL, JOANE and OLZAK, SUSAN (1981) 'Ethnic Mobilization in New and Old States: An Extension of the Competition Model', Paper presented to the annual meeting of the American Sociological Association.
NNOLI, OKWUDIBA (1978) *Ethnic Politics in Nigeria* (Enugu: Fourth Dimension Publishing Company).
NORDLINGER, ERIC (1972) *Conflict Regulation in Divided Societies.* Occasional Papers in International Affairs, No. 29 (Cambridge, MA: Harvard University Center for International Affairs).
O'DONNELL, GUILLERMO (1973) *Modernization and Bureaucratic-Authoritarianism: Studies in South American Politics.* Institute of International Studies, University of California (Politics of Modernization Series, No. 9).
OLSEN, MARVIN E. (1968) 'Multivariate Analysis of National Political Development', *American Sociological Review* 33(5): 699–712.
OLZAK, SUSAN (1978) 'An Ecological-Competitive Model of the Emergence of Ethnicity: The French-Canadian Example'. Unpublished thesis, Stanford University.
POPKIN, SAMUEL (1979) *The Rational Peasant* (Berkeley: University of California Press).
POWELL, C. BINGHAM, JR. (1982) *Contemporary Democracies: Participation, Stability and Violence* (Cambridge MA: Harvard University Press).
RABUSHKA, ALVIN and SHEPSLE, KENNETH (1972) *Politics in Plural Societies: A Theory of Democratic Instability* (Columbus, Ohio: Charles E. Merrill).
SCHUMPETER, JOSEPH A. (1942) *Capitalism, Socialism and Democracy*, 3rd ed. (New York: Harper & Row).
SKLAR, RICHARD L. (1967) 'Political Science and National Integration – A Radical Approach', *Journal of Modern African Studies* 5(1): 1–11.
- (1979) 'The Nature of Class Domination in Africa', *Journal of Modern African Studies* 17(4): 531–52.

- (1982) 'Democracy in Africa' Presidential Address to the 25th Annual Meeting of the African Studies Association, Washington, D.C. (Published in 1983 in the *African Studies Review* 26 (3/4): 11–24).
SKOCPOL, THEDA (1979) *States and Social Revolutions* (Cambridge: Cambridge University Press).
- (1982) 'Bringing the State Back In: False Leads and Promising Starts in Current Theories and Research', Working Paper for the SSRC Conference on 'States and Social Structure', Mount Kisco, New York, February 25–27.
- (1984) 'Emerging Agendas and Recurrent Strategies in Historical Sociology', in Theda Skocpol, (ed.), *Vision and Method in Historical Sociology* (Cambridge: Cambridge University Press).
STEPAN, ALFRED (1978) 'Political Leadership and Regime Breakdown: Brazil', in Juan J. Linz and Alfred Stepan, (eds), *The Breakdown of Democratic Regimes: Latin America* (Baltimore: The Johns Hopkins University Press).
TILLY, CHARLES (1978) *From Mobilization to Revolution* (Reading, MA: Addison-Wesley).
VERBA, SIDNEY (1965) 'Conclusion: Comparative Political Culture', in Lucian W. Pye and Sidney Verba (eds), *Political Culture and Political Development* (Princeton: Princeton University Press).
- (1971) 'Sequences and Development', in Binder *et al.*, *Crises and Sequences in Political Development* (op. cit.).
WALLERSTEIN, IMMANUEL (1964) 'Voluntary Associations', in James S. Coleman and Carl G. Rosberg, Jr, *Political Parties and National Integration in Tropical Africa* (Berkeley: University of California Press).
YOUNG, CRAWFORD (1976) *The Politics of Cultural Pluralism* (Madison: University of Wisconsin Press).

II. The Nigerian Case

ABERNETHY, DAVID B. (1964) 'Nigeria Creates a New Region', *Africa Report* (March).
- (1969) *The Political Dilemma of Popular Education* (Stanford, CA: Stanford University Press).
- (1982) 'Bureaucratic Growth and Economic Decline in Sub-Saharan Africa'. Paper presented to the 26th Annual Meeting of the African Studies Association, Boston, Massachusetts, December.
ACHEBE, CHINUA (1960) *No Longer at Ease* (Greenwich, CT: Fawcett Books).
- (1966) *A Man of the People* (Garden City, NY: Anchor Books).
ACTION GROUP (1954) 'NCNC: Their Black Record'.
- (1960) 'Democratic Socialism, Being the Manifesto of the Action Group in Nigeria for an Independent Nigeria', Lagos.
ADEDEJI, A. (1969) *Nigerian Federal Finance* (London: Hutchinson).
ADEMOYEGA, ADEWALE (1981) *Why We Struck: The Story of the First Nigerian Coup* (Ibadan: Evans Brothers).
AFRICA REPORT, Various Issues, 1962–66.
AGUNBIADE-BAMISHE, O. (1953) 'The Case for the Action Group – Party of the Masses' (Ibadan: African Press Limited).

AHMADU BELLO, THE SARDAUNA OF SOKOTO (1962) *My Life* (Cambridge: Cambridge University Press).

AKE, CLAUDE (1981) Presidential Address to the 1981 Conference of the Nigerian Political Science Association, in *West Africa*, 25 May: 1162–3.

– (1981b) *A Political Economy of Africa* (Harlow: Longman).

AKEREDOLU-ALE, E. O. (1976) 'Private Foreign Investment and the Underdevelopment of Indigenous Entrepreneurship in Nigeria', in Gavin Williams (ed.), *Nigeria: Economy and Society* (London: Rex Collings).

AKINTUNDE, J. O. (1967) 'The Demise of Democracy in the First Republic of Nigeria: A Causal Analysis', *ODU* (Journal of African Studies of the University of Ife) 4(1): 3–38.

ALLEN, V. L. (1966) 'Nigeria: Coup on a Tightrope', *The Nation*, February 7: 143–5.

ALUKO, S. A. (1965) 'How Many Nigerians? An Analysis of Nigeria's Census Problems, 1901–63', *Journal of Modern African Studies* 3(3).

ANBER, PAUL (1967) 'Modernization and Political Disintegration: Nigeria and the Ibos', *Journal of Modern African Studies* 5(2): 1963–79.

ANIFOWOSE, REMI (1982) *Violence and Politics in Nigeria: The Tiv and Yoruba Experience* (Enugu and New York: NOK Publishers).

ARIKPO, OKOI (1967) *The Development of Modern Nigeria* (Baltimore, MD: Penguin Books).

AWOLOWO, OBAFEMI (1947) *Path to Nigerian Freedom* (London: Faber and Faber).

– (1959) 'Action Group 14-Point Programme', (Ibadan: Action Group).

– (1960a) *Awo: The Autobiography of Obafemi Awolowo* (Cambridge: Cambridge University Press).

– (1960b) 'Presidential Address to the Seventh Congress of the Action Group', September 19, 1960.

– (1961) 'Call to Rededication and Reconstruction', Statement to the meeting of Federal Executive Council of the Action Group, 18 December 1961.

– (1968) *The People's Republic* (London: Oxford University Press).

AZIKIWE, NNAMDI (1959) 'Address of the National President of the NCNC, Dr the Honourable Nnamdi Azikiwe, delivered at the NCNC 1959 Convention held in Kano' (Lagos: NCNC).

– (1960) 'Respect for Human Dignity', Inaugural Address by His Excellency Dr Nnamdi Azikiwe, Governor-General and Commander-in-Chief, Federation of Nigeria, 16 November 1960.

– (1961) *Zik: A Selection from the Speeches of Nnamdi Azikiwe* (Cambridge: Cambridge University Press).

– (1965) 'Essentials for Nigerian Survival', *Foreign Affairs* 43(3).

BAKER, PAULINE (1974) *Urbanization and Political Change: The Politics of Lagos, 1917–67* (Berkeley: University of California Press).

BALEWA, SIR ABUBAKAR TAFAWA (1961) 'Foreword', in Chief H.O. Davies, *Nigeria: Prospects for Democracy* (London: Weidenfeld & Nicolson).

– (1964) *Nigeria Speaks* (Ikeja: Longmans of Nigeria).

BATES, ROBERT H. (1981) *Markets and States in Tropical Africa* (Berkeley: University of California Press).

BOHANNAN, PAUL (1965) 'The Tiv of Nigeria', in James L. Gibbs, Jr, (ed.), *Peoples of Africa* (New York: Holt, Rinehart & Winston).

BRETTON, HENRY L. (1962) *Power and Stability in Nigeria* (New York: Frederick A. Praeger).

BROWN-PETERSIDE, GALLY (1966) 'Why Balewa Died', *Africa Report* 11(3): 15–17.

CALLAWAY, ARCHIBALD (1962) 'School Leavers and the Developing Economy of Nigeria', in Robert O. Tilman and Taylor Cole (eds) *The Nigerian Political Scene* (Durham, NC: Duke University Press).

CANTRIL, HADLEY (1965) *The Pattern of Human Concerns* (New Brunswick, N.J.: Rutgers University Press).

COHEN, ROBIN (1974) *Labour and Politics in Nigeria 1945–71* (London: Heinemann).

COHEN, RONALD (1966) 'Power, Authority and Personal Success in Islam and Bornu', in Marc J. Swartz *et al.* (eds), *Political Anthropology* (Chicago, IL: Aldine).

COKER, G. B. A.; KASSIM, J. O.; and WILLIAMS, AKINTOLA (1962) *Report of the Coker Commission of Inquiry into the Affairs of Certain Statutory Corporations in Western Nigeria.*

COLE, TAYLOR (1962) 'Emergent Federalism in Nigeria', 'The Independence Constitution of Federal Nigeria', and 'Bureaucracy in Transition', in Robert O. Tilman and Taylor Cole (eds), *The Nigerian Political Scene* (Durham, NC: Duke University Press).

COLEMAN, JAMES S. (1958) *Nigeria: Background to Nationalism* (Berkeley: University of California Press).

COMMISSION APPOINTED TO ENQUIRE INTO THE FEARS OF MINORITIES AND THE MEANS OF ALLAYING THEM (1958) *Report* (London: Her Majesty's Stationery Office).

CONSTITUTION OF THE FEDERATION OF NIGERIA (1963) In Oluwole Idowu Odumosu, *The Nigerian Constitution: History and Development* (London: Sweet & Maxwell).

DAVIES, H. O. (1961) *Nigeria: The Prospects for Democracy* (London: Weidenfeld & Nicolson).

DENT, J. M. (1966) 'A Minority Party – the United Middle Belt Congress', in John P. Mackintosh, (ed.) *Nigerian Government and Politics* (Evanston, IL: Northwestern University Press).

– (1971) 'The Military and Politics: A Study of the Relation Between the Army and the Political Process in Nigeria', in Robert Melson and Howard Wolpe (eds) *Nigeria: Modernization and the Politics of Communalism*: 267–99 (East Lansing: Michigan State University Press).

DIAMOND, LARRY (1980) 'The Social Foundations of Democracy: The Case of Nigeria', Unpublished Ph.D. Dissertation, Stanford University.

– (1982) 'Cleavage, Conflict and Anxiety in the Second Nigerian Republic', *Journal of Modern African Studies* 20(4): 629–68.

– (1983a) 'Class, Ethnicity and the Democratic State: Nigeria, 1950–66', *Comparative Studies in Society and History* 25(3): 457–89.

– (1983b) 'Social Change and Political Conflict in Nigeria's Second Republic', in I. William Zartman (ed.), *The Political Economy of Nigeria*: 25–84. (New York: Praeger).

– (1984a) 'Nigeria in Search of Democracy', *Foreign Affairs* 62(4): 905–27.

– (1984b) 'The Political Economy of Corruption in Nigeria', Paper

presented to the 27th Annual Meeting of the African Studies Association. Los Angeles, October 25–28.
− (1985) 'Nigeria Update', *Foreign Affairs* 64(2): 326–36.
DIAMOND, STANLEY (1962) 'Collapse in the West', *Africa Today* (September).
− (1963) 'The Trial of Awolowo', *Africa Today* (November).
− (1964) 'Notes for the Record', *Africa Today* (May).
− (1966) 'The End of the First Republic', *Africa Today* (February): 5–9.
DIEJOMAOH, V. P. and ANUSIONWU, E. C. (1981) 'The Structure of Income Inequality in Nigeria: A Macro Analysis', in Henry Bienen and V.P. Diejomaoh, (eds), *Inequality and Development in Nigeria:* 77–114 (New York and London: Holmes and Meier).
DILLON, WILTON (1966) 'Nigeria's Two Revolutions', *Africa Report*, 11(3): 9–14.
DOOB, LEONARD W. (1966) *Communications in Africa: A Search for Boundaries* (New Haven, CT: Yale University Press).
DUDLEY, B. J. (1966) 'Federalism and the Balance of Political Power in Nigeria', *Journal of Commonwealth Studies*, 4: 16–29.
− (1968) *Parties and Politics in Northern Nigeria* (London: Frank Cass & Company).
− (1973) *Instability and Political Order* (Ibadan: Ibadan University Press).
EKEH, PETER P. (1975) 'Colonialism and the Two Publics in Africa: A Theoretical Statement', *Comparative Studies in Society and History* 17(1): 91–112.
ELEAZU, UMA O. (1977) *Federalism and Nation-Building: The Nigerian Experience, 1954–64* (Elms Court, Great Britain: Arthur H. Stockwell Ltd).
EMERSON, RUPERT (1960) *From Empire to Nation* (Boston MA: Beacon Press).
FEINSTEIN, ALAN (1973) *African Revolutionary: The Life and Times of Nigeria's Aminu Kano* (New York: Quadrangle/The New York Times Book Company).
FIRST, RUTH (1970) *The Barrel of a Gun: Political Power in Africa and the Coup d'Etat* (Harmondsworth: Penguin).
FLOYER, R. K.; IBEKWE, D. O. and NJEMANZE, J. C. (1955) *Report of the Commission of Inquiry into the Working of the Port Harcourt Town Council* (Enugu: Eastern Region Government Printer).
FOSTER-SUTTON, SIR STAFFORD WILLIAM POWELL (1957) *Report of the Tribunal appointed to inquire into allegations reflecting on the Official Conduct of the Premier of, and certain persons holding Ministerial and other Public Offices in, the Eastern Region of Nigeria* (London: Her Majesty's Stationery Office).
FREE, LLOYD A. (1964) *The Attitudes, Hopes and Fears of Nigerians* (Princeton: Institute for International Social Research).
FRIEDLAND, WILLIAM H. (1965) 'Paradoxes of African Trade Union-ism: Organizational Chaos and Political Potential', *Africa Report* (June).
GRANT, P. F. (1955) *Report of the Inquiry into the Allocation of Market Stalls at Aba* (Enugu: Eastern Region Government Printer).
GREEN, REGINALD H. (1965) 'Economic Policy of the Political Class', *Nigerian Opinion* (December).

GUNNING, O. P. (1955) *Report of the Inquiry into the Administration of the Affairs of the Onitsha Urban District Council* (Enugu: Eastern Region Government Printer).

HARRIS, RICHARD (1965) 'Nigeria: Crisis and Compromise', *Africa Report* 10(3).

HATCH, JOHN (1970) *Nigeria: The Seeds of Disaster* (Chicago, IL: Henry Regnery).

HELLEINER, GERALD K. (1964) 'The Eastern Nigeria Development Corporation: A Study in Resources and Uses of Public Development Funds, 1949–62', *Nigerian Journal of Economic and Social Studies* 6 (1): 98–123.

– (1966) *Peasant Agriculture, Government and Economic Growth in Nigeria* (Homewood, IL: Richard D. Irwin, Inc).

HERRING, PENDLETON (1962) 'The Future for Democracy in Nigeria', in Robert O. Tilman and Taylor Cole (eds), *The Nigerian Political Scene* (Durham, NC: Duke University Press).

HERSKOVITS, JEAN (1979) 'Democracy in Nigeria', *Foreign Affairs* 58(2): 314–335.

HIMMELSTRAND, ULF (1973) 'Tribalism, Regionalism, Nationalism and Secession in Nigeria', in S.N. Eisenstadt and Stein Rokkan (eds), *Building States and Nations*, Vol. II: 427–67 (Beverley Hills, CA: SAGE).

IBRAHIM, OMAR FAROUK (1983) 'The Impact of the PRP Government on Traditional Institutions in Kano State', M.Sc. Dissertation, Bayero University, Kano.

IDEM, OKON (1962) 'What Next in Western Nigeria?', *Africa Report*, 7(7).

– (1965) 'Tribalism and Politics . . . The University of Lagos', *Africa Report*, 10(10).

KILSON, MARTIN (1966) 'Behind Nigeria's Revolt', *The New Leader* (January 31): 9–12.

KINGSLEY, J. DONALD (1963) 'Bureaucracy and Political Development, with Particular Reference to Nigeria', in *Bureaucracy and Political Development* (Princeton: Princeton University Press).

KIRK-GREENE, A. H. M. (1967) 'The Peoples of Nigeria: Cultural Background to the Crisis', *African Affairs* 66(1): 3–12.

– (1971) *Crisis and Conflict in Nigeria, Vol. 1*. (London: Oxford University Press).

KWITNY, JONATHAN (1967) 'Nigeria in Focus', *The New Leader* (January 16): 14–18.

LEGUM, COLIN (1962) 'Deceptive Calm in Nigeria', *Africa Report*, 7(10).

– (1966) 'Can Nigeria Escape Its Past?' *Africa Report*, 11(3): 19.

LEVINE, ROBERT A. (with the assistance of Eugene Strangman and Leonard Unterberger) (1966) *Dreams and Deeds: Achievement Motivation in Nigeria* (Chicago, IL: University of Chicago Press).

LEWIS, L. J. (1965) *Society, Schools and Progress in Nigeria* (London: Pergamon Press).

LEYS, COLIN (1965) 'What is the Problem about Corruption?' *Journal of Modern African Studies* 3(2): 215–30.

LLOYD, P. C. (1960) 'Sacred Kingship and Government among the Yoruba', *Africa* 30(3).

– (1970) 'The Ethnic Background to the Nigerian Crisis', in S.K. Panter-Brick (ed.), *Nigerian Politics and Military Rule: Prelude to Civil War* (London: Athlone Press).

– (1974) *Power and Independence: Urban Africans' Perception of Social Inequality* (London: Routledge & Kegan Paul).

LOW, VICTOR N. (1972) *Three Nigerian Emirates: A Study in Oral History* (Evanston, IL.: Northwestern University Press).

LUBECK, PAUL (1979) 'Islam and Resistance in Northern Nigeria', in Walter L. Goldfrank, (ed.), *The World-System of Capitalism: Past and Present*: 189–205 (Beverley Hills: SAGE).

LUCKHAM, ROBIN (1971) *The Nigerian Military: A Sociological Analysis of Authority and Revolt, 1960–67* (Cambridge: Cambridge University Press).

MACKINTOSH, JOHN P. (1962) 'Federalism in Nigeria', *Political Studies* 10(3).

– (1966) *Nigerian Government and Politics* (Evanston, IL: Northwestern University Press).

MAFEJE, ARCHIE (1971) 'The Ideology of "Tribalism"'. *Journal of Modern African Studies* 9(2): 253–61.

MARKOVITZ, IRVING LEONARD (1977) *Power and Class in Africa* (Englewood Cliffs NJ: Prentice-Hall).

MAZRUI, ALI (1983) 'Francophone Nations and English-Speaking States: Imperial Ethnicity and African Political Formations', in Donald Rothchild and Victor Olorunsola, (eds), *State vs. Ethnic Claims: African Policy Dilemmas*: 25–43 (Boulder: Westview Press).

McEWEN, F. S. (1960) 'NCNC on the March', National Secretary's Report to the 1960 Annual Convention in Lagos, September 10–11, 1960 (Lagos: NCNC Bureau of Information).

MELSON, ROBERT (1970) 'Nigerian Politics and the General Strike of 1964', in Robert I. Rotberg and Ali A. Mazrui, (eds), *Protest and Power in Black Africa* (New York: Oxford University Press).

– (1971) 'Ideology and Inconsistency: The 'Cross-pressured' Nigerian Worker', in Robert Melson and Howard Wolpe, (eds), *Nigeria: Modernization and the Politics of Communalism*: 581–605 (East Lansing: Michigan State University Press).

– (1973) 'Political Dilemmas of Nigerian Labor', in Ukandi C. Damachi and Hans Dieter Seibel, *Social Change and Economic Development in Nigeria* (New York: Praeger).

MELSON, ROBERT and WOLPE, HOWARD (1971) 'Modernization and the Politics of Communalism', in Robert Melson and Howard Wolpe (eds) *Nigeria: Modernization and the Politics of Communalism*: 1–42 (East Lansing: Michigan State University Press).

MINERS, N. J. (1971) *The Nigerian Army 1956–66* (London: Methuen & Company).

MUFFETT, D. J. M. (1982) *Let Truth Be Told: The Coups D'Etat of 1966* (Zaria: Hudahuda Publishing Co.)

NICHOLSON, E. W. J. (1955) *Report of the Commission of Inquiry into the Administration of the Ibadan District Council* (Ibadan: Western Region Government Printer).

NICOLSON, I. (1966) 'The Machinery of the Federal and Regional Government', in John P. Mackintosh, *Nigerian Government and Politics*

(Evanston, IL: Northwestern University Press).

NIGERIAN OPINION (1965) Vol. 1 (1–12).

– (1966) Vol. 2 (1–3).

NIGERIAN YOUTH CONGRESS (1962) 'The Crisis and the People: (Being a Commentary on the Action Group Crisis of May 1962)'. (Information and Publicity Bureau, Nigerian Youth Congress).

NJAKA, MAZI ELECHUKWA N. (1974) *Igbo Political Culture* (Evanston, IL: Northwestern University Press).

NNOLI, OKWUDIBA (1978) *Ethnic Politics in Nigeria* (Enugu: Fourth Dimension Publishing Company).

NWANKWO, ARTHUR A., AND IFEJIKA, SAMUEL U. (1969) *The Making of a Nation: Biafra* (London: C. Hurst & Company).

O'CONNELL, JAMES (1962a) 'Some Social and Political Reflections on the Plan', *Nigerian Journal of Economic and Social Studies* 4(2).

– (1962b) 'Northern Regional Elections, 1961: An Analysis', *Nigerian Journal of Economic and Social Studies* 4(3).

– (1965) 'Political Parties in Nigeria', in L. Franklin Blitz (ed.) *The Politics and Administration of Nigerian Government* (New York: Frederick A. Praeger).

– (1966) 'The Political Class and Economic Growth', *Nigerian Journal of Economic and Social Studies* 8(1): 129–40.

– (1967) 'Political Integration: The Nigerian Case', in Arthur Hazelwood (ed.) *African Integration and Disintegration: Case Studies in Economic and Political Union*: 129–84 (London and New York: Oxford University Press).

– (1970) 'The Fragility of Stability: The Fall of the Nigerian Federal Government, 1966', in Robert I. Rotberg and Ali A. Mazrui, (eds), *Protest and Power in Black Africa*: 1012–34 (London and New York: Oxford University Press).

ODUMOSU, OLUWOLE IDOWU (1963) *The Nigerian Constitution: History and Development* (London: Sweet & Maxwell).

OFFODILE, CHRIS (1980) *Dr M. I. Okpara: A Biography* (Enugu Nigeria: Fourth Dimension Publishers).

OGBEIDE, UYI-EKPEN (1985) 'The Expansion of the State and Ethnic Mobilization: The Nigerian Experience', Unpublished Ph.D. Dissertation, Vanderbilt University.

OGUNADE, ERNEST ADELUMOLA (1981) 'Freedom of the Press: Government-Press Relationships in Nigeria, 1900–1966', Unpublished Ph.D. Dissertation, Southern Illinois University.

OGUNSHEYE, AYO (1965) 'Nigeria', in James S. Coleman (ed.), *Education and Political Development* (Princeton: Princeton University Press).

OHONBAMU, O. (1966) 'The Rise and Fall of Nigerian Federalism', *African Quarterly* 5(4).

OKIGBO, P.N.C. (1965) *Nigerian Public Finance* (Evanston, IL: Northwestern University Press).

OKOYE, MOKWUGO (1961) 'Nigeria in Crisis', *Africa South* 6 (October-December).

OKPARA, MICHAEL I. (1960) 'Before the Dawn', Address to the NCNC Annual Convention at Lagos, September 10–11, 1960 (Lagos, NCNC Bureau of Information).

- (1962) 'The Responsibilities of Independence', Address to the NCNC Annual Convention at Port Harcourt, January 15, 1962.
- (1964) 'A Crusade for Total Freedom', Speech by Dr the Honourable M. I. Okpara on the Launching of the UPGA Campaign at Yaba, Lagos, 10 October.
OLISA, M. S. O. (1971) 'Political Culture and Stability in Igbo Society', in M. J. C. Echeruo and E. N. Obiechina, (eds), *Igbo Traditional Life, Culture, and Literature* (Owerri: Conch Magazine, Ltd).
OLORUNSOLA, VICTOR A. (1967) 'Nigerian Cultural Nationalisms', *African Forum* 3(1): 78–9.
- (1972 'Nigeria', in Victor A. Olorunsola (ed.), *The Politics of Cultural Sub-Nationalism in Nigeria* (Garden City, NY: Anchor Books).
OSOBA, SEGUN (1977) 'The Nigerian Power Elite, 1952–65', in Peter C. W. Gutkind and Peter Waterman (eds), *African Social Studies* (New York: Monthly Review Press).
OSTHEIMER, JOHN, M. (1973) *Nigerian Politics* (New York: Harper & Row).
OSUNTOKUN, AKINJIDE (1982) *Chief S. L. A. Akintola: His Life and Times* (Ibadan and London: Evans Brothers Publishers Ltd.) (Page references are to original manuscript).
OTTENBERG, SIMON (1959) 'Ibo Receptivity to Change', in William R. Bascom and Melville J. Herskovits (eds.), *Continuity and Change in African Cultures* (Chicago: University of Chicago Press).
OYINBO, JOHN (1971) *Nigeria: Crisis and Beyond* (London: Charles Knight & Company, Ltd).
PADEN, JOHN (1971) 'Communal Competition, Conflict and Violence in Kano', in Melson and Wolpe (eds) *Nigeria: Modernization and the Politics of Communalism:* 113–44.
- (1973) *Religion and Political Culture in Kano* (Berkeley: University of California Press).
PEIL, MARGARET (1976) *Nigerian Politics: The People's View* (London: Cassell Ltd).
PESHKIN, ALAN (1971) 'Education and National Integration in Nigeria', in Melson and Wolpe (eds) *Nigeria: Modernization and the Politics of Communalism*: 433–47.
PHILLIPS, ADEDOTUN (1971) 'Nigeria's Federal Financial Experience', *The Journal of Modern African Studies* 9(3).
PLOTNICOV, LEONARD (1971) 'An Early Nigerian Civil Disturbance: The 1945 Hausa-Ibo Riot in Jos', *Journal of Modern African Studies* 9(2): 297–305.
POST, K. W. J. (1960) 'Forming a Government in Nigeria', *Nigerian Journal of Economic and Social Studies* 2(1).
- (1961) 'Nigeria – The First Decade', *Africa South* 6 (October-December).
- (1962) 'Nigeria Two Years After Independence', *The World Today* 18(11–12).
- (1963) *The Nigerian Federal Election of 1959* (London: Oxford University Press).
- (1964) 'Nationalism and Politics in Nigeria: A Marxist Approach', *Nigerian Journal of Economic and Social Studies* 6(2).

- (1966) 'The National Council of Nigeria and the Cameroons, and the Decision of December 1959', in John P. Mackintosh (ed.), *Nigerian Government and Politics* (Evanston, IL: Northwestern University Press).
POST, K. W. J., AND VICKERS, MICHAEL (1973) *Structure and Conflict in Nigeria* (London: Heinemann).
SCHATZ, SAYRE P. (1977) *Nigerian Capitalism* (Berkeley: University of California Press).
SCHWARZ, FREDERICK A. 0. (1965) *Nigeria: The Tribes, the Nation or the Race – The Politics of Independence* (Cambridge, MA: Massachusetts Institute of Technology Press).
SCHWARZ, WALTER (1966) 'Tribalism and Politics in Nigeria', *World Today* 22(1): 460–6.
- (1968) *Nigeria* (New York: Frederick A. Praeger).
SEIBEL, H. DIETER (1967) 'Some Aspects of Inter-ethnic Relations in Nigeria', *Nigerian Journal of Economic and Social Studies* 9(2) (July).
SHARWOOD-SMITH, BRYAN (1969) *But Always as Friends* (London: Allen & Unwin).
SKLAR, RICHARD L. (1960) 'The Contribution of Tribalism to Nationalism' *Journal of Human Relations* 8: 407–18.
 (1963) *Nigerian Political Parties* (Princeton: Princeton University Press).
- (1965a) 'Contradictions in the Nigerian Political System', *Journal of Modern African Studies* 3(2): 201–13.
- (1965b) 'For National Reconciliation and a United National Front', *Nigerian Opinion* 1(1).
- (1966) 'The Ordeal of Chief Awolowo', in Gwendolen M. Carter (ed.), *Politics in Africa: Seven Cases*: 119–65 (New York: Harcourt Brace and World).
- (1967) 'Political Science and National Integration – A Radical Approach', *Journal of Modern African Studies* 5(1): 1–11.
- (1971) 'Nigerian Politics in Perspective', in Melson and Wolpe, (eds) *Nigeria: Modernization and the Politics of Communalism*: 43–62.
- (1976) 'Postimperialism: A Class Analysis of Multinational Corporate Expansion', *Comparative Politics* 9(1): 75–92.
- (1979) 'The Nature of Class Domination in Africa', *Journal of Modern African Studies* 17(4): 531–52.
- (1981) 'Democracy for the Second Republic', *Issue* 11(1/2): 14–16.
SKLAR, RICHARD L. AND WHITAKER, C. S. (1966) 'The Federal Republic of Nigeria', in Gwendolen M. Carter (ed.), *National Unity and Regionalism in Eight African States* (Ithaca, NY: Cornell University Press).
SMITH, M. G. (1955) *The Economy of Hausa Communities of Zaria* (London: Her Majesty's Stationery Office).
- (1959) 'The Hausa System of Social Status', *Africa* 29(3).
SMOCK, AUDREY C., AND SMOCK, DAVID B. (1969) 'Ethnicity and Attitudes toward Development in Eastern Nigeria', *The Journal of Developing Areas* 3 (July): 499–512.
SMYTHE, HUGH P., AND SMYTHE, MABEL M. (1960) *The New Nigerian Elite* (Stanford, CA: Stanford University Press).

STAPLETON, C. BRIAN (1967) *The Wealth of Nigeria* (Ibadan: Oxford University Press).

STOREY, BERNARD (1953) *Report of the Commission of Inquiry into the Administration of the Lagos Town Council* (Lagos: Government Printer).

TAYLOR, DON (1960) 'Nigeria 1960', *New Commonwealth* (July).

UCHENDU, VICTOR C. (1965) *The Igbo of Southeast Nigeria* (New York: Holt, Rinehart and Winston).

UWANAKA, CHARLES U. (1955) *Zik and Awolowo in Political Storm* (Lagos: Pacific Printing).

— (1964) *Awolowo and Akintola in Political Storm* (Yaba: John Okwesa and Company).

VAN DE WALLE, ETIENNE (1970) 'Who's Who and Where in Nigeria', *Africa Report, (15)1*.

WALLERSTEIN, IMMANUEL (1962) 'Nigeria: Slow Road to Trouble', *The New Leader* (July 23).

— (1963) 'Ethnicity and National Integration in West Africa' in Harry Eckstein and David Apter (eds), *Comparative Politics* (New York: Free Press).

— (1964) 'Voluntary Associations', in James S. Coleman and Carl G. Rosberg, Jr, *Political Parties and National Integration in Tropical Africa* (Berkeley: University of California Press).

WATTS, MICHAEL (1983) *Silent Violence: Food, Famine and Peasantry in Northern Nigeria* (Berkeley: University of California Press).

WEST AFRICA (1960–66) Numerous issues.

WHEARE, K. C. (1953) *Federal Government*. 3rd Edition (London: Oxford University Press).

WHITAKER, C. S., JR. (1965) 'Three Perspectives on Hierarchy', *The Journal of Commonwealth Political Studies* 3(1) Reprinted in Melson and Wolpe (eds) *Nigeria: Modernization and the Politics of Communalism* (1971): 530–56. Page citations refer to the latter.

— (1970) *The Politics of Tradition: Continuity and Change in Northern Nigeria, 1946–66* (Princeton: Princeton University Press).

— (1981) 'Second Beginnings: The New Political Framework', *Issue* 11(1/2): 2–12.

WILLIAMS, BABATUNDE A. (1960) 'Where Does Nigeria Go from Here?' *Africa Report* 5(10).

WILLIAMS, DAVID (1960) 'Nigeria on the Eve of Independence', *World Today* 16(3).

— (1982) *President and Power in Nigeria: The Life of Shehu Shagari* (London: Frank Cass).

WILLIAMS, GAVIN (1976) 'Nigeria: A Political Economy', in Gavin Williams (ed.), *Nigeria: Economy and Society*. (London: Rex Collings).

WOLPE, HOWARD (1974) *Urban Politics in Nigeria: A Study of Port Harcourt* (Berkeley: University of California Press).

WORLD BANK (1983) *World Development Report 1983* (New York and Oxford: Oxford University Press).

WORRALL, DENNIS (1965) 'The Breakdown of Government in the Western Region of Nigeria and Its Aftermath', *Africa Institute Bulletin* 3(5).

WRAITH, RONALD AND SIMPKINS, EDGAR (1963) *Corruption in Developing Countries* (New York: W. W. Norton & Company).
YOUNG, CRAWFORD (1976) *The Politics of Cultural Pluralism* (Madison: University of Wisconsin Press).
— (1982) *Ideology and Development in Africa* (New Haven: Yale University Press).

Index

356

Mbadiwe land scandal, 252, 254
Mbanefo, Sir Louis (Chief Justice, Eastern region), 221
Mbanugo, Dr G. C. (NCNC Working Committee Chairman), 143
MDF, *see* Mid-West Democratic Front
Meany, George, and Adebola, 166
Middle Belt State (Region), demands for, 53, 115
Middle Belt tribes, relative independence of, 24, 115
middle class,
  absence of, 312
  and democracy, 12, 14, 328
  see also bourgeoisie
Mid-West Democratic Front (MDF)
  and elections, 192, 202
  establishment of, 108–9, 147
Mid-West Region, 118, 190, 195
  contest for control of, 129
  demands for, 53
  election in 118, 147, 190–3
  political violence in, 97
  support of, 106
Mid-West People's Congress, alliance with UPP of, 190
Mid-Western Executive Committee, AG, 100
military, 81, 92
  governmental powers of, 2
  as impartial referee, 287, 323
military coups, 2, 92, 244, 287, 288, 334n10
minority politics, 52–5, 61
  see also ethnic minorities
missionaries, goals of, 28
modernisation,
  northern control of, 50, 301, 330n3
  process of, 14, 299
Mojekwu, C. C. (Eastern Attorney General), 213
Morgan, Sir Adeyinka (Chairman of Commission of Inquiry), 171
Morgan Commission of Inquiry
  delayed release of report, 172–3
  expense cutting suggestions of, 185

members of, 170–1
terms of, 181
wage-scale recommendations of, 171, 177
Motor Transport Owners' Union, 163
Muffett, David, account of Sardauna's actions, 341n10
Muhammed, General Murtala, 324
Muslim aristocracy, 34–5, 240
Muslims, Northern region, development gap of, 26–7
Muslims, Yoruba, separate state demands of, 53

National Council of Nigeria and the Cameroons (NCNC; renamed in 1961 National Convention of Nigerian Citizens), 40, 43, 58, 62, 72, 78–9, 82, 88, 89, 97, 103, 107, 116–17, 135, 147, 148, 150, 155–61 *passim*, 196, 197, 198, 209, 213, 218, 224, 225
  and AG, 94, 108, 118, 194–5, 251
  and Azikiwe, 222
  broad support base of, 46, 47, 53, 105
  cabinet role of, 228
  and the census dispute, 134, 135, 139–41, 145–6
  and the constitutional review, 256, 257
  defeat in the West of, 57, 143, 149
  and elections, 48, 192, 203–6, 226–7
  and Igbos, 47, 55, 229, 335n4
  independence of, 191, 211, 293
  and the Mid-West, 229
  –NEPU alliance, 57
  –NPC alliance, 57, 97, 116, 123, 128–9, 141, 189, 196
  policies of, 51, 122, 201–22, 251, 258
  press of, 226
  problems of, 193, 200, 212
  regional power of, 55, 108–9, 273
  strike support of, 176
  support of, 53, 105, 106, 164

steel mill location of, 146
nouveaux riches, 43
NPC, *see* Northern People's
Congress
NPF, *see* Northern Progressive Front
NTUC, *see* Nigerian Trade Union
Congress
Nupe (ethnic group), 21
Nzeribe, Gogo, 165, 167, 168

Oba, definition of, 68, 69, 205
Obande, Jacob (Minister of
Establishments), 172
Obasanjo, General Olusegun, 324
Obi, Dr Chike, 77, 332n6
O'Connell, J. (associate editor,
Nigerian Opinion), 254, 312
Odebiyi, Chief Jonathan, 101
Ogunsanya, Chief Adeniran (NCNC
leader), 224
Ogunsheye, Ayo (Director, Extra-
Mural Department of
University of Ibadan), 92
oil production, 338n12
conflict over, 337–8n4
revenue from 146, 339n4
Oke, E. O. (Akintola supporter),
101
Okotie-Eboh, Chief Festus (Federal
Finance Minister), 191, 192,
194, 196, 223, 225, 226
cabinet appointment of, 224, 228
policy of, 276, 377
and Mid-West state movement,
108, 139, 150, 176
NPC sympathies of, 129
personal fortune of, 311
pro-federalism of, 229, 318
and unions, 165, 180
Okoye, Mokwugo (Gen. Secretary
of Zikist movement), 215
Okpara, Dr Michael (Premier,
Eastern Region), 79, 86, 105,
122, 134, 148, 155, 156, 203,
208, 209, 225
alliance formations by, 194–9
and Awolowo, 97, 128, 130
and census crisis, 138–40, 141–2,
145, 150

coalition government concept
support of, 216, 237, 256, 316,
339n3
criticism of, 224–5
and elections, 206, 215, 216, 223,
225, 286
increasing domination of NCNC,
212
and Mbadiwe house-warming
gala, 276
and the President, 217
quoted, 131, 200, 201
State of Emergency declaration
of, 121
strike support of, 178–9, 180
warnings of, 214, 216, 267
Omo-Osagie, Chief Humphrey, 192,
193, 211
Onabanjo, Bisi, 103
one-party system, idea of, 87–8, 256,
339n2
'Operation No Mercy', 272
opposition, *see* political opposition
Organisation of African Unity
(OAU), 201
organised labour, weakness of, 230
Orishas (tribal deities), 22
Osadebay, Chief Dennis (Premier,
Mid-Western Region), 146, 152,
153, 194, 216, 223, 269
and census (1963), 139, 145
and coalition government concept
of, 229, 237
criticism of, 224–5
and elections, 219–20, 286
and one-party system, 256
regional activities of, 108–9, 191, 193
Otegbeye, Dr Tunji, 78, 148, 195
leader of Socialist Workers' and
Farmers' Party, 167
Otu Edo (Benin), 191, 193, 211
Oyemade, Justice, 284
Oyo (Yoruba ethnic group), 113
Oyo, Alafin of, 202

Pan Africanism, 120, 166, 167
Parliament
constitutional powers and
structure, 83–4, 85